The Postreform Congress

The Postreform Congress

Edited by Roger H. Davidson

UNIVERSITY OF MARYLAND,
COLLEGE PARK

ST. MARTIN'S PRESS   NEW YORK

Senior editor: Don Reisman
Managing editor: Patricia Mansfield
Project editor: Suzanne Holt
Production supervisor: Alan Fischer
Graphics: G&H Soho
Cover design: Nadia Furlan-Lorbek
Cover art: Library of Congress

For information, write:
St. Martin's Press, Inc.
175 Fifth Avenue
New York, NY 10010

ISBN: 0-312-06521-3 (cloth)
       0-312-05673-7 (paper)

Library of Congress Cataloging-in-Publication Data

The Postreform congress / edited by Roger H. Davidson.
        p.   cm.
    Includes bibliographical references and index.
    ISBN 0-312-06521-3.—ISBN 0-312-05673-7 (pbk.)
    1. United States. Congress. 2. United States. Congress—Reform.
    3. United States—Politics and government—1977–   I. Davidson, Roger H.
    JK1061.P66   1992
    328.73—dc20   91-61134
                                                         CIP

To
Richard W. Bolling
Morris K. Udall

Preface

The idea for *The Postreform Congress* came to me several years ago in the midst of a panel discussion at a professional meeting. Several earnest and capable scholars were presenting papers analyzing the reform-era Congress of the 1970s. They accurately detailed its decentralizing tendencies—reactions against the harsh reign of the conservative coalition that dominated the post–World War II generation. All this was well and good, I thought, but the descriptions soon exceeded the bounds of reality and took on an exaggerated quality. Terms like "fragmented," "atomistic," and "centrifugal" were tossed about with abandon. Surely, I thought, an institution such as they described would be so lacking in coherence and cohesion that it could not long survive. This was by no means the Congress I knew at close range—decentralized as always, but nonetheless elaborately structured and routinized. Indeed, it was gradually, but perceptibly, moving away from the "big bang" explosion that marked the revolt against the barons of the previous generation.

Today's Congress faces an environment that differs significantly from what has gone before. The advent of what economist Lester Thurow calls the zero-sum society—a sluggish economy combined with costly entitlements and, after 1981, tax cuts and program reallocations—no doubt lies at the root of this changed political atmosphere. Although the shift is popularly associated with Ronald Reagan's victory in 1980, it was already well under way in the late 1970s and survives into the 1990s.

Earlier congressional eras have been vividly described by scholars and journalists. What Kenneth Shepsle termed the "textbook Congress"—the conservative coalition's domination of Capitol Hill policy-making from the second Roosevelt administration through the early 1960s—was well researched and colorfully reported. Scholars such as Donald R. Matthews, Richard F. Fenno, Jr., and Charles O. Jones and journalists such as William S. White constructed a picture of the legislative process that was descriptively rich and conceptually persuasive.

The frenetic activism and structural fragmentation of the reform period (1960s and 1970s) were also well reported and still dominate most textbook treatments of the subject. Important analyses of this period include David Mayhew's provocative essay *Congress: The Electoral Connection* (1974), Thomas E. Mann's and Norman J. Ornstein's collection *The New Congress*

(1981), and Hedrick Smith's book *The Power Game: How Washington Works* (1988).

A number of studies, reported at scholarly meetings over the past several years, reflect an emerging consensus on the nature of the contemporary postreform era. Elements that have received attention include: shifts in legislative workload; stress on the budget process; "blame-avoidance" techniques; reinvigorated partisanship; stronger party leadership, combined with weakened committee leadership; contraction of certain policy-making arenas; and tighter management of floor procedures, especially in the House. In contrast to the prior reform era, innovations of recent years represent not a concerted reform effort but rather a gradual, piecemeal adaptation to alterations in Congress's political environment and legislative agenda.

While articles on aspects of the postreform Congress have appeared in various scholarly journals, no collection has been available for a wider audience—for example, for students and nonspecialist scholars. There is nothing comparable to Mann and Ornstein's important and widely cited 1981 collection. Therefore, this volume brings together a group of leading scholars who illuminate various aspects of the postreform era in essays especially designed for a wide readership.

Such a collaborative enterprise is the product of many hands. My thanks go to my colleagues who contributed to this volume; they willingly met a demanding schedule and endured my extensive editorial intrusions. Don Reisman and his staff at St. Martin's Press were consistently helpful and supportive. Especially valuable were the contributions of Frances Jones, Suzanne Holt, and copyeditor Wendy Polhemus-Annibell, who carefully reviewed the entire manuscript and imposed stylistic consistency upon our disparate contributions. I am grateful also to those who critiqued the manuscript in substantive terms: Herbert Weisberg, Ohio State University; Linda L. Fowler, Syracuse University; and Michael L. Mezey, DePaul University.

This volume is dedicated to Richard W. Bolling and Morris K. Udall. I worked for the first of them; I admired and learned from both of them. Two more different personalities could hardly be imagined. Yet both individuals shared a passion for public policy and a commitment to legislative processes. Both shaped the reform movement on Capitol Hill during the 1960s and 1970s. Both gained formal leadership posts as the reform era ebbed, helping Congress to adapt to the demands of the postreform policy agenda. Both of them received a measure of public acclaim, and yet both failed to achieve their highest aspirations. They deserve to be remembered as among the finest lawmakers and public servants of their generation.

Roger H. Davidson

Contents

The Postreform Congress

PART · I

Introduction

1 / The Emergence of the Postreform Congress

ROGER H. DAVIDSON

Innovation in Congress's structures, procedures, and practices is a persistent theme in writing and commentary about the institution. Scholars, journalists, reformers, and ordinary citizens have publicly complained about how badly Congress works since even before the Progressive Era at the turn of the twentieth century. Manifestos, issued periodically, declare that various changes must be adopted to cure legislative ills (most recently, campaign finance reform). These worries have spawned an enormous literature on *congressional innovation*, typically reflecting a reformist viewpoint.

Other analysts have investigated what can be called the *mechanics of legislative innovation*. They are less interested in reforming the institution than in describing and understanding whatever changes take place within it. In the earliest days of political science as an organized discipline, scholars trained in public law naturally concentrated on formal structures: rules, precedents, and procedures. It was this legalistic and formalistic tradition that the young Woodrow Wilson sought to replace with the study of politics' "rough practice," in order to discover "the real depositories and the essential machinery of power" (1885, 30). Following Wilson's lead, succeeding generations of investigators exposed the "rough practice" of Capitol Hill politics with ingenuity, skill, and a wide range of theoretical assumptions and methodological tools.

The most recent generation of congressional scholarship has zealously explored what Hedrick Smith (1988) calls the "power earthquake" of the 1960s and 1970s: a multifaceted onslaught of changes, or reforms, that shattered the older seniority leaders' power, opened up the decision-making game to wider circles of players, and dramatically recast House and Senate rules and procedures. Political analysts have described and explained the contours of the *reform-era Congress* in enormous detail (Mann and Ornstein 1981; Rieselbach 1986). Given the rich and varied character of the era's institutional changes, it is not surprising that scholars still find in these developments material for detailed and insightful analyses (Smith 1989, especially chaps. 2, 4; Sinclair 1989c).

Increasingly, however, it is evident that Congress has embarked on a postreform period of adjustment and development. To be sure, most of the reform-era innovations remain formally in place and continue to shape the assumptions and expectations of both observers and members about how the system operates. Nonetheless, the evidence of continued change and

3

adaptation is undeniable. In ways both subtle and profound, Congress has changed markedly since the reform era of the 1960s and 1970s; it is, among other things, more routinized, more partisan, and even more hierarchical (Davidson 1988b). While explicit tinkering with rules and procedures is not as pronounced as in the prior era, the postreform Congress has acted to minimize or reverse some of the central reformist trends. In the House of Representatives, this has meant stronger leadership and stricter management of floor business (Bach and Smith 1988). The Senate has undergone more subtle but still noticeable shifts in its operations.

CONGRESS AS AN ORGANIZATION

To understand innovation on Capitol Hill, it is useful to think of Congress as a complex organization responding to an equally complex environment. However, the term *Congress* is used only for convenience's sake; more precisely we mean the *House* and *Senate*, which operate as two distinct, though closely linked, organizations, jealous of their prerogatives and distinctive in their procedures.

Congress exhibits many of the attributes of other large-scale organizations. For one thing, it is large in scale. If somehow transferred into the business sector, Congress's 25,000 members and employees would rank it as a moderately large firm. In the governmental sphere, though, it resembles one of the smaller cabinet departments—the State Department, for example, is almost exactly the same size. Congress relies heavily on complicated sets of rules, procedures, precedents, and practices. It divides its work load among a variety of discrete task groups, and it contains at least a modest hierarchy of power. In the political marketplace, Congress produces distinctive "commodities" in order to satisfy public expectations or demands. In doing so, it faces competition from rival institutions.

The House and Senate, of course, differ in many respects from other complex organizations, public or private. Most importantly, they are less hierarchical in leadership and management than all but a few other organizations. And while the chambers reflect highly elaborated organization and a large measure of functional specialization, the subunits' decisions and even activities are usually known and subject to review by other participants in the system. Members tend to behave as generalists, relying on staffs or outsiders for specialized expertise. Finally, the organization's work is uncommonly exposed to intervention by outside interests, including lobbyists, constituents, executives, and the press.

All organizations have the imperative of maximizing their competitive position in the markets or arenas in which they operate. Ultimately, the question is one of institutional survival: Will the doors be open for business tomorrow morning, or next week, or next year? For an established political institution like the U.S. Congress, the challenge is more subtle. It is not one of surviving but of maintaining or even expanding its autonomy (control over its own decisions) and its scope of operations (extent or sphere of its influence).

No organization, of course, enjoys the luxury of pure autonomy or unlimited scope of influence. In our constitutional framework of blended powers, the House and Senate compete with many other power centers—among them the White House, executive agencies, the courts, state and local governments, the media, and even talk-show hosts. If Congress cannot or does not respond to the demands placed on it, other institutions are poised to take action. Congress temporized when President Harry S. Truman seized the nation's strike-bound steel mills to assure the flow of production during the Korean War. Musing on the lessons of the resulting 1952 Steel Seizure Case (*Youngstown Sheet & Tube Co. v. Sawyer*), the great constitutional scholar Edward S. Corwin noted that "just as nature abhors a vacuum, so does an age of emergency. Let Congress see to it, then, that no such vacuum occurs. The best escape from presidential autocracy in the age we inhabit is not, in short, judicial review, which can supply only a vacuum, but timely legislation" (1957, 157). Corwin's words, uttered in the context of a constitutional confrontation, are a pointed warning to institutions confronted with insistent demands for action. To put the challenge in everyday language: "Don't just stand there! Do something!"

EXTERNAL FORCES, INTERNAL TENSIONS

In order to maintain a position in the marketplace, organizations—whether a family business or the U.S. Congress—must adjust to *external demands* while at the same time coping with *internal stresses*. That is, an institution must adapt to outside demands and expectations in ways that further the discrete goals of its members or employees. As for Congress, this balance between external and internal imperatives is especially problematic because of the "two Congresses" dilemma: the fact that every legislator is recruited separately and pursues incentives largely independent of the institution as a whole.

External Demands

Social, economic, and political developments generate demands that the legislature enact laws or take other actions to meet constitutional and public expectations concerning the general welfare. Wars, economic cycles, demographic shifts, international or domestic crises, and accumulating technological developments intensify pressures on Congress. The unprecedented period of prosperity following World War II, coupled with demographic shifts (migration from farms to cities and suburbs, the rise of the baby boomers), propelled demands for government services that spilled over into the 1960s and 1970s in the form of new laws and programs. Likewise, the economic downturns since the mid-1970s have inhibited program innovation and curtailed spending increases.

Political or governmental shifts—aggressive presidential leadership, partisan realignments, scandals, and far-reaching court rulings—also drive the congressional work load. Before the upheavals of the reform era, policymaking was shaped by the peculiar tripartite division of the political parties: mainstream northern Democrats versus southern conservatives aligned with Republican stalwarts. The reform-era upheavals signaled a victory of the former over the latter. Since then, demographic and political changes have moderated the clashes between wings of the Democratic party, leading to more "coherent" two-party confrontations (see Rohde, this volume, Chapter 2).

Agenda is a shorthand way of measuring external demands on Congress. Historically, Congress has experienced long-term growth in its work-load demands. According to Galloway, "the business of Congress in modern times is as varied and multifarious as the affairs of the American people. Once relatively limited in scope, small in volume, and simple in nature, it has now become almost unlimited in subject matter, enormous in volume, and complex in character" (1962, 108). This long-term picture of Congress—accurate in general terms, though subject to numerous short-term exceptions—is buttressed by such statistics as the rising numbers of public laws and the lengthening of annual sessions. Additional testimony is provided by senior lawmakers who recount their experience with mounting legislative and nonlegislative burdens. There is little quarrel with the overall judgment that Congress today confronts a volume and variety of demands unmatched in all but the most turbulent years of its earlier history. "What is equally true, as the history of [Congress] readily demonstrates, is that the volume of output demands, as well as the degree of their complexity, uniformity, and volatility, vary greatly over time" (Cooper 1981, 332). Examining modern-day statistics on legislative proposals and legislative products casts light on the demands placed on Congress.

In the years following World War II, overall House and Senate work-load indicators were marked first by a gradual buildup (roughly, 1951–64), then by an era of extraordinarily high legislative activity (1965–78), and most recently (since 1979) by a sudden and steep decline (Davidson 1986b).

Overall work-load demands reverberate, to a greater or lesser degree, in the committee rooms of the two houses of Congress. Here the overall pattern is equally clear, with most committees conforming to it. Committee activity and work load soared in the boom years of the 1970s, as a crowded policy agenda synchronized with a newly decentralized power structure that featured multiple channels for action. The number of measures referred to five representative House committees rose by more than 20 percent in the 1970s, even though House rules by this time allowed unlimited cosponsorship of measures (Davidson 1986a, 29–31). These committees scheduled more than twice as many hearing days in the mid-1970s as they had a decade earlier.

By the mid-1980s this frenetic activity had subsided: referrals were cut almost in half, while days of hearings were down by about one-third. Not even Representative John Dingell's Energy and Commerce Committee was immune from the work-load reversal. From 1985 to 1986 this panel, regarded as one of the most active and aggressive Capitol Hill powerhouses, spent only half as many hours in hearings, and a third as many hours in markups, as it had logged a decade earlier (Davidson 1986b, 14).

Internal Pressures

Other pressures for change emanate from forces within Congress itself—centering mainly on the goals and careers of individual members. Foremost among members' goals is reelection, a premise no less powerful because it is so obvious (Bianco, this volume, Chapter 4). However, members (like the rest of us) harbor a number of personal goals, some of them altruistic but most tinged with self-interest. They want to shape public policy, watch their ideas come to fruition, and make their mark in history; they also desire some measure of order, convenience, and comfort in their private lives. Hence, legislators make a wide variety of claims on the institution, shaping its structures and procedures to serve their own needs as well as external demands.

Sometimes the effects of external demands ricochet, causing interpersonal stresses within Congress. For example, a ballooning work load (external demand) can cause personal or committee scrambles for jurisdiction (internal stress). Other tensions flow from growth in size, shifts in personnel, factional or partisan disputes, and members' attitudes or norms. Elections and retirements alter the generational or factional balance, exerting pressure on the established ways of doing things. Such conflicts surface in recurrent debates over salaries, perquisites, committee jurisdictions, rules, scheduling, and budgetary procedures. Over time, these conflicts yield changes—obvious or subtle, profound or trivial—in the way Congress goes about its work.

Instances of innovations that serve one set of demands yet jeopardize other needs can be cited. Efforts aimed at adapting to outside legislative demands can raise the human costs for members. Increased constituency attention, for example, undeniably meets voter demands but inhibits members' ability to focus on legislative work and adds to their personal wear and tear. Likewise, arrangements that accommodate members can hinder the institution in coping with its work load or in meeting public expectations. The opening up of committee rooms and floor proceedings in the mid-1970s made it possible for more members to participate in shaping legislation, but it also jeopardized orderly processing of the legislative work load. Party and committee leaders soon fashioned new tactics for managing the legislative agenda (Weingast, this volume, Chapter 8).

Reform is an attractive label for selling proposed innovations. Reform connotes change for the better; but whether change is reform depends on where you are standing. One person's reform is another's stumbling block. Further, it is not possible to predict with any certainty whether a given innovation will resolve the problem for which it was designed or even whether it will produce positive or negative results. Change usually brings costs and benefits; intended and unintended consequences. Moreover, the passage of time may render even the most useful innovations obsolete. History is strewn with examples of one generation's reforms that exacerbated the next generation's problems.

Thus the term *reform* is used here with caution. The reform era of the 1960s and 1970s was indeed a time of massive change and structural upheaval. The innovations responded to political demands and shifting alignments, but their legacy is ambiguous. The postreform Congress, too, has adapted to its environment with mixed success, to say the least (Quirk, this volume, Chapter 15).

Types of Innovation

The stresses caused by the buildup of external and internal pressures can be moderated or relieved by *organizational innovation*, defined as a variation in the substance or structure of organizational behavior (Gawthrop 1966, 239). There is nothing foreordained or automatic about such innovation. Indeed, capacity for innovation is one of the critical variables that differentiate organizations. Pressures or strains on an organization may go unrelieved for long periods of time, or they may be mitigated by noninnovative developments (for example, changes imposed on recruitment of the organization's personnel).

Substantive accommodation is certainly the most direct and visible manifestation of change. Pressures can be relieved if the organization visibly alters its product or output. A manufacturer designs a new model, or recalls an old one, in response to consumer complaints or regulatory warnings. Lawmakers pass a bill or resolution in response to public pressure or presidential initiative; or they rewrite an act's language to shift or conceal the policy's purposes or effects; or, as in the case of the controversial 1989 pay-raise scheme, they scurry to overturn the product of a prescribed procedure (Bianco, this volume, Chapter 4).

Outside and inside pressures for change produce two distinct types of innovation: adaptation and consolidation (Davidson and Oleszek 1976, 40–41). *Adaptation* responds to conditions imposed by the external environment; it embraces structural or procedural alterations designed to satisfy or moderate the demands imposed on the organization. Adaptation may involve a highly rational process of analyzing the nature of the external challenge, diagnosing organizational weaknesses, and searching for ways of improving the organization's performance.

Major adaptive innovation is typically entrusted to a special subunit— a task force, study group, or special committee—charged with gathering information and sifting through proposed solutions. Many noteworthy re- organization efforts of the post–World War II era emerged from just such a concerted inquiry—among them the Legislative Reorganization Acts of 1946 and 1970; the House and Senate committee realignments of 1974 and 1977, respectively; and the work of the House Democrats' Committee on Organization, Study and Review, mainly in the early 1970s. Concentrated efforts like these can pinpoint institutional problems somewhat indepen- dently of established power centers or subunits. This very quality is also the prime drawback of such efforts, which in their zeal for adaptive in- novations tend to underestimate the goals and needs of entrenched indi- viduals and subgroups within the organization. In other words, such efforts elevate adaptation above consolidation. Because of their high informational costs and potential disruption of established ways of doing things, such deliberate adaptive reform efforts must be regarded as radical solutions, not as everyday occurrences.

Most adaptive changes result not from deliberate planning but from conscious or unconscious adaptive behavior on the part of the institution. Such alterations are less coordinated or coherent than planned innovation, but because they tend to emerge naturally from behavior within the insti- tution they are more likely to meet consolidative needs. The advent of the postreform Congress reflects this type of largely unplanned adaptive be- havior. Although some postreform developments entailed formal changes in rules, procedures, or statutes (for example, budgetary procedures and limits on legislative riders on the House floor), most came about in response to specific situations rather than as part of a coordinated plan for organi- zational change.

The second form of innovation, *consolidation*, is designed to relieve an organization's internal stresses and strains. Such innovations are normally intended to contain conflict or to conform to shifting balances of power, accommodating insofar as possible the individual participants' needs and goals. Consolidative changes imply efforts to resolve members' demands for change within existing organizational structures and traditions, if at all possible. Some such changes are hotly contested; others may be uncon- troversial. Organizations are constantly engaged in making consolidative adjustments, some of them quite significant. One example of consolidative change on Capitol Hill is the curtailment of the seniority leaders' prerog- atives in the 1960s and 1970s (to accommodate newer members and their career needs). Another example is the augmentation of members' resources for traveling between Washington and their home bases and for conducting constituency business. "As Congress accommodated to the needs of its mem- bers to maintain contact with their constituents," Parker explains, "it facilitated changes in attention by reducing the direct costs associated with it" (1986, 94).

THE CONSERVATIVE COALITION ERA (1937–1964)

From Franklin Roosevelt's second administration through the mid-1960s, Congress was dominated by an oligarchy of senior leaders—sometimes called "the barons" or "the old bulls." Whichever party was in power, congressional leaders overrepresented safe, one-party regions (the Democratic rural South, the Republican rural Northeast and Midwest) and reflected the narrow legislative agenda of the bipartisan conservative coalition that controlled so much domestic policy-making. This created a hostile environment for activist presidents and their legislative allies. "Deadlock on the Potomac" was how James MacGregor Burns described the situation in Roosevelt's second term. He cited this anecdote: " 'For God's sake,' a congressional spokesman telephoned the White House in April 1938, 'don't send us any more controversial legislation!' " (1956, 337, 339). Here spoke the authentic voice of the post–New Deal Congress.

Harry Truman's clashes with Capitol Hill began early and lasted throughout his presidency. "Except for the modified Employment Act of 1946," relates Donovan, "the [Democratic] Seventy-ninth Congress had squelched practically every piece of social and economic legislation Truman had requested" (1977, 260). Truman's other Congresses were equally frustrating, though in different ways. The Republican Eightieth Congress "gave [Truman] his most enduring image. Facing an opposition-controlled legislative body almost certain to reject any domestic program he proposed, he adopted the role of an oppositionist" (Hamby 1989, 46). Truman campaigned successfully in 1948 by excoriating the "awful, do-nothing Eightieth Congress." Yet the Democratic Eighty-first Congress rejected virtually all of Truman's major Fair Deal initiatives; his final congress, the Eighty-second, marked by depleted Democratic majorities and the Korean War stalemate, was even more hostile to new legislative initiatives.

The 1950s were years of outward quiescence accompanied by underlying, yet accelerating, demands for action and innovation. Dwight Eisenhower, whose legislative goals were far more modest than Truman's, was increasingly placed in the position of offering scaled-down alternatives to proposals floated on Capitol Hill by coalitions of activist Democrats and liberal Republicans. The legislative work load through this period was relatively stable and manageable from year to year. A large proportion of the bills and resolutions were routine—immigration, land claims, and private legislation, categories of questions not yet delegated to the executive branch for resolution. Demands were building, however, for new legislation to address civil rights and other urban and suburban concerns.

Internally, the key committees of the 1950s (the taxing and spending panels plus House Rules) tended to be cohesive groups—"corporate," to use Richard F. Fenno's (1973, 279) term—boasting firm leadership and rigorous internal norms of behavior. These committees kept a tight lid on new legislation, especially in fiscal affairs. The appropriations panels, in particular, served as guardians of the U.S. Treasury, holding in check the more rapacious inclinations of the program-oriented authorizing panels.

Journalists and political scientists closely studied the postwar Congress, constructing a detailed picture of its operations. The picture that emerged was so persuasive that one scholar labeled it "the textbook Congress" (Shepsle 1989). The leading intellectual framework saw the institution as an interlocking pattern of personal relationships in which structure and function worked in rough equilibrium. Ironically, by the time observers got around to completing this coherent portrait of a tight, closed, internally coherent congressional world, that world was already being turned upside down. Pressures for change and reform mounted, heralding a remarkable period of reformist politics.

THE REFORM ERA (1965–1978)

The cozy domains of the barons were eventually pulled apart by nothing less than a "power earthquake," as journalist Hedrick Smith (1988) calls it. The earthquake touched virtually every corner of the political landscape: the presidency, courts, parties, interest groups, and media, not to mention citizens themselves.

The boundaries of this reform era, as of other eras, are somewhat imprecise. The course of change began in earnest after the 1958 elections, which enlarged the Democrats' ranks by sixteen senators and fifty-one representatives, many of them programmatic liberals. The elections had an immediate impact in both chambers. Senate Majority Leader Lyndon Johnson's autocratic rule softened perceptibly; two years later, Johnson relinquished his leadership post to the mild-mannered liberal Mike Mansfield (D-Mont.). In the House a small band of liberal activists formally launched the Democratic Study Group, which subsequently spearheaded efforts for procedural reforms. Speaker Sam Rayburn (D-Tex.) resolved in 1961 to break the conservatives' hold on the powerful House Rules Committee. The reform era reached its climax in the mid-1970s with successive waves of changes in committee and floor procedures and, in 1975, the ouster of three of the barons from their committee chair positions.

One underlying cause of the upheaval was a series of unmet policy demands pushed by urban and suburban voting blocs as well as minority groups, and adopted by activist presidents (Sundquist 1968). The spirit of the era was reflected in the popular movements that came to prominence: civil rights, environmentalism, consumerism, and opposition to the Vietnam

War. Longer-range causes included reapportionment and redistricting, widened citizen participation, social upheaval, and technological innovations in transportation and communications.

Internally, the resulting changes pointed Congress in the direction of a more open, participatory legislative process: greater leverage for individual lawmakers, and dispersion of influence among and within the committees. More leaders existed than ever before, and more influence was exerted by nonleaders. More staff aides were on hand to extend the legislative reach of even the most junior members.

Individual senators and representatives, while enjoying their enhanced legislative involvement, were obliged at the same time to devote greater attention to their constituents back home. No longer was frantic constituency outreach confined to a few large-state senators and representatives from swing districts; now it was practiced by all members (or their staffs) to purchase electoral security in an age of dwindling party support. In their home styles, members tended to exchange the workhorse role for that of the show horse.

The reforms were propelled by, and in turn helped to facilitate, an ambitious and expansionary congressional work load. It was the era of such presidential themes as the New Frontier and the Great Society, witnessing a host of landmark enactments in civil rights, education, medical insurance, employment and training, science and space, consumer protection, the environment—and five new cabinet departments and four constitutional amendments. Legislative activity soared in those years by whatever measure one chooses to apply—bills introduced, hearings, reports, hours in session, floor amendments, recorded floor votes, and measures passed (Davidson and Hardy 1987a, b). The processing of freestanding bills and resolutions became the centerpiece of committee and subcommittee work.

The decentralization of the 1960s and 1970s was accompanied by a weakening of the appropriations committees' grip over spending, at the same time building up the authorizing committees' power. The ascendant authorizing panels engineered a revolution in federal spending practices through ingenious use of "backdoor spending" provisions in much of this new legislation—such as contract authority, budget authority, direct Treasury borrowing, and especially entitlements—thus stripping the appropriations panels of much of their formal fiscal guardianship role (Schick 1980, 424–36). One analyst (Ellwood 1985) calculates that three-quarters of the domestic spending growth between 1970 and 1983 occurred in budget accounts lying outside annual appropriations; that is, beyond the appropriations committees' reach.

Like the earlier period, the reform era of the 1960s and 1970s was well documented by journalists and scholars (Davidson and Oleszek 1977; Sundquist 1981; Rieselbach 1986). Symptomatic of the decentralization and fragmentation of the reform era was its most popular scholarly paradigm, drawn from economics (Mayhew 1974). Lawmakers were now seen not as role players in a complex system of interactions in equilibrium, but as individual entrepreneurs in a vast, open marketplace that rewarded self-interested competitiveness with little or no regard for the welfare of the whole.

THE POSTREFORM ERA (1979–   )

By the 1980s Congress again faced an environment that diverged in significant ways from what had gone before. Although the shift is popularly associated with the Reagan administration, it was under way by 1979 or 1980 (the Ninety-sixth Congress).

The advent of the so-called *zero-sum society* (Thurow 1980) no doubt lay at the root of the changed political atmosphere. The economy no longer seemed to support the federal government's array of services, many of them enacted during the reform period. The core problem was productivity—the engine that over the long haul enables a nation to raise its standard of living and underwrite an expanding array of public services. After 1973 the nation's productivity stagnated in comparison with both its economic rivals and its previous record. The 1970s and 1980s were the poorest productivity decades of the twentieth century (Krugman 1990).

Lagging productivity affected not only government tax receipts but also citizens' attitudes toward their economic well-being. In the late 1970s the economy was buffeted by *stagflation,* a double whammy of high inflation and high unemployment. A serious recession occurred in the early 1980s and again a decade later. Meanwhile, the government's costly and relatively impervious system of entitlements and, after 1981, tax cuts and program reallocations turned the fiscal dividends of the postwar era into structural deficits.

Intellectual fashions and political realities repudiated the notion that government intervention could solve all manner of economic and social ills. Disenchantment with the results of government programs, many of which had been shamelessly oversold to glean support for their enactment, led to widespread demands for a statutory cease-fire: disinvestment, deregulation, and privatization. At the same time, spurred by "bracket creep"—which raised the marginal and real tax rates of millions of U.S. citizens—a series of tax revolts swept through the states to the nation's capital. The "no new taxes" cry of Presidents Reagan and Bush, however unrealistic and misleading, was politically a long-running hit with politicians and voters.

The advent of zero-sum politics is popularly associated with the Reagan administration, which took office in 1980 with the pledge of cutting taxes, domestic aid, and welfare programs. Reagan's election was, to be sure, interpreted at the time as a major change in American politics; certainly, Reagan's policies—especially the 1981 revenue cuts and the repeated threats to veto new taxes and domestic spending—hastened the trend toward constricting the legislative agenda. However, deteriorating economic conditions and shifting attitudes had already propelled former President Jimmy Carter in some (though not all) of these policy directions (Jones 1988, chap. 7); by the Ninety-sixth Congress (that is, by 1979–80), the altered environment had already produced a decline in legislative work load. Had Carter been reelected in 1980, it is probable that he, and Congress, would have traveled further along the road toward zero-sum politics.

The president and Congress were preoccupied in the postreform period with resolving fiscal and revenue issues, rather than designing new programs or establishing new agencies. In the domestic realm, the emphasis was on reviewing, adjusting, refining, or cutting back on existing programs. "There's not a whole lot of money for any kind of new programs," remarked Mississippi GOP Senator Thad Cochran, "so we're holding oversight hearings on old programs . . . which may not be all that bad an idea" (qtd. in Dewar 1989a, A4). Accordingly, individual members were less tempted to put forward their ideas as freestanding bills or resolutions. Such new ideas as were saleable were more apt to be conveyed in amendments to large-scale legislative vehicles: reauthorizations, continuing appropriations, debt limit, or reconciliation bills.

The environment of the 1980s reversed the previous era's liberal activism. Few new progams were launched and few domestic programs were given added funding. Although the public continued to expect Congress to take action to solve problems, there was equal sentiment for cutting back "big government" and reducing public-sector deficits. Faith in government activism plummeted in the wake of criticisms of waste and ineffectiveness in government programs.

The economic predicament and its attendant intellectual shift severely curtailed legislative productivity. "Rarely in peacetime has a single issue dominated politics here the way the budget deficit is doing now," observed a *New York Times* correspondent. "The most important legislative measures of the year [1989]—tax cuts, expansion of child-care benefits, changes in Medicare and Medicaid and many others—are paralyzed" (Rosenbaum 1989, E1). In some cases zero-sum politics was practiced literally, as members bartered such items as congressional mailing costs with the war on drugs. Senate Majority Leader George J. Mitchell characterized the budget dilemma as "the whale in the bathtub that leaves no room for anything else" (Dewar 1989b, A4).

ELEMENTS OF
THE POSTREFORM CONGRESS

The results of what some observers call *cutback politics* are predictable: (1) fewer bills are sponsored by individual legislators; (2) key policy decisions are packaged into huge "mega-bills," permitting lawmakers to escape adverse reactions to individual provisions; (3) techniques of blame avoidance are employed to protect lawmakers from the adverse effects of cutback politics; (4) noncontroversial, commemorative resolutions are passed into law—nearly half of all laws produced by recent Congresses; (5) driven by budgetary concerns, party-line voting is at a modern-day high on Capitol Hill; and (6) leadership in the House and Senate is markedly stronger now than at any time since 1910. Today's leaders not only benefit from powers conferred by reform-era innovations of the 1960s and 1970s, they also respond to widespread expectations that they are the only people who can, and should, untangle the legislative schedule.

Decline of Individually Sponsored Measures

The downturn in the number of measures introduced in the two chambers is one of the most obvious characteristics of the postreform Congress. This is particularly striking because it occurred in the wake of heightened bill introduction during the previous era. (House trends have been exacerbated by shifts in rules pertaining to cosponsorship of bills and resolutions.)

The overall bill-introduction pattern—a long-term increase followed by a precipitous decline—is similar for both senators and representatives. An average of about thirty-seven bills and resolutions per senator were introduced in 1947–48, reaching a peak of fifty-five in 1969–70; by the mid-1980s, the average was down to about forty-one bills and resolutions. The trend line in the House began at about twenty bills and resolutions, peaked at nearly fifty-six (1967–68), and then dropped to about seventeen per Congress. The current trend was well established before 1978, when the House first allowed unlimited cosponsorship of measures, causing the rate to plummet still further. The bottom line is that, on average, senators now introduce 25 percent fewer bills and resolutions than they did a generation ago, and representatives on average introduce only a third of the measures they used to.

It is no great task to locate the cause of declining legislative initiatives. "When the first thing you have to ask is what does it cost and where do you get the money, it totally distorts the policy process," observes Robert Reischauer, director of the Congressional Budget Office. "Congress doesn't do what it used to do, look at problems and try to fashion solutions" (qtd. in Raskin 1990, E1). This budgetary preoccupation has shifted the thrust of legislative creativity from policy-making to budgetary legerdemain. Lawmakers "have learned that there is little percentage in inventing programs for which there is no money, and little reward in making things work better when what matters politically is the appearance that the deficit is being reduced" (Rasking 1990, E1).

Some observers discern also a new emphasis on oversight of ongoing programs rather than innovation of new ones (Oleszek 1983; Aberbach 1989), though measuring oversight activities is quite difficult. Attention to oversight is promoted also by the persistence of divided government, in which the House (since 1981) and the Senate (since 1987) are thrust into the role of loyal opposition. Oversight need not lead to legislative products; indeed, it offers lawmakers a soapbox for making programmatic stands without necessarily providing legislative remedies or allocating funds.

Another apparent trend is the emphasis placed on symbolic domestic and foreign policy issues—especially those involving negligible or only modest outlays of funds. Such topics include various domestic social issues, arms control, terrorism, foreign trade, nuclear power, and international human rights. While expenditure of funds may be implied by some of these enactments, their chief value is that they allow politicians to position themselves without committing significant federal resources.

Legislative Packaging

Another attribute of postreform lawmaking is the rise of mega-bills—legislation that runs to hundreds or thousands of pages in length. Increasingly, Congress's most significant enactments are folded into a small number of omnibus bills, such as omnibus reauthorizations, continuing resolutions, or reconciliation bills. A related trend is the decrease of measures embodying substantive policy decisions. The proportion of substantive public laws peaked in the 1970s and has since declined to less than one-third of the public laws produced in the Ninety-ninth Congress (1985–86). The slack was taken up by the boom in commemorative measures (see Figure 1-1). "We're simply spending more and more time doing less and less," complained Arkansas's Democratic Senator David H. Pryor (qtd. in Peterson 1985, A13).

The postreform shift in the legislative agenda is largely a function of the politics of fiscal austerity. With the nation facing huge fiscal deficits, it is difficult to gain acceptance for freestanding initiatives that involve expenditures. As a result, these initiatives are often incorporated into mega-bills to improve their chances of enactment. A president may sign such measures even if they contain offensive provisions because a veto could cause the entire national government to shut down temporarily.

Omnibus bills also have the effect of recentralizing authority among party leaders and helping them manage legislative business. The leaders are the only ones who possess the resources and prerogatives needed to assure coordination in processing such complex measures. Mega-bills usually engage several committees. Therefore, committee leaders (as well as rank-and-file members) look to party leaders to assist in formulating a package acceptable to at least a majority of lawmakers. As one House member put it: "Our goal is to find something that's 60-percent acceptable to 52 percent of the members and I think we have a 75-percent chance of doing that" (qtd. in Kenworthy 1988, A22). This is why House and Senate leaders often appoint *ad hoc* party task forces to mobilize support behind these priority bills.

Figure 1-1 / Major Categories of Public Laws, 1947–1986

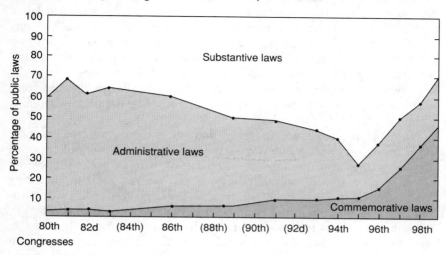

Definitions of categories of public laws:

Substantive: Major or general policy decisions, including appropriations, authorizations, or substantive amendments to authorizations.

Administrative: Includes administrative decisions not involving major policy decisions. Examples include native American tribal claims settlements, land conveyances, interstate compacts, actions pertaining to the legislative process, and other administrative actions such as pay adjustments and income disbursements.

Commemorative: This category includes designation of federal buildings or other facilities; authorization of commemorative days, weeks, or months; authorization of special medals or coins; and granting of federal charters to organizations.

From Claiming Credit to Avoiding Blame

Legislative packaging serves another purpose in a zero-sum environment: It helps to achieve consensus and to protect lawmakers from the repercussions of unpleasant policy alternatives (like freezes or cutbacks in funding or services). Senator Mark O. Hatfield (R-Oreg.), then chair of the Appropriations Committee, once announced that he would "hold [his] nose and do certain things here for the purpose of getting the job done, but certainly not with enthusiasm or anything other than recognizing that we are doing things under emergency conditions" (qtd. in Tate 1982b, 2379). Rather than alienating the clients or beneficiaries of programs facing cutbacks, freezes, or stretch-outs, lawmakers find it prudent to vote for omnibus measures that embody across-the-board formulas or complex compromises. As long as everyone else is taking their lumps, it is argued, it is easier to accept damage to one's own favored programs.

Legislative packaging is thus a parliamentary tactic well suited to an era of fiscal stringency. In a more expansionary atmosphere, individual law-makers have numerous opportunities to link their names with legislative proposals authorizing new government programs or services. For this "credit claiming," freestanding measures offer the highest payoff. But in a cutback era there are fewer opportunities for claiming credit; hence, law-makers' energies are devoted less to advertising their decisions than to de-vising ways of avoiding or disguising them. Weaver calls this "blame avoid-ance" (1988, 22–25). And for escaping or spreading the blame, omnibus measures are clearly preferable.

Other blame-avoidance strategies flourish in the postreform era. One of the most prominent is *indexing*—automatic adjustments of public policy outputs according to the movement of cost-of-living or other supposedly objective economic or social indicators. As Weaver explains, indexing "flows from a 'pass-the-buck' strategy, as policymakers cede to an auto-matic process the responsibility for politically painful choices" (1988, 32). While hardly a new technique, indexing has proved particularly useful in insulating politicians from the anguish of making specific allocations in a zero-sum atmosphere. On the one hand, it helps justify unpopular decisions; on the other, it imposes automatic limitations on the scope of permissible decisions (akin to the plea of "stop me before I kill again"). The Gramm-Rudman-Hollings formula, aimed at confining spending within boundaries imposed by revenues and deficits, might be thought of as a particularly ingenious use of indexing to redefine the congressional agenda.

Another strategy useful for blame avoidance is the establishment of au-tomatic procedures that yield policy results that can be overturned only by deliberate intervention. This might be called the "Look, Ma! No hands!" approach to policy-making. One example is the complicated quadrennial process for adjusting the pay of high-level executive, judicial, and legislative officials—a process that was thwarted in early 1989 by public outcry over what was deemed an excessive congressional pay raise. Another example is the 1988 statute designed to insulate military base closings from congres-sional pressure by creating a bipartisan commission to draw up a list of installations slated for closure. The list then has to be accepted or rejected *in toto*, a requirement aimed at making the commission's recommendations difficult to overturn. The initial "hit list" of eighty-three obsolete bases, announced after Congress had adjourned, was accepted by the secretary of defense and ultimately survived Capitol Hill efforts to scuttle it.

The Urge to Commemorate

In addition to the small number of massive legislative packages, Congress in the 1980s produced unprecedented numbers of *commemorative enact-ments*, defined as "those bills, resolutions, and laws which provide for spe-cial recognition of individuals, places, things, or events" (Richardson 1987, 1). Most commonly, these measures designate special commemorative days, weeks, or months—for example, National Asparagus Month, National Dairy Goat Awareness Week, or National Catfish Day. Other measures that should be placed in this category are those that, for instance, name federal buildings or sites, grant congressional charters for organizations, or authorize special medals or coins.

Once quite rare, commemorative measures enjoyed runaway popularity in the postreform era. In the Ninety-ninth Congress (1985–86) no less than 307 commemorative bills and joint resolutions became public laws—46 percent of all public laws enacted in that two-year period. Such measures comprised no more than 4–5 percent of all public enactments in the 1940s and 1950s, and 8–9 percent in the late 1960s and 1970s (see Figure 1-1). In the 1980s commemoratives accounted for at least a quarter of all enactments in any given Congress.

Commemorative measures are yet another response to the fiscal stringency that limits new substantive programs or spending to satisfy constituent demands. They placate lobby groups' interests, they express noncontroversial sentiments, they publicize certain causes, and, best of all, they cost virtually nothing. Such measures, of course, take up very little time in either chamber. The resolutions are brief, noncontroversial, and considered under expedited procedures such as unanimous consent or suspension of the rules. They are approved after perfunctory debate, involving at most a few laudatory remarks from their sponsors. Even so, their popularity has engendered some embarrassment and retrenchment: The two chambers have tightened the guidelines and procedures for approving the measures, and there have been proposals to curtail them even more drastically.

The Revival of Partisanship

Stronger parties and leaders are conspicuous features of the postreform Congress. Throughout most of the twentieth century, the term *congressional leadership* could have been regarded, without much exaggeration, as an oxymoron. With a few notable exceptions, leadership in the two chambers remained weak and scattered. After Franklin D. Roosevelt's first administration, a bipartisan conservative coalition dominated Capitol Hill through the seniority system's hold on the standing committees' ladders of advancement; opposition from many of these entrenched committee barons sealed the doom of numerous provisions of the 1946 Legislative Reorganization Act. The long-term decline of the political parties in commanding voter loyalty and controlling candidate recruitment compounded the problems faced by party leaders in promoting cohesion in their ranks.

Yet partisanship is alive and well in the postreform Congress. The party conferences (or caucuses) are firmly and elaborately institutionalized—a reform-era legacy that has outlived its reformist objectives. Robust, too, are the parties' campaign committees, which individually and in concert have become major forces in recruiting candidates and providing them with campaign support, financial and otherwise (Herrnson 1988, and this volume, Chapter 3). Once elected, members attend party-sponsored orientation programs, rely on party bodies for committee assignments, and are enmeshed in the parties' extensive whip systems.

Not surprisingly, then, party voting in the two chambers has enjoyed a renaissance. *Congressional Quarterly*'s party-unity scores for the late 1980s were the highest since the index was devised three decades earlier (Cranford 1988, 3334–35); other measures reflected the same story (Cohen and Schneider 1989, 203). Party-line voting, of course, still falls short of the levels customary under parliamentary systems; but by American standards, current levels of partisanship in floor voting are quite remarkable.

The reasons for the lively partisanship now manifested on Capitol Hill, while open to contention, are not unrelated to the agenda phenomenon. Part of the explanation surely lies in the nationalization of the two parties and the concomitant decline of the bipartisan conservative coalition. Many southern Democrats, who used to be called "Boll Weevils," now dependent on black voters for their reelection, have moved closer to the national party's left-of-center mainstream. The most conservative areas are quite willing to send Republicans to Washington; in a few cases, Democrats from such areas have simply switched parties. On the Republican side of the aisle, the ranks of the northeastern liberals (sometimes called "Gypsy Moths") have thinned, many of their seats now held by Democrats. The result is congressional parties that are more coherent ideologically than in earlier times (Rohde, this volume, Chapter 2).

More specifically the postreform agenda, centering on budget and deficit issues, has a heavy partisan content. Budgetary decisions are centralizing, integrating processes. Most obviously, party leaders are intimately involved in shaping the budget panels' membership and monitoring their activities. Budget packages are labeled by party, with voting on budget resolutions overwhelmingly following party lines. In a Congress where so many factions and pressures cross party lines, preoccupation with budgetary issues tends to polarize issues and factions (Thurber, this volume, Chapter 13).

The persistence of divided government in the 1980s contributed to the heightened partisanship of the postreform era. As long as the White House and one or both chambers are in different parties' hands, there is an inevitable temptation to regard legislative products as partisan declarations. Party strategists, majority and minority, sometimes frame major issues in partisan terms because they see potential bonuses in terms of public attitudes or electoral outcomes. Democratic leaders in the 100th Congress, for example, were anxious to compile a record of achievement that they hoped would carry them to victory in the 1988 elections. GOP strategists used issues advantageous to them—taxes, crime, and flag desecration, for example—to cultivate support for future elections.

Resurgence of "The Leadership"

The postreform Congress manifests a resurgence not only of partisanship but also of "the leadership"; that is, institutionalized party leadership (Sinclair and Palazzolo, this volume, Chapters 5 and 6, respectively). The earlier reform era, though its central thrust was to empower rank-and-file members at the expense of the committee leaders, bequeathed a legacy of stronger prerogatives for party leaders—again, mainly at the expense of committee leaders. As a result of 1970s innovations, Democratic Speakers nominate all majority members of the Committee on Rules, subject to caucus approval. (The Republican floor leader has been given similar power.) Staffed with loyalists, the committee became an arm of the leadership, crafting rules for floor consideration of measures that restricted floor amendments and promoted final legislative products reflecting party leaders' preferences or judgments. Closed and so-called restrictive or complex rules rose from about 16 percent of all rules in 1975–76 to nearly half of all rules in 1985–86 (Bach and Smith 1988, 56–57). Rules Committee efforts to contain and shape House floor deliberations expanded qualitatively as well as quantitatively with the appearance of such novel devices as self-executing and "king-of-the-mountain" rules that stack the deck to favor majority-party outcomes (this volume, Chapter 7).

Leadership prerogatives are augmented by increased use of mega-bills and bills referred to two or more committees (Davidson and Oleszek, this volume, Chapter 7). When multiple referrals were first allowed in 1975, they were intended to spread the action on bills to more committees and members. But the practice also buttressed House leaders' most fundamental power: scheduling. The Speaker has the responsibility of assigning bills or resolutions to two or more committees—jointly, sequentially, or in split fashion. In sequential referrals, the Speaker routinely sets deadlines for consideration by all but the initial committee—an astounding power for the House to bequeath to its chief officer. Although they are only a tiny portion of all multiple referrals, sequential referrals are almost always applied to important leadership packages. Further, multiple-referral bills are more likely to require the Rules Committee's assistance in facilitating floor approval. More than two-thirds of all multiple-referred bills come to the House floor with closed or restrictive rules, compared with about 38 percent of all other bills (Bach and Smith 1988, 60). Thus, such legislative packages directly involve the Speaker from referral through committee deadlines to floor scheduling and final voting.

Exploitation of the full range of leadership prerogatives did not occur overnight. Thomas P. (Tip) O'Neill (D-Mass.), who played a modest though pivotal role in the 1970s reforms, became Speaker in 1977, but it was not until 1983 that circumstances propelled him into a more aggressive leadership style. His successor, Jim Wright (D-Tex.), had fewer inhibitions about exploiting his powers of office. Taking office in 1987, Wright announced an ambitious list of legislative goals, including highway improvement, clean air, trade, and catastrophic health insurance. Two years later, nearly all the bills had passed the House and many had been signed into law. Wright's personal combativeness and extreme partisanship, to be sure, made him a host of enemies, not all of them in the opposing party. His demise in mid-1989, in the wake of questions about his financial ethics, had as much to do with his personal style as with his admittedly aggressive use of prerogatives. Wright's rise and fall was closely paralleled by that of Majority Whip Tony Coelho (D-Calif.). And while the new team—Speaker Thomas S. Foley (D-Wash.) and Majority Leader Richard A. Gephardt (D-Mo.)—betokened a "kinder, gentler" House leadership, the change was more one of style than substance. Foley surprised everyone by fulfilling his pledge to get all thirteen appropriations bills passed before the August 1989 recess, seven of them in one week alone. "The new Speaker was following through on a degree of discipline first imposed by his predecessor . . ." (Madison 1989, 2067). Firm central direction may well be a functional requirement of the postreform House.

Leadership in the Senate is typically more muted and constricted than in the House (Smith, this volume, Chapter 9). In the 1980s, Senate leaders sought to manage day-to-day business while struggling against the delays dictated by the Senate's traditions. Majority Leader Howard Baker (R-Tenn.) for a time waged war on "holds," whereby individual senators halt the progress of certain measures. Robert C. Byrd attacked the rules, sought to control filibusters, brokered agreements for processing key measures considered by multiple committees, and tried to establish a four-day business week. Later the Senate decided to operate on a five-day workweek, with every fourth week off for constituency visits.

A survey of twenty-six senators in late 1987 uncovered widespread support for even tighter scheduling and floor management (Center for Responsive Politics 1988, 1, 13). A majority of the respondents were dismayed by the inefficiency of the chamber. Among the leading demands of Senate leaders were (1) more advance scheduling of legislative activity, (2) stronger discipline for members, and (3) more attention to the partisan and congressional agenda. Support for change was especially strong among former House members, accustomed to the tighter discipline of the larger chamber.

CONCLUSION

The premise of this analysis is that Congress is motivated by the need to respond—through structural or procedural changes, legislation, or other activities—to demands emanating from the larger economic, social, political, and government environment. The largely uncoordinated and unexpected evolution of what we call the postreform Congress provides a compelling illustration of this premise.

The postreform Congress betokens not a concerted reform effort but a gradual adaptation to radically altered political and legislative agendas. Confronted by a lagging economy, divided government, and divisions over the efficacy of government programs, Congress markedly changed the way it approached its legislative work load, in the process retreating from the decentralized system established by the reforms of the 1960s and 1970s.

One message conveyed by this story is the institution's resiliency in adapting to the demands made upon it. Confronted with stresses brought on by changes in its external environment, an organization normally does not willingly choose to emasculate its mission or radically transform its work (Cooper 1981, 341–43). Rather, the typical organization pursues one or more adaptive strategies. It may seek to adopt structural or operational changes that will adjust its output capability upward or downward, as the case may be. Or it may seek to reshape its effective domain by contracting or expanding it—sloughing off categories of work load in the former, appropriating new tasks in the latter. Both strategies are designed to achieve an equilibrium between the expectations and demands and the institution's work-load capacities.

Consider the kinds of institutional innovations adopted by Congress in the postreform years. Beginning in the late 1970s, Congress confronted an altered set of demands for legislative action. The political agenda shrank, narrowing the prospects for new programs or spending priorities. While many of the structural innovations of the earlier reform era remained intact, Congress adjusted its activities to meet the altered environment. Committee and floor agendas contracted. Key decisions were more apt to be contained in lengthy omnibus vehicles, often processed by more than one committee and usually superintended by party leaders. Members and committees explored new categories of policy-making, or they exploited existing categories—oversight, commemoratives, indexing, and symbolic measures— that were well suited to the policy environment.

Whether Congress adjusts quickly enough or effectively enough to preserve its constitutional position remains an open question. Yet the variability of legislative structures, procedures, and products is impressive. Today's legislative work load is very different from what it was in previous decades. This and the following chapters in *The Postreform Congress* are intended to sensitize the reader to those differences, and to help explain how those changes occurred and how Congress remade itself because of them.

PART · II

Electoral Currents in the Postreform Era

2 / Electoral Forces, Political Agendas, and Partisanship in the House and Senate

DAVID W. ROHDE

Until recently, congressional analysts considered political parties in Congress to be largely inconsequential.[1] They argued that support for party positions among members of the House and Senate was low, largely because they had few incentives to take account of those positions when making legislative choices. Instead, senators and representatives made decisions on the basis of their own political interests, particularly their desire to be re-elected. The weakening of traditional party loyalties in the electorate produced conflict within the parties, particularly between northern and southern Democrats. Moreover, party organizations and their leaders had few rewards or sanctions at their disposal to encourage members' support, and the decentralized congressional system fostered many competing power centers that could urge members in the opposite direction.

The 1980s, however, witnessed a marked increase in partisanship in the House.[2] Interparty conflict and intraparty cohesion in floor voting increased. Party leaders became more aggressive, often encouraged by rank-and-file members. Relationships between the Democratic majority and the Republican White House became more confrontational, with the Democrats more and more frequently choosing policy options the president opposed. Little attention has been given to the degree to which corresponding developments have occurred in the Senate (Hurley 1989 is an exception). This analysis looks at recent findings regarding partisanship in the House and offers some comparative evidence on the Senate. While space does not permit a complete and definitive analysis here, it is hoped that the results will prove useful for future research.

INFLUENCES ON PARTISANSHIP: SOME THEORETICAL CONSIDERATIONS

What is meant by the term *partisanship*? It refers to the influence and impact of political parties on members' choices and on the operation of the two houses. Partisanship is not an attribute that is present or absent; it is a

27

matter of degree. We can speak of some aspect of congressional operations as being more or less partisan compared to some other aspect, or relative to that same aspect in another time period. We can also refer to some individual, activity, or institutional arrangement as being partisan (or nonpartisan), indicating that we regard the connection to political parties to be relatively strong (or weak). For example, we might characterize the House as partisan, meaning that parties (and particularly the majority party) are important influences on institutional operations, individual decisions, and legislative outcomes. *Partisan* would imply that conflict along party lines was relatively frequent. If, however, we labeled the Senate as nonpartisan, we would imply that parties are not particularly influential and that disagreements over policy are mostly shaped by other considerations.

Similarly, we can say that an action or activity is partisan, indicating that it is intended to benefit one party (often, but not always, at the expense of the other). A clear example is the choice of the Speaker of the House at the beginning of each Congress. The Democrats all vote for their candidate, and the Republicans for theirs, because each party wants to use the powers of the office for their benefit. This choice is thus a partisan decision.

Finally, we can speak of an individual as partisan, meaning that the person's decisions and behavior are strongly influenced by his or her attachment to a party. Thus Speaker Jim Wright (D-Tex.) could be labeled partisan because much of his leadership activity was directed at securing legislation favored by Democrats and blocking alternatives supported by the Republicans.

In addition to this definition of partisanship, though, it is useful to distinguish between *policy partisanship* and *process partisanship*. The former relates to the degree to which policy decisions—on the floor, in committee, or elsewhere—are characterized by partisan disagreement. Thus if the House were characterized by frequent policy conflicts between cohesive Democrats and cohesive Republicans, we would say that it exhibited strong policy partisanship. Process partisanship, however, refers to the degree to which each institution is structured or operates in a partisan fashion. For example, when Congress convened in 1981 with a new Republican majority in the Senate and a substantially reduced Democratic majority in the House, the party balance on every Senate standing committee matched the balance in the full chamber as closely as possible. In the House, while many committees reflected the chamber balance (56 percent Democratic), five of them (including the four most important) had Democratic majorities substantially above that.[3] In this case, the House exhibited much greater process partisanship by allocating disproportionate power to the majority party. Most of the discussion and evidence in this chapter deal with policy partisanship, though process matters are briefly examined as well.

In an earlier analysis of parties and partisanship in the House (Rohde 1991b), I argued that the level of partisanship is the consequence of three, or possibly four, factors. These three factors, in hypothesized order of importance, are *electoral forces*, *institutional arrangements*, and *personal influences*. The fourth factor involves possible variations in the agenda. That is, the degree of apparent partisan conflict may vary along with variations in the types of issues or vote choices that members confront. These variations may be the consequence of either systematic political forces or simply chance. It is important to keep this factor in mind, in order to control for these variations when possible.

Electoral Forces

The overwhelming majority of members of Congress desire to be reelected and seek reelection when the opportunity arises. These members must constantly perform their jobs with an eye toward constituents' reactions to what they do. Every legislative choice is an opportunity to build support at home or to provide a potential opponent with an issue for the next election.

Thus electoral forces are an important—the majority of analysts would say the most important—influence on legislative decision making. Policy partisanship is high within a legislative body when the constituency preferences of the members of a party are similar to one another and different from those of the other party.[4] Within the Democratic party in the 1950s, northerners and southerners differed on a range of domestic issues. These differences deepened during the 1960s with the national Democratic commitment to civil rights, the launching of the Great Society, and the conflict over the Vietnam War and national defense issues.[5] These deep divisions were reflected in the Congress, where Democrats were sharply split along regional lines (Sinclair 1982, 1989c).

The 1960s, however, also sowed the seeds of further change. The Voting Rights Act of 1965 set the stage for the political equality of black Americans in the South. As the impact of the law was gradually felt, black electoral participation increased during the 1970s and into the 1980s. Black voters overwhelmingly identified with the Democratic party because their policy views were markedly more liberal than the views of white southern voters. Meanwhile, the national Democratic party's identification with the liberal position on civil rights and other issues pushed many conservative white southerners to align with the Republicans. These two trends had the effects of liberalizing southern Democratic constituencies and making them more like their northern counterparts (Rohde 1988, 1989).

As these sectional conflicts receded, we would expect to observe a resurgence of interparty conflict and intraparty cohesion. The increased similarity between northern and southern Democratic constituencies would likely affect both the recruitment of new legislators and the behavior of continuing members, resulting in responses on issues by southerners that were increasingly similar to those of northern Democrats.

There are, however, reasons to expect that the effects would not be precisely the same in the House and Senate. One involves systematic differences in the nature of House and Senate constituencies. Senate districts are fixed geographic entities, varying enormously in terms of population. Although House constituencies are variable, with their lines adjusted periodically, they all contain approximately the same number of people, The geographic constituencies of senators, on average, are considerably more heterogeneous than those of representative, containing a greater variety of social, political, and economic characteristics.[6] No state can be as dominated by urban interests as a Manhattan House district. No state has a majority black population, but a number of House districts do. Heterogeneous Senate "districts" offer politicians the opportunity to build a variety of winning coalitions—what Fenno (1978) terms *reelection constituencies*—while those opportunities are more limited in House districts. This Senate-district heterogeneity can lead to winning coalitions being constructed by both parties within a single state, resulting in one Senate seat being held by each,[7] or to coalitions with different characteristics and emphases being represented by two senators from the same party. In the latter case, two senators (North or South) representing different constituencies would probably respond differently to some of the choices they faced, so one would probably exhibit more partisanship than the other. The partisanship of House members, who represent more homogeneous constituencies, depends on the degree of similarity of the preferences of those constituencies across districts. Because representatives are less vulnerable to electoral defeat, and their elections less issue-oriented than those of senators (Fenno 1982, chap. 2; Baker 1989, 115–122), their partisanship may depend more heavily on their own policy preferences and orientations (Rohde 1991b, chap. 3). Electoral conditions that tend to foster partisanship in the House may have less impact in the Senate. However, electoral conditions leading to intraparty divisions in the House have less clear results in the Senate, where partisanship may actually be greater.

Another potential reason for a contrast between the houses is the differing impacts of the enfranchisement of black voters and the realignment in the South. The liberalizing effects of the Voting Rights Act were unequally distributed across House districts within states. In some districts the impact of the act was strong, while in others it was virtually nonexistent. For example, the election of a black Democratic congressman, Mike Espy, in 1986 was linked to the fact that 58 percent of the population of Mississippi's Second District is black. The Fifth District, though, is only 19 percent black, so it was represented for 16 years by conservative Republican Trent Lott. The overall black population of the state is between these two extremes— 35 percent—and both senators are conservative Republicans. Thus electoral changes in the South appear to have produced a number of Democratic districts with political preferences closer to those in northern Democratic districts, as well as several conservative districts largely represented by Republicans. The statewide effects, however, are more mixed and may tend to produce a larger proportion of moderate-to-conservative Democrats.

The houses also differ in the length of members' terms of office. Representatives, who serve a two-year term, must campaign constantly. As the founders intended, this renders them sensitive to constituency opinions. The next election is always just around the corner, and the risks of taking an unpopular stand on salient issues are great. Senators, though, face the voters less frequently. For the majority of senators at any given time, the next election is from three to six years away. Senators do stop campaigning (Fenno 1982, 27), but there are indications that the House and Senate variations in this regard are less substantial than they once were (Baker 1989, 187–95). To the degree that there are differences among members' own preferences on issues and those of their constituents (Rohde 1990, 1991b), senators, being more insulated from electoral pressures, may be more inclined to follow their own views than are representatives. Thus electoral changes may have a less predictable and less powerful effect in the Senate than in the House.

Institutional Arrangements

Institutional differences between the House and the Senate are likely to affect the levels of partisanship in many ways (see Smith, this volume, Chapter 9).[8] For the purposes of this analysis, the most profound institutional difference is that, in the House, a cohesive majority party can almost always work its will, even if its margin of control is minuscule, while the same is not true in the Senate. It is here that both the distinction and the connection between policy and procedural partisanship become clear.

Power in the Senate is more equally distributed between the parties than it is in the House. The potential for extended debate (commonly known as *filibusters*), which has no parallel in the House, gives the minority a potent potential weapon (along with the other procedural-delaying devices available to individuals). Because of the threat of delaying or blocking tactics, and the related need to employ unanimous-consent agreements to deal with bills on the floor (Smith 1989, chap. 4), the Senate majority party usually must make accommodations with the minority. House debate, however, is limited by rules or by specific resolutions adopted by majority vote, and the availability of other delaying tactics to the minority is relatively limited. Aside from a few major bills introduced each year, most legislation in the House is routinely disposed of in an hour or two; and if a House rule stands in the way of the majority party accomplishing its goal, that too can usually be overridden by a simple majority.

Within most Senate committees, partisanship is more muted than in their House counterparts (Fenno 1973, chap. 5). The majority rarely has incentives to try to "roll over" the minority because the barrier of floor consideration must be faced. In this more accommodating atmosphere, bipartisan action in support of significant legislation is commonplace, even between ideologically divergent senators. For example, Fenno (1989a) describes the alliance between Senators Dan Quayle (R-Ind.) and Edward M. Kennedy (D-Mass.) behind a major job-training bill in 1982. Such bipartisanship is rare in the House. While House committees vary in how partisan they are, reform rules passed by Democrats in the 1970s gave the majority party in each committee the power to control all facets of structure and procedure (Rohde 1991b, chap. 2). When it is in their interests, and when they are cohesive, the majority can exercise this power. As Representative Henry A. Waxman (D-Calif.) said, "If we have a united Democratic position, Republicans are irrelevant" (Hook 1986, 1393). Even senior committee Republicans have relatively little impact. John McCain (R-Ariz.), who left the House in 1986 for a Senate seat, commented that "the only difference between a freshman Republican and a ranking Republican is that the ranking Republican gets to ask questions first" (Hook 1986, 1393).

When bills come to the floor, minority party senators have the opportunity to alter the committee's product. Unless restrictions are imposed by unanimous consent, a senator can offer an amendment even if it does not deal with the subject of the bill. House floor amendments must be germane, and a resolution from the Rules Committee (known as a "special rule" and adopted by majority floor vote) can bar amendments entirely, or restrict what amendments can be offered, by whom, and in what order (see Bach and Smith 1988; Rohde 1991b, chap. 4). This institutional contrast is carried over to the powers that each body grants to its majority leadership. Cohesive majority parties in the House have incentives to give their leadership strong powers, while divided parties tend to keep their leaders weak (Cooper and Brady 1981; Rohde and Shepsle 1987). the Democrats strengthened their leadership by giving the Speaker control over appointments to the Rules Committee and increasing the leadership's influence over other committee assignments.[9] The Speaker also has the authority to refer bills to more than one committee and to set deadlines for committee action (Cooper and Collie 1989). The Senate majority, however, has little ability or reason to grant its leaders strong powers. Such a move would require a wholesale change in the Senate's rules, which could itself be blocked by the minority's current advantages, while more modest changes would probably have little effect if they could pass. Thus Senate leaders are left with few formal powers to enhance the chances of partisan policy positions. They generally try to serve the diverse individual interests of their members (Davidson 1985).

Personal Influences

The personalities, styles, and ideological orientations of the particular actors involved at any given time have a noticeable but less significant impact on the level of partisanship in the two chambers. For example, the 100th Congress (involving House Speaker Jim Wright, Senate Majority Leader Robert Byrd, and President Ronald Reagan) was more partisan than the 101st

Congress (with Speaker Tom Foley, Majority Leader George Mitchell, and President George Bush) because of personal influences. Reagan was more ideologically rigid and less inclined to compromise than Bush; he was also more aggressive in his attacks on Democrats and their policies. Wright was extremely partisan, willing to use his leadership powers to advance the Democratic agenda. Speaker Foley was personally inclined to be less combative with the Republicans (both in the House and the White House) and more willing to compromise to reach a viable result, being disinclined toward procedural partisanship.[10]

With respect to Senators Byrd and Mitchell, the expectations are less clear. Byrd was willing from time to time to engage in some procedural partisanship (to the limited degree the Senate makes it feasible) and sought to foster party unity (Calmes 1987). However, he exhibited comparatively little personal interest in advancing particular policy positions and was strongly inclined toward a service orientation (Davidson 1985). Mitchell, with strong interests in a variety of policy areas, indicated when he took office that a policy agenda for Senate Democrats was a priority (Cohen 1989). Yet he began by further fragmenting his personal resources by parceling out the chairmanships of the party's Steering Committee and Policy Committee to others. Mitchell, too, was willing to take procedural initiatives on occasion to advance party priorities. When he succeeded in getting the Senate to invoke cloture (that is, terminate debate) on the 1990 Civil Rights Bill to speed its passage, Minority Leader Bob Dole complained that the Republicans were being treated "like of bunch of bums" and threatened to block future interparty agreements on scheduling (Dewar and Devroy 1990).

The personal factor involves complex relationships; taking account of it in an analysis involving decades of activity would be a major task. The fragmentary evidence available, however, indicates that it is potentially important, at least after accounting for other major influences.

Variable Agendas

The potential impact of variations in the legislative agenda over time is relevant to any longitudinal analysis of decision making or outcomes, but it is easiest to discuss in the context of floor voting. To measure partisanship, groups of roll calls organized by periods (years or Congresses) are used. The mix of votes varies among periods; for example, by issue area or by type of vote. That is, at one point there may be more votes on defense issues or amendments than at another point. This is further complicated by the attempt to compare the House and Senate, because the sets of votes over which members make choices differ between the two bodies.

As noted earlier, variations in the legislative agenda can be random or systematic. They are systematic because the roll-call agenda itself—which issues get to the floor, which get voted on with roll calls or voice votes, and what type of vote is involved—is determined by the choices of legislators

Table 2-1 / Percentage of Party Votes in the House and Senate, 84th–100th Congresses

Congress (Years)	House (N)[a]	Senate (N)[a]	Difference (House-Senate)
84th (1955–56)	42% (149)	44% (217)	−2
85th (1957–58)	49% (193)	41% (307)	+8
86th (1959–60)	54% (180)	42% (422)	+12
87th (1961–62)	48% (240)	51% (428)	−3
88th (1963–64)	52% (232)	41% (534)	+11
89th (1965–66)	47% (394)	43% (497)	+4
90th (1967–68)	35% (478)	33% (596)	+2
91st (1969–70)	28% (443)	35% (666)	−7
92d (1971–72)	33% (649)	39% (955)	−6
93d (1973–74)	36% (1,078)	41% (1,138)	−5
94th (1975–76)	42% (1,273)	41% (1,311)	+1
95th (1977–78)	37% (1,540)	44% (1,156)	−7
96th (1979–80)	43% (1,276)	46% (1,054)	−3
97th (1981–82)	37% (812)	45% (966)	−8
98th (1983–84)	52% (896)	41% (663)	+11
99th (1985–86)	53% (766)	51% (740)	+2
100th (1987–88)	52% (847)	42% (799)	+10

[a] N is the number of roll-call votes taken in that Congress.
Source: Inter-University Consortium for Political and Social Research (ICPSR) roll-call data.

responding to incentives that are similar in nature to those that are involved in the actual roll-call choices. The choice of what to vote on is just as much a legislative decision as is which policy option to choose (see Van Doren 1990; Rohde 1990). Accounting for these kinds of variations when using roll-call data involves a substantial but worthwhile investment in data gathering.[11] Controlling for agenda variations helps determine whether relationships hold in the same way across categories or institutions and whether the impact of changing agendas is systematic over time.

ELECTORAL CHANGES AND PARTISANSHIP IN FLOOR VOTING

Important to this analysis are the changing levels of party voting and party unity in the House and Senate.[12] Table 2-1 shows the percentage of party votes in the House and Senate from the 84th Congress through the 100th Congress (1955–88).[13] The time series for both the House and Senate exhibit the expected decline and resurgence of partisanship. Party voting declined substantially during the late 1960s and early 1970s, then rose in the 1980s. There was little overall difference between the two series. Over the seventeen-Congress period, the average difference in party votes between the House and Senate was only 1.2 percentage points.

However, there are period effects worth noting. The average levels of voting when the congresses are grouped are as follows:

	House	Senate	Difference
84th–88th Congresses	49.0	43.8	+5.2
89th–93d Congresses	35.8	38.2	−2.4
94th–97th Congresses	39.8	44.0	−4.2
98th–100th Congresses	52.3	44.7	+7.6

Average party voting had a much greater range in the House, falling lower when it declined and reaching a higher peak when it increased. The level in the House, moreover, was higher than in the Senate before Johnson's election in 1964 and after Reagan's first Congress, and it was lower in between. This is consistent with the argument that the impact of electoral change is mitigated in the Senate, and that the effects of changing constituency preferences are less powerfully felt. It may also be due, in part, to agenda differences.

Table 2-2 (see p. 36) shows average party-unity scores for both parties in the two chambers. All four party groups exhibit the same temporal pattern, with loyalty being higher on average before the Eighty-ninth Congress and after the Ninety-seventh Congress. Here, however, the interchamber differences are not as pronounced as with party voting. Within each party, the two time series are quite similar and large differences within a Congress tend to be scattered. Among the few comparisons worth noting are (1) House Republicans were noticeably more loyal than their Senate counterparts during the Carter presidency and (2) House Democrats were more loyal in the Ninety-eighth and Ninety-ninth Congresses.

The data in Table 2-2 also show that Democratic unity scores peaked in the 98th through the 100th Congresses in the House and in the 100th Congress in the Senate. As argued earlier, the resurgence of partisanship among Democrats was due in large measure to electoral changes in the South. Table 2-3 (see p. 37) presents unity data for Democrats by section.[14] The patterns are consistent with expectations, and similar (albeit not identical) between the houses. Northern Democrats had high levels of loyalty and exhibited comparatively little variation over time, although representatives reached higher average levels than senators. Southerners in both chambers demonstrated the sharp decline and strong resurgence of party loyalty. In both the House and Senate, the level of unity achieved by southern Democrats in the 100th Congress was the highest in the entire series.

Thus it is clear that the substantial gap between northern and southern Democrats on partisan issues has closed. Issues that once divided the party either no longer do so or their impact is reduced. Southern Democrats are

Table 2-2 / Average Party Loyalty in the House and Senate, by Party, 84th–100th Congresses

Congress (Years)	Democrats		Republicans	
	HOUSE	SENATE	HOUSE	SENATE
84th (1955–56)	80	81	78	81
85th (1957–58)	78	80	74	77
86th (1959–60)	80	75	81	79
87th (1961–62)	81	79	80	80
88th (1963–64)	83	76	82	78
89th (1965–66)	79	74	81	77
90th (1967–68)	75	73	79	72
91st (1969–70)	71	73	72	71
92d (1971–72)	70	74	76	73
93d (1973–74)	74	76	73	70
94th (1975–76)	75	76	76	71
95th (1977–78)	73	73	77	70
96th (1979–80)	76	76	79	73
97th (1981–82)	78	76	78	82
98th (1983–84)	82	76	78	80
99th (1985–86)	83	77	76	80
100th (1987–88)	86	86	81	76

Source: ICPSR roll-call data.

more likely to support social programs than they were in the past, and liberals and conservatives have found more common ground on budget matters. On defense issues, southerners are more supportive of cuts in spending (though most do not favor reductions as large as northerners seek) and more willing to restrict presidential discretion on substantive matters.

The most striking change involves the issue of civil rights. By the late 1970s, majority support among southern Democrats for civil rights measures was routine, while among Republicans (even northerners) support had declined from previous levels. When the Voting Rights Act was up for renewal in 1981, efforts to weaken the bill in both chambers came from Republicans and were generally opposed by southern Democrats, who also strongly supported passage of the final bill. Southern Democrats also provided substantial support for efforts to impose economic sanctions on South Africa for its system of apartheid. More recently, Congress in 1990 considered a civil rights measure designed to reverse or restrict six Supreme Court decisions that had narrowed the application of laws prohibiting employment discrimination. Despite Republican charges that the bill would lead to racial quotas, southern Democrats in the House supported the con-

Table 2-3 / Average Party Loyalty among Democrats in the House and Senate, by Region, 84th–100th Congresses

Congress (Years)	House		Senate	
	NORTH	SOUTH	NORTH	SOUTH
84th (1955–56)	86	73	85	77
85th (1957–58)	85	70	83	77
86th (1959–60)	86	70	83	62
87th (1961–62)	92	68	88	61
88th (1963–64)	94	68	84	61
89th (1965–66)	91	55	85	55
90th (1967–68)	90	51	81	60
91st (1969–70)	83	50	84	53
92d (1971–72)	82	46	85	53
93d (1973–74)	85	54	86	53
94th (1975–76)	85	53	87	52
95th (1977–78)	81	55	83	53
96th (1979–80)	83	61	82	63
97th (1981–82)	86	60	83	63
98th (1983–84)	89	67	80	67
99th (1985–86)	89	71	82	63
100th (1987–88)	91	76	89	79

Source: ICPSR roll-call data.

ference report seventy to twelve; among southern Democratic senators support was unanimous.[15] This is particularly remarkable in light of the fact that the 1990 candidacies of Jesse Helms in North Carolina and David Duke in Louisiana demonstrated that quotas are a politically potent issue.

Intraparty unity among Democrats substantially increased during the last two decades in both houses of Congress. How did this come about? Did these changes in aggregate party loyalty occur because certain members changed their behavior over time, because new members replaced old ones, or because of a combination of these factors? The data in Table 2-2 show that the period from the 95th Congress to the 100th Congress produced a strong increase in average unity among House and Senate Democrats. By comparing these two Congresses in terms of average party unity of members who served in either both or only one of them, insight is gained into the relative impact of changed behavior versus replacement. These data are presented in Table 2-4 (see p. 38).[16]

First, note in Table 2-4 the differences in average party unity for members who served only in the 95th Congress versus those who continued on through the 100th Congress. In the House, the differences are small: in each

Table 2-4 / Party Unity in the 95th and 100th Congresses

Congress	When Members Served	Party and Region (N)[a]			
		SOUTHERN DEMOCRATS	NORTHERN DEMOCRATS	SOUTHERN REPUBLICANS	NORTHERN REPUBLICANS
House					
95th	95th only	53 (52)	81 (120)	84 (21)	74 (76)
95th	Both	56 (36)	82 (77)	87 (10)	76 (39)
100th	Both	77 (36)	91 (77)	83 (10)	74 (39)
100th	100th only	75 (48)	91 (95)	90 (33)	80 (93)
Senate					
95th	95th only	48 (10)	83 (27)	84 (5)	63 (16)
95th	Both	55 (9)	81 (16)	90 (2)	72 (15)
100th	Both	81 (9)	89 (16)	89 (2)	69 (15)
100th	100th only	78 (9)	88 (20)	86 (6)	78 (23)

[a] N is the number of members in each category.
Source: ICPSR roll-call data.

of the four categories scores for those who continued serving were one to three points higher. For the Senate, the results are similar, but the differences are a bit larger: for all except northern Democrats average party unity of members who continued was five to seven points higher. Next, consider the corresponding comparisons for the 100th Congress. For Democrats in both Houses the differences are all small, from zero to three points. Among Republicans, however, the contrast is notable. With the exception of southern senators (where the number of cases is small), average unity scores are six to nine points higher among members who entered after the Ninety-fifth Congress than among continuing members.

It is also necessary to examine the changes in scores among members who served in both Congresses and to compare the scores of members who served only in the Ninety-fifth Congress with those who entered later. These comparisons are presented in Table 2-5. For continuing members the changes are remarkably similar in both chambers. Southern Democrats demonstrated an enormous increase in average party loyalty, while northern Democrats exhibited a smaller but still substantial gain. Among Republicans, though, there are small decreases across the board.

Also in Table 2-5 are the parallel comparisons for groups of members who served in only one of the two Congresses in question. For Democrats, the differences are similar to the shifts among continuing members. Thus the aggregate changes in loyalty among Democrats were not due solely to the replacement of one type of member with another. Instead, the effects

Table 2-5 / Changes in Party-Unity Scores for Senators and Representatives, 95th and 100th Congresses

	A. Continuing Members (served in both Congresses)			
	SOUTHERN DEMOCRATS	NORTHERN DEMOCRATS	SOUTHERN REPUBLICANS	NORTHERN REPUBLICANS
House	+21	+9	−4	−2
Senate	+26	+8	−1	−3

	B. Members Who Served in the 95th and 100th Congresses[a]			
	SOUTHERN DEMOCRATS	NORTHERN DEMOCRATS	SOUTHERN REPUBLICANS	NORTHERN REPUBLICANS
House	+22	+10	+6	+6
Senate	+30	+5	+2	+13

[a] The cells in part B give the average score for the 100th Congress minus the average score for the 95th, and thus parallel the data in part A for continuing members.
Source: ICPSR roll-call data.

of member replacement and of changed behavior among continuing members were virtually identical. These results suggest that Democrats' resurgent party unity responded to shifts in voter alignments in their electoral constituencies. As their supportive constituencies in both the House and Senate became less sectionally distinct, long-serving Democrats adjusted their behavior accordingly; and newly elected members, responding to the same electoral environment, exhibited similar behavior.

The pattern of change among Republicans sheds further light on the matter. Among continuing members, there were small decreases in unity scores (Table 2-5). Comparing "departed" members of the 95th Congress to new members of the 100th Congress shows consistent (and larger) increases in average unity. Together these results suggest that the increased unity among Democrats was not simply an artifact of a changed agenda. As we will see later in the chapter, there were noteworthy variations in the roll-call agendas between the chambers and over time, but the evidence does not support a conclusion that the character of the roll calls that divide the parties was systematically different. For example, if increased loyalty among southern Democrats had occurred because democratic proposals had become more moderate in nature (that is, less reflective of the preferences of the liberal wing of the party), then those proposals should also have become more attractive to moderate Republicans, causing a correspondingly large drop in unity among continuing GOP members from the North. But this did not occur; indeed, the trend was in the opposite direction among new Republican members relative to their predecessors.[17] This evidence, of course, is inconclusive, but it can be argued that these data do not support the counterhypothesis that behavioral differences were primarily due to agenda changes rather than electoral changes.

SOME CONTRASTS RELATED TO AGENDAS AND INSTITUTIONS

While the analysis of changes in party-unity scores does not indicate the systematic effects of variations in the agenda or of variations between chambers, this does not foreclose the issue. Specifically, it does not address the question of whether institutional or agenda differences affect the likelihood of a vote or an issue producing partisan conflict. Party-unity scores only relate to that subset of votes on which party majorities are opposed. The preceding analysis suggests that the nature of these two subsets is similar between the houses over time, but the chambers could still differ systematically on the probability that a given matter gets into that subset.

One way to address the issue is to make comparisons between the House and Senate on the same issues. Of course, this is difficult because of the bicameral arrangement of the houses; each deals independently with legislative issues. However, one vehicle that does permit such a comparison is the conference report; it is identical in both chambers.

Table 2-6 compares twenty-four conference reports from the 100th Congress that were decided by roll-call votes in both the House and Senate. The second and third columns of the table provide comparisons based on all twenty-four reports; the last two columns exclude reports decided by consensual votes (that is, majorities on 90 percent or more)[18] in both houses. In the Senate, the average majority was larger and the average party difference[19] was lower. House votes on these issues were more than twice as likely to produce opposed-party majorities than in the Senate. On only one Senate vote was the majority less than 60 percent, whereas this occurred six times in the House. Further, when votes that were consensual in both chambers are excluded, only one other House vote and four Senate votes were consensual. These data indicate that senators are less likely to divide along party lines than are representatives, even when they are presented with identical stimuli.

Of course, conference reports may be unrepresentative of other types of votes, and voting divisions on them may have as much to do with the dynamics of how each house got to that point as with the substance of the report.[20] In this sense the stimuli may not be identical. Moreover, conference reports constituted only a small proportion (about 3 percent) of the roll calls from the 100th Congress. Thus it is necessary to examine a broader

Table 2-6 / Comparison of Votes on Conference Reports Decided by Roll Calls in Both Houses, 100th Congress

	All Votes (N = 24)		Consensual Votes in Both Houses Excluded (N = 16)	
	HOUSE	SENATE	HOUSE	SENATE
Average majority	77%	84%	69%	78%
Average party difference	29%	22%	40%	32%
Proportion of party votes	46%	21%	69%	31%
Proportion of votes with less than two-thirds majority	33%	17%	50%	25%
Distribution of majorities				
90–100%	38%	50%	6%	25%
80–89%	13%	17%	19%	25%
70–79%	13%	4%	19%	6%
60–69%	13%	25%	19%	38%
50–59%	25%	4%	38%	6%
	102%	100%	101%	100%

Source: ICPSR roll-call data.

representation of the roll-call agenda, even if the votes are not identical between the House and Senate.

The ideal comparison would involve House and Senate responses to roll-call agendas across the time period in question here. In order to make some more limited comparisons, though, data have been coded for three Congresses in Table 2-7 (see p. 42): the 91st Congress (1969–70, just before the period of reform), the 96th Congress (Carter's second Congress), and the 100th Congress (Reagan's last Congress). Roll calls from these Congresses were grouped into three categories by issue area—domestic policy, foreign policy, and defense—and into three categories by type of vote—passage votes, amendments, and procedural votes.[21]

Table 2-7 shows the proportion of party voters within each category for each Congress. A number of general points of interest can be inferred from the data. First, passage votes in both houses are much less likely to be partisan than other votes, and within that category House votes are consistently more partisan than those in the Senate. This is consistent with the data on conference reports. Clearly, the decisions related to whether a program should exist are less likely to provoke partisan disagreement than are decisions regarding the particulars of a program. Furthermore, most passage votes involve not the institution of new programs or policies but

Table 2-7 / Percentages of Party-Unity Votes in the House and Senate in Three Congresses, by Issue and Vote Type

Issue	Vote Type[a]			
	PASSAGE	AMENDMENT	PROCEDURAL	TOTAL
91st Congress (1969–70)				
Domestic	15/10	59/43	52/60	27/35
	(255/144)	(22/336)	(94/40)	(371/520)
Foreign policy	50/10	75/46	53/100	54/32
	(20/21)	(4/24)	(15/2)	(39/47)
Defense	0/0	50/40	40/31	18/33
	(16/13)	(2/70)	(10/13)	(28/96)
Total	16/9	61/42	51/55	28/35
	(291/178)	(28/430)	(119/55)	(438/663)
96th Congress (1979–80)				
Domestic	37/16	58/56	40/56	45/47
	(363/202)	(329/527)	(275/133)	(967/862)
Foreign policy	27/18	69/59	37/100	50/42
	(55/49)	(95/58)	(41/3)	(191/110)
Defense	20/0	16/41	13/63	17/63
	(20/12)	(31/49)	(15/16)	(66/16)
Total	35/16	58/55	39/57	45/46
	(438/263)	(455/634)	(331/152)	(1,224/1,049)
100th Congress (1987–88)				
Domestic	28/11	69/50	64/53	49/40
	(266/146)	(189/242)	(140/133)	(595/521)
Foreign policy	16/17	67/35	71/33	46/29
	(50/42)	(43/82)	(21/9)	(114/133)
Defense	53/31	65/60	82/65	68/59
	(15/13)	(89/86)	(34/46)	(138/145)
Total	28/13	68/49	68/55	52/42
	(331/201)	(321/410)	(195/188)	(847/799)

[a] Each cell gives the proportion of party-unity votes in that category for the House first and the Senate second. The respective Ns (numbers of roll-call votes) are in parentheses.
Source: ICPSR roll-call data.

the renewal or revision of existing ones. Such previously existing programs tend to have built up support in both parties, rendering their renewal relatively noncontroversial.[22] The interchamber variation is consistent with the hypothesis that the Senate's institutional arrangements compel its members to approach most decisions in a way that treats proponents on both sides fairly and accommodates the intense preferences of significant minorities, even when there are disagreements on particulars along party lines.

Further, the data in Table 2-7 suggest that the mix of votes varies considerably across time and between chambers, and that these variations shape the overall levels of party voting. This was most apparent in the Ninety-first Congress because the House's rules at that time made it difficult to have a record vote on amendments (see Smith 1989, chap. 2). In the House, 66 percent of the votes were passage votes and 14 percent were on amendments; whereas in the Senate, 65 percent were on amendments and 27 percent were on passage. Therefore, even though House votes in both categories were more likely than Senate votes to be partisan, the overall proportion of party votes was higher for the Senate. Indeed, the House's proportion of party votes was higher in almost every subcategory.

The data in Table 2-7 indicate that, once variations in the mix of votes are taken into account, party voting was stronger in the House in all of the three Congresses. Even in the 100th Congress, when the overall level for the House was clearly higher (52 versus 42 percent), the magnitude of the difference is understated by that margin. The average difference between the chambers (the seven cells in the table with 20 or more votes in both houses) was +14.3 points for the House. Only for passage votes on foreign policy (which typically exhibit low partisanship in each chamber) was the level approximately equal. Variations in the makeup of the roll-call agenda masked a consistent pattern of interchamber differences in partisanship.

SUMMARY:
TRENDS AND FUTURE DIRECTIONS

This analysis has made an initial comparison of partisanship in the House and Senate. The level of partisanship in each chamber is the result of three major factors, the impact of which differs between the chambers. The most important factor is electoral forces because the configuration of constituency opinion exerts a powerful influence on members' legislative choices. During the 1960s and 1970s, the Democratic party was beset by deep sectional conflicts on policy at the constituency level, but these constituency differences were substantially reduced by the 1980s. Based on these variations, a decline of partisanship in Congress in the first period, followed by a resurgence in the second, would be expected. Indeed, this is what occurred.

The second major influence on partisanship is institutional arrangements. Because of the strong powers given to each individual senator and to minorities of the membership, the ability of the Senate's majority party to proceed in a procedurally partisan fashion is severely limited. In the House, however, the rules are structured to permit the majority party to work its will. If its members are cohesive, they can do largely what they please and ignore the minority. Thus, one would expect policy partisanship to be greater in the House, and the evidence regarding party voting is consistent with this expectation.

While important personal influences have no clear interchamber impact, they are not accounted for in the data analysis. Finally, because variations in the agenda, over time or between the House and Senate, may also be important, they are taken into account whenever possible. The comparisons made using data from three Congresses support this view and provide additional insights beyond the aggregate totals.

The most important conclusion generated by this analysis is that partisanship in Congress has at least two distinct aspects, reflected separately in the data on party voting and party unity. While these two aspects may be conditioned by the same factors, the level of party voting (that is, whether members' responses on a particular issue divide along party lines) seems to be more strongly affected by institutional arrangements (see Patterson and Caldeira 1988). As we saw earlier, once agenda variations are controlled for, the evidence suggests that the House is consistently more likely than the Senate to produce partisan splits. However, with respect to party loyalty (that is, the pattern of individual members' responses to matters that do split the parties), there are no significant chamber differences. Instead, electoral forces seem to be paramount. Similar types of members in both houses exhibit similar variations in loyalty over time, variations that are consistent with changes in the electoral environment. (There is, however, at least some evidence that senators may be somewhat more insulated than representatives from those electoral forces.)

Based on this analysis, then, what can we expect in terms of congressional partisanship in the future? Assuming no significant change in the electoral alignments (and there appear to be no major changes in prospect), and assuming no important institutional changes, we can expect process partisanship to remain lower in the Senate than in the House. This should continue to yield less consistent divisions on policy along party lines in the upper chamber. However, on those policy matters that do produce partisan division, the parties in each body are likely to exhibit similar levels of internal homogeneity, levels that are fairly close to those in the recent past and (especially for Democrats) much higher than in the 1970s.

An examination of data from the 101st Congress is relative to these expectations. In the two sessions of the 101st Congress, party voting was down in the House and up somewhat in the Senate compared to the 100th Congress, though the level remained higher in the House (51 percent versus the Senate's 45 percent).[23] Of course, because we cannot control for agenda variations, we cannot determine whether this contrast is applicable to the data for previous years. Regarding party-unity scores, the House exhibited levels for all party or regional groups in both sessions of the 101st Congress that were similar to those in the 100th Congress.[24] In the Senate, however, there was a noticeable shift in the first session (relative to the same session of the 100th Congress). Republican unity was up and Democratic unity was down (the drop was particularly pronounced among southern Democrats).[25] In the second session, average unity scores reverted to levels similar to those of two years earlier. The second session results, combined with the systematic way that first-session unity increased among both groups of Republicans and decreased among both sets of Democrats, suggest that these variations may have been due to idiosyncratic variations in the Senate's agenda for that year.

Therefore, the preliminary roll-call results from the 101st Congress confirm our expectations in certain respects but exhibit potentially important variations in other respects. These contrasts, coupled with the preliminary nature of the analysis contained here, point to the need for further research. For example, it would be beneficial to compile data for the Senate on issues and type of vote for all years since the 1950s, thus permitting full comparisons to the House data. But the potential impact of variable agendas calls for a more focused analysis. More specifically, a shift in the unit of analysis to individual bills, with parallel legislative vehicles selected from each chamber on a single, narrowly defined issue, would be a more fruitful way to proceed. Data would then be gathered on all bills dealing with the issue over a given number of Congresses. This would permit comparisons between chambers and over time, as well as (with the selection of a number of representative policy areas) across issues. Such data would account for biases caused by variations in the frequency of roll calls. More important, the data, which would not focus on the floor as roll-call analysis requires, would permit comparisons across all the major stages of decision making in each chamber. This kind of analysis would also consider the impact of the personal influences discussed earlier and take into account more fully institutional arrangements and their effects.

The research design proposed here would explore more completely the link between policy partisanship and process partisanship. While process partisanship ought always to be greater in the House than in the Senate, the level almost certainly varies over time in each chamber. The more internally homogeneous parties are on policy within a chamber, and the more different they are from each other, the greater the inclination toward process partisanship. There is strong evidence in support of this hypothesis with regard to the House as well as some fragmentary evidence for the Senate. As noted earlier, Senator Dole protested the treatment of the minority during consideration of the civil rights bill in 1990, and in the same context he vigorously complained about Republican defections in favor of cloture.[26] Partly because of that kind of defection, and partly because of a more general desire to enhance party regularity, Senate Republicans elected a more conservative leadership team for the 102d Congress. This included dumping moderate Senator John Chafee (R.I.) from his post as chair of the Republican Conference.[27]

In summary, the theoretical arguments presented here offer a basis for comparing partisanship in the House and Senate and the data analysis provides the initial evidence in support of the theory. The next step is to shift the analysis to a broader base of data so that the full range of the theory's implications can be discussed and tested.

Acknowledgments

The major support for the project of which this paper is a part came from the National Science Foundation through grant SES 89-09884. During the project's initial stages, support was also received from the Dirksen Congressional Center and Michigan State University's Research Initiation Grant program. I want to acknowledge the research assistance of James Meernik throughout the development of the project. More recent assistance was provided by Renee Smith. Roll-call data were supplied by the Interuniversity Consortium for Political and Social Research, which bears no responsibility for the analyses or interpretations presented here.

Notes

1. For discussions of the weakness of parties in Congress see Cooper, Brady, and Hurley 1977; Brady, Cooper, and Hurley 1979; Cooper and Brady 1981; Brady and Ettling 1984; Collie and Brady 1985; and Collie 1986. These studies deal almost exclusively with the House.

2. Some examples of research discussions of these changes include Davidson 1988b; Bach and Smith 1988; Hurley 1989; Sinclair 1989a, 1989b; Smith 1989; and Rohde 1988, 1989, 1991a, 1991b.

3. For example, Rules was 69 percent Democratic, and Ways and Means was 66 percent Democratic.

4. See Brady, Cooper, and Hurley 1979; Cooper and Brady 1981; and Brady and Ettling 1984.

5. Some particularly useful works from the vast literature on this subject include Petrocik 1987; Stanley 1988; Carmines and Stimson 1989; and Aldrich and Niemi 1990.

6. For discussions of this contrast in constituency heterogeneity, see Fenno 1982, chap. 2; and Baker 1989, chap. 3.

7. As Bullock and Brady (1983, 32) show, the likelihood of split Senate delegations increases as state heterogeneity increases.

8. See also Froman 1967, chap. 1; Ornstein 1981; and Baker 1989, esp. chap. 2.

9. See Bach and Smith 1988; Sinclair 1989a, 1989b; and Rohde 1991b, chaps. 2 and 4.

10. For contrasts of Reagan and Bush and of Wright and Foley with regard to partisanship, see Rohde 1991b, chaps. 4–6.

11. The problem is even more difficult when analyzing other decisions, such as whether bills get sent to the floor from committee. See Van Doren 1990.

12. The level of party voting is the percentage of votes on which majorities of both parties take opposite positions. Party-unity scores are the percentage of all votes with opposed-party majorities on which a member supports his or her party. Scores through the Ninety-fifth Congress were obtained from ICPSR file 7645 ("Voting Scores for Members of the United States Congress, 1945–1982"), and were recomputed for each member to remove the effect of nonparticipation. From the Ninety-sixth Congress on, the scores were computed directly from the ICPSR roll-call tapes for each Congress. In the House in the 99th and 100th Congresses there were many purely procedural votes that were used by Republicans to protest what they regarded as unfair treatment by the Democrats. These votes are excluded in computing scores to make the data more comparable over time. (Including these votes would have increased the level of party voting in the House. It also would have made northern and southern Democrats appear to be even more similar to each other, and more different from the Republicans, than the data actually used.) In both Congresses, all votes on approval of the House Journal were excluded, and in the Ninety-ninth Congress, votes protesting House decisions on the seating dispute in an Indiana House election were also excluded. For the party-unity data, if more than one member occupied a seat during a Congress, only the one who served longest was counted.

13. The Eighty-fourth Congress was chosen as the starting point because it represents the beginning of the yet unbroken period of Democratic control of the House.

14. The definition of *the South* employed here is the one used by the *Congressional Quarterly*: the eleven states of the Confederacy, plus Kentucky and Oklahoma.

15. Those senators also unanimously supported the effort to override President Bush's veto of the bill, which failed by a single vote.

16. Four members of the House who served in both Congresses who switched parties or whose scores were unavailable are excluded from Table 2-4.

17. The sectional breakdown in the table masks the relevant division among Republicans: the Northeast versus the rest of the country. Northeastern Republicans historically have been much more moderate to liberal than their colleagues in other parts of the country. Between the 95th and the 100th Congresses, the proportion of Republicans in both Houses who came from the Northeast decreased; this largely accounts for the aggregate increase in loyalty among new members from the North.

18. Collie 1988 analyzes variations in the proportion of these votes (which she terms "universalistic") over time in the House.

19. The *party difference*—defined as the absolute difference between the percentage of Democrats voting aye and the percentage of Republicans voting aye on a roll call—is a measure of the degree of party conflict.

20. For a recent analysis of conference committee politics, see Longley and Oleszek 1989.

21. Because purely procedural votes such as approval of the House Journal are rare in the Senate, they are omitted from the data for both chambers.

22. See, for example, Evans 1991 for a discussion of routine reauthorization decisions in the Senate Commerce Committee.

23. The figure for the House is not adjusted to remove the impact of purely procedural votes, which may reduce the results by 3–4 percentage points.

24. Since data are unavailable for computor analysis, we can only compare the aggregate data for each session compiled by the *Congressional Quarterly*.

25. The party-unity support scores for 1987–90 in the Senate were:

	1987	1988	1989	1990
Northern Democrats	88	89	84	85
Southern Democrats	80	78	69	75
Northern Republicans	76	72	77	75
Southern Republicans	90	84	91	86

26. Dole even implied that such behavior could lead to his stepping down as leader ("maybe we should get together and elect another leader"), and he went on: "If we're going to let Democrats run the Senate and throw away eight or nine Republican votes to help them, then I don't want any part of it" (Dewar and Devroy 1990, A6).

27. Chafee not only voted for cloture and to override Bush's veto on the civil rights bill, but he also was one of the only three Republican senators to support cloture on the campaign finance bill. More generally, conservative Senator Dan Coats (Ind.) said that the leadership elections "may reflect the fact that there is a sense that business as usual is not going to serve us in 1992. We need an aggressiveness in defining differences between the two parties" (Hook 1990b, 3871).

3 / National Party Organizations and the Postreform Congress

PAUL S. HERRNSON

The postreform era brought with it new challenges for national party organizations and the party leaders in Congress. Partisan de-alignment, the introduction of new technology into the political arena, a more aggressive news corps, and reforms within Congress itself changed many of the ways that candidates campaign for the House and Senate. These changes encouraged party officials to recognize that the national party organizations—the Democratic and Republican national, congressional, and senatorial campaign committees—needed major institutional transformations if they were to become more useful to the representatives, senators, and nonincumbent House and Senate candidates they sought to serve. Party leaders both in and out of government also recognized that improvements in the relationships between party organizations external to Congress and certain leadership organizations within the House and Senate would better serve the interests of their colleagues and themselves.

This chapter examines some of the changes that have taken place in the national party organizations since the mid-1970s. It focuses primarily on the congressional and senatorial campaign committees, describing their institutional adaptation and their new roles and activities. It also discusses developments in the national parties' relationships with policymakers in Congress.

THE INSTITUTIONALIZATION OF THE NATIONAL PARTIES

Prior to their institutionalization in the 1980s, national party organizations lacked much of a presence in Washington, D.C., and they had very few resources at their command. For most of their history, the Democratic National Committee (DNC) and the Republican National Committee (RNC) were located in rented office suites, moving from place to place in search of affordable space at the end of each election cycle. The four Capitol Hill committees—the Democratic Congressional Campaign Committee (DCCC), the Democratic Senatorial Campaign Committee (DSCC), the National Republican Congressional Campaign (NRCC), and the National Republican Senatorial Committee (NRSC)—were located in congressional office buildings. The parties' lack of permanent headquarters created security problems, made it difficult to conduct routine business, and hindered long-range planning. The committees' homelessness did little to promote their stature in Washington. They were "renters in a city where many lesser political groups ha[d] their own grand and imposing buildings" (Cotter and Hennessy 1964, 10).

For most of their history, the national parties also had very limited staff resources. The DNC and RNC had skeletal staffs that swelled enormously in preparation for the presidential election and shrunk once the election was over. The four Hill committees also had small staffs. Their executive directors were official employees of the Clerk of the House or the Secretary of the Senate (Clapp 1963). Many of the committees' day-to-day operations were conducted primarily by staff assigned in the personal offices of individual members of Congress. Some of these staffs had to perform routine, nonpartisan, legislative duties associated with working in a congressional office as well as the overtly political activities connected with the congressional elections. The committees' dependence on Congress for staff and other resources provides insight into their lack of organizational strength.[1]

National party organizations historically played fairly modest roles in congressional elections. Most Hill committee activity consisted of arranging for prominent party spokespersons to attend campaign events and of giving small campaign contributions to incumbents. The committees rarely assisted nonincumbents, leaving them largely to fend for themselves. Local and state party organizations occasionally gave House and Senate candidates some campaign assistance, particularly with voter mobilization activities. When progressive reforms, declining immigration, changing communications patterns, and other systemic changes in the political environment caused large numbers of these organizations to collapse, many congressional candidates found themselves receiving virtually no party support.

The national parties changed dramatically during the late 1970s and 1980s. All six national party organizations displayed a flurry of activity as they attempted to adapt to the rise of the technologically sophisticated, capital-intensive, new-style politics (Agranoff 1972; Sorauf 1980; Adamany 1984). The restructuring of the congressional and senatorial campaign committees was driven by the needs of House and Senate candidates. The new-style politics emphasized campaign activities requiring technical expertise and in-depth research. Many candidates lacked the money or technical know-how needed to run a modern congressional campaign. Some candidates, mostly incumbents, were able to turn to political consultants, political action committees (PACs), and interest groups for assistance. Others, especially challengers, found it difficult to assemble the money or expertise needed to wage a competitive bid for the House or Senate. The increased needs of candidates for greater access to specialized election services and money created an opportunity for national party organizations to become

Table 3-1 / National Party Finances, 1976–1988 (in $ millions)

Party	1976	1978	1980	1982	1984	1986	1988
Democratic							
DNC	$13.1	$11.3	$ 15.4	$ 16.5	$ 46.6	$ 17.2	$ 52.3
DCCC	0.9	2.8	2.9	6.5	10.4	12.3	12.5
DSCC	1.0	0.3	1.7	5.6	8.9	13.4	16.3
Total	$15.0	$14.4	$ 20.0	$ 28.6	$ 65.9	$ 42.9	$ 81.1
Republican							
RNC	$29.1	$34.2	$ 77.8	$ 84.1	$105.9	$ 83.8	$ 91.0
NRCC	12.2	14.1	20.3	58.0	58.3	39.8	34.5
NRSC	1.8	10.9	22.3	48.9	81.7	86.1	65.9
Total	$43.1	$59.2	$120.4	$191.0	$245.9	$209.7	$191.4

Source: Federal Election Commission.

the repositories of these resources (Schlesinger 1985). The massive electoral defeats the Republicans suffered in 1974 and 1976 and the electoral trouncing the Democrats took in 1980 created opportunities for political entrepreneurs to change the missions of the national party organizations and develop their institutional and electoral capacities (Herrnson 1990b; Herrnson and Menefee-Libey, forthcoming).

The *institutionalization* of the national party organizations refers to their becoming fiscally solvent, organizationally stable, larger, and more diversified in their staffing. It also refers to their adopting professional and bureaucratic decision-making procedures. In the cases of the four Hill committees, institutionalization also is marked by their declining dependence on Congress for staff, office space, and other resources. The Republicans were the first to develop organizationally, but the Democratic committees subsequently made major progress toward catching them.

Since the late 1970s, the national party organizations have raised more money from more sources using more varied approaches than ever. Table 3-1 indicates that Republican committees raised more money than their Democratic rivals in all seven election cycles, but that following the 1982 election the Democrats also began to raise substantial sums of money. Data published by the Federal Election Commission (1990c) indicate that the Republicans possessed a four-to-one advantage in fund-raising as of 17 October 1990. This is a significant improvement over the six-to-one advantage the Republicans enjoyed in 1982.

The GOP's financial advantage reflects a number of factors. Republican committees began developing their direct-mail solicitation programs earlier and have displayed a more businesslike approach to fund-raising. The

Table 3-2 / Sources of National Party Receipts during the 1988 Election Cycle (in $ millions)

Party	Contributions from Individuals	Contributions from PACs	Contributions from other Party Committees
Democratic			
DNC	$46.6	$1.5	$0.9
	(95%)	(3%)	(2%)
DCCC	$6.3	$2.6	$1.0
	(64%)	(26%)	(10%)
DSCC	$11.2	$3.0	$1.1
	(73%)	(20%)	(7%)
Republican			
RNC	$85.2	$1.0	$0.5
	(98%)	(1%)	(1%)
NRCC	$31.8	$0.7	$1.5
	(94%)	(2%)	(4%)
NRSC	$60.8	$0.7	$1.4
	(87%)	(1%)	(2%)

Source: Federal Election Commission.

greater wealth and homogeneity of their supporters also make it easier for Republican committees to raise money from individuals. Finally, the Republicans' minority status in Congress enables them to make fund-raising appeals that attack the government, which are usually more successful in fund-raising than appeals that advocate the maintenance of the status quo (Godwin 1988). Although Republican fund-raising appears to have reached a plateau and the Democrats have taken strides to improve their fund-raising programs, the advantages possessed by the Republicans make it unlikely that the Democratic national party organizations will be able to catch up to the GOP committees.

Most national party money is raised in contributions of under $100, but large contributions from individuals, PACs, and other groups continue to play an important role. Individual contributions typically account for the vast majority of national party receipts (see Table 3-2). Republicans raise substantially more than Democrats from individual contributors. Democratic congressional and senatorial campaign committees, however, have been able to capitalize on their party's control of Congress, raising substantially more money from PACs. The Democratic Hill committees also rely more on monetary transfers from other party committees than do the Republican committees.

The national parties use a variety of fund-raising techniques. Direct-mail and telephone solicitations are used mainly to raise small contributions. Individual givers typically are enrolled in contributor clubs and sent membership cards and other paraphernalia to encourage a feeling of group membership designed to encourage repeat contributing. By enrolling individual givers in clubs, the parties are able to improve the success rate of their follow-up requests by informing the individual that his or her membership fee is due. Tiered membership systems that offer larger contributors more attractive privileges are used to encourage donors to give more money.

Traditional fund-raising dinners, parties, and other events continue to be used by the national parties. In fact, an industry-wide decline in direct-mail fund-raising was largely responsible for the revival of personalized fund-raising events as vehicles for collecting large contributions during the 1988 and 1990 elections. Many individuals and PACs pay dues of up to $5,000 per year to belong to one of the national committees' labor or business councils, the DCCC's Speaker's Club, the DSCC's Leadership Council, the NRCC's Congressional Leadership Council, the NRSC's Senate Trust Club, or some other club created by one of the national party organizations for the purpose of raising large contributions. Some clubs require contributors to give money directly to a party committee; others encourage them to give money to groups of candidates, party committees, or both.

Unlike small direct-mail contributors, club members get to meet with members of Congress, cabinet secretaries, prominent party officials, and even foreign ambassadors in return for their donations. In September 1990, for example, members of the NRSC's Senatorial Inner Circle were invited to attend a "V.I.P. dinner" at Vice President Dan Quayle's home in Washington, D.C., that featured Housing Secretary Jack Kemp and other high-ranking administration officials. The NRSC provides its 1,800 active Inner Circle members (who give $1,000 per year to the NRSC or Republican Senate candidates) with access to a special toll-free hot line they can use to learn about the latest developments in administration policy or to check the status of legislation pending in Congress. In addition, congressional and senatorial campaign committee staffs routinely brief members of the Inner Circle and other big contributor clubs on the status of House and Senate races. These briefings are particularly useful to PACs because the information they are given helps them to identify candidates who are running in competitive races. PAC participation in party contributor clubs is indicative of the symbiotic nature of the relationships that have emerged between the national parties and many PACs (Sabato 1984; Herrnson 1988).

Soft money contributions—donations that are given and spent outside of the contribution and spending limits that the Federal Election Campaign Act of 1971 and its amendments (collectively referred to as FECA) set for federal candidates—make up another source of national party money. Most soft money is collected in large contributions by the two national committees or some auxiliary party committee, such as the Republicans' Victory '88 or the Democratic Victory Fund, and then distributed to state or local party committees that are required to abide by less stringent financial regulations than the FECA.[2] These committees spend soft money on nonfederal election activities such as party building, party-focused advertising, voter-mobilization drives, and other programs that strengthen the committees and help them to campaign for the party ticket.

The Hill committees also collect soft money contributions.[3] These have been used to purchase television and radio studies and other campaign equipment, to improve the organizational and electoral strength of state and local parties, and to finance party-focused campaign activity in states that contain marginal House or Senate seats. Soft money provides a means for businesses, unions, and other wealthy groups and individuals to make contributions in excess of the FECA's contribution limits (Drew 1983; Sorauf 1988). The $1 million check that Joan Kroc, heiress to the McDonald's fast-food chain, gave to the DNC in 1987 is typical of the contributions that made up the $20 million to $30 million that each national committee collected in soft money contributions in 1988 (Barnes and Cohen 1988; Cook 1988; Jackson 1988).

National party fund-raising success has fueled the parties' organizational development. All six national party organizations now reside in party-owned buildings on Capitol Hill. The buildings provide the committees with a secure location in which to house their records, computers, and other campaign equipment. They serve as convenient places to hold meetings with candidates, PACs, and political consultants. They also give the national parties a sense of permanence and prestige.

The postreform national parties are organizationally more complex and more professionally staffed than their predecessors were. Each committee has a two-tiered structure consisting of members and professional staff. The members of the Republican and Democratic national committees are selected by their state parties. The members of three of the four Hill committees are congressional incumbents who are selected by their colleagues in the House or Senate. The NRCC created an exception of sorts in 1989 by naming Edward J. Rollins, a professional political consultant, rather than a House member as its cochair and most visible spokesperson. Committee members serve as the governing boards that oversee the operations of the national parties. The committee chairs (the cochair in the case of the NRCC) serve as the committees' principal spokespersons.

The staffs that comprise the second tier of the national party organizations are now larger and more professional than they were prior to the reform period. The staffs are comprised of political consultants, administrators, and clerical workers who are paid by the party committees. Federally paid congressional staff no longer work for the Hill committees. In 1990 the DNC, DCCC, and DSCC employed 130, 80, and 45 full-time staff, respectively, while their Republican counterparts had 400, 110, and 101 full-time employees (estimates provided by committee staffs).

The staffs have a great deal of autonomy over the day-to-day operations and are extremely influential in formulating their campaign strategies (Herrnson 1989). Each committee's staff is split into five or six divisions, with each division being responsible for performing one or more specialized tasks. The executive division oversees administration of the committee. The finance division is responsible for fund-raising. The political (or campaign) division is the largest; its responsibilities include compiling a list of competitive races at the beginning of each election cycle, modifying that list as the campaign season progresses, recruiting candidates, providing candidates with strategic advice and money, and offering campaign services. The political division has specialized subdivisions that assist candidates in the field, maintain relations with PACs, provide legal help, and distribute other forms of campaign assistance.

The research and communications divisions work closely with the political division. The research division distributes issue and opposition research to candidates. The communications division acts as the committee's news center and public-relations firm, distributing press releases and maintaining relations with journalists. In addition, the communications divisions of the two congressional campaign committees oversee the operation of the committees' media centers. The RNC, NRCC, and NRSC also have divisions for coalition development that help Republican candidates identify associations, clubs, and other groups in their districts that are likely to provide endorsements, volunteer workers, or financial contributions.

The institutionalization of the national parties has altered relations within the party apparatus. The national party organizations now cooperate with each other on a variety of projects, though cooperation remains higher among the Democratic committees. The national parties' executive, political, communications, and other divisions meet regularly to discuss strategy and the political climate in various states. Some party strategy is developed jointly. The FECA's contribution and coordinated spending limits force the committees to work together when spending money in congressional races.[4] The committees have been known to piggyback questions on polls commissioned by one another. Voter registration and get-out-the-vote drives also have been cooperative endeavors run by the national party organizations in conjunction with state and local party committees.

DNC and RNC party-building programs have succeeded in strengthening and modernizing many state and local party organizations. In 1990 the DNC and RNC transferred $1.1 million and $1.2 million, respectively, to their state party committees. The NRSC and DSCC transferred an additional $2.5 million and $430,000, respectively, to state party organizations (Federal Election Commission 1990c).[5] Agency agreements that allow Hill committees to make state party organizations' contributions and coordinated expenditures further contribute to party-building efforts because they encourage state parties to spend their money on organizational development, state and local elections, and party-focused campaigning rather than on House and Senate elections. The institutionalization of the national parties has bolstered their influence in party politics and led to a greater federalization of the American party system (Wekkin 1985; Epstein 1986).

Institutionalization also has transformed the national parties' relations with political consultants and PACs. As noted earlier, PACs provide the national parties with money, while the national parties give PACs information about individual congressional races that help PACs formulate their contribution strategies. The national parties also facilitate agreements between candidates and political consultants, hire outside consultants to help with polling and advertising, and furnish candidates with campaign services. In addition, the parties often work with PACs when formulating long-range plans. Even before the 1990 election was over, for example, DCCC political director Doug Sosnik and staff from the National Committee for an Effective Congress—one of the nation's oldest liberal PACs—were formulating the Democrats' redistricting strategy. The symbiotic relationships that have emerged among party committees, PACs, and political consultants enable the parties to draw from the resources and expertise of these groups while providing them with strategic information and gainful employment.

PARTY CAMPAIGNING

National party campaign activity increased greatly during the 1980s. The Hill committees currently play important roles in candidate recruitment and in assisting congressional candidates with their campaigns. National, state, and local party committees assist candidates by conducting voter mobilization drives and conducting other activities connected with the parties' coordinated campaigns. Nevertheless, it is important to remember that the electoral activities of American political parties are restricted by election law, established custom, and resources.

Recruiting Candidates

Most candidates for Congress are self-recruited and conduct their own nominating campaigns. The national party organizations, however, typically get involved in some nominating contests for the House or Senate. They actively recruit some candidates and just as actively discourage others from running for the nomination.[6] Most candidate recruitment is focused on competitive districts, but sometimes committee officials encourage a candidate to run in a district that the party has little likelihood of winning so that the election will be contested. Party staff in Washington and regional coordinators in the field meet with state and local party leaders to identify potential candidates and encourage them to run. The promise of party campaign money and assistance, favorable surveys, and telephone calls from party leaders, members of Congress, and even presidents are used to influence the decisions of potential candidates.[7] In 1990, for example, DCCC member Representative Mike Synar of Oklahoma traveled with DCCC Deputy Political Director Karen Hancox to thirty-five states to recruit candidates to run for the House.

The DCCC and NRCC are each believed to have had a major hand in persuading about two dozen candidates to run for the lower chamber in 1988 and 1990. The DCCC is credited with being instrumental in persuading Faye Baggiano to challenge Republican incumbent Bill Dickinson in her near-successful bid in Alabama's Second Congressional District. The committee also played an important role in supporting challenger Mike Kopetski in a successful rematch against Representative Denny Smith in Oregon's Fifth District.[8]

The NRCC has been somewhat less successful than its Democratic counterpart in recruiting top-quality challengers during the last few election cycles. The GOP's recruitment difficulties stem from the relatively small number of Republicans who serve in state legislatures, the opposition that many potential Republican candidates feel toward the federal government, and the reticence of many Republicans to leave successful private-sector careers to run for Congress.[9] Nevertheless, the committee did succeed in getting a number of good candidates to run in 1990. It helped recruit John Linder, who lost a competitive contest to incumbent Ben Jones in Georgia's Fourth District. It encouraged several candidates to enter into rematches with the Democratic incumbents who had beaten them in the 1988, one of whom, Wayne Gilchrest, succeeded in winning a House seat.[10] The committee also persuaded three promising black Republicans to run for the House, including Gary Franks, who won an open-seat race in Connecticut's Fifth District.[11]

The DSCC did not have a particularly good recruitment year in 1990. It failed in its attempt to recruit Idaho Representative Richard Stallings to run in the state's open-seat Senate race. It also was unable to convince its preferred choices to run in some other states, including Colorado and Minnesota.[12] The NRSC was more successful. It helped to persuade eight House members to run for the Senate. Three of those candidates—Hank Brown, Larry Craig, and Robert Smith—succeeded in capturing open seats in Colorado, Idaho, and New Hamsphire, respectively. The other five went down in defeat to Democratic incumbents occupying Senate seats in Hawaii, Illinois, Iowa, Michigan, and Rhode Island.

National party candidate-recruitment programs are not designed or intended to change the dominant pattern of self-selected candidates assembling their own campaign organizations in order to compete for their party's nomination. Nor are the programs designed to restore to state or local party leaders the power to select their party's nominees. Rather, most national party recruitment activity is largely concentrated on influencing the decisions of a small group of politicians who are considering running in competitive districts. Less focused recruitment efforts are designed to inform a broader group of party activists about the types of campaign assistance that are available to candidates who make it to the general election.

Targeting Competitive Races

The energy and resources that the Hill committees invest in candidate recruitment reflect major changes the committees have made in their focus and objectives. No longer do the committees focus exclusively on incumbent races; they now concern themselves with challenger and open-seat contests, too. The imperative is to maximize the number of seats the party controls in the House and Senate, rather than merely to reelect incumbents.[13] In pursuing this goal, postreform Hill committees expend most of their resources in elections they expect to be competitive, including challenger and open-seat contests.

The committees use a variety of information to compile their lists of targeted, competitive races. Election returns from previous congressional and presidential races are used to categorize districts (or states in the case of Senate races) as marginal; that is, potentially winnable for either party. Seats being vacated by an incumbent who has decided not to run for re-election are almost always considered up for grabs. Surveys may be used to evaluate the competitiveness of a seat, especially if there has been significant population movement since the previous election.

The quality of the candidates and their campaign organizations are also taken into consideration, especially when nonincumbents are being evaluated. Candidates who possess previous office-holding experience, celebrity status, or came close to winning a seat in the House or Senate are expected to run more strongly than others (Canon 1990; Jacobson 1990). A candidate who assembles a professional organization early in the election cycle also is looked upon favorably (Herrnson 1989, 1990a). Incumbents who are just completing their first term, have been tainted by scandal, whose previous margin of victory was uncomfortably close, or whose congressional voting records are perceived to be out of step with their district also draw special attention, both from their own party's committee and their opponent's committee. Committee staff contact state and local party officials, local elites, and members of the local press to gather information about candidates and their districts. Regional coordinators in the field meet with these people and other local political activists to get an accurate picture of the candidates' strengths and weaknesses and the nature of their districts.

Finally, larger strategic considerations also may influence the categorization of election contests and the distribution of party resources. The national party organizations, for example, may decide to undertake a special effort in one region of the country. In 1984 both parties attempted to strengthen their positions in the South. Alternatively, a party might dedicate extra resources to protecting its incumbents if indicators such as the state of the economy, the president's popularity, or a nationwide anti-incumbency fervor (like the one that emerged in 1990) indicate that sitting members of Congress could be especially at risk. Other events, like redistricting, also may have an impact on the distribution of party resources. According to executives at the DCCC, the NRCC, and the two national committees, few decisions were made in 1990 without considering the impact that they might have on redistricting and the competitiveness of the "redrawn" districts House candidates will run in during the 1992 elections.

Over the course of the 1980s, the Hill committees greatly refined their ability to identify and participate in competitive races. In 1984, for example, each House campaign committee identified approximately one hundred "opportunity," or competitive, races. Distinctions were made among these races, but party resources were not narrowly targeted. Some noncompetitive candidates received more campaign assistance than was warranted given the competitiveness of their race; others received less (Herrnson 1988, 1989). Party resources were targeted more narrowly in ensuing election cycles. Organizational improvements, such as the DCCC's adding a team of regional field coordinators and improvements in the staff and equipment possessed by both congressional campaign committees, helped to improve targeting. The discovery of new ways of working within the confines of FECA's spending limits also enabled the Hill committees to deliver campaign resources more effectively. In 1990 the DCCC and the NRCC each compiled a list of approximately forty "first-tier" races. The committees directed the lion's share of their campaign assistance to candidates in competitive contests.[14] Nevertheless, all four committees failed to allocate appropriate levels of resources in a few contests. The DCCC, for example, gave a mere $5,000 to Democratic challenger David Worley, who came within 958 votes of defeating House Minority Whip Newt Gingrich in Georgia's Sixth District House contest.

National party campaign assistance can take a variety of forms. The congressional and senatorial campaign committees contribute money and campaign services directly to congressional candidates. They also provide candidates with transactional assistance that helps them obtain additional campaign resources from political consultants and PACs. The DNC and RNC may furnish candidates with lesser sums of money and services and often help congressional candidates indirectly by investing in state and local party-building and helping to finance a party-focused, coordinated campaign.

Party Money in Campaigns

It is important to note that the FECA limits party activity in congressional races. National, congressional, and state party organizations are each allowed to contribute no more than $5,000 to House candidates during the general election.[15] The parties' national and senatorial campaign committees are allowed to give a combined total of $17,500 to Senate general election candidates; state party organizations can give them an additional $5,000. National party organizations and state party committees also are allowed to make coordinated expenditures on behalf of their candidates. Unlike the independent expenditures of PACs, party-coordinated expenditures are made in cooperation with a candidate's campaign committee, giving both the party and the candidate a measure of control over them. Originally set at $10,000 each for a state and national committee, the limits for coordinated expenditures on behalf of House candidates are adjusted for inflation and reached $25,140 in 1990.[16] The limits for coordinated expenditures in Senate elections vary by the size of a state's voting-age population and are indexed to inflation. In 1990 they ranged from $50,280 in the smallest states to $605,271 in Texas. If a Senate race had been held in California duing the 1990 election cycle, the coordinated spending limit would have been set at $1,073,478 each for a state and national committee (Federal Election Commission 1990b). The national parties give virtually every competitive House or Senate candidate the maximum contribution and most also benefit from a large coordinated expenditure.

Data collected from the 1988 general election and the 1989 special elections provide insights into the spending activities of postreform party committees. As Table 3-3 (see p. 60) indicates, most party money is distributed as coordinated expenditures, reflecting the higher amounts allowed by the FECA. Republican party organizations spent substantially more than their Democratic rivals, but the Democrats have made significant progress in closing this gap over the past few election cycles (Federal Election Commission 1989). National-level GOP committees outspent their Democratic rivals by substantial sums. The four Capitol Hill committees account for the bulk of national party spending in congressional elections. They routinely enter into agency agreements that allow them to make their national and state party committees' contributions and coordinated expenditures. In 1988 the four Hill committees accounted for over 90 percent of all party spending in congressional elections (Sorauf and Wilson 1990). This pattern probably will persist.

The figures for the NRCC and NRSC call attention to a relatively new phenomenon known as *crossover spending*. This occurs when a senatorial campaign committee spends money in a House election, a congressional campaign committee spends money in a Senate race, or a state party committee spends money on the election of a candidate in another state. During the 1988 election cycle, most crossover spending consisted of in-kind contributions that took the form of shared polls or other coordinated activities that were conducted by one Hill committee in cooperation with the party's other Hill committee, a Senate candidate, or one or more House candidates who resided in the same state.

During the 1989 special elections, all four Hill committees made crossover expenditures. The DSCC gave $5,000 to each of three House candidates who ran in special elections; its Republican counterpart gave four House

Table 3-3 / Party Contributions and Coordinated Expenditures in the 1988
Congressional Elections[a]

| | House | | Senate | |
PARTY	CONTRIBUTIONS	COORDINATED EXPENDITURES	CONTRIBUTIONS	COORDINATED EXPENDITURES
Democratic				
DNC	$ 120,000	$ 30,000	$ 0	$ 0
DCCC	593,849	2,251,449	0	0
DSCC	0	0	418,620	6,197,037
State and local	400,475	342,363	70,219	310,820
Total	$1,118,740	$2,623,812	$488,839	$ 6,507,857
Republican				
RNC	$ 291,480	$ 0	$ 0	$ 0
NRCC	1,429,856	3,868,586	55,731	0
NRSC	195,000	0	520,960	10,247,724
State and local	553,310	51,389	111,695	6,992
Total	$2,469,646	$3,919,975	$688,386	$10,254,716

[a] Includes only general election activity. Figures are calculated from a preliminary version of
campaign finance data, which may be subject to minor revision.
Source: Federal Election Commission.

candidates contributions of $10,000 each and three candidates contribu-
tions of $5,000. Unlike the contributions made in 1988, many of those
given in 1989 were made in cash. In addition to the crossover expenditures
made by the Hill committee, ten candidates running in six special elections
for the House received contributions from state party committees from outside of their state.[17] Although state party committees provided the money
that was distributed, the national parties played a major role in selecting
the candidates who received it. Crossover spending played an important
role in the 1989 special elections, but it is unlikely that it will play as large
a role during normal general election cycles because the Hill committees
and state party organizations will probably not have much money to distribute to candidates other than their own. Nevertheless, the emergence of
crossover spending demonstrates that the parties have found new ways to
expand their influence in congressional contests.

The information in Table 3-4, also from 1988, provides further insights
into the parties' role in campaign finance. Republican candidates generally
received more financial assistance from party committees than Democratic
candidates did. Both parties spent substantial sums of money in connection
with campaigns waged by candidates in open-seat races. The next largest

Table 3-4 / Average Party Spending in the 1988 Congressional Elections[a]

Party	House			Senate		
	INCUMBENT	CHALLENGER	OPEN SEAT	INCUMBENT	CHALLENGER	OPEN SEAT
Democratic						
DNC	$ 291	$ 596	$ 1,739	$ 0	$ 0	$ 0
DCCC	8,101	9,297	19,116	0	0	0
DSCC	0	0	0	154,291	257,728	272,568
State and local	1,490	3,215	5,497	2,299	7,873	50,675
Total	$ 9,882	$13,108	$26,352	$156,590	$265,601	$323,243
Percent[b]	2.2%	6.3%	5.0%	5.0%	10.9%	12.2%
(N)	(189)	(109)	(23)	(14)[c]	(12)	(5)[d]
Republican						
RNC	$ 504	$ 1,010	$ 4,477	$ 0	$ 0	$ 0
NRCC	12,430	18,304	48,935	0	3,000	1,789
NRSC	213	698	3,636	313,890	320,153	366,617
State and local	1,098	2,403	5,550	3,560	2,346	6,794
Total	$14,246	$22,415	$62,599	$317,451	$325,500	$375,200
Percent[b]	3.2%	13.9%	13.9%	7.5%	17.6%	12.6%
(N)	(164)	(129)	(22)	(12)	(15)	(6)

[a] Includes only general election contributions and coordinated expenditures for elections in which one or more party organizations spent money; the averages would be lower, obviously, if all races were included. Figures are calculated from a preliminary version of campaign finance data, which may be subject to minor revisions.

[b] Denotes percentage of candidate-controlled money (candidate receipts and party-coordinated expenditures) composed of party money.

[c] Spark Matsunaga (Hawaii) took no party money.

[d] Herbert Kohl (Wis.) took no party money.

Note: Some numbers do not add up because of rounding.

Source: Federal Election Commission.

sums were spent in connection with campaigns waged by challengers. Substantially less was spent in connection with incumbent campaigns. The percentages indicate that the importance of party money varies by the party, candidate status, and the office sought. Party money accounted for almost 14 percent of the general election funds spent by, or on behalf of, Republican nonincumbent candidates for the House. It accounted for over 12 percent of the funds spent by, or on behalf of, Republican Senate challengers, and for an impressive 17.6 percent of the money spent in connection with the campaigns of Republican Senate challengers. Democratic party money provided less of the funds spent in connection with Democratic House campaigns, yet it comprised a substantial share of the money spent in connection with races waged by Democratic challengers and open-seat contestants for the Senate.

As mentioned earlier, the national parties target most of their money to candidates in competitive elections. Challengers who show little promise and incumbents who are considered shoo-ins usually receive only token sums. In 1988, for example, the parties spent over $40,000 in connection with each of 107 House candidacies and spent no money in connection with 178 others (Federal Election Commission 1989). The discrepancies in party spending in Senate elections were even greater, reflecting party strategy and the FECA's contribution and spending limits. At one extreme, the 1988 race for the Senate in Hawaii, the Democratic party contributed no money to incumbent Spark Matsunaga and the Republican party contributed only a token $5,000 to challenger Maria Hustace.[18] At the other extreme, the parties spent approximately $1.9 million each in the California race between Republican incumbent Pete Wilson and Democratic challenger Leo McCarthy, accounting for 21.4 percent and 12.9 percent, respectively, of all the money spent in the campaigns over which the candidates had some control (Federal Election Commission 1989).[19] In 1990 virtually every Senate candidate competing in a close race benefited from the legal maximum in party contributions and coordinated expenditures.

Individuals and PACs continue to furnish candidates with most of their campaign funds. Nevertheless, political parties are currently the largest single source of campaign money for most candidates. Party money comes from one, or at most a few, organizations that are concerned solely with the election of their candidates. Individual and PAC contributions, however, come from a multitude of sources and are motivated by a variety of concerns. Moreover, dollar for dollar, national party money has greater value than the contributions of other groups. National party contributions are frequently given early in the election cycle and function as "seed money" that candidates can use to raise funds from other sources. National party contributions and coordinated expenditures often take the form of in-kind campaign services that are worth many times more than their reported value. National party money and transactional assistance also help candidates attract additional money from PACs.

Campaign Services

The Hill committees also provide candidates with a variety of campaign services. They hold training colleges for candidates and campaign managers, introduce candidates and political consultants to each other, and frequently provide candidates with in-kind contributions or coordinated expenditures in the form of campaign services. Under some circumstances, a Hill committee will make a coordinated expenditure consisting of a political consultant who has been hired to work on a candidate's campaign. The committees also help congressional campaigns file reports with the Federal Election Commission (FEC) and perform other administrative, clerical, and legal tasks. Most important, the national parties furnish candidates with strategic assistance. In 1990 the DCCC had five and the NRCC had eight field workers who visited local campaign headquarters to help candidates develop campaign plans, plan and respond to attacks, and perform other crucial campaign activities.

The national party organizations assist congressional candidates with gauging public opinion in three ways: (1) they distribute the results of national polls to inform candidates of the electorate's mood, (2) they conduct district-level analyses of voting patterns exhibited in previous elections to help congressional candidates locate where their supporters reside, and (3) they conduct surveys for their most competitive candidates. These activities help candidates ascertain their levels of name recognition, electoral support, and the impact that their campaign communications are having on voters. The NRCC conducted 204 surveys in eighty-five districts during the 1990 election cycle and the 1989 special elections. Included among these are tracking polls conducted for thirteen incumbents, nine challengers, and eight candidates in open-seat contests.

National party assistance in campaign communications can take many forms. All six national party organizations conduct issue and opposition research. DNC and RNC research revolves around traditional party positions and the issue stands of presidents, presidential candidates, or other party leaders. Both committees distribute talking points to congressional candidates and local party leaders. Congressional and senatorial campaign committee research is more specialized. The Hill committees furnish competitive candidates with issue packets consisting of hundreds of pages of issue research. The packets include suggestions for attracting certain voting blocs and exploiting an opponent's weaknesses. Some of the committees' issues research is stored on electronic bulletin boards that candidates and party activists can use to learn about congressional activity, examine members' voting records, gain access to the latest party research or press releases, or download specialized election research conducted specifically for their campaign. The bulletin boards are especially useful to challengers and open-seat candidates, providing them with resources similar to those that incumbents can access through their congressional offices.

In response to the wave of negative campaigning that has gripped American politics, the national parties have devoted more resources to opposition research during the last few elections. During the 1990 election, the DCCC provided opposition research packages for fourteen incumbents, twenty open-seat candidates, and four challengers. The GOP conducted opposition research for an even larger group, consisting of seven incumbents, fourteen open-seat candidates, and thirty challengers. Not all opposition research is used solely by the candidates. Occasionally, a Hill committee will use it to attack a candidate on its own. In 1990 the NRCC went on the offensive against Representative Frank Annunzio, the second highest–ranking Democrat on the House Banking Committee, linking him to the savings and loan scandal and filing a complaint with the FEC alleging that he failed to disclose that twenty of his campaign contributors were associated with a savings bank.[20] The DCCC filed a similar complaint against Representative Denny Smith of Oregon (Kenworthy 1990). As noted earlier, Annunzio staved off a serious challenge by Walter Dudycz, but Smith fell victim to challenger Mike Kopetski in a race that focused largely on the incumbent's connection to the savings and loan crisis. The growth in negative campaigning also has encouraged the Hill committees to help their candidates respond to attacks and learn to inoculate themselves against future "hits."

The national party organizations also furnish congressional candidates with assistance in mass-media advertising and establishing good relations with the press. In 1990 the NRCC produced a total of 328 television commercials for twenty-four incumbents, thirteen challengers, and seven open-seat candidates, and it arranged for many other House candidates to receive media assistance from professional consultants at its expense.[21] The DCCC's Harriman Center serviced many more campaigns, but the services it provided to candidates were not nearly as comprehensive as those provided by the NRCC. The Republican committee helped develop advertising themes, wrote scripts, and arranged for its candidates' advertisements to be aired on local stations. Democratic candidates, in contrast, were given use of the Harriman Center's recording facilities and technical staff, but had to supply their own creative talent. Both committees made satellite services available to their candidates and House members, so that they could conduct live "town meetings" with constituents back in the district and stage live, mock press conferences that local television stations could air on the evening news. The committees also held press lunches in Washington to help House candidates get favorable coverage in newsletters that many political reporters and PACs rely on for information.

The DSCC and NRSC generally do not get as deeply involved in their candidates' campaign communications. They offer advice, criticisms, and occasionally pretest their candidates' television and radio advertisements. The senatorial campaign committees play more of an advisory role because Senate candidates are visible enough to gain adequate attention from the press, and Senate campaigns typically have enough money, expertise, and experience to produce their own campaign commercials.

The national parties help their congressional candidates raise money from individuals and PACs both in Washington and in their election districts. The Hill committees help congressional candidates organize fund-raising events and develop direct-mail lists. During the 1990 election cycle, the NRSC broke new ground by transforming its Inner Circle from a party fund-raising organ into a joint party–candidate fund-raising operation. The committee gave names of its major donors to a joint fund-raising committee organized with fifty senators and Senate candidates. The committee handled the fund-raising arrangements, took 1 percent of the Inner Circle's proceeds, and funneled the rest of the money to candidates using a formula that favored those involved in close elections. The program, which is the most recent of many NRSC conduit activities, is estimated to have raised roughly

$2 million during the 1990 elections and is currently under legal challenge (Alston 1990; Federal Election Commission 1990c).

The Hill committees also assist candidates with raising money from PACs. The committees help design the PAC kits that many candidates use to familiarize members of the PAC community with their campaigns, hold "meet and greet" sessions to personally introduce candidates to PAC managers, and mail, telephone, and fax campaign progress reports to PAC managers. The goals of these activities are to get PAC money flowing to the party's most competitive contenders and away from their candidates' opponents. National party endorsements, communications, contributions, and coordinated expenditures serve as decision-making cues that help many PACs decide which candidates will receive their money. National party services and transactional assistance are especially important to House challengers and open-seat candidates. They often do not possess fund-raising lists from previous campaigns, are generally less skilled at fund-raising than incumbents, have none of the clout with PACs that comes with holding a House seat, and begin the election cycle virtually unknown to members of the PAC community.

Coordinated Campaigning

The last set of activities the national parties conduct in conjunction with congressional elections is referred to as the *coordinated campaign*. Unlike the candidate-centered campaign programs discussed earlier, the coordinated campaign consists of generic, or party-focused, election activities that are designed to benefit all candidates on the party ticket. Party-focused television and radio commercials, like those for broadcast by the RNC in 1980, are the most visible of these activities. They are designed to deliver a thematic message about an entire political party and to activate voters nationwide.

Electronic broadcasts, press releases, and issues research may help to reinforce a party's image among voters and have some influence on the political agenda. The Republican national party organizations encourage their congressional candidates to focus more on national themes and issues than do their Democratic counterparts. This strategy paid off for the GOP in 1980, when a large number of Republican candidates succeeded in getting elected to Congress by tapping into a ground swell of populist dissatisfaction with big government. Nevertheless, activities that seek to impose a national agenda on congressional elections—which are, after all, local and statewide races—are not without risk.[22] This strategy appears to have harmed a number of Republican candidates in 1990. After having defined campaigns around the "no-new-taxes" position staked out by President Bush and GOP congressional leaders, these candidates found themselves caught in the uncomfortable position of either having to flip-flop on their main issue or oppose their president and party leaders after Bush suddenly reversed his stand. The national GOP's floundering on the tax issue was especially harmful to Republican challengers and open-seat candidates because nonincumbents must base their campaigns on issues; unlike incumbents, they do not have the luxury of stressing experience, constituent service, or the federal projects they have brought to their district or state.

Party-sponsored voter registration and get-out-the-vote drives also reached unprecedented levels in recent years. Most of these activities are spearheaded by the national committees and conducted in cooperation with congressional, senatorial, state, and local party committees and candidates. Republican efforts in grass-roots campaigning, as in most other areas of campaigning, overshadow those of the Democrats. In 1984 the Republican national parties invested more than $10 million to register over four million previously unregistered Republican identifiers and encourage almost thirty million households to vote Republican (Herrnson 1988). In 1986 the NRCC and NRSC set up a $10 million program to help Republican state parties develop or refine their lists of Republican-leaning voters (Bibby 1990). During that election, the Democrats made some significant attempts to try to catch up with the GOP. By 1988 DNC field operatives had helped state party organizations in thirty states develop computerized voter files and formulate plans to register and turn out new voters. DNC staff estimate that these efforts resulted in the registration of over two million new Democratic voters.

The parties' newest voter mobilization efforts are designed to use absentee ballots for partisan advantage. The national parties have spearheaded programs that register supporters for absentee ballots in California, Florida, Oregon, Texas, and other states that have liberal absentee-voter requirements. These programs played critical roles in determining the outcomes of several close elections during the late 1980s. In 1988 absentee ballots enabled Republican House member Denny Smith to squeak by Mike Kopetski by a margin of 707 votes. Absentee-ballot programs also were a crucial contributor to the less than one-half of a 1 percent victory that Connie Mack had over Buddy MacKay in the open-seat Senate race in Florida. During the 1989 special elections, absentee-ballot programs accounted for the margins of victory that enabled Democrats Pete Geren and Gary Condit to win in Texas' Twelfth District and California's Fifteenth District (Donovan 1989). According to DCC Political Director Doug Sosnik and NRCC Executive Director Marc Nuttle, party organizations and candidates at the national and state levels invested substantial resources in signing up voters for absentee ballots during the 1990 midterm elections. In addition, the RNC and DNC undertook efforts to register supporters living abroad.

The institutionalization of the national parties has made them important players in congressional elections, but it has not changed the balance of power in Congress. The Democrats continue to dominate the House and the Senate remains Democratically controlled, but competitive. This is partially due to the fact that the Republicans have been unable to capitalize on their party's organizational advantages. Candidate recruitment difficulties, caused in part by the absence of a strong farm team at the state and local levels, have hindered the GOP's ability to field strong congressional candidates. Official "perks," such as WATS lines, franked mail, and congressional staff, have contributed to the high reelection rates of national legislators. The ability of incumbents to amass huge campaign chests well ahead of the start of the election cycle has given them tremendous advantages over challengers and discouraged many politicians from running for Congress. The national parties may have contributed to the seeming invincibility of House members and the high reelection rates for the Senate because they deliver larger amounts of resources to incumbents who are expected to face stiff challenges.

PARTY ORGANIZATIONS AND THE PARTIES-IN-CONGRESS

Just as the institutionalization of the national party organizations has altered their relationships with state, and local party committees, PACs, political consultants, and congressional candidates, it also has altered the national parties' relationships with the party members and party leadership organizations in Congress. Here, however, the changes have been of a much smaller magnitude and are more subtle.

The Hill committees have become important forums for members of Congress to discuss partisan issues and develop election strategies. The congressional campaign committees help House leaders of both parties formulate their partisan press strategies and coordinate their messages with those being disseminated by other party leaders. DCCC and DNC staff, for example, participate in leadership organizations such as the Democrats' Message Board, which helps House leaders develop a daily message theme and coordinate one-minute and special-order speeches given on the House floor. In 1990 DCCC and DNC staff participated in House Democratic Caucus task forces and helped produce *Investing in America's Future* (1990), the Caucus's issues handbook. The Republican national party organizations were involved in similar activities. National party staffs also distribute issues briefs, talking points, survey results, partisan responses to major news events, and summaries of party accomplishments to members of Congress and other party activists.

In addition to their formal participation in party leadership activities, Hill committee staffs furnish members of Congress with political advice on a less formal basis. Some House members routinely ask Hill committee staff how their constituents can be expected to react to difficult congressional votes. Most of the questions are raised by junior House members who represent marginal districts. In answering such questions, Hill committee staff normally address the repercussions associated with a yes or a no vote and attempt to help members formulate ways to defend both positions rather than try to influence the way the member ultimately votes.

Not all national party activity results in a party's congressional membership or a president delivering the same message. Constituent pressures continue to encourage members of Congress to focus much of their energy and most of their public-relations efforts on their districts or states. Electoral considerations also may discourage members from the same party from voting together on key policy votes. The Hill committees fully understand the importance that local politics plays in congressional life. They occasionally even may advise members of Congress to break ranks with their party leadership in order to solidify their support at home. During the 1990 budget debate, the NRCC went to the extreme of drafting a memo advising Republican House members and candidates to oppose the bipartisan budget package that was backed by President Bush and Republican congressional leaders. Congress's rejection of the budget package was viewed as a major defeat for the Bush administration. The budget debacle shows the general independence of the Hill committees from the parties' national committees, each other, and the executive branch. It also demonstrates that the national party organizations can exacerbate, as well as help overcome, the problems associated with divided government.

While national party support for congressional leadership and member activity generally has grown, this increase can be easily overstated. The national parties continue to be election-oriented organizations. They are not concerned with the formulation of public policy, nor do they take members' policy positions into consideration when distributing campaign money or services. National party activities are aimed at the attainment or expansion of electoral majorities, not the building of policy majorities. The increase in the support that the national parties provide for members' congressional activities pales next to the increase in their support for congressional candidates' election-related ventures.

CONCLUSION

The national party organizations of the postreform era are wealthier, more professional, and more influential with PACs, political consultants, and state and local party committees. They also are better equipped to assist congressional candidates with campaigning. The national party organizations have adapted to the technologically sophisticated, capital-intensive demands of the new-style politics. The parties furnish their candidates with campaign money and election services in areas of campaigning requiring technical expertise, in-depth research, or connections with political consultants, PACs, and other organizations that possess the resources needed to wage a congressional campaign. Most national party resources are distributed to candidates running in competitive elections. The Republican national party organizations are wealthier and able to give candidates more assistance than can their Democratic rivals, but the Democratic committees are narrowing the gap and possess sufficient resources to play an important role in congressional elections. The national parties now play a slightly larger supporting role in House and Senate politics, but this role is miniscule compared to their increased electoral functions. The development of stronger Democratic and Republican national, congressional, and senatorial campaign committees demonstrates the parties' abilities to adapt to the electoral politics of the postreform Congress.

Notes

1. The importance of congressional resources and the committees' incumbency focus have led some researchers to categorize the Capitol Hill committees as congressional organizations rather than as part of the extragovernmental party apparatus (see Kolodny 1990). For the more widely accepted view that the committees are party organizations see, for example, Clapp 1963; and Cotter and Hennessy 1964.

2. Soft money cannot be spent in federal elections. It should be noted that some of the Republicans' Victory '88 accounts were hard money accounts, which were subject to FECA regulations, rather than soft money accounts. The term *soft money* was coined by Drew 1983; see also Sorauf 1988.

3. The amounts of soft money collected by the Capitol Hill committees vary. DSCC staff report that their committee collects little soft money, while staff at the other three Hill committees indicate that their committees accept considerable sums of soft money.

4. The law provides individual limits for national, congressional, senatorial, and state campaign committees; however, the congressional and senatorial campaign committees have assumed the responsibility for providing most of the party money spent in House and Senate elections. Agreements allowing the Capitol Hill committees to take over the other committees' contributions and coordinated expenditures are made early in the election cycle.

5. The DCCC transferred $2,000 to Democratic state committees. The NRCC did not transfer any funds to Republican state committees (Federal Election Commission 1990c).

6. For further information on the candidate recruitment activities of the national party organizations see Herrnson 1988.

7. The national parties gave money and campaign assistance to few candidates competing for contested primary contests since the 1984 election cycle. Prior to the 1984 election, the Republican national party organizations backed a number of candidates in contested primaries. Protests registered by state and local party activists in 1984 led RNC members to pass a rule prohibiting committee involvement in House and Senate nominating contests and led the NRCC to institute a policy requiring primary candidates to have the support of their state delegation in the House and local party leaders before they are given support. The NRSC continues to get involved in a small number of primaries. The DCCC's bylaws bar it from becoming involved in contested primaries, and the DNC and DSCC rarely get involved in them.

8. Kopetski lost to Smith by 707 votes in 1988.

9. In addition, the Iran-contra scandal discouraged some potential GOP candidates from running in 1988, and the low probability that a member of the president's party will win a House seat during a midterm election year discouraged others from running in 1990.

10. Gilchrest defeated the scandal-plagued Roy Dyson in Maryland's First District.

11. Franks defeated Toby Moffet by a 5 percent margin in Connecticut's Fifth District. The other two, Al Brown and J. Kenneth Blackwell, did not fare so well. Brown lost by a 22 percent margin to incumbent Romano Mazzoli in Kentucky's Third District and Blackwell lost the open-seat contest in Ohio's First District to Charles Luken by 2 percent of the vote.

12. The Minnesota Senate election was unique among modern Senate contests. Political neophyte, college professor Paul Wellstone, a Democrat, ran a largely grass-roots campaign that was able to defeat the highly professional and well-financed campaign of incumbent Republican Rudy Boschwitz.

13. Incumbent pressures sometimes interfere with the committees' ability to pursue this objective (Jacobson 1985–86; Herrnson 1989).

14. It is important to recognize that the committees continuously revise their lists of competitive races throughout the election cycle. Elections are added to or dropped from the lists in response to poll results indicating that individual candidates have become more or less competitive, because candidates have failed to meet or have surpassed the fund-raising and organizational goals set by their congressional campaign committee, or because some other development is believed to have improved or reduced their chances of winning.

15. The parties also can give $5,000 in a primary or run-off election.

16. The coordinated expenditure limits for states with only one House member were set at $50,280 for each committee during the 1990 election cycle (Federal Election Commission 1990b).

17. John Vinich and Craig Thomas, the Democratic and Republican candidates vying for Wyoming's at-large district, received the most out-of-state party money. Vinich raised $76,000 in out-of-state money from sixteen Democratic state party committees, while Thomas received $45,000 in out-of-state contributions from nine Republican state party committees (Federal Election Commission 1990a).

18. Democrat Herb Kohl of Wisconsin also took no party money.

19. These figures exclude independent expenditures made by PACs, which are made without candidates' knowledge or consent, and party spending on party-focused television commercials, voter-mobilization drives, and other forms of coordinated, party-focused campaigning.

20. The law requires candidates to make "best efforts" to identify the employers of contributors who give $200 or more to their campaigns.

21. The NRCC's media center also produced ads for seven Senate candidates and a small group of state and local candidates.

22. Republican leaders and campaign operatives are well aware of the risks involved with imposing a national agenda on congressional elections, and there is considerable disagreement over this matter within the party. In 1990 House Minority Leader Newt Gingrich, who favored campaigning for Congress on the basis of a broad, ideological, national agenda, publicly feuded with NRCC Cochair Ed Rollins, who favored instructing GOP candidates to campaign on local issues.

4 / Representatives and Constituents in the Postreform Congress: The Problem of Persuasion

WILLIAM T. BIANCO

Policy-making in Congress has two distinct stages: (1) legislators agree on a proposal and (2) they try to convince their constituents that it is worthy of enactment. Because most members of Congress want the constituents to approve of their actions, expectations about the saleability of different proposals are a critical influence on policy-making.

This chapter focuses on *persuasion*. It uses *information economics* (Rasmussen 1989)—a series of techniques developed to study choices under uncertainty—to explain the factors that create and enhance representatives' ability to persuade or explain proposals to their constituents. The chapter also addresses how the 1970s procedural reforms, combined with trends in congressional elections and media coverage of Congress, have increased the need for, and difficulty of, constituent persuasion. These findings are supported with quotes from interviews conducted with lawmakers concerning their votes on the Ethics Act of 1989, which raised congressional pay. In addition, there is discussion of the leadership tactics that made it easier for members to persuade constituents in favor of the virtues of the Ethics Act.

THE PROBLEM: INFORMATION AND RETROSPECTIVE EVALUATIONS

The mechanics of congressional persuasion are connected to the concept of *retrospective evaluations*. Constituents make retrospective evaluations when they determine whether their representative has voted to enact bills they support and against bills they oppose (Key 1965; Fiorina 1981). This evaluation helps constituents to rate their representative's performance and decide whether he or she deserves reelection.

Retrospective evaluations can also influence a member's voting behavior. Unfavorable evaluations are costly to a representative who values reelection, as most members of the modern Congress do. A representative who wants to achieve a policy end by casting a particular vote, but who knows the vote will anger the constituents, must balance the cost of un-favorable evaluations against the benefits of improved policy. For example, if a proposal is salient to large numbers of constituents, legislators will probably vote the way their constituents want so to preserve their reelection chances, regardless of their assessment of the resulting outcome.[1] They are likely to ignore retrospective evaluations if only a few of their constituents care about a proposal, if they consider the policy end at stake to be extremely important, or if they are uninterested in reelection. High levels of constituent satisfaction with an incumbent's overall performance can reduce the loss in political support from one set of unfavorable evaluations, thereby allowing an occasional vote against constituent wishes.

While retrospective evaluations can influence how an elected represen-tative votes, the constituents' influence may not make them better off. For instance, this problem arises when constituents are mistaken in their eval-uation of a proposal—when they believe enactment of a certain proposal would hurt them when it would actually make them better off, or when they believe a proposal is beneficial when the opposite is true. When con-stituents misjudge a proposal in this way and incorporate the error into their retrospective evaluations, the threat of unfavorable evaluations, if it has any effect at all, will force their representative to vote against their interests.

Unfortunately, survey evidence suggests constituents are rarely well in-formed about legislative proposals (Jacobson 1987, chap. 5; Powell 1982). In contrast, legislators enjoy many sources of information unavailable to constituents: hearings and debates, committee reports, interest group ar-guments, and the efforts of their staffs—not to mention their own expertise. Elected officials are thus usually better informed about proposals than are their constituents.

Information economists (Rasmussen 1989) argue that elected officials have "private information"; that is, information constituents will not learn unless the officials choose to share it with them. Even if an official shares some information, constituents have no way to verify that he or she is telling the truth.

The combination of congressional expertise and constituent uncertainty produces a critical problem for constituents. On the one hand, they would like their representative to use private information when he or she votes. Reelection-minded representatives will do this only if they believe that they can persuade their constituents that they have acted in their interest. On the other hand, if constituents allow themselves to be persuaded, they lose their ability to influence representatives' behavior.

Suppose, for instance, a representative votes for a proposal that con-stituents dislike, explaining that private information indicated that the pro-posal would actually enhance constituents' welfare. Assume also that the representative values reelection over policy, so he or she is unwilling to vote yea if the vote will be judged unfavorably by the constituents. In this case, the representative will vote yea only if he or she expects constituents to be persuaded and to evaluate the vote favorably. If the representative expects that the explanation will be disregarded, he or she will vote nay to receive a favorable constituent evaluation, regardless of the impact of the vote on constituents' welfare or personal policy goals.

However, explanations based on private information are unverifiable; constituents will never learn whether their representative is telling the truth. Therefore, representatives who are able to explain votes can disregard constituent interests and vote however they want without worrying about unfavorable evaluations.

Constituents thus face an inevitable and problematic choice. On the one hand, they can use retrospective evaluations to try to influence how their representative votes, but this tactic, if it has any effect at all, leads the representative to act in accordance with constituent interests only if constituents have accurate information about proposals. On the other hand, constituents can forswear influence over their representative's behavior by allowing themselves to be persuaded. Then the representative can use private information but will act in accordance with constituent interests only if he or she shares those interests.

Successful persuasion is also described as *explanation, trust,* or *voting leeway* (Fenno 1978; Jewell 1982; Kingdon 1981; Parker and Parker 1989). All of these terms describe the same things: Constituents, by allowing themselves to be persuaded, or by accepting explanations, granting leeway, or choosing to trust, permit their elected representative to cast votes free of electoral constraints and accept the representative's evaluations of legislative proposals. In terms of retrospective evaluations, this implies that constituents will evaluate their representative's vote favorably regardless of what it is.

MORE PROBLEMS: CHANGES IN CAMPAIGNS AND PROCEDURES

The number of situations in which persuasion is necessary has increased in recent years due to secular trends that focus constituent attention on their representative's performance in office, as well as reforms that make congressional actions more visible to the public.

The secular trends include the decline of presidential coattails, the erosion of voter's party identification, and the rise of candidate-centered campaigns (Hinckley 1981; Jacobson 1987). These trends reduced the influences of party identification and evaluations of presidential performance on vote decisions in congressional elections. The changes imply that representatives' performance in office looms larger in constituents' vote decisions. If representatives cast enough politically damaging votes, presidential popularity or a favorable party balance will not save them from defeat. Therefore, representatives have to worry more today than they did in the past about persuading constituents of the correctness of their voting record.

Congressional voting behavior has also become more visible to constituents because of changes in legislative procedure during the 1970s that changed the number of recorded votes. These reforms reduced the number of members who must agree to call for a recorded vote and allowed for recorded votes on amendments (Oleszek 1989). Votes on almost all major pieces of legislation and most important amendments are recorded.

Interest groups and the media have also intensified their efforts to inform citizens about congressional votes (Schlozman and Tierney 1986). Interest groups inform citizens by publicizing individual votes (Keller 1981). The representatives interviewed for this analysis thought it inevitable that their constituents would learn how they voted—after all, they said, this information is printed in the local newspapers.

Unfortunately, though, many local papers and other sources of news do not inform citizens about the details of legislation. As a result, citizens are aware of their representatives' votes but remain relatively uninformed about what their representatives are voting on. Thus, the problem of persuasion remains.

CHOOSING LEEWAY

Three factors influence whether constituents should grant leeway to their elected representatives (Bianco 1991):[2]

1. *Constituent uncertainty*—how sure can constituents be about what a proposal will do if it is enacted?
2. *Private information*—how likely is it that representatives have more accurate information about a proposal than constituents do?
3. *Common interest*—how likely is it that constituents share common interests with their representatives?

Constituent Uncertainty

Constituents have no reason to grant leeway to a representative when they have full information about how a proposal will affect them. Similarly, no motive for leeway exists when constituents are uncertain about the exact impact of a proposal but know for sure that it will make them better or worse off. In both cases, constituents have enough information to determine which outcome (and vote) will be best for them.

However, when constituents do not know whether enacting a proposal will improve their welfare, they may incorrectly determine which vote serves their interests. Demands or evaluations based on this determination may force representatives to vote against constituents' interests. The level of constituent uncertainty is measured as the probability that constituents are mistaken in their assessment of which outcome (enactment or defeat) will make them better off.

Private Information

Constituents will grant leeway to their representative when they think there is some chance that the representative has private information about the impact a proposal will have on them. When constituents believe their representative has no such information, they have no reason to tolerate a vote that is inconsistent with their judgments, however uncertain those judgments may be.

Constituent uncertainty, coupled with the belief that the representative has relevant private information, is a motive for granting leeway. By doing so, constituents allow their representative to cast votes based on the representative's private information, rather than on uncertain constituent perceptions.

Common Interest

To grant leeway, constituents must believe there is some chance that the representative will use that leeway to act in their interest. Given leeway, though, a representative could vote to achieve his or her personal policy goals. Therefore, constituents should grant leeway only when they share common interests with their representative.

Formally, a representative and the constituents have a common interest on a proposal if the same outcome (enactment or defeat) is considered optimal by both actors given their respective policy goals. A common interest does not mean that a representative and the constituents have the identical policy goals, just that they share a preference about what should be done with a particular proposal. Suppose, for example, that a representative favors increases in the defense budget while the constituents prefer no change in spending. They have a common interest in defeating bills that will reduce defense spending. No common interest exists on bills that will increase spending—the representative prefers to enact such increases, while the constituents prefers to defeat them.

Uncertainties about the impact of a proposal and a representative's policy preferences make it impossible for constituents to be sure that a common interest exists.[3] However, uncertain constituents can assess the likelihood of a common interest using whatever information is available to them about proposals and the representative, and then act on the basis of that assessment.

Putting the Factors Together

Analyzing constituent strategies-given policy uncertainty, private information, and perceptions of the representative reveals that constituents sometimes do better by granting leeway. That is, to grant leeway, constituents must be uncertain enough about a proposal, believe their representative has relevant private information, and believe there is a high enough chance that a common interest exists. If so, the benefit of leeway—allowing the representative to use private information—outweighs the cost—the representative may vote counter to constituents' interests.

The probability of a common interest must be better than even for constituents to prefer leeway. This value makes leeway preferable only when constituents have no idea of whether enacting a proposal will make them better or worse off.[4]

As constituent uncertainty declines, the likelihood of a common interest needed to make leeway preferable increases. The reason is that, as constituents gain information, the value of the representative's private information declines, and with it the potential gains from leeway. Therefore, constituents must be more certain that a common interest exists for leeway to be preferable.

In substantive terms, these results mean that the perception of a common interest is a critical factor for leeway or successful persuasion. If constituents believe that a common interest exists, they will grant leeway even if they are extremely confident of what a proposal will do and believe it extremely unlikely that their representative has private information.

Constituent perception of whether a common interest exists should be based on the information they have about their representative's policy preferences. Information may be obtained directly from the representative, through his or her presentation of self (Fenno 1978). A representative's demographic and other observable characteristics are other sources of information about preferences. Voter's policy preferences are correlated with demographic characteristics such as age, race, religion, and socioeconomic status (Nie, Verba, and Petrocik 1979; Stanley, Bianco, and Niemi 1986). Constituents may believe the same is true for their representative, and make inferences about his or her preferences based on observed characteristics.

Empirically, lawmakers who are successful at presenting themselves, or who have the "right" demographic characteristics, should be given leeway by their constituents. These lawmakers usually vote however they wish on a proposal without receiving unfavorable evaluations. In addition, constituents who grant leeway may alter their perceptions of a proposal in response to their representative's vote.

At the other end, lawmakers who are unsuccessful at presentation, or who have the "wrong" characteristics, are not given leeway. These representatives must vote according to constituents' demands or face a loss of political support. They are also unable to modify constituents' perceptions of the proposal through persuasion or explanation.

INFORMATION AND REPRESENTATION: THE ETHICS ACT OF 1989

The Ethics Act of 1989 provided a 35 percent pay raise for members of Congress and senior members of the executive branch. It also imposed a variety of ethics reforms on members of Congress and their staffs. The reforms included limits on earned outside income, a ban on honoraria for members and staff, a 1993 deadline for members to convert campaign funds to private use on retirement, and new restrictions on the value of gifts or travel that members and staff can accept.[5]

Perhaps the most surprising thing about the Ethics Act was that anyone in Congress was willing to vote for it. Most citizens oppose pay raises for elected officials (Mills 1989). Intense constituent opposition forced the defeat of an earlier attempt to raise pay by a 48 to 380 vote (Hook 1989). Yet the Ethics Act passed the House by a margin of 252 to 174. Furthermore, many members who voted for the act reported that their constituents were not angry with their vote and that some were even pleased.

Despite constituent opposition, then, some representatives had leeway on the Ethics Act. While in some cases leeway was the product of the representatives' overall reputation, most members were given leeway because of characteristics that signaled a common interest to constituents, such as personal wealth, outside income, and substantial honoraria. For members who had these characteristics, their constituents inferred that they would vote for the Ethics Act only if it implemented meaningful ethics reform or had other beneficial effects on Congress. Most constituents in most districts would accept a trade of pay for ethics reform. Wealth, outside income, and honoraria signaled that members would vote for a raise only if it was part of such a trade, and thus signaled a common interest.

Congressional Support

Almost all of the supporters of the Ethics Act believed the pay raise was a good idea. The central argument in favor of the raise was that it would motivate qualified, middle-class people to run for Congress, give them the incentive to stay and develop policy expertise, and reduce the financial lure of outside activities and interests. A senior northeastern Democrat described the pay raise this way:[6]

> [The raise] gives members of Congress more time to tend to their congressional business, and be less beholden to the special interests. Not that they're bought, but if they're flown first class to a beach resort, put in a luxury hotel, have their greens fees paid, and treated like they're special, it develops a personal relationship that arguably makes them less independent. . . . When people go into public service, they should be able to provide for their family. It's expensive to be a member of Congress because of the need to live in two places. . . . I didn't want Congress to become a body for rich people.

The reader may wish to discount this argument on grounds that proponents just wanted a larger salary. Self-interest was clearly the driving force for some members. One freshman argued that

> the leadership felt the raise was necessary to keep regular people in Congress. A guy like me, without much wealth, not much net worth, couldn't afford to maintain two households without it. There's a tremendous amount of start-up costs. You need to buy new furniture, dining room sets, new plates, a new toaster. I had to buy a new set of suits for up here. So you're either well-off, or you struggle.

However, self-interest cannot explain the senior Democrat's support of the raise. His net worth is in the millions of dollars; the honoraria income that he lost because of the Ethics Act outweighed the increase in his congressional pay.

Supporters of the Ethics Act were divided on the benefits of ethics reform. Many proponents felt the reforms merely supplied political cover for the raise, by responding to constituent perceptions of the dangers of honoraria. The two comments that follow, the first by a junior Republican and the second by a senior Democrat, are typical:

> Ethics was a snare and an illusion as always. . . . The thought was, if we have all this ethics stuff that doesn't matter, we can get a pay raise through. It lets you make a speech where you say that the raise was tough to swallow, but we needed it to get the ethics reforms through.

> On the question of banning honoraria, I have mixed feelings. Enough people think it's wrong, it makes people feel less good about government, so we should get rid of them. But we lose some benefit—Congress used to go out, meet with people they wouldn't otherwise meet with, and learn things they wouldn't otherwise learn. On balance, the package was all right. Not an unmitigated good, but good, the pay raise being the better part.

Some proponents of the Act, such as the freshman Democrat quoted next, felt that the ethics reforms would reduce the influence of lobbyists and special interests on the policy process:

> When I speak on an issue I know about, I see nothing wrong with honoraria. But it's way too complicated to write an honoraria restriction to limit talks to things you know about. On the other side, I had lunch with three lobbyists and when I got up, there was an honoraria, an envelope with a thousand dollars in it. I gave it back, but that's wrong. I'm on banking, so they call me and ask if I want to have lunch and get an honoraria for talking with them. It's hard to shut that out, so we have to blanket it.

The overall picture from the interviews is one of overwhelming majority in Congress supporting the Ethics Act out of either self-interest or concern with the composition and behavior of the institution. Estimates of the percentage of members who supported the act usually ran in the 80–99 percent range.

Constituent Opposition

Constituent opposition to the Ethics Act was widespread. The opposition argued that congressional salaries were high enough already or that the act would not alter the composition or performance of Congress. The following two comments are from members representing midwestern districts:

> [Pay raises] are just the biggest fishhook issue around. . . . It's just a lose, lose, lose issue. They equate it with the salary they make and the problems the nation has, and they resent the hell out of it. They say, "You knew what the salary was when you ran." It's just a fishhook they swallowed, and it won't come out. They're eighty to twenty against it, and you might convince 10 percent more if you worked at it.

> People were not very focused on the ethics, but they were very focused on the pay hike. People in my neck of the woods are not interested in pay hikes for congressmen, cabinet officials, or judges. Some were almost offended that they were put together. Folks knew the honoraria limit and knew just how much most members make in honoraria, so they knew the pay hike was more. Honoraria are not a big issue in my district.

The only exceptions came from constituents who are affluent, "professionals," government employees, or who lived in areas with a high cost of living. A member representing a district in southern California put it this way:

> I got a lot of mail and calls from people expressing empathy. They still think we're not getting paid enough. They know we need to keep two homes, plus they have higher salaries. They make $700,000 working for a law firm, they know I used to make that much, but now I don't. So there's some sympathy.

Similarly, a representative from an urban district said his constituents had some sympathy for a raise: "Coming from New York, people understand how expensive it is to live [in Washington]. Even a lot of poor people understand."

But support for the pay raise was the exception rather than the rule. In addition, constituents were skeptical of the ethics reforms or unaware of them entirely. Overall, constituents opposed the Ethics Act. Many members of Congress attributed constituent opposition to the Ethics Act to ignorance about the expenses they faced or to envy of the magnitude of congressional salaries. While there may be some truth in these arguments, other members advanced a more likely explanation—that constituents' opposition was rational given the information available to them. Arguments that a raise was necessary to keep qualified or middle-class legislators in Congress were negated by casual observation. There is no sign of mass retirements from Congress; indeed, a diverse group of challengers run for Congress in each election. Thus constituents had no evidence that a pay raise would change the composition of Congress. In addition, most constituents have a low opinion of Congress in general, so they had no reason to reward members with a pay raise.[7]

Arguments based on the ethics proposals faced a similar appeal to facts: previous ethics reforms did not eliminate congressional misdeeds. The session in which the Ethics Act was enacted included numerous examples of ethical lapses—violations of honoraria rules by then-Speaker Jim Wright (D-Tex.) and Senator David Durenburger (D-Minn.) and the "Keating Five" involvement in the savings and loan scandal, to name a few. Constituents who knew about the ethics proposals had little reason to believe they would have much of an effect.

In sum, then, the typical member of Congress faced constituents who were opposed to the pay raise and skeptical or unaware of the proposed ethics reforms. Exceptions were constituents in affluent or high-cost areas and high-income professionals, who were more apt to sympathize with the idea of raising pay. This is not to say that the public was opposed to trading a pay raise for ethics reform and improved congressional performance. Some people did not support a pay raise for Congress under any circumstances, though this group was only a small minority in most districts. The remaining constituents were willing to accept the trade. The problem was that these constituents thought the Ethics Act would not raise ethical standards, lessen the influence of special interests, or increase the number of middle-class people in Congress. All they thought it would do is raise congressional pay.

Leeway on the Ethics Act

Characteristics such as personal wealth, outside income, and honoraria receipts led constituents to grant leeway to their representatives on the Ethics Act. Wealthy members were given leeway because their constituents inferred that personal wealth reduced the members' financial incentive to vote for the act. In addition, most constituents tend to make favorable evaluations of their own representative's ethical judgment. Taken together, these perceptions led constituents to believe that a wealthy member would vote for the Ethics Act only if it was a worthwhile pay-for-ethics trade. In this case, then, constituents who favored the trade had a common interest with the member, and a grant of leeway was justified.

Two southern Democrats described the link between leeway and personal wealth as follows:

> One reason my situation is atypical is that I've given a substantial amount of money to my district each year. My constituents might not think that's a big deal, but they know I'm not dependent on my congressional pay. With my friends I make the argument that for me, a vote for the pay raise is unselfish because I didn't need it. . . . I've always been up-front about my income. It's pretty well known that I have the second-largest net worth in the delegation. Some of my constituents don't like that I was born with a silver spoon in my mouth, but the others just think it's harder to buy me.

> I got criticized during the campaign for spending $450,000 of my own money. So I told them, "If you're upset about that, you can't say I voted yes only so I could take a $25,000 raise."

Both members believe that their constituents were happy with their vote on the Ethics Act. The argument for leeway based on personal wealth is thus supported.

In contrast, middle-class lawmakers who wanted or needed a pay raise found it difficult to justify a yea vote. Most constituents believed that these members supported the Ethics Act because they wanted a raise, regardless of the whatever other effects the act might have. As a result, middle-class representatives were usually perceived as having no common interests with their constituents on the Ethics Act. As a result, they were not given leeway.

Members of Congress with substantial honoraria or outside income were also perceived as having interests in common with their constituents. These members successfully argued that they did not vote to increase their pay because their loss in income from the act's restrictions on outside income and honoraria outweighed the pay raise. A northwestern Democrat put it this way:

> [My constituents] think I acted in the interests of the country. The raise was overdue; it had to be dealt with.
>
> [*Would it be easier to vote against it?*] It would be a slam-dunk. It would be easy to vote against the raise. I won't make a nickel more—it's a wash for what goes into my pocket.
>
> [*Did you make that argument?*] Yes, I argued that. They responded favorably.

As with personal wealth, once pay is removed as a motive, constituents are more likely to believe they have a common interest with their representative: improving congressional ethics and performance. This inference may be incorrect, but it represents efficient use of available information by constituents.

Personal wealth, outside income, and honoraria were not the only factors that generated leeway on the Ethics Act. Some members said they were given leeway because of their reputation of acting in constituents' interest. The same urban Democrat quoted earlier described his situation as follows:

> I've been fairly confident that my constituents will understand [a vote for the raise], and they do. . . . People sort of understand, they accept that if I voted against something I must have had a good reason. They have confidence in my representation.

This quote supports evidence of leeway, though the reason is unclear. This does not mean that the member's constituents were ineffective information users; rather, it suggests that the constituents' perceptions of this particular representative's preferences were based on a variety of factors including demographic characteristics. Attempting to understand what these factors are is a significant challenge for future research.

The Role of Electoral Safety

As noted earlier, a high level of constituent satisfaction with an incumbent's overall performance may allow the representative to disregard constituents' wishes on an occasional vote, even one that is highly salient to the constituents. Overall, the interviews conducted for this analysis suggest there is some truth to this claim. For example, one freshman representative described his constituents' reaction to a vote in favor of the Ethics Act as follows:

> [*Did they approve of your vote?*] If you asked them in a straight-out poll, you'd get 80 percent no.

> [*From the guys who brought you the savings and loan mess?*] Ninety-six thousand looks like a lot of money. For most people it's three times their salary.

> [*Then why did you vote for it?*] Because if you got 75 percent of the vote last time [like I did], you have a responsibility to the country—a broader responsibility than if you just scraped by with 51 percent.

This member, facing a trade-off between policy and political support, chose the former.[8]

However, it is also important to understand that representatives' election margin does not insure that they have leeway or that their cost of voting against constituents' wishes is small. Election margins, therefore, are not a good predictor of how representatives will react to the threat of unfavorable evaluations.

The idea that leeway is unrelated to representatives' election margins can be seen by comparing two members' statements during 1990 interviews. Both members supported the Ethics Act, although both reported that their constituents were initially opposed to it.

> I don't know why they included me in the article about the pay raise because I haven't heard from my opponent about it. If he includes that in the campaign, he'll lose. . . . I haven't heard a whole lot of anything. There's a talk show back home that bangs away on it, but I haven't heard much at town meetings. I've spoke a couple of hundred times, and it hasn't happened once. As best I can tell, it's not a problem.

> I couldn't even attempt to sell the pay raise. . . . I'm a sitting target at all those town meetings, and I don't need the hassle. No, it's not worth the hassle to attempt to do it. I can walk one step on water, but not three or four.

The first statement is from a freshman member who won with about 60 percent of the vote and was rated as vulnerable in the 1990 election. The second is from a ranking minority member of a committee who was reelected with over 70 percent of the vote in the previous seven elections. The vulnerable freshman believed he had leeway on the Ethics Act; the safe senior member did not. Thus election margin (or seniority) does not determine whether a member has leeway.

The costs of voting against constituents' wishes on the Ethics Act are described by a northeastern Democrat in the following quote from a 1990 interview:

> I don't vote for pay raises, I just don't. I just vote politically on them, which gives me the freedom to do other things like [voting against repeal of] catastrophic health insurance. Constituents pay attention to votes like the pay raise, and they get exercised if you vote for them. . . . It's kind of a litmus test of whether you're antiestablishment, whether you're part of the problem in Congress or not. Privately, I'm certainly for it, but I'm locked into voting against it.

Unfavorable evaluations thus have two effects: (1) they cause constituents to lower their opinions of incumbents' performance in office and (2) the vote reduces incumbents' chances of getting leeway on other votes. This occurs because constituents update their perceptions of representatives' policy preferences based on voting behavior.

However, these costs have nothing to do with incumbents' election margins. Rather, they are a function of constituents' evaluations of proposals and their beliefs about incumbents' policy preferences. Scholars need to examine these factors carefully so to explain why reelection-minded incumbents are able to cast politically sensitive votes. A single-minded focus on election margins is misguided.

MANAGING CONSTITUENT UNCERTAINTY: LEADERSHIP TACTICS

The congressional leadership used its agenda-setting powers to make it easier for members of Congress to sell the Ethics Act to their constituents. The leadership's involvement with the Ethics Act and other legislation flows from changes in the postreform Congress that have decentralized policy-making authority to individual members (Sinclair 1983).[9] During the coalition-building process, the leadership facilitates negotiation and compromise. Once a proposal has attracted majority support, the leadership works to structure the legislative process to enact the proposal as efficiently as possible.

Leadership involvement with the Ethics Act began with the leadership-appointed task force that wrote it. The leadership then used three tactics to facilitate persuasion and explanation. First, the leaders structured the proposal by combining pay and ethics proposals into one measure rather than voting on them separately. Second, they coordinated the voting process to minimize the number of members who needed to cast potentially costly votes in order to enact the Ethics Act. Third, they worked to get conservative politicians to endorse the Ethics Act.[10]

Structuring the Proposal

The most obvious feature of the Ethics Act was the trade: pay for ethics. Nothing made this package inevitable; pay raises and ethics reforms were usually considered separately in the past. Further, packaging pay with ethics did not change the proposals; the pay raise was just as large as it would have been if enacted by itself, and none of the ethics reforms were weakened by the simultaneous passage of the raise in pay.

By combining the proposals, the leadership limited the demands constituents could make of their representatives. Recall that most constituents opposed the pay raise and favored the ethics reforms. Because the two items were packaged together, constituents had to accept one to get the other. If the proposals had been voted on separately, constituents could have demanded that their representatives vote for ethics reform and against the pay raise. With packaging (and a closed rule), constituents had to accept both or neither.

The effects of packaging are clear when the enactment of the Ethics Act is compared with the defeat of the Quadrennial Commission recommendations for a pay raise. Then-Speaker Jim Wright (D-Tex.) promised that if the recommendations were approved, he would bring an ethics proposal to the floor. Wright's procedure created uncertainty about whether the ethics reforms would follow a pay raise and whether a pay raise was needed to induce a majority to vote for ethics reform. These uncertainties did not affect constituent evaluations of the two proposals. However, by making constituents uncertain of the inevitability and the necessity of the trade, the procedure made it harder for members to explain a vote in favor of the pay recommendations.

Coordination

Another leadership tactic involved coordinated voting on the Ethics Act. Recorded votes in the House take at least fifteen minutes to conduct.[11] The leadership told different types of members to vote at different times.[12]

Members who were confident they had leeway or determined to vote yea regardless of the political costs were encouraged to vote as early as possible. Members who were going to vote no because of policy or reelection concerns were encouraged to vote late. Finally, members who were prepared to vote yea but at some risk politically were told to wait and see whether the bill would pass before they cast their vote. This coordination tactic had two benefits. First, members who were unsure they had leeway or who would offend their constituents by voting yea could hold off voting until it was clear their votes were needed. Once a majority had voted for the proposal, these members could play it safe and vote against the package without affecting its chance of passage. Second, stacking yea votes early maximized bandwagon effects. These effects would occur if members engaged in cue-taking (Matthews and Stimson 1975); that is, an early wave of yea votes might cue late voters that a vote for the proposal would not be so difficult to explain and thus lead them to vote yea. The leadership's tactics ensured that any bandwagon effect that did occur would push members toward a yea vote.

Endorsements

The leadership also gathered endorsements from political actors who usually opposed pay raises. In particular, the leadership enlisted the endorsement of Newt Gingrich (R-Ga.), the Republican party whip. Gingrich may have supported the proposal on its merits or because he was coerced by members of the Republican caucus. Regardless of his motive, several members from Gingrich's home state of Georgia and several surrounding states reported that his endorsement helped them convince their constituents that the proposal was worthwhile.

The effect of Gingrich's endorsement is understood in terms of constituent perceptions and private information. Constituents who knew of Gingrich generally thought of him as a fiscal conservative, unwilling to vote for a pay raise unless it improved the quality of congressional ethics and performance. Gingrich's endorsement of the Ethics Act was seen by these constituents as evidence that the trade of pay for ethics was worthwhile. As a result, the endorsement helped some members to vote for the Ethics Act: they faced constituents who were more favorably disposed toward the proposal.

The importance of constituent perceptions is seen clearly when the effect of Gingrich's endorsement is contrasted with the effect of Common Cause's endorsement of the Ethics Act. During 1990 interviews, only a few legislators indicated that Common Cause's endorsement had an effect on district opinion. One obvious reason is that constituents were largely unaware of the endorsement. However, even informed constituents had reason to disregard the endorsement. Common Cause has been a consistent supporter of ethics reform. Faced with this record, constituents may have inferred that Common Cause supported the proposal only because of the ethics reforms, not because a pay-for-ethics trade was worthwhile on balance.

Leadership tactics work at the margin: some proposals cannot be explained regardless of how they are packaged, voted on, or endorsed. But the Ethics Act shows that the postreform congressional leadership can play a valuable role in both stages of the policy process, helping members to develop acceptable proposals and persuading constituents of their merits.

CONCLUSION

This chapter has addressed the problems representatives face when they try to persuade constituents of the virtues of legislative proposals. Using the tools of information economics, it has been shown that well-informed constituents will accept a representative's explanations and thus grant leeway even though they cannot be certain that the elected representative will act in their interest. Doing so helps legislators to further citizen interests, a central element of democratic theory.

The analysis also has shown that constituents are sometimes wise to ignore attempts at persuasion. Doing so may lead representatives to forgo good policies in favor of maintaining their political support. However, constituents who believe that they do not share common interests with their legislators should evaluate proposals based on the available information, however scanty. In this regard, citizens' refusal to believe what politicians tell them may reflect calculation, not myopia or ignorance.

Finally, the analysis has outlined the tactics that legislators in the post-reform era use to enact complex policy proposals. The difficulties of enacting complex proposals have increased because of certain trends, such as the increase in constituents' information about representatives' voting behavior and the decline in voter partisan identification.

Members of Congress have responded to these trends by increasing direct and indirect contacts with their constituents (Jacobson 1986) and by highlighting the interests they have in common. In addition, members have empowered the congressional leadership to structure the legislative process in a way that reduces the need for, and thereby the success of, constituent persuasion.

Acknowledgments

I would like to thank my colleagues John Aldrich, David Canon, and Patrick Sellers, as well as Roger Davidson, for their thoughtful comments. I would also like to thank Tom Mann and his staff at the Brookings Institution for their valuable assistance during my fieldwork in Washington.

Notes

1. Only a few proposals each year will pass this salience test, which both narrows and sharpens the problem of persuasion. Representatives need not worry about constituent reactions to most of their votes. However, they will be unable to use an overall favorable voting record to justify unpopular votes on the proposals that attract widespread attention.

2. Three assumptions are made in the game-theoretic analysis: (a) representatives are pivotal—proposals are enacted if they vote yea and defeated if they vote nay; (b) representatives are motivated by goals of reelection and policy, with reelection taking precedence—thus, they will always vote to satisfy constituents' demands, if the latter choose to make them; and (c) constituent policy preferences are homogenous, and constituents all have the same information about proposals. Each of these assumptions could be relaxed without changing the results described here.

3. Examples of policy uncertainty in the case of defense spending include uncertainty about the cost of open-ended deployments of troops and the future costs of a weapons system.

4. Formally, at this point constituents believe it is equally likely that enacting the proposal will make them better or worse off.

5. Following the lead of the congressional leadership, I refer to HR 3660 as the "Ethics Act."

6. This and the following quotations are taken from interviews conducted with ninety-

three members of Congress from January to June 1990. All respondents requested and were promised anonymity.

7. Many comments were consistent with Fenno's assertion that the public "loves their congressmen and hates Congress" (1975). One member even cited Fenno on this point.

8. This member was reelected in 1990 with a similar margin, so it may be that his cost of voting for the Ethics Act was fairly small.

9. In general, these tactics are used by the Democratic party leadership, which controls various aspects of the legislative process in the House. The Republicans frequently oppose Democrats' efforts at structuring floor proceedings. The Ethics Act is an exception: it was enacted by a bipartisan coalition, and the leadership in both parties worked to facilitate the result.

10. A fourth leadership tactic, coercion, is not discussed here. Members in positions of power in Congress were expected to vote for the Ethics Act as partial payment for their position.

11. It is not clear whether there are records of the order of voting. A member could be embarrassed by revelation of the timing of a vote if, for example, he or she waited to vote until the Ethics Act was sure to pass, then voted nay. Several members interviewed believe these records exist. However, no one in the Office of the Clerk of the House would say so.

12. Some coordination would occur without any leadership effort. Strong supporters and opponents of a proposal would vote early to promote bandwagon effects, while those on the fence would wait until the result became more certain. However, the leadership worked against this pattern by telling opponents to vote late. In addition, the leadership used the whip system to inform members of their expectations about coordination.

PART · III

Party Leaders and Followers

5 / House Majority Party Leadership in an Era of Legislative Constraint

BARBARA SINCLAIR

The Speaker of the House sits at the president's side, with other congressional leaders arrayed around a large oval table in the White House, prepared to begin a negotiation session on the budget. The Speaker, majority leader, and whip are interviewed on the Sunday talk shows. At a stakeout in the White House driveway, reporters question the leaders about their responses to the president's foreign policy moves. Having sat behind the president while the State of the Union address was delivered, the Speaker then usually presents the party's response. All these now common television images suggest that the role of the House majority party leadership has changed in recent years. The leadership has become more active, more visible, and more consequential in the legislative process than it was twenty, even ten years ago.

Much current commentary on Congress, particularly that of journalists and textbook writers, still portrays a resource-poor majority party leadership trying to cope, not very successfully, with a reformed House inimical to all leadership (see, for example, Smith 1988). Having stripped the committee chairs of much of their power and endowed themselves with increased resources especially in the form of staff, rank-and-file members are described as eager to participate actively in all aspects of the legislative process and refuse to countenance any restraints; so the story goes. They follow their own agendas and make their own voting decisions totally unconstrained by party. Because party leaders can do little to help or hurt a member's reelection chances, they have little influence over members' behavior. Given the ideological heterogeneity of the Democratic party, the leadership is, thus, frequently unsuccessful in carrying out its primary task of building winning coalitions on major legislation.

Although reasonably descriptive of the House in the immediate postreform period of the mid- to late 1970s, this portrait is no longer accurate. This chapter describes House majority party leadership in the early 1990s and explains why the highly decentralized portrait of the House evolved toward centralization and stronger leadership during the 1980s.

Since the late 1980s and early 1990s, the House majority party leadership has been more actively and more comprehensively involved in the legislative process than its predecessors of the post–World War II period.

91

Today it is involved in a larger proportion of the major legislation and at more stages of the legislative process. No longer does the party leadership focus primarily on building winning coalitions at the floor stage; rather, it is frequently engaged in coordinating the work of multiple committees on a given bill, often working out disagreements among them. The leaders not infrequently become involved in negotiating the substance of particularly vital and contentious legislation with the Senate and the White House. In addition, the party leaders are more visible as public spokespersons for their membership.

In searching for an explanation of this change, it is important to remember that congressional party leaders are the elected agents of their members. Because they are dependent on the votes of their membership to attain and retain their positions, party leaders try to satisfy their members' expectations. Consequently, if a change in leaders' behavior is observed, the expectations of members should be examined.

The development of strong leadership is the result of a significant change in the costs and benefits to Democratic members of such leadership and of a consequent change in what members expect of their leaders. The 1970s reforms, combined with the constraints of the 1980s political environment, greatly increased the difficulty of enacting legislation, especially legislation Democrats favored. The decline in intercommittee reciprocity and the rise of floor amending activity, split control, and the huge deficits made passing major legislation more difficult. The 1970s reformers, most of them liberal Democrats, were motivated by concerns about both policy and participation. The changes they instituted would, they believed, produce better— more representative and more liberal—policy and provide greater opportunities for the rank and file to participate in the legislative process. By the late 1970s many had concluded that unrestrained participation, particularly on the House floor, hindered rather than facilitated the production of good public policy. And in the more hostile political climate of the 1980s, the policy costs of unrestrained and uncoordinated legislative activism rose further (see Sinclair 1991).

The party leadership possesses critical resources that, if Democratic members acquiesce in their use, can significantly increase the probability of legislative success. Through control of the Rules Committee, the leadership can structure the floor choice situation so as to reduce uncertainty and advantage the committee majority's position. Through the expanded whip system, the leadership can collect information and mobilize votes and thereby provide important aid to a bill's proponents. To the extent that passing legislation is necessary to the advancement of their goals, the Democratic membership, Democratic committee contingents, and Democratic committee leaders all can at least potentially benefit from strong leadership.

Moreover, during this same period, the costs of strong leadership declined as the effective ideological heterogeneity of the Democratic membership declined (see Rohde 1988, and this volume, Chapter 2). As the policy differences among Democrats declined, so did fears that the exercise of strong leadership would pose a threat to individual policy or reelection goals.

The adverse political climate of the 1980s, which resulted in House Democrats requiring help to pass legislation, also convinced them they needed a spokesperson to counter the president in the media. President Ronald Reagan effectively used his access to the media to shape the political agenda and to sell a highly negative image of the Democratic party. Unable to counter this threat to their policy and electoral goals individually, House Democrats expected their party leaders to take on the task.

PARTICIPATION AND ORGANIZATION

Members of the House expect their leaders to facilitate the passage of legislation they favor but without unduly narrowing their opportunities to participate in the legislative process. To be sure, House Democrats in the 1980s allowed their leaders to place restrictions on floor participation because such limits, they were convinced, had become a prerequisite to legislative success. This retreat from the wide-open floor decision-making process that characterized the mid- to late 1970s by no means signaled a waning of the desire for broad active participation in the legislative process. The challenge leaders have faced since the beginning of the reform era, and continue to face today, is reconciling members' desire to participate broadly with the dictates of coalition-building success. Over time, through a strategy of inclusion, the party leadership has developed ways of satisfying members' desires to participate that also contribute to, rather than hinder, legislative success (Sinclair 1983). From the leaders' perspective, including as many members as they can in leadership efforts has a twofold payoff: satisfying members' desire for participation and enlisting the help needed to meet expanded demands on leaders.

Traditionally, the Speaker, majority leader, and whip made up the party leadership. Recently, however, the chief deputy whip and the chair and vice-chair of the Democratic caucus have been incorporated into the inner circle. In the case of the caucus officers, their inclusion is in part an acknowledgment of their status derived from being elected by the full party membership. More important is the top leaders' need for help. The coordination and negotiation tasks the leadership is increasingly expected to take on are highly time-consuming. One response has been to expand the inner circle and parcel out those tasks among its members.

The whip system and the caucus are important vehicles for two-way communication and for participation by rank-and-file members. The whip system that in the early 1970s consisted of the whip, an assistant whip, and eighteen or so regionally elected zone whips had, by the 101st Congress (1989–90), expanded to include 102 members: the whip, the chief deputy whip, fifteen deputy whips, three task force chairpersons, sixty-four at-large-whips, and eighteen zone whips. The leadership meets with the whips every Thursday morning when the House is in session. Because of the number and representativeness of the whips, these meetings provide leaders with a quick, efficient way of getting information to their members directly, and they give members the opportunity to communicate their views—and gripes—to the leaders firsthand.

The whip system collects information on House members' voting intentions on major legislation, which forms the basis of the persuasion effort. Whip task forces, charged with rounding up the votes on bills deemed important but vulnerable, offer junior members a chance to participate in the legislative process beyond their committees.

The Democratic caucus—the organization of all House Democrats—also serves as a forum for communication and participation. When important but controversial legislation is ready for floor consideration, the leadership sometimes calls a caucus meeting to explain the legislation and ask for support. At the behest of a group of members or the leadership, a caucus to discuss any topic or problem can be held. The caucus Committee on Party Effectiveness holds open lunches about every two weeks, during which members can discuss specific policy problems among themselves and sometimes with outside experts. Every Congress, the caucus produces a party platformlike document through a series of broadly representative issue task forces (see Herrnson, this volume, Chapter 3).

The Democratic party organization in the House has in recent years evolved toward greater inclusiveness. In response to their own needs and to pressure from members, leaders have expanded the opportunities for two-way communication and for member participation under the aegis of the party. As the 1980s progressed, providing members with these opportunities became increasingly important because meeting their expectations for legislative output required leaders to curtail participation in more traditional forums and on some of the most important legislation of a session.

THE LEADERSHIP'S EXPANDED ROLE IN THE LEGISLATIVE PROCESS

Most legislation proceeds through the legislative process in the House with no leadership involvement beyond the routine task of scheduling the measure for floor consideration. To warrant extensive leadership involvement, legislation usually must be highly consequential or highly controversial and often both. Bills that their members badly want for policy or reelection reasons, or ones the party collectively needs for its reputation's sake, will elicit leadership activity, particularly if passage is problematical. If Democratic committee contingents can write a bill with broad appeal to the party membership and pass it on the floor without help, the party leaders will seldom intervene. It is their increasing difficulty in doing so that has fostered the party leadership's more activist role.

In the mid-1970s, as the floor became a more active decision-making arena and legislation became more vulnerable to attack and significant alteration on the floor, it became more important to bring to the floor bills carefully crafted to command broad support (Smith 1989). Once the amending process started on the floor, it could easily get out of hand. Because not all committees were capable of putting together such carefully crafted legislation, the party leaders found it necessary to become engaged in the legislative process before the floor stage, persuading committee leaders to compromise and sometimes working out the contours of the compromise themselves. The minimum-wage case studied later in the chapter offers an example. When the unrepresentatively liberal Education and Labor Committee reported a too-generous bill, leaders oversaw the drafting of a substitute that would command broader support.

The multiple-referral rule instituted in the mid-1970s has also had the effect of drawing party leaders more deeply into the prefloor legislative process. A considerable proportion of the most important legislation is now referred to more than one committee (see Davidson and Oleszek, this volume, Chapter 7). In the 101st Congress, for example, clean air, child care, and the Americans with Disabilities Act were all multiple-referred legislation. When the number of committees is large, leadership coordination is frequently necessary. Even when only two committees are involved, committee leaders are not always able to resolve their differences through negotiation. If they and their membership want the legislation at issue to be enacted, the party leaders must, through negotiation and pressure, get the committees to come to an agreement. During the 101st Congress, disagreement between the Ways and Means Committee and the Education and Labor Committee blocked the child-care bill for months. Party leaders tried to persuade the principals to resolve their differences; finally, the lack of noticeable progress and resultant criticism of the leadership convinced Speaker Thomas S. Foley that stronger measures were called for. Without consulting the committee leaders, Foley announced a date for floor consideration. With the committees now under great pressure to settle, he personally brokered the package taken to the floor.

In the 1980s deep policy divisions between President Reagan and House Democrats resulted in much more frequent employment of omnibus measures. The major battles came to revolve around budget resolutions, reconciliation bills, and other omnibus measures centering on questions of basic priorities. During the Ninety-seventh Congress, Reagan used these measures as vehicles for his agenda. After the 1982 elections, in which Democrats won back twenty-six House seats, stalemate became an ever-present threat. The inability of the president and House Democrats to agree on individual appropriations bills, or of either to impose its preferences on the other, resulted in frequent use of *continuing resolutions* (*CRs*), which are omnibus appropriations bills. Because such CRs are must-pass legislation and thus difficult for a president to veto, they also provided Democrats with a vehicle for enacting into law provisions that Reagan would have vetoed had they been sent to him as freestanding legislation. Much the same is true of *reconciliation bills*: they, too, are major, multiprovision measures that are difficult for presidents to veto and thereby can be used to force on presidents legislation they would not otherwise accept. Reconciliation bills became a prominent part of the congressional agenda because they provided the vehicle through which the unpalatable decisions necessitated by the huge deficits could be bundled. A package in which all shared the pain was passable, though often with difficulty, whereas separate bills cutting popular programs and raising revenues might well not have been passable. Finally, in their effort to compete with the White House for media attention and public credit, House Democrats began to package legislation on issues such as trade and drugs into high-profile omnibus measures. As a result of all these processes, omnibus measures increased as a proportion of the congressional agenda.

Because of the number and magnitude of issues and sometimes the number of committees involved in omnibus measures, putting together and passing such legislation often require negotiation and coordination activities beyond the capacity of committee leaders. Furthermore, on such broad, high-stakes measures, committee leaders lack the legitimacy to speak for the membership as a whole. As such omnibus measures became more prominent on the congressional agenda, the need for leadership involvement increased.

In the late 1980s and early 1990s, continued divided control and the Gramm-Rudman Act, which stipulated across-the-board spending cuts if the deficit was not reduced by a specified amount each year, forced a resort to budget summits for making overall decisions on spending and taxes (Gilmour, this volume, Chapter 12). The magnitude of the issues involved and the partisan stakes dictated that party leaders speak and act for their membership in these negotiations with the administration.

The growing demand for the leadership's coordinating and negotiating services has been met by an expansion in the inner circle and by delegation beyond it. Informally and sporadically under Speakers Thomas P. O'Neill and Jim Wright, and more systematically under Speaker Thomas S. Foley, a member is designated to take the lead role on each major bill. As a leadership staffer explained:

> It's the way Tom Foley operates. When there is legislation he is interested in that he knows there's going to be a problem with, he turns it over to someone to be coordinator, designated hitter. The point is Foley knows it will eventually come to his office, but this way it will get there much later in the process and there will be some one person who has spent a lot of time and energy working on it in a hands-on way. So it will be in better shape when it does get to him.[1]

During the mid- to late 1980s, for example, David Bonior (Mich.), a deputy whip and later chief deputy whip, took the lead on behalf of the party leadership on the issue of contra aid. Similarly, in the 101st Congress, Steny Hoyer (Md.), caucus chair, was designated hitter on the Americans with Disabilities Act (ADA); Bill Gray (Pa.), whip, played that role on the voter-registration bill; and Vic Fazio (Calif.), caucus vice chair, assumed the role on the ethics and pay raise bill.

The leadership's greater involvement in legislation at the prefloor stage has not reduced its obligations at the floor stage. The Speaker's decisive influence over the Rules Committee enables the leadership to control the flow of business to the floor and to structure the choices that confront members there. In the mid-1970s the Democratic Caucus granted the Speaker power to name all Democratic members of Rules subject only to caucus ratification, thereby giving the leadership predominant influence over the content of the special rules the committee reports. These resolutions, which set the ground rules under which legislation can be debated on the floor, must be approved by a majority vote of the House. In the immediate postreform period, Democrats were eager to participate actively on the floor and balked at approving rules that restrict amending activity. By the late 1970s, however, many had become convinced that the policy costs of un-restricted floor participation were too high. Members from both parties and all parts of the ideological spectrum—but especially conservative Republicans—were using the amending process to pick apart legislation written in Democratic-controlled committees, to put members on record on politically difficult issues, and to delay action on the floor (see Sinclair 1983). In response, majority party members increasingly backed their party leadership's use of special rules to restrict floor-amending activity.

Currently, major legislation in which the leadership is involved is almost never brought to the floor under a simple open rule allowing all germane amendments. Because restrictions on amendments reduce the uncertainty and the danger of major changes, committee leaders and the bill's other proponents are often eager for restrictive rules. Those who lost out in committee, however, want to offer amendments on the floor. The party leadership's control of this decision gives it leverage with committee proponents and sometimes with opponents, especially if they are Democrats. This leverage is sometimes used by the leadership to induce committee contingents and other participants to compromise so to produce a bill the leadership believes makes political as well as substantive sense.

Control of the Rules Committee allows the Speaker to make strategic use of floor scheduling and of the character of special rules. The timing of floor consideration can affect a bill's probability of passage. In the summer of 1990, when the Supreme Court declared unconstitutional a federal statute protecting the flag, Democratic leaders quickly brought to the floor a constitutional amendment banning flag desecration. Republican proponents, who had clamored for a vote on such a constitutional amendment since the

Court in 1989 had ruled a state statute unconstitutional, were caught un-prepared. The amendment was defeated as the Democratic leadership had hoped (Biskupic 1990, pp. 1962–64).

Over the last decade, the strategic use of special rules has become not only more frequent but also more sophisticated (see Bach and Smith 1988). By allowing some amendments but not others, by specifying the order in which amendments will be considered, by using special devices such as the king-of-the-hill procedure (in which alternatives are voted on *ad seriatim*, but if more than one receives a majority only the last is considered as passed), and by waiving points of order, rules can advantage one outcome and dis-advantage another. On major legislation, these are decisions the party lead-ership makes, though in consultation with Democratic committee leaders and Democrats on Rules. In making these decisions, the leadership is con-strained by the need for a majority vote. As Republicans increasingly vote against restrictive rules on principle, a large majority of Democrats must support a rule for it to pass.

When floor action on major legislation is contemplated, the party lead-ership forms a task force by inviting all the whips and Democratic members of the committee or committees of origin to participate. Working together, party and committee leaders will have decided which roll calls are most likely to be problematical—on the rule, on specific amendments, or (rarely) on passage—and will have asked the zone whips to ascertain their members' voting intentions. The task force, which consists of those members who responded to the invitation to participate, will work from this information to refine the count and attempt to assure a majority for the party position. Each task force member takes a list of names of Democrats not recorded as supporting the party position; from personal conversations with those on the list, the task force member is expected to ascertain the target De-mocrat's precise position and, where necessary and possible, to persuade him or her to support the leadership.

The elaborateness of the effort varies with the perceived difficulty of passing the legislation at issue as well as with the time available. A refine-ment of the initial zone-whip count by the task force may reveal that no floor problem exists. On more difficult legislative battles, a variety of strate-gies may be pursued. Interest groups may be brought into the persuasion effort, attempts to influence the character of the debate through the media may be made, and, if a majority cannot be rounded up through persuasion, the legislation may be altered so as to garner the needed support.

Such vote-mobilization efforts clearly benefit the proponents of the leg-islation. The leadership's command of the whip system allows it to provide this service to its members and thereby gives it leverage. During the 100th Congress, for example, the party leadership agreed to mount mobilization efforts against amendments that made across-the-board cuts in appropri-ations bills so long as the Appropriations Committee reported bills that were in compliance with the budget resolution.

The party leadership is able to mount frequent vote-mobilization efforts because it involves a large proportion of the membership in the process. About seventy task forces involving about 60 percent of the Democratic members functioned during the 100th Congress; about thirty task forces were in operation in 1989. The strategy of inclusion is a necessary *modus operandi* in the contemporary House.

PARTY LEADERS AS MEDIA SPOKESPERSONS

In the 1980s House Democrats came to expect their leaders to act as their spokespeople, countering the president in the media. Since at least Franklin Roosevelt's time, presidents have attempted through the mass media to influence elite and mass perceptions so as to shape the political agenda and party images. In the early 1980s President Reagan's media skills, in combination with the political climate, allowed him to dominate the agenda and to communicate a negative image of the Democratic party. Unable as individuals to counter this threat to their policy, power, and reelection goals, Democrats expected their leaders to take on the task. Unlike rank-and-file House members, the party leaders did have considerable access to the national media. In fact, in the aftermath of the 1981 Republican takeover of the Senate, the press anointed Speaker Thomas P. O'Neill as chief Democratic spokesperson.

George Bush's election as president did not reduce Democrats' expectations of their leaders' media role. Although less adept as a television performer than Reagan, Bush certainly attempted to use the president's media advantage to further his goals at the congressional Democrats' expense.

Even beyond meeting their members' expectations, the party leaders have a direct interest in performing this function effectively. To the extent the leaders can influence the issues and problems on the agenda, as well as shape the definition of those issues, they ease the task of passing legislation that furthers their members' policy and reelection goals. How the choice is defined often determines the electoral risks inherent in a particular vote. Thus in the 1990 controversy over funding for the National Endowment for the Arts, opponents of content restrictions attempted to define the issue as one of artistic freedom and opposition to censorship; those who favored restrictions cast the choice as favoring or opposing federal funding of pornographic art.

The majority party leaders' regular contact with the press provides them with many opportunities to attempt to influence perceptions. Every day that the House is in session the Speaker holds a short press conference. When, after ten or fifteen minutes of answering questions, the Speaker leaves to open the House, other leaders remain to answer further questions individually. The leaders appear frequently on Sunday talk shows and on programs like the "MacNeil/Lehrer Newshour." They give interviews at reporters' requests and sometimes hold media lunches to which selected reporters are invited for a wide-ranging discussion.

A congressional party seldom speaks with one voice. As much as members want their leaders to act as spokespersons, they do not thereby commit themselves to silence. And with the expansion of leadership positions, the coordination of messages even within the leadership circle has become more difficult. In the last few years, a formal attempt to "harmonize the various communications operations . . . of the various leaders and the caucus" has been instituted, an involved staffer explained. "If nothing is done, Democrats' worst instincts come out. You get people talking about the Democrats in disarray. . . . You certainly miss opportunities for presenting a unified front," the staffer added. Every morning that the House is in session, a group of about eighteen members—"midlevel activists who understand the media"—meet in the majority leader's office. The aim is to link the major items on the week's legislative schedule—"the anchor"—to one of the general themes the House Democrats are attempting to develop. The unified theme that emerges, if the process is successful, is then conveyed to other members and to the media through a variety of means. The staffer in charge gave this example:

> Last week's anchor was parental leave. We did the rule on Wednesday, passage on Thursday. We did one-minutes all week; we had a press conference on Tuesday in which we had [two victims of the lack of parental leave] tell their stories. We got on two network news shows on Tuesday and the other on Wednesday. Our press conference defined the coverage [as a family and a fairness issue], it made us look good and the president the bad guy. . . . You want to define yourself and the other guy. That's what the struggle is all about.

The more elaborate task force efforts also often involve attempts to shape the debate through the media. In the months before the 1990 vote on the constitutional amendment to ban flag desecration, the task force working to defeat it contacted newspaper editors around the country and argued that such an amendment would, in its attempt to bar isolated acts, do irremediable damage to the Bill of Rights (Biskupic 1990, pp. 1962–64). As soon as the Supreme Court handed down its decision, task force members held a news conference and appeared on talk shows making the same argument. Partly as a result, newspaper coverage, editorial opinion, and constituents' views changed. "This year you could hardly find a hometown paper that was editorializing for the amendment," Don Edwards (Calif.), a leader of the task force, reported (qtd. in Biskupic 1990, p. 1963).

Despite occasional successes such as these, however, the congressional leadership's ability to influence the terms of the debate when competing with the president is severely limited. The president's standing as head of state and government and the president's greater media access are enormous advantages in having an administration's interpretation of complex and abstruse matters accepted by the public over that of the congressional opponents. The impossibility of getting all the members to "sing from the same hymn book," the media's lesser coverage of the congressional leadership, and their tendency to cover the Democratic leadership in response to the president all contribute to the congressional party's problem in conveying a clear message to the public. The president's action, proposal, or position is most frequently the lead in newspaper and television stories, with the congressional leaders being quoted about their reactions to the president's move but rarely about their own initiatives. The president's actions or circumstances may carry a message that redounds to the credit of the majority party in Congress, but such positive spin-off is not under the leadership's control. Consequently, party leaders are only seldom able to satisfy their members fully with how they carry out the spokesperson role.

THE LEADERSHIP IN ACTION

The range of leadership activities and the variety of contextual factors that affect leadership success can best be illustrated by case studies of specific legislative efforts.

Minimum Wage Legislation (1989)

In the mid- to late 1980s, raising the minimum wage was a top legislative priority of organized labor, a major Democratic constituency. President Reagan's adamant opposition retarded congressional action, even during the 100th Congress when Democrats controlled both chambers. President Bush's support for a modest increase encouraged the Democratic leadership to put the proposal high on their agenda. Speaker Wright cited the legislation as a top priority in his speeches in late 1988 and early 1989, including his reply to Bush's first address to Congress. Wright assigned the bill the symbolic low number HR 2, and early in the session he met to discuss timing with Augustus F. Hawkins (Calif.), chair of the Education and Labor Committee; Austin J. Murphy (Pa.), chair of the Labor Subcommittee; and Pat Williams (Mont.), the leadership-designated labor whip whose charge included liaison with organized labor.

In keeping with the decision to move quickly, the Education and Labor Committee on 14 March 1989 approved HR 2 on a straight party-line vote. The legislation raised the minimum wage considerably more than Bush wanted and did not include the subminimum or training wage he had demanded, even though Bush had insisted earlier that he would veto any bill that did not closely conform to his proposal.

Although the whip system's count indicated that the committee bill might well pass, political circumstances dictated moderating the measure. As a leadership staffer explained, "We might actually have passed the bill but it would have been a very tough narrow victory. . . . We would have looked like we were pushing everyone to the wall for something that couldn't be held. Everyone knows that a compromise with the administration will eventually be required." Another staffer explained that "we needed as big a vote as possible to send a strong signal to the administration." In this case, the whip's office took the lead in working out a compromise. Initially, a southern member was asked to "inventory" the South—to talk to all the southern Democrats for whom supporting the legislation presented the greatest constituency problem—and come up with a bill they could vote for. Although this member's efforts were successful, the resulting legislation was unacceptable to the liberal Education and Labor Committee and to other Democratic liberals. The leadership next turned to Arkansas Democrat Tommy Robinson, who, with Republican Tom Ridge of Pennsylvania, was sponsoring an alternative bill. The compromise amendment to be offered as a substitute on the floor was worked out in negotiations among selected committee Democrats, Whip Tony Coelho (Calif.) and his staff, Robinson and Ridge, and the American Federation of Labor and Congress of Industrial Organizations (AFL-CIO). The amendment cut the size of the minimum wage increase and included a two-month training wage, but the measure was still distant from Bush's proposal.

Another whip count indicated that passage of the minimum wage legislation was assured. Labor Whip Pat Williams and Chief Deputy Whip David E. Bonier cochaired the task force but, as an involved staffer explained, "after the compromise was in place, not a lot of work needed to be done. There was high turnout at task force meetings. You can always tell when you're going to win; you get large numbers of people willing to work."

Although defeating Bush's alternative and passing the compromise substitute were not in doubt, the leadership decided on a king-of-the-hill procedure in the rule. The Republican alternative would be voted on first, the Democratic compromise second; if both received majorities, the second would prevail. This procedure enabled members to vote for both and thus provided cover to those who were leery of voting against Bush's version. The substitute supported by the president was defeated 198 to 218; the Democratic substitute prevailed on a 240 to 179 vote. Twenty Democrats—mostly southerners—and five Republicans voted for both.

Democrats had hoped Bush would be willing to negotiate, but when he showed no sign of flexibility, the Senate passed a bill similar to the House version; the conference quickly worked out the few differences between the two bills.

During the 1988 presidential race and continuing over the months in which the legislation worked its way through the House and Senate, Democrats attempted to publicize the minimum wage increase, hoping to make it a major issue and to frame it as a "fairness" issue, thereby pressuring Bush to approve a more generous increase than he initially proposed.

Congressional leaders made innumerable public statements; they contrasted Bush's stinginess toward low-wage workers with his support for a capital gains tax cut that would benefit primarily the rich; they signaled their willingness to compromise and called on Bush to do the same. A coalition of labor, civil rights, and women's groups ran radio ads urging the president to sign HR 2 and coordinated a letter-writing protest by low-wage workers.

The effort was unsuccessful. Even after Bush vetoed the bill, no public indignation was evident. "Nobody has hassled the president over this veto. Nobody," an aide to Subcommittee Chair Austin Murphy said (*Congressional Quarterly Almanac* 1989, 334). The House failed to override. Given its disadvantage vis-à-vis the president in media access, the congressional majority party leadership is highly dependent in its efforts to pressure the president on how the media decide to frame their stories. When the media emphasized presidential decisiveness rather than the Democrats' preferred line—presidential insensitivity to workers—there was little the leadership could do.

Despite the Democrats' failure, many congressional Republicans were "uneasy" about Bush's hard line and did not "want to go to the wall a second time" (*Congressional Quarterly Almanac* 1989, 333); they pressured the administration to talk. Democrats, aware they would not be able to override a veto, were willing to make more extensive compromises. Late in 1989 talks among administration officials, the AFL-CIO, and congressional leaders produced a compromise somewhat closer to the Democrats' than to Bush's initial position.

The leadership's capacity for orchestrating the process inside the House and producing substantial House majorities was sufficient to enact a bill that Democrats preferred over no legislation at all. To enact the strong bill they really wanted and to reap significant political benefit from the confrontation would have required success in the public-relations battle, which the leadership could not deliver.

Americans with Disabilities Act (ADA) of 1990

Bipartisan support does not always make leadership involvement unnecessary. Democratic Whip Tony Coelho was the chief sponsor of the Americans with Disabilities Act (ADA) outlawing discrimination against the disabled. President Bush endorsed the concept during his election campaign, and support was widespread on both sides of the aisle. However, the referral of the bill to four different committees in the House and the adamant opposition of small business meant that passage was far from assured.

When Tony Coelho resigned from the House he asked Steny Hoyer (Md.), then vice chair of the caucus, to take over the task of shepherding the bill to passage. Foley, on becoming Speaker, designated Hoyer the leadership's point man on the legislation. With four committees involved, the task encompassed monitoring multiple subcommittee and full committee meetings, encouraging action, and negotiating over substance. Such coordination enhances the prospects of passage for any bill referred to a number of committees because multiple referral entails enormous procedural and jurisdictional complexities. In the case of ADA, though, there were additional potential problems. A participant explained Hoyer's task and why it was crucial:

> The disability rights groups just wanted us to pass the Senate bill. But House members felt this was a major piece of legislation that really shouldn't be passed in a cavalier fashion and that the Senate bill had too much a cavalier, pasted-together character to it. It wasn't even that the chairs were insisting on their jurisdictional rights but a feeling it needed some careful going over. And that's what Hoyer's job was—to work with the chairs in a bipartisan fashion and come up with deals. They went over the entire bill and came up with a much more careful piece of work. There was a major deal with Education and Labor, then one with Energy and Commerce—both bipartisan. Another with Transportation. Not all the problems were worked out on that—there were a couple of floor amendments. And then a smaller deal with Judiciary. If this hadn't been done we might have had a lot more trouble on the floor. There was some unease with the bill anyway. Members felt it was the kind of bill that if no one knew what was in there, there could be some real problems. Every few years there's some kind of legislation passed that produces a major political problem. Last year it was Catastrophic, before that interest withholding. People know that can happen and it makes them nervous.

Because Hoyer was successful in maintaining bipartisan support throughout the committee process, the leadership hoped they could obtain a bipartisan rule for floor consideration. Bipartisan support seldom means agreement on all aspects of a bill, however. On ADA many Republicans wanted to offer floor amendments. When the Republicans insisted on virtually an open rule, Democrats demurred, unwilling to open such a complex bill to any and all amendments on the floor.

The most difficult rule-related decision facing the leadership and other ADA proponents concerned the Chapman amendment. Jim Chapman, a Texas Democrat, wanted to offer an amendment, strongly supported by the National Restaurant Association, that would allow employers to move an AIDS-infected worker out of a food-handling position provided the employer offered the worker an equally remunerative alternative position. Because AIDS cannot be transmitted through food, ADA proponents opposed the amendment as catering to customer prejudices. Nevertheless, the amendment would be difficult to defeat on an up-or-down vote, so many ADA proponents hoped the leadership would make in order a substitute that would render the Chapman amendment innocuous. A number of those who opposed the amendment on substance but feared the reelection costs of voting against it wanted the leadership to provide cover for them via a substitute. A leadership aide explained the decision to forego a substitute:

> We could have beaten it with a substitute but Chapman and Republicans wanted an up-or-down vote on his amendment [if the substitute wins, there is no such

vote] and so doing that would have meant stepping on a Democrat in the rule and Chapman would have been ballistic on that. So it would have required a big effort to do a count to make sure we had the votes [to pass the rule and the substitute]. It would have required putting off the bill for a week or so to let people cool down. So we called the [disability rights] groups and asked them what they wanted to do and they in effect agreed to go ahead. Our AIDS coalition held together on that and opposed Chapman. That's why the vote was so close and that means there's a good argument for removing it in conference.

In addition to the rule and the Chapman amendment was an amendment introduced by F. James Sensenbrenner, Jr. (R-Wis.), incorporating President Bush's preferred alternative on the remedies available to those found to have suffered discrimination because of their disabilities. It was expected to provoke controversy on the floor.

Hoyer chaired the task force charged with defeating the amendments and passing the bill. Coordinating the efforts of both members and the many outside groups was an important aspect of the task. In addition to the groups that traditionally represent the disabled, the Leadership Conference on Civil Rights, a coalition of 185 organizations, was active (Rovner 1990b, c).

The rule passed on a largely party-line vote of 237 to 172; the Sensenbrenner amendment was rejected 192 to 227; and the Chapman amendment passed on a close 199 to 187 vote. By an overwhelming vote of 403 to 20, the bill passed the House.

In the end, after a few more legislative twists and turns, the bill became law without the Chapman amendment. Compromise language acceptable to ADA supporters was agreed on in conference; and the House, on a 224 to 180 vote, in effect, endorsed the change (Rovner 1990a, d).

ADA illustrates how changes in the legislative process—the institution of multiple referral, in this case—have drawn the party leadership more deeply into the prefloor legislative process. When a number of committees are involved, the coordination and even the quality-control tasks necessary to get a broadly satisfactory bill to the floor may be beyond the capabilities of the committee leaders. In such cases proponents, including committee leaders and committee contingents, expect their party leadership to perform those tasks.

Budget Politics (1990)

The process of reaching a budget agreement in 1990 illustrates particularly well several points about contemporary majority party leadership in the House. It shows how the political environment has in effect forced the party leadership to play a more central role in the legislative process. It demonstrates the importance of how the debate is framed and consequently why members are so eager for their leaders to seek control of the debate, yet it also shows how limited leaders' capacity is for affecting the debate. In addition, the 1990 budget process illustrates the fine line leaders must tread in attempting to satisfy members' policy goals while not restricting too much their participation; and it clarifies the character and the limits of the party leadership's ability to influence its members' votes and, as a result, legislative outcomes. Because the 1990 budget process was extraordinarily prolonged and complex, only the most revealing aspects and episodes are discussed in detail here.

In 1990 the policy and political stakes of budget decision making were enormous. A budget is a statement of priorities; when resources are tight, budget decisions involve painful trade-offs. The Gramm-Rudman requirement—that either the deficit be cut by a specified large amount or sequestration take place—ensured that the costs of president and Congress failing to reach an agreement would be very high, inasmuch as sequestration would involve automatic across-the-board spending cuts of draconian proportions.

Most independent experts agreed that a serious budget-reduction package would have to include significant revenue increases. Yet in decisions about taxes, the parties saw their future electoral prospects at stake. Attempting to shake the high-tax image that Republicans had successfully pinned on them, Democrats were determined to refuse to take the initiative—and the blame—in proposing new taxes. A great many Republicans believed that their "no new taxes" image accounted for their party's electoral success; Bush had pledged himself to that course during his 1988 presidential campaign. As they saw it, Republicans had a great deal to lose by reneging on that promise and very little to gain, given the lack of public demand for action on the deficit.

In 1990 congressional Democrats were eager to reach budget decisions through the normal budget process. In 1989—and several times previously during the 1980s—such decisions were made by the congressional party leadership and top administration officials in closed negotiations. Most Democrats considered the 1989 summit agreement substantively disappointing; consequently, their being cut out of the decision-making process was all the more galling. Sensitive to members' complaints and believing administration officials had been less than straightforward in the 1989 negotiations, House Democratic leaders were leery of another summit. Yet, because President Bush could veto the reconciliation and appropriations bills that would implement the congressional budget resolution, his assent was needed to avoid a sequester. Furthermore, so long as Democrats were unwilling to take the initiative on new taxes, they could not proceed alone with the congressional budget process very far. Almost everyone realized that eventually some sort of talks would be necessary. But most believed that the further along the congressional budget process was when talks did start, the greater the Democrats' leverage would be; certainly, there also would be greater opportunity for the member participation made possible by the normal budget process.

House Democrats passed their budget resolution on 2 May. Through an arduous series of talks, Majority Leader Richard A. Gephardt (Mo.) had negotiated a defense-spending figure acceptable to both liberals and conservatives within the party. The resolution specified the same amount in new revenue as the president's budget (but not, Bush said, new taxes); however, to alleviate concerns that Republicans would again label Democrats as big taxers, the report stated that the House would not act on the proposed tax increase "unless and until such time as there is bipartisan agreement with the President of the United States on specific legislation to meet or exceed such reconciliation requirements" (qtd. in Fessler 1990b, 1332). The same day, the Senate Budget Committee reported its budget resolution.

Almost immediately, President Bush invited the congressional leadership to the White House for preliminary talks. Estimates of the deficit were rising, the U.S. economy showed signs of slowing, and the forward movement in the Democratic-dominated congressional budget process threatened to decrease the president's leverage. Though Democrats were reluctant, their leadership could not refuse President Bush's request to talk. Given the president's greater media access, explaining a refusal to the American public was impossible. Democrats publicly and repeatedly pushed the president to define the problem that necessitated the summit: "The president needs to clarify for the country what the problems are and how he thinks they should be resolved," said House Budget Committee Chair Leon E. Panetta (Calif.) (qtd. in Fessler 1990a, 1457). Democrats insisted that everything would have to be put on the table, and they agreed among themselves that any proposals for higher taxes would have to come from the Republicans.

Because in 1989 not only rank-and-file members but also committee chairs had felt cut out of the action by summit decision making, the congressional party leaders in 1990 appointed seventeen members—including chairs and ranking minority members of Budget, Appropriations, and the tax-writing committees—as negotiators. Treasury Secretary Nicholas F. Brady, Office of Management and Budget (OMB) Director Richard G. Darman, and White House Chief of Staff John H. Sununu represented the president. The first talks were held on 17 May and sessions continued through much of June. Estimates of the likely size of the budget continued to increase but no progress toward a plan to deal with it was made.

Democrats and Republicans were engaged in an intense struggle to frame the debate and position themselves favorably. Because serious deficit reduction would require highly unpopular proposals, almost certainly including tax increases, neither Republicans nor Democrats wanted to lay out a plan first. Democrats called on President Bush to exert leadership. The president and congressional Republicans repeatedly asserted that it was the Democrats' responsibility, as the majority party in Congress, to move first. On 26 June the Democrats' firmness paid off when Bush issued a statement conceding that tax-revenue increases would be necessary. A storm of protest from Republican officeholders and activists followed. The president's statement was clearly a prerequisite to budget agreement, which Bush badly needed in the weakening economy. Yet, as many Republicans feared, the statement proved in retrospect a turning point in the decisive battle for public opinion.

On 30 September, the day before the beginning of the new fiscal year (when a new budget must be in place to keep the government functioning), President Bush and congressional leaders announced a deal had been reached. Even after the president's 26 June statement, differences over taxes and domestic-spending cuts continued to block progress. Finally, the negotiating group was pared down to include only the top party leaders. Again the requisites for policy results conflicted with the dictates of the leadership's preferred strategy of inclusion. The primary barrier to an agreement, Democrats claimed, was the president's continued insistence on a cut in the capital gains tax without an offsetting income tax rate increase for the wealthy. Media attention increasingly focused on the capital gains issue and on President Bush's opposition to any rate increase for the rich. The Democratic leadership refused to give in; nervous Republican congressional leaders, perceiving that Democrats were winning the public-relations war on the issue of a tax break for the wealthy when everyone else was being asked to sacrifice, began to back away from insisting that such a tax change be included in the package. Bush capitulated.

After congressional leaders briefed their members in party caucuses, prospects for passage in the Senate appeared favorable. House passage, it immediately became clear, would be much more difficult. Many Republicans opposed the package because it included any new taxes. Democratic liberals were upset with the big Medicare cuts and the regressive character of the new taxes—primarily excise taxes, including a gas tax increase.

The Democratic leadership attempted to sell the agreement to its members and deliver the number of yea votes—about 130, or 50 percent of the membership—that had been part of the deal. The Speaker met with the committee chairs and the Appropriations Committee subcommittee chairs; three caucus meetings were held during the two days prior to the vote. A task force chaired by the whip counted and attempted to persuade Democrats to vote for the agreement. With President Bush's assent, Speaker Foley intimated that some of the details of the agreement could be redone. The vote was put off for a day, but when the whip count showed an erosion rather than a pickup in support, the leadership brought the agreement to the floor. While the count never showed enough votes, leaders hoped that, if Republicans delivered their 50 percent, Democrats might go along. In any case, nothing was to be gained by further delay.

When the House vote was taken, the budget resolution incorporating the summit agreement was voted down 179 to 254 with majorities of both parties voting in opposition (Hager 1990; Hook 1990a). Many House Democrats saw the agreement as bad policy and bad politics and, because they had again been excluded from the decision-making process, they felt little obligation to vote for it.

Democratic leaders' strong belief that Democrats would be blamed if the summit talks broke down led them to agree to a package that some found abhorrent and that all knew would be difficult to pass. Now the leaders feared that Democrats would be blamed for the House defeat. The Speaker, in a caucus on the morning of the vote, warned members that by voting the resolution down they would be providing the Republicans with an "alibi" for not supporting it themselves and a "machine gun" for Bush to shoot the Democrats (staff interview).

The big media story, however, was House Republicans' desertion of the president. Even with a full-court press by the White House and personal appeals by the president himself, Bush failed to persuade even a majority of fellow partisans in the House to support him. Then, as Congress got to work on a budget plan to replace the defeated bipartisan package, Bush sent out a stream of mixed signals as to what he would accept—especially with respect to a possible trade-off of a cut in capital gains for an increase in tax rates for the wealthy. When, in response to a reporter's question, a jogging Bush quipped, "Read my hips," devastating headlines about the president's flip-flopping appeared across the country.

By this time, the character of the public debate over taxes had clearly changed. The media no longer portrayed it as a question of whether there would be new taxes but as a struggle about whom those new taxes would fall on most heavily. With the debate thus framed the Democrats were strongly advantaged: their position of taxing the wealthy was now the popular one. Democrats had not brought about this transformation; rather, the president's reneging on his "no new taxes" pledge had begun the change, and his later strategic missteps contributed to rekindling the perception of Republicans as the party of the rich. The Democratic leadership's unwillingness to agree to a capital gains tax cut unless offset by higher income tax rates on the wealthy, and congressional Democrats' near unity in spreading that message, allowed them to take advantage of the situation.

House Democrats moved swiftly to put together their own budget plan. President Bush's possible agreement to a package that included new taxes inoculated Democrats against the charge that they alone were high taxers, many Democrats believed; and most thought that, in the public exchange over the type of taxes to be levied, Democrats were the clear winners. Ways and Means Democrats, in consultation with the Speaker, put together a package that included no gas tax, significantly decreased the cut in Medicare, and raised tax rates for the wealthy. The bill was brought to the floor under an unusual rule that denied Republicans a motion to recommit with instructions, which is a means of offering and getting a vote on an alternative plan. While the Republican alternative included no new taxes, it cut the deficit by much less than had been agreed to in the summit. Democrats thus argued that the Republican alternative did not deserve consideration because it did not meet the mutually agreed-on target; in addition, the leadership did not want to confront its members unnecessarily with a tough vote just before the election. The House approved the Democratic reconciliation bill on 16 October by a 227 to 203 vote, with 217 Democrats and 10 Republicans voting for it.

The conference to work out differences between the House bill and a more conservative Senate version began on 19 October with administration officials integrally involved. The resulting bill had to be acceptable to the president or he could veto it. Yet the strategic situation had shifted significantly since the earlier budget negotiations. One of two proposals now on the table was a liberal, House-passed version with higher tax rates for the wealthy that had considerable support among Senate Democrats. Crucially, any package that emerged from conference would have to command the support of a large majority of House Democrats because few House Republican votes were likely. Furthermore, Democrats clearly commanded the high ground in the battle for public opinion.

The compromise that emerged from conference included a hike in the tax rate for high-income taxpayers (a proposal the president had bitterly opposed) and other provisions that indirectly raised the taxes the wealthy would pay; capital gains taxes were not cut. Gas taxes were increased less and Medicare was cut less than was proposed in the summit agreement.

Throughout the process of putting together a Democratic alternative and negotiating a conference agreement, the chair of the Ways and Means Committee and the Democratic party leaders kept in contact with their members through frequent caucus meetings. "There were lots and lots of caucuses," a participant explained, "for two-way communication." Practicing the strategy of inclusion to the extent possible under the circumstances, the leaders not only kept their members informed but sought members' advice as well. By the time a final conference agreement was reached, the leadership was in the midst of a full-court press aimed at ensuring passage. The task force had been at work; a list of "if-you-really-need me" votes had been compiled; the Speaker as well as lower-ranking leaders had made calls to persuade members to vote yea. "We knew we were in pretty good shape going into the vote," a participant said. At 7 A.M. on Saturday, 28 October, only hours after final agreement on the five-year, $490-billion deficit-reduction bill was reached, a weary House voted approval 228 to 200. Democrats split 181 to 74 in favor; Republicans, 47 to 126 against. That Saturday afternoon, by a vote of 54 to 45, the Senate concurred.

THE CHARACTER AND LIMITS OF MAJORITY PARTY LEADERSHIP IN THE 1990s

The 1980s saw the emergence of a strengthened House majority party leadership, one that is today more active and more consequential in the legislative process. These mini-case studies in this chapter illuminate the character and the limits of this stronger leadership. Congressional party leaders are the elected agents of their members; their increased involvement in the legislative process is a response to the needs and demands of the Democratic membership in an era of legislative constraint. The help that the leadership can provide in enacting legislation gives the leaders leverage with Democratic members, committee chairs, and committee contingents.

However, because of the party leaders' dependence on members for their positions, that leverage must be used to further members' goals, not the leaders' goals. To be sure, it is leaders who interpret what their members want and, given the frequent lack of clarity and consensus among an opinionated and diverse membership of 250 or more, leaders' own values, beliefs, and judgments affect their interpretations. Yet leadership misjudgments quickly become evident because the party leaders' capacity to affect legislative outcomes depends on almost continuous member acquiescence and assent. When many Democrats concluded that the 1990 budget summit agreement was bad policy and dangerous reelection politics, the leadership possessed no rewards or sanctions sufficient to produce a wholesale change of mind. To the extent they believed members correctly perceived a yes vote to endanger their reelection chances, leaders would not have used coercion had they been capable of doing so.

So long as members' reelection chances remain more dependent on their own behavior than on the decisions of party leaders, members will refuse to give their leadership power sufficient to coerce. By the same token, however, so long as members continue to need help in attaining their policy goals, they will expect their leaders to provide it and, so long as they continue to be reasonably homogeneous in their policy preferences, they will, much of the time, behave in such a way as to make it possible for party leaders to do so.

Acknowledgments

This chapter is based, in part, on participant observation in the office of the Speaker in 1987–88 and on interviews with House members, staff, and informed observers over a number of years. I am grateful to Jim Wright and his staff for giving me the opportunity to see the operation of the speakership from the inside. I also thank all those who gave up some of their valuable time to talk with me. Grants from the Academic Senate Research Committee of the University of California-Riverside greatly facilitated the research for this chapter.

Note

1. This quotation and all other unattributed quotations in Chapter 5 are from interviews conducted by the author with House members, staff, and informed observers (1989–90), who requested to remain anonymous.

6 / From Decentralization to Centralization: Members' Changing Expectations for House Leaders

DANIEL J. PALAZZOLO

Before the reforms of the 1970s, at least since the revolt against Speaker Joseph G. Cannon in 1910, party leaders of the House of Representatives performed tasks designed to mediate party interests both within and outside of the House. Within the House, their most important functions included organizing the party, scheduling bills, building coalitions, distributing and collecting information, and maintaining party harmony (Ripley 1967). Meanwhile, committee chairs exercised the most discretion over specific policy issues. Outside of the House, the Speaker acted as a mediator between the majority party and the president, especially if the president was of the same party (Ripley 1969a). Again, however, presidents dealt directly with committee chairs on most policy matters.

In the immediate aftermath of the 1970s budgetary reforms, party leaders continued to concentrate on mediating functions within the House—coalition building and party maintenance (Sinclair 1983). But as the postreform period extended into the 1980s, leaders began to perform *policy-oriented* tasks both internal and external to the House. Internally, leaders participated in formulating the details of budget resolutions. Externally, they were called on to settle conference disputes with Senate leaders and to negotiate budget priorities with the president.

How can the evolution toward policy-oriented leadership tasks in the postreform House be explained? This chapter argues that the answer lies in the expectations of House members (see Jones 1968; Rohde and Shepsle 1987; Sinclair 1983), which can emanate from two sources. First, expectations arise partly from individual members' electoral, political, and policy goals. Members expect leaders to help them attain such goals; leaders, in turn, work with their colleagues' objectives in mind. The other source of members' expectations is the context that shapes House politics (Cooper and Brady 1981; Jones 1981). Leaders not only respond to individual member goals but also adapt their activities to institutional changes, electoral trends, partisan developments, and the policy agenda. This chapter concentrates primarily on this source of member expectations.

In the current postreform era, leaders are expected to perform tasks aimed either at resolving institutional problems or advancing party priorities. In the decentralized House of the immediate postreform period, party leaders engaged in traditional leadership activities in response to problems *within* the House. But in the more centralized context of the 1980s, party leaders also took advantage of policy-related opportunities within the House and were expected to respond to demands coming from *outside* the institution. Consequently, their functions expanded to include policy formulation and negotiation with outside actors, particularly Senate leaders and the president. To understand how party leaders adapted their activities to problems and opportunities as budget policy-making evolved from a decentralized to a centralized context, a broad overview of the variations in conditions of the postreform period is necessary.

THE POSTREFORM CONTEXT

The context surrounding party leaders' involvement in the budget process can be traced partly to the institutional reforms of the 1970s. These reforms were deliberate attempts to structure the formal organization and procedures of the two chambers, the informal norms of members, and the relationship between Congress and the president. In addition to institutional reforms, other conditions, both internal and external to the House, were the products of electoral results, partisan developments, and the policy agenda. These postreform institutional, political, and policy conditions expose the problems members expect House leaders to address and create the opportunities leaders may capitalize on.

Taken together, the 1970s reforms lacked a clear and coherent prescription for arranging decision-making power in the House. On the one hand, in order to topple powerful committee chairs and the entrenched seniority system, reformers further decentralized power by spreading it across subcommittees. On the other, reformers attempted to coordinate the committee system in order to centralize power in the party leadership. "Whereas earlier reform periods appeared to swing in one direction or the other—toward centralization or decentralization, responsibility or responsiveness—the elaborate changes enacted in the 1970s seemed to go in both directions at once," observed Charles O. Jones (1981, 121). One of the objectives of the 1974 Budget Act, for example, was to create a budget process that could potentially integrate the separate appropriations, authorization, and tax legislation into a coherent budget plan. Yet the new process maintained the traditional legislative powers of the tax-writing, appropriating, and authorizing committees. Reforms that broadened the Speaker's powers included a Steering and Policy Committee chaired by the Speaker (and including many members nominated by the Speaker), the power of multiple referral, and the prerogative to nominate members of the Rules Committee.

To complicate further the decentralization–centralization paradox of the reforms, Steven Smith (1989) suggests that the reforms actually pulled in three directions. He argues that some rule changes aimed at enhancing members' legislative prerogatives buttressed a third center of power—the House floor. A substantial increase in floor amendments following the reforms indicated a "collegial" pattern of decision making that differed from a purely decentralized subcommittee arrangement. While a subcommittee system features many actors deliberating on policy issues in many decision-making units, collegial decision making brings many participants together in only a few decision-making units. Thus, the House floor became a central forum for all members to participate in shaping legislation.

Given the mixed intentions of the reforms, decision making in the post-reform House could take several paths: centralized, decentralized, collegial, or some combination of the three. The bulk of the reforms clearly favored a subcommittee structure and encouraged members to participate actively on the floor. Consequently, the immediate effects of the reforms were exhibited in either *subcommittee government* (Davidson 1981; Deering and Smith 1981) or *collegial decision making* (Smith 1989). Subcommittee government increased the number of places where policies originated, thereby limiting the interaction between party leaders and subcommittee chairs to scheduling decisions (Deering and Smith 1981). Increases in floor amendments made the final fate of committee-sponsored bills more uncertain than before (Sinclair 1983; Bach and Smith 1988). Also, ideological divisions within the majority party made final passage of legislation less predictable. Leaders addressed these uncertainties by devising ways to maintain party harmony and build coalitions on the floor.

But during the 1980s these tendencies gradually declined, and the latent power of centralized party leadership was aroused by unanticipated changes in the political landscape and the policy agenda (Davidson 1988b; Dodd and Oppenheimer 1989). The 1980s were marked by split party control of government; Republicans held firm control of the White House and, for six years, the Senate, while Democrats continued to control the House. Ronald Reagan's presidential election ignited a conservative fiscal policy movement that was simmering since the late 1970s. Reagan's agenda of tax breaks, domestic-spending cuts, and large defense-spending increases was expected to fix the sluggish economy, balance the budget, and strengthen the military. As it turned out, though, these policies exacerbated the deficit problem already underway during the Carter years. Annual deficits exploded during the 1980s, jumping from about $80 billion in fiscal year (FY) 1981 to $127 billion a year later to $207 billion by FY 1983. By FY 1986 the deficit climaxed at $220 billion. Large deficits placed constraints on new federal spending (see Schick 1983). The deficit, combined with increasing homogeneity of policy preferences among House Democrats (Rohde 1988), also polarized the parties. As Table 6-1 indicates, high levels of party unity on roll-call votes for first budget resolutions became the norm by 1983 (see Ellwood 1985).

Table 6-1 / Party Unity among House Democrats, 1975–1988

Calendar Year	Fiscal Year	Party Unity[a]	Annual Change	Party Unity on First Budget Resolutions	Annual Change
Period I					
1975	1976	75	—	74	—
1976	1977	75	0	82	+8
1977	1978	74	−1	78	−4
1978	1979	71	−3	76	−2
1979	1980	75	+4	81	+5
Period II					
1980	1981	78	+3	77	−4
1981	1982	75	−3	65	−12
1982	1983	77	+2	73	+8
Period III					
1983	1984	82	+5	86	+13
1984	1985	81	−1	89	+3
1985	1986	86	+5	94	+5
1986	1987	86	0	92	−2
1987	1988	88	+2	92	0
1988	1989	88	0	90	−2

[a] Party unity is the percentage of members voting with a majority of their party when a majority of one party is arrayed against a majority of the other party (party unity votes). See Chapter 2.

Source: Party unity scores from Ornstein, Mann, and Malbin 1990, 199. Party unity scores for first budget resolutions compiled by author from data published in *Congressional Quarterly Almanac* 1975–88, vols. 31–44.

PERIODS OF THE POSTREFORM HOUSE

An examination of budget policy-making in the context of institutional reforms, electoral trends, partisan changes, and agenda factors reveals that the postreform era evolved through roughly three periods. Period I, the *decentralized–collegial* period (1975–79), consisted of high levels of member participation, weak majority party (Democratic) unity, and dwindling support for traditional liberal policies. Period II, the *decentralized–centralized* period (1980–82), as its label suggests, contained elements of both decentralization and centralization. The majority party was still divided, and members continued to offer amendments when they could; at the same time, though party leaders began to restrict floor amendments to budget resolutions, the deficit became a salient issue, and reconciliation procedures

Table 6-2 / Leader Activity in the Budget Process during the Three Periods of the Postreform Era

Activity	Period		
	I. DECENTRALIZED—COLLEGIAL (1975–79)	II. DECENTRALIZED—CENTRALIZED (1980–82)	III. CENTRALIZED (1983–88)
Policy formulation	Secondary activity	Slightly more active	Active to very active
Coalition building	Very active	Very active	Secondary activity
Settling differences with the Senate	Inactive	More active	Active
Negotiating with the president	Inactive	Active	Active

were used to reduce the deficit. Period III, the *centralized* period (1983–88), was marked by split party control, high levels of party unity, large budget deficits, and continued use of restricted rules and reconciliation. Each period presented institutional problems that members expected party leaders to address or created opportunities for leaders to exploit.

The tasks of party leaders changed as budget politics evolved from the decentralized to a centralized mode. Leaders are potentially involved in four stages of the budget process: policy formulation, coalition building, settling conference disputes, and negotiating budget agreements with the president. Table 6-2 outlines how leaders' tasks evolved during the three periods of the postreform era.

The Decentralized–Collegial Period: 1975–1979

Under the Budget Act (1974), the House Budget Committee is formally responsible for drafting a first budget resolution, which establishes the basic guidelines for the authorizations, appropriations, and revenue bills to be considered for the upcoming fiscal year. The first resolution includes both aggregate estimates (for budget outlays, revenues, annual deficit, and total debt) and nineteen separate budget functions (broad categories defined in terms of budget priorities, such as defense, education, and the like). In the process of formulating budget resolutions, Budget Committee members typically consider the preferences of the majority party caucus, the president (if of the same party as the House majority), or party leaders. Once the committee's work is complete, the first budget resolution is reported to the floor, where it is normally endorsed by majority party leaders. On the floor, the committee's budget resolution is usually subject to amendment or challenge by alternative budget resolutions, depending on the floor rules framed by the Rules Committee and approved by the House.

During the decentralized–collegial period, the role played by party leaders in formulating first budget resolutions was limited by several factors. First, the reforms aimed mostly toward expanding opportunities for members to participate in the legislative process. Rather than state the party's priorities outright, party leaders were expected to let members express their views on the budget. Second, House Democrats were divided ideologically. As Speaker Thomas P. O'Neill (D-Mass.) indicated, the party actually was comprised of "five parties in one. We've got about 25 really strong liberals, 110 progressive liberals, maybe 60 moderates, about 45 people just to the right of the moderates, and 30 conservatives" (qtd. in Arieff 1980, 2696). Hence, the Speaker was poorly positioned to advocate one set of priorities over another. Third, for most of this period, Jimmy Carter was president. Even though the Budget Act gave Congress a legitimate claim to challenge the executive's budget, many still considered the president to be the leading agenda setter for his party in Congress. His presence inhibited party leaders from trying to define the party's priorities.

Because budget resolutions essentially define the priorities of the House majority party, leaders—despite these restrictions—had more input into budget policy at the Budget Committee level than with other policy issues treated by House standing committees (see Sinclair 1981a). Unlike other committees, the Budget Committee includes one leader from each of the two parties. The majority leader naturally participates in the budget-formulation process. On one occasion, Speaker O'Neill took a direct role in the committee's business; in 1979, the first year members gave serious consideration to trimming the budget, O'Neill met with Budget Committee Democrats and "made an impassioned plea for saving social programs" (Sinclair 1983, 176).

Nevertheless, party leaders did not regularly intervene in the committee's business in the decentralized–collegial period. Their main job was to help the committee pass its resolutions on the floor, a task complicated by members' expectations to participate actively in floor debate over budget priorities. Numerous floor amendments on first budget resolutions (LeLoup 1980) and partisan divisions over budget priorities (Schick 1980) increased the uncertainty of gaining approval for the Budget Committee's resolution on the House floor. During this period the committee's first budget resolution passed by an average margin of only twenty-eight votes per year (see Table 6-3, p. 118), even though Democrats outnumbered Republicans by an average of 138 seats. Two particular cases reveal clearly the problem of passing budget resolutions on the floor: (1) the Budget Committee's first attempt at passing the FY 1978 first budget resolution was rejected by the

Table 6-3 / House Roll-call Votes and Margins of Victory for House Budget
Committee's First Budget Resolutions, 1975–1988

Calendar Year	Party Ratio (D–R)	House Vote (Yea-Nay)	Vote Margin	Average Vote Margin for Period
Period I				
1975	291–144	200–196	4	
1976	—	221–155	66	
1977	292–193	84–320	Rejected	28.8
1977	—	213–179	34	
1978	—	201–197	4	
1979	277–158	220–184	36	
Period II				
1980	—	225–193	32	
1981	242–167	270–154	Republican	32
1982	—	219–206	Substitutes	
Period III				
1983	268–167	229–196	33	
1984	—	250–168	82	
1985	254–179	258–170	88	61.4
1986	—	245–179	66	
1987	259–174	230–192	38	
1988	—	319–102	Summit budget	

Source: Compiled by the author from data published in the *Congressional Quarterly Almanac*, 1975–88, vols. 31–44.

House by a vote of 84 to 320, and (2) in 1979 the House rejected the initial conference version of the first budget resolution.

Yet passing budget resolutions is essential to the survival of the congressional budget process. Hence party leaders directed their attention to the floor stage of the budget process, where they performed traditional coalition-building and party-maintenance functions. During this period, majority party leaders engaged in numerous vote-gathering activities: they provided more services to members, expanded the whip system, and set up task forces designed to build party support for first budget resolutions (Sinclair 1981b, 1983).

It was appropriate for majority party leaders to concentrate on tasks aimed toward resolving problems within the House. Leaders had traditionally engaged in coalition building; now they were needed to ensure that Congress fulfilled its responsibility to pass a budget. To be sure, there were problems outside of the House as well. House Democrats frequently disagreed with President Carter's fiscal policy, and House and Senate Democrats differed over the proper balance of defense versus domestic spending. But because there were no protracted disputes between the two chambers, the House and Senate budget committee chairs could be counted on to settle differences between the chambers. Once these differences were settled, party leaders concentrated on maintaining the coalition that approved the House's version of the budget resolution.

The Decentralized–Centralized Period: 1980–1982

The deficit problem in 1980 led to the first steps toward centralizing power in the hands of party leaders. Alarmed by rising inflation, unemployment, and interest rates, Carter administration officials met with congressional budget policymakers to discuss ways of curbing the growing federal deficit. Although Budget Committee Chair Robert N. Giaimo (D-Conn.) was the leading representative of the House Democratic party, Majority Leader Jim Wright (D-Tex.) participated in the first presidential-congressional summit meeting, held in late February and early March of 1980. During the Ninety-seventh Congress (1981–82), split party control of government complicated the deficit problem and propelled party leaders into more active negotiations with the president. But because ideological differences among House Democrats persisted, party leaders continued to contend with the internal problems of party maintenance and coalition building. Member expectations for party leaders were shaped by both decentralizing and centralizing forces.

Budget Policy Formulation Conflicts among House Democrats continued to limit leaders' input into first budget resolutions. Speaker O'Neill sat on the sidelines during the summit meetings in 1980. He withheld support for the summit agreement reached by Carter officials and congressional leaders, which contained reconciliation instructions to reduce spending by $6.4 billion. O'Neill objected that the cuts would "dismantle the programs I've been working for as an old liberal" (qtd. in Gregg 1980, 641).

In the following year, conditions continued to thwart O'Neill's role in formulating the House budget resolution. Reagan's 1980 electoral victory made O'Neill the opposition party leader, but it also carried a conservative fiscal policy message that moved the House Democratic party further away from the traditional liberal agenda O'Neill championed. Republicans had picked up thirty-four House seats and won a majority in the Senate for the first time since 1952. Conservative southern Democrats formed the Conservative Democratic Forum (CDF) and pushed Speaker O'Neill to appoint more conservatives to the House Budget Committee. Under these conditions, O'Neill deferred to committee Democrats, led by conservative chair James R. Jones (D-Okla.), to draft a moderate alternative to Reagan's budget.

Speaker O'Neill's heaviest participation in formulating a budget resolution came in 1982, in response to a minor crisis in the budget process. The House initially rejected all eight budget resolutions voted on the floor, including the original package offered by the Budget Committee. The committee went back to the drawing board to formulate another budget resolution. The prospect of failing to approve a budget gave O'Neill a chance to put his mark on the first budget resolution. He commissioned the Steering and Policy Committee to draft a "true Democratic budget," including spending increases for housing, jobs, unemployment compensation, Medicare, and education. This budget marked the Speaker's first attempt at an active role in formulating a first budget resolution.

Passing Budget Resolutions The primary task of party leaders during this period, however, was to build support for resolutions drafted by the Budget Committee. The heavy amending activity of the collegial–decentralized period was curtailed somewhat by the deficit problem. Party leaders issued complex rules for floor debate, including restrictions on the number of amendments members could offer (Bach and Smith 1988). But party leaders continued to struggle to satisfy the conflicting priorities of conservative and liberal Democrats. In the Ninety-seventh Congress (1981–82), a coalition of conservative Democrats and minority party Republicans took control of the House floor.

In 1980 the House approved the Budget Committee's first budget resolution (which incorporated the elements of the presidential-congressional summit agreement) by a vote of 225 to 193. But the House-passed resolution fell apart in conference as Senate Budget Committee Chair Ernest F. Hollings (D-S.C.) pressed to increase defense spending. Several House Democratic conferees refused to endorse the conference report, and both O'Neill and Carter disapproved the measure. The House defeated the conference version of the resolution by a vote of 141 to 245.

However, after Giaimo, Hollings, and Carter resolved the major issues dividing the party, Speaker O'Neill fully supported the revised conference report. He mobilized the support of the Steering and Policy Committee Democrats and the party whips, and he appointed a task force to build support for the conference budget resolution (Sinclair 1983, 186–88). O'Neill dispatched a letter to House Democrats that reflected his duties to address institutional problems and advance party interests. "Failure to adopt the first resolution," he warned, "would demonstrate clearly that the Democratic Congress cannot deal with the budget. It would discredit the party and the Congress" (qtd. in Sinclair 1983, 187). The House approved the conference report on a 237 to 161 vote, with only twelve Democrats voting nay.

During the first two years of the Reagan administration, Democratic party leaders tried numerous coalition-building strategies to offset the conservative movement (Sinclair 1983; Smith 1982). They offered amendments to attract conservative Democrats, mobilized interest group support, and made personal appeals to party unity. Their efforts failed, however, in both 1981 and 1982. In 1981 President Reagan rode the wave of his electoral victory to gain congressional approval for a first budget resolution—a reconciliation bill including unprecedented spending cuts and a three-year plan to reduce taxes. Combining his personal popularity, persuasive bargaining skills, and an effective White House staff, Reagan executed a vote-gathering drive that overwhelmed Democratic leaders.

In 1982 the Rules Committee crafted a rule that allowed sixty-eight floor amendments and seven substitutes to the Budget Committee's first budget resolution. The rule included a king-of-the-mountain feature—it established the voting order for amendments and substitutes and decreed that the last budget resolution to receive a majority vote would be declared the House-passed resolution. Naturally, the Rules Committee placed the Budget Committee's resolution last in order. After the seven substitutes were rejected, O'Neill spoke in favor of the committee's resolution, urging the House to perform its duty and pass the budget. But the House rejected the committee's resolution by a vote of 159 to 265. The unsuccessful first round gave way to O'Neill's "true Democratic budget," which the House also rejected by a vote of 202 to 225. Finally, the House passed a Republican budget alternative for the second consecutive year. Despite their efforts, party leaders were unable to perform effectively even their most fundamental tasks.

Presidential-Congressional Relations In the context of split party control and growing deficits, the Speaker participated actively in policy-related tasks outside of the House. Budget Chair Jones defined the expectations of the speaker's role as opposition party leader:

> The Speaker is the lightning rod, the chief spokesman. He is the one who predominantly has to draw the lines of difference between the [Reagan] administration's policies and the House. Because the budget is the guts of government, the heart and soul of government. And, how it is configured shapes the differences in the [Democratic] party's view toward the country. (Interview, 13 February 1989)

As chief spokesperson for the majority party, Speaker O'Neill represented the policy interests of the House majority party in budget negotiations with the president. In 1981, of course, President Reagan bypassed Democratic leaders altogether and took advantage of favorable conditions to push his budget package through Congress. But when the deficit became the core issue of budget politics, the two parties became locked in continual stalemate over budget priorities. Bipartisan summit meetings involving the president and party leaders became the primary means of trying to break the stalemate and negotiate ways to reduce the deficit.

The need for a principal majority party spokesperson became clear as early as 1982. Reagan's budget for the upcoming fiscal year was tagged "dead on arrival" on Capitol Hill. But neither Senate Republican nor House Democratic budget makers, acting alone, could devise an adequate substitute to reduce the menacing deficit. The two parties came together at the so-called "Gang of Seventeen" meetings, comprising seventeen high-level White House officials and congressional leaders. Behind closed doors, the group made progress toward an agreement. But no bargains could be struck without the consent of the president and the Speaker. Senate Budget Committee Chair Pete V. Domenici (R-N.Mex.), a leading participant in the meetings, noted that a budget agreement could be reached "if we can get both Speaker Tip O'Neill and the president on board" (qtd. in Tate 1982, 787). But Reagan was unwilling to raise taxes in the midst of a recession, and O'Neill refused to reduce Social Security benefits. With the two leaders reluctant to budge, the meetings ended in stalemate.

Soon after the Gang of Seventeen meetings broke up, Reagan invited O'Neill to the White House for a one-on-one meeting. The two haggled over ideological differences—Reagan argued in favor of conservative fiscal philosophy, while O'Neill cited the virtues of the New Deal and Great Society programs. Even though this meeting also ended in deadlock, it symbolized a new task for the Speaker—as opposition party leader, representing House Democrats in negotiations with the president.

Later in 1982 the Speaker and the president reached a rare compromise on a $98 billion tax-increase bill crafted by O'Neill, Senate Majority Leader Howard H. Baker, Jr. (R-Tenn.), and Senate Finance Chair Bob Dole (R-Kans.). The Speaker was thus established as a key player in negotiations over major policy decisions with the Senate and the White House.

The Period of Centralization: 1983–1988

The pattern of centralized leadership that emerged during the 1980s was encouraged by the continuation of divided government combined with growing deficits and increasing party cohesion. Reconciliation procedures used to reduce the deficit required leaders to play a more active role in coordinating the committees.

The Rules Committee continued to restrict amendments to first budget resolutions (Bach and Smith 1988). The deficits squeezed new spending initiatives and increased partisan conflict, creating stalemate over budget priorities. Yet the two parties were forced to the bargaining table, first by the concern for deficits, then by the threat of automatic spending cuts in the Gramm-Rudman-Hollings (GRH) deficit-reduction law. Budget summit meetings thus became vehicles for trying to resolve fundamental policy differences, with House Democrats relying on party leaders to negotiate with Republican Senate leaders and White House officials. The same centralizing conditions that encouraged party leaders to perform more policy-related tasks also reduced the need for leaders to concentrate their efforts on traditional coalition-building and party-maintenance functions.

Policy Formulation High levels of party unity are typically reflected in more homogenous preferences among party members, allowing leaders to exercise stronger party leadership (Rohde and Shepsle 1987). By 1982 Speaker O'Neill was taking a more active role in formulating the priorities of the House Democratic party. But his actions sprang in large part from the House's failure to pass a budget resolution. Weak party cohesion limited O'Neill's capacity to initiate priorities on behalf of the Democratic party. After the Democrats regained twenty-six House seats in the 1982 midterm elections, however, O'Neill was better positioned to lead the party. Backed by a unified party (see Table 6-1, p. 115), the Speaker participated more actively than ever before in formulating Democratic budget priorities.

The most impressive example of active policy-oriented leadership came in 1987 from Speaker Jim Wright (D-Tex.) (Sinclair 1989b). A former member of the Budget Committee, Wright established his priorities almost immediately after being elected Speaker in December 1986. At his first press conference, Wright announced that the Democratic party should propose a tax-revenue increase for higher-income earners. When the 100th Congress convened in January 1987, the new Speaker submitted a detailed list of initiatives that he believed the Budget Committee should include in its first budget resolution for the upcoming fiscal year. Wright's priorities included spending increases for welfare programs, health care, assistance for the homeless, relief for AIDS victims, drug prevention, and federal job training. He proceeded to lobby Democratic caucus and Budget Committee members to support the tax increase and the new spending initiatives. Ultimately, the House Budget Committee endorsed, and the House approved, a first budget resolution encompassing Wright's agenda.

Wright's ability to define the majority party's priorities indicated how far the Speaker's policy-making tasks had evolved since the creation of the budget process in 1974. For years a divided House Democratic party prohibited the Speaker from participating actively in formulating the House Budget; the Speaker's job was to mediate interests, not to define policies. With the party more unified, especially in terms of budget matters, Speaker O'Neill was able to take a more active role in stating his preferences. But Wright was even more willing and able than O'Neill to take advantage of the conditions that upheld policy-oriented leadership.

Passing Budget Resolutions The same conditions that permitted the Speaker to play a more active role in formulating budget resolutions also removed obstacles to floor passage. As the House Democrats' budgetary preferences became more homogenous, party leaders spent far less time and effort on coalition building and party maintenance. Leaders used the Rules Committee more aggressively to prohibit amendments on the floor and to manage the uncertainty of passing legislation (Bach and Smith 1988). The closed rules marked a shift from the wide-open collegial process of the 1970s toward the centralized leadership of the 1980s.

One way to measure the predictability of passing budget resolutions on the floor is to examine the margins of victory or defeat on the Budget Committee's first budget resolutions. As Table 6-3 shows, from 1983 to 1988 the Budget Committee's first budget resolutions were approved by impressive margins in comparison with previous years. Armed with strong party unity and restrictive rules for floor debate, leaders had little trouble passing the committee's first budget resolutions. The Speaker made less use of task forces and the whip system to build partisan support for budget resolutions. Instead, the Speaker's emphasis shifted to policy-oriented activities.

Settling Conference Disputes Ever since the creation of a congressional budget process, the Senate and the House have supported different budget priorities, even when Democrats controlled both chambers. House budgets normally contained lower defense spending and higher figures for domestic programs than the Senate preferred. These differences were usually resolved in conference by members of the two budget committees, with little intervention by party leaders. However, between 1981 and 1986, when Republicans controlled the Senate, the gap between the parties was at times too wide to be bridged through normal conference committee proceedings. Bicameral deadlocks were so prolonged in 1984 and 1985 that the Speaker was called on to negotiate agreements with Republican Senate leaders and the president.

In 1984 conferees fought over a wide gap between each chamber's proposals for total defense and domestic spending. On the one hand, the Senate backed a Reagan-endorsed plan to place caps, or ceilings, on spending levels that would pare defense spending by $41 billion and domestic spending by $43 billion over a three-year period. The House budget, on the other hand, reduced defense spending by $95 billion and domestic expenditures by only $15 billion over three years. As the conference talks began, Speaker O'Neill announced, "We absolutely will not go along" with the Senate's plan (qtd. in Tate 1984, 1295).

The opposing sides were deadlocked until Congress was forced to pass a debt-limit increase bill on 28 June 1984. Conferees agreed to a partial deficit-reduction reconciliation bill that increased revenues by $50 billion and reduced domestic spending by $13 billion. But because the defense issue remained unsettled, conferees failed to complete the first budget resolution. The impasse lasted until O'Neill met privately with Senate Majority Leader Baker during the final two weeks of September. The two leaders agreed on Baker's proposal to delay a vote on appropriations for the MX missile until the spring of 1985, in exchange for O'Neill's commitment to support the Senate's overall defense figure for FY 1985. With this issue decided, the conferees quickly finished their business and the two chambers approved the conference report on 1 October 1984.

In 1985 conferees haggled over a Senate proposal, also endorsed by

President Reagan, to freeze cost-of-living adjustments (COLAs) for Social Security benefits. "I am bitterly opposed [to capping the COLAs]," Speaker O'Neill sharply announced, "and I will so notify and instruct my conferees" (qtd. in Calmes 1985, 971). After seven weeks of stalemate, President Reagan intervened. He invited Speaker O'Neill to the White House, along with Majority Leader Wright, House Minority Leader Robert H. Michel (R-Ill.), Senate Majority Leader Bob Dole, and Senate Minority Leader Robert C. Byrd (D-W.Va.). At that meeting, Reagan dropped the Senate initiative to freeze COLAs for Social Security, and he and O'Neill agreed to a budget package that would increase the House defense figure, freeze tax increases, and reduce other domestic programs.

The compromises reached by the Speaker and the president were at first resisted by many Senate Republicans and House Democrats. Senate Republicans criticized the president for abandoning the freeze on Social Security COLAs; House Democrats balked at some of the proposed domestic spending cuts. The differences were finally ironed out in private meetings that included the two Budget Committee chairs, Representative William H. Gray (D-Pa.) and Senator Domenici (R-N.Mex.), and the committee's ranking minority party members, Representative Delbert L. Latta (R-Ohio) and Senator Lawton Chiles (D-Fla.). The group endorsed a budget resolution that incorporated the major points of the deficit-reduction package endorsed by Reagan and O'Neill. The conference budget resolution was finally approved by both chambers.

Presidential-Congressional Relations As the preceding example indicates, meetings between the president and House leaders were essential to resolving budgetary disagreements during the period of centralized decision making. Speaker O'Neill met with President Reagan on several occasions either to discuss the broad outlines of the budget or to consider ways of reducing the deficit. For the most part, the two leaders bargained over national priorities under the constraints of large deficits. Reagan advocated large defense expenditures, while O'Neill sought to protect traditional liberal programs. More often than not, their meetings failed to produce an agreement. Although Reagan and O'Neill were recognized as the leaders of their parties, neither was able to build a consistent, loyal following. Their positions indicated the peculiar nature of leadership during a period of stalemate. As Aaron Wildavsky put it:

> President Reagan and Speaker O'Neill, the elder statesmen, serve as lodestars; their agreement gives permission to people on their right and left respectively to follow suit. But by refusing permission the president and the Speaker are better at stopping what they don't like than in getting what they want because, like other would-be leaders, they lack majorities. (1988, 207)

Thus the Speaker's main task was to accept or reject budget proposals on behalf of the Democratic party.

One of the most memorable budget summits occurred after the stock-market crash of October 1987. The president and Congress were compelled by the situation to consider ways to reduce the deficit. The summit meetings involved key White House officials, party leaders, and chairs of the budget, appropriations, and tax committees. Majority Leader Thomas S. Foley (D-Wash.) was the leading representative for the House Democratic party. Although Speaker Wright and President Reagan did not participate directly in the summit, the fate of the meetings rested on the consent of the two leaders. Their disagreement partly explains why it took over a month to reach a summit agreement. As one House Democrat said, "You've got two exceedingly inflexible men, Wright and Reagan" (qtd. in Wehr 1987, 2707). The stalemate finally broke under the threat of a sequester—automatic spending cuts necessary to meet the requirements of the Gramm-Rudman-Hollings law. The participants approved a two-year deficit-reduction plan with $30 billion in savings for FY 1988 and $46 billion for FY 1989.

CONCLUSION

As a result of the conditions that shaped the postreform period in Congress, party leaders now perform a wider variety of functions. Coalition-building and party-maintenance tasks continue to be critical to the internal workings of the House. It was natural for leaders to continue to execute these tasks in response to the problems arising in the decentralized, participatory mood of the immediate postreform period.

However, party leaders need not be restricted to such traditional functions. This is attested by the wider range of leaders' activities in the centralized context of the 1980s—especially their participation in formulating budget priorities, settling conference disputes, and negotiating budget meetings with the president. Members expect leaders to adapt, as the institution itself must, to changes in the policy agenda and the political environment. Divided government, a contracted agenda, and intense partisanship posed a new and different set of conditions. These conditions, in turn, encouraged party leaders to assume policy-oriented functions both within and outside of the House. In general, then, the functions of party leaders tend to reflect the problems and opportunities encountered by Congress itself.

PART · IV

Rules of the Game

7 / From Monopoly to Management: Changing Patterns of Committee Deliberation

ROGER H. DAVIDSON AND WALTER J. OLESZEK

When most people think of how legislation is processed by Congress, they visualize a measure being referred to a single specialized committee that considers and perhaps reports it. While this is an accurate picture of what occurs with the majority of bills and resolutions, the 1970s reforms created multiple-committee review of legislation. Today a sizeable portion of measures are considered jointly or sequentially by two or more committees. On average, nearly a quarter of the work load of House committees and about a tenth of the work load of Senate committees consist of bills and resolutions shared with one or more other panels (Davidson, Oleszek, and Kephart 1988).

The two chambers have distinctive ways of treating legislation that spans the jurisdictions of more than a single committee. The Senate has a long history of making multiple referrals by unanimous consent, its preferred mode of doing business. In 1977 its rules were altered to provide explicitly for multiple referrals on a motion by the joint leadership (that is, the majority and minority leaders acting jointly). Although this provision has yet to be invoked, the chamber continues to refer, by unanimous consent, a small but significant portion of bills, resolutions, and nominations to two or more committees (Davidson 1989). Some unanimous consent agreements are prospective in effect and cover a certain category of legislation or nomination. For instance, Senate Majority Leader George Mitchell (D-Maine) asked and received unanimous consent "that nominations to the Offices of Inspector General, excepting the Office of Inspector General for the Central Intelligence Agency, be referred during the 101st Congress in each case to the committee having substantive jurisdiction over the department, agency, or entity, and if and when reported in each case, then to the Committee on Governmental Affairs for not to exceed 20 days" (*Congressional Record*, 27 September 1990, S14154).

If the Senate makes little use of formal multiple referrals, it has other mechanisms for intercommittee coordination: overlapping committee memberships, for example, and a tradition of involving noncommittee senators in policy-making through informal negotiations and floor amendments.

Before 1975 the House of Representatives had no formal rule for sharing measures among two or more committees making jurisdictional claims or for reconciling the jurisdictional claims of competing committees for the same bill. House committees are more autonomous than their Senate counterparts, and more jealously guard their jurisdictional boundaries. From Woodrow Wilson to the present day, observers have regarded House panels as "islands of decision" with few direct linkages to other committees. "These miniature legislatures," wrote one student, ". . . are largely autonomous of the House itself which created them and whose agents they are supposed to be" (Galloway 1962, 87).

Committee compartmentalization was a major target of the 1960s and 1970s reformers. Walls surrounding the committee feifdoms were breached in a number of ways—for example, through caucus approval of committee chairs, greater use of floor amendments, and recorded floor votes on those amendments. In its 1974 overhaul of committee jurisdictions, the House amended its rules to permit, for the first time in its history, the reference of legislation to more than one committee. The new rule (House Rule X, clause 5) was intended to (1) bring the wisdom and perspective of several different committees to bear on complex public issues, (2) make the committee system more flexible in handling policies that cut across jurisdictional boundaries, and (3) encourage intercommittee cooperation and contain jurisdictional conflicts (U.S. Congress, Select Committee on Committees 1980, 59–61). But the core purpose of the rule was to break committee monopolies over important legislation. As Speaker Thomas P. O'Neill (D-Mass.) explained, "The object at the time was to take power out of the hands of the few and give it to more people" (O'Neill 1980, 24).

The rise of multiple referrals has placed greater stress on intercommittee relationships. Nearly all such referrals involve some form of cross-committee communications—even if they are merely initiatives taken to anticipate another committee's actions. This raises a host of questions rarely mentioned by those who examine the operations of a single committee: Which committees tend to interact with which other committees, and on what issues? Are their relationships marked by cooperation or conflict? How do such relationships affect overall legislative output?

Multiple referrals have also given chamber leaders, especially in the House, new opportunities to coordinate and even manage the work of committees. The act of referring a measure involves the leadership, usually acting through the parliamentarians of the respective chambers. If multiple-referred measures are to have any chance of passage, leaders must coordinate or at least oversee the committees' actions.

When time limits are placed on the deliberations of one or more committees, it is a matter of scheduling—fundamental to the power of the leadership. Time limits are "akin to a 'discharge power,' the potent capability to override a committee trying to bottle a bill up" (Tiefer and Murray 1989, 38). Measures subject to time limits often require careful floor management—through special rules from the House Rules Committee or Senate

Figure 7-1 / Types of Multiple Referrals in the House of Representatives

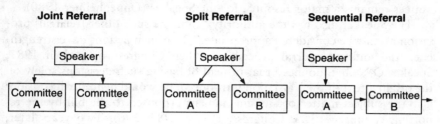

unanimous-consent agreements. These tools of legislative management are controlled by or exercised through the leaders, especially the House Speaker. To what extent, then, has the multiple-referral device provided resources for leaders to manage and schedule the work of Congress?

MULTIPLE REFERRALS IN THE HOUSE

Bills and resolutions introduced in the House and delivered to the Speaker are referred by the Speaker to the appropriate committee (House Rule XXII, clause 4a). The actual referral is typically made by the parliamentarian, acting for the Speaker in accordance with House rules and precedents. Most referral decisions are routine. When the precedents are unclear or conflicting, however, the Speaker (or parliamentarian) sometimes mediates between committees having claims on the jurisdiction.

Types of Multiple Referrals

The House's multiple-referral rule (Rule X, clause 5c) permits the Speaker to make three types of multiple referrals: joint (or concurrent), split, and sequential (see Figure 7-1). In a *joint referral*, the most common type, a bill or resolution is referred to two or more committees simultaneously. *Split* (or *divided*) *referrals* involve sending various titles or sections of a bill to two or more committees. Some such referrals grant one panel authority over the whole bill while others receive the bill solely to consider certain titles or sections. Split referrals are rare because many bills are not readily divided by sections or titles. In a *sequential referral*, a measure reported by a committee (whether initially referred singly or jointly) is then assigned to one or more additional committees.

House Rule X also permits the Speaker, subject to House approval, to establish *ad hoc* committees to consider policies that overlap the jurisdiction of several standing committees. Only two such panels have been established: (1) on the outer-continental shelf (1975) and (2) on energy policy (1977). These panels drew such bitter controversy from the standing committees that they have not been replicated. However, the power to create such committees remains a major resource for the Speaker (Oppenheimer 1980).

The Speaker also has the authority "to make such other [referral] provision as may be considered appropriate." Two such actions have strengthened the multiple-referral procedure. When Congress opened in 1981, Speaker O'Neill announced that instead of basing such decisions solely on the original text of the legislation introduced, he would henceforth consider also the subject matter of any amendment proposed to the bill by the reporting committee (U.S. Congress, House 1983, 396). Two years later, O'Neill announced that he would designate a primary committee among those to which a bill was jointly referred in appropriate situations and impose time limits on committees having a secondary interest following the primary committee's report (*Congressional Record*, 3 January 1983, H25–H26).

The Growth of Multiple Referrals

Since their inception in the House, multiple referrals have become a significant part of the legislative work load. Of all the measures introduced in the Ninety-eighth Congress (1983–84)—bills, simple resolutions, joint resolutions, concurrent resolutions—11.4 percent were referred to more than a single committee (see Figure 7-2). This was twice the proportion of such measures when the provision was first added to the House rules. Four out of five multiple-referred measures go to two committees, but sometimes more panels are involved—the largest number remains the fifteen committees that handled the 1981 Budget Reconciliation Act. With so many committees involved in budget matters, the 1980s witnessed the emergence of centralizing processes: congressional leadership–White House summits that bypassed regular committee review of fiscal policy (see Gilmour, this volume, Chapter 12).

Multiple referrals have a greater impact on committees than chamber-wide figures suggest. Each bill in this category generates two, three, or more referrals involving the equivalent number of committees and many subcommittees. Seen this way, about a quarter of the average committee's legislative work load consists of measures shared wholly or in part with other committees. The impact varies dramatically among committees. The champion is the Select Committee on Intelligence, which deals with relatively few bills but shares most of them with Armed Services and Foreign Affairs (see Kaiser, this volume, Chapter 14). Committees with broad mandates—such as Energy and Commerce; Science, Space and Technology; and Government Operations—also receive high proportions of such bills. In contrast, some committees handle a few highly focused measures that are rarely shared with other panels. These include the Budget, Veterans' Affairs, House Administration, and Judiciary committees. Like other committee attributes, mul-

Figure 7-2 / Multiple-referred Measures and Total Measures Introduced, House of Representatives, 1975–1986

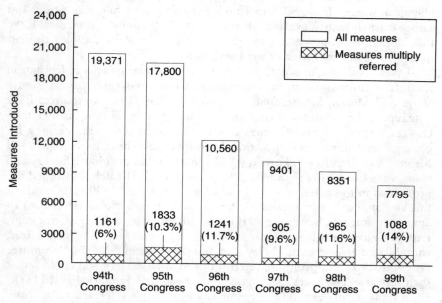

NOTE: Measures include all bills, simple resolutions, joint resolutions, and concurrent resolutions listed as "referred" in the House Legis data base.
Source: Legis computerized data base.

tiple referrals validate Fenno's dictum that "congressional committees differ from one another" (1973, 280).

The extent of overlapping work load lends new meaning to the notion of committee permeability. Fenno distinguished between "corporate" committees that display internal coherence and "permeable" ones that respond to outside forces (1973, 278–79). The parent chamber and its leadership are among those outside forces. However, the influence of other committees with adjacent or overlapping duties is also important. Committees that commonly share legislation with other committees are no doubt more permeable than those with work loads over which they exercise total control.

Patterns of Intercommittee Relations

Intercommittee relationships vary widely. The Agriculture and Interior panels, for example, share jurisdiction over public lands, parks, forests, and wildernesses—an overlap that accounts for most of the multiple-referred bills sent to these two committees. Fairly settled procedures have evolved for handling shared bills. In other cases, committees' divergent perspectives, arising from different membership mixes, inhibit the passage of legislation. In 1985 Energy and Commerce fought fiercely with Public Works over chemical waste cleanup ("superfund") legislation, while Education and Labor clashed with Ways and Means over a 1990 family and medical leave bill. Difficulties in processing multiple referrals mirror the complex content or controversial character of the legislation.

Taxes are a case in point. Any time the word *tax* appears in legislation it is referred automatically in each chamber to the tax-writing panels (House Ways and Means; Senate Finance). However, legislative committees have long reported measures that contain provisions raising revenue through fees, charges, or assessments. Needless to say, what constitutes a tax versus a fee has produced numerous jurisdictional controversies. For example, Ways and Means Chair Dan Rostenkowski (D-Ill.) charged that the House Energy and Commerce Committee, headed by John D. Dingell (D-Mich.), included tax provisions in the guise of fees in the Clean Air Act of 1990. The result of this and similar controversies led Speaker Thomas S. Foley (D-Wash.) to announce a new policy at the start of the 102nd Congress. Legislative committees "have jurisdiction to consider user, regulatory, and other fees, charges, and assessments," Foley said, but the Ways and Means Committee "is entitled to an appropriate referral of broad-based fees and could recast such fees as excise taxes" (*Congressional Record*, 3 January 1991, H31).

Several factors explain the popularity of multiple referrals. First, many current issues—education, energy, crime, drug control, environmental protection, trade, and transportation—span numerous separate topics. Second, House committee jurisdictions, as laid out in the rules, are outmoded and thus often fail adequately to delineate these complex, interdependent issues. Third, some committees' jurisdictions were deliberately worded to promote multiple-committee review. The Foreign Affairs Committee, for instance, has jurisdiction over international economic policy; Energy and Commerce handles foreign commerce generally; and Ways and Means considers reciprocal trade agreements. Further, these are not the only panels active in international trade.

Finally, the multiple-referral rule encourages committees to assert their claims over legislation. With more active subcommittees, capable and aggressive staffs, computerized information sources, scores of interest groups, and independent-minded legislators, today's committees are better able to monitor bills as they are introduced and reported from other committees. Chairs seek to have measures referred to their committees on the ground that they affect directly or indirectly their panels' responsibilities.

WHAT HAPPENS TO MULTIPLE-REFERRED BILLS?

Two-thirds of the measures that are referred to more than one committee go no farther. In this respect they resemble all other measures, though their chances of passage are even lower than for single-referred measures. During

Table 7-1 / Procedural Routes to the House Floor, Ninety-eighth Congress

Method	Multiple-referred Measures	Single-referred Measures
Suspension of the rules	59%	29%
Rules from the Rules Committee	31	9
Unanimous consent	9	37
Other procedures	1	5
Privileged matter	—	20
Total	100%	100%
(N)	(106)	(1461)

Sources: Figures for multiple referrals are from House LEGIS computerized data base; figures for single referrals were compiled by Ilona Nickels and reprinted in Davidson and Oleszek 1985, 271.

the Ninety-fourth to Ninety-ninth Congresses, no more than 14 percent of all multiple-referred measures were reported by one or more of the panels that considered them; no more than 10 percent were eventually passed by the House.

When a committee wants to take a tentative first step on the measure, the chair requests comments from one or more executive agencies. This is a way of putting a toe in the water without getting very wet. In the Ninety-eighth Congress, comments were received on 37 percent of all bills involving two or more committees—an average of 3.2 executive agencies per bill. Agency jurisdictions, it seems, are as scattered as those on Capitol Hill.

Hearings or business meetings are the next level of attention that a committee can direct to a bill. In the Ninety-eighth Congress, a third of the multiple-referred measures were actually taken up by one or more committees. In most cases, one of the panels took the lead in the issue. For instance, one committee may use as its markup vehicle the substitute reported by another panel.

Once a bill has been reported by a committee, it has a good chance of being accepted by the full House. Table 7-1 analyzes the fate of measures reported during the Ninety-eighth Congress by at least one of the committees of reference. Sixty-nine percent of these were acted on by the chamber, and all but five passed. Six out of ten were taken up under suspension of the rules, an expedited procedure requiring a two-thirds vote. Three of ten were granted a rule by the Rules Committee; one of ten passed under the abbreviated unanimous-consent procedure. Compared to all measures taken up on the House floor, multiple-referred measures made more use of suspensions of the rules and rules from the Rules Committee, but they were less likely to come up under unanimous consent. This reinforces the view that measures handled by more than one committee are, as a group, more complex than the total body of legislation considered on the House floor.

The multiple referral has become a major weapon in the arsenal of legislative strategists. Among its uses are the following:

1. A committee's request for sequential referral of a measure reported by another committee may slow down or even kill the measure.
2. A sequential-referral request (sometimes stimulated by lobbyists or executive branch officials) may reflect a committee's desire to modify a measure, redirect its content, or add new provisions.
3. Submitting a broadly drafted bill, which goes to several committees, may prod reluctant panels to deliberate or take action that they might not otherwise do. Alternatively, committees may draft measures to avoid or limit multiple referrals.
4. The policy-making biases of committees can be offset by the diverse viewpoints or alternative expertise embodied in the committee structure.
5. Committees acquire leverage through multiple referrals that enables them to promote policy compromise or refine another panel's handiwork.

The most frequently claimed effect of multiple referrals is that they add to the veto points on Capitol Hill, compounding the difficulties of enacting legislation. (However, when two or more committees favorably report the same bill, this may add to the measure's political momentum and chances of passage.) While it is true that multiple-referred measures are less likely to succeed than single-referred ones, they can be used as a lever to stimulate policy innovation and prod committees to consider problems that they might not otherwise do. Examples of cross-fertilization are common. One example is the enactment that modified antitrust laws to encourage joint ventures among U.S. firms to engage in research and development needed to compete on the world market (P.L. 98-462). Science, Space and Technology pushed the bill at the behest of the scientific community; but the committee lacked experience with antitrust law, which Judiciary supplied. In addition, House leaders sometimes put together an orchestrated effort embracing a series of committees to produce a large-scale measure with partisan or public appeal. Indeed, leadership involvement is perhaps the most intriguing aspect of the multiple-referral process.

LEADERSHIP AND MULTIPLE REFERRALS

Multiple referrals, as noted earlier, were urged on the House as a means of giving more committees—and members—access to decisions on given legislation. Thus they conformed with the main thrust of the 1960s and 1970s reforms: dispersion of initiative and influence. Yet the device has a direct impact on the leadership, especially the Speaker and the Rules Committee, and it buttresses House leaders' most fundamental power: scheduling.

The Speaker's Role

Multiple-referral authority today ties the House Speaker more closely into committee decision making than at any time since the 1910 "revolt" against Speaker Joseph G. Cannon (R-Ill.). (Before that revolt, the Speaker named the chairs and members of the standing committees.) Committee chairs lobby the Speaker about referral decisions—to raise issues and to sensitize the Speaker to their concerns. Similarly, committee staff aides consult with the parliamentarian about legislative referrals and are adept at protecting or even expanding their committees' jurisdictional boundaries through artful drafting of bills.

The Speaker employs multiple referrals to achieve a variety of objectives. The device can be used, for instance, to build credits among colleagues by protecting certain jurisdictional prerogatives, to impose deadlines on committees for reporting legislation, to coordinate the fragmented committee system, to promote integrated public policy, and to expedite or delay action on certain measures. One GOP study called multiple referrals the Speaker's "line-item veto" (Gingrich and Gregorsky 1985).

The objectives of multiple referrals were evident in the House's 1986 consideration of an omnibus trade bill designed to take advantage of the trade deficit issue. Because of the growing trade deficit, Speaker O'Neill and other Democratic leaders worked to develop and pass legislation aimed at strengthening the nation's international competitiveness and combatting unfair foreign trading practices. Six House committees considered nine separate trade bills (five were sequentially referred), which were eventually consolidated into a single measure (HR 4800). To alleviate turf battles among the committees, the Speaker "directed Majority Leader Jim Wright of Texas to coordinate the activities of House committees working on different pieces of an overall trade measure" (Pressman 1986, 557). As early as March 1986, the Speaker promised that comprehensive trade legislation would reach the House floor by mid-May (Farnsworth 1986). Keeping that commitment required an expedited "fast track" for sequential review—for example, trade bills reported from the Banking and Foreign Affairs committees were sequentially referred for only three days.

In contrast, the Speaker's decision to refer a bill sequentially to another committee late in a congressional session can place it in jeopardy. This occurred in 1983 after President Reagan dispatched U.S. troops to Lebanon. After months of wrangling, the White House reached an informal (later formal) agreement with congressional leaders to keep the troops in Lebanon for another eighteen months. Subsequently, the House Appropriations Committee added to a continuing resolution a provision cutting off funds for the U.S. forces unless the president invoked the 1973 War Powers Resolution. The Speaker took two unique actions: He sequentially referred the appropriations bill to a legislative committee (Foreign Affairs) and imposed no time limit for Foreign Affairs' review (Granat 1983, p. 1973). Another continuing resolution without the offending provision was later reported by Appropriations.

Multiple referrals present challenges and opportunities for the leadership. The Speaker can devise referral arrangements that promote policy and political objectives. With many policy areas routinely shared by several committees, however, the Speaker must balance additional demands from members—scheduling their reported bills, extending the time for sequential review, or reviewing requests for the multiple reference of legislation. By fostering policy-making by inclusion, multiple referrals make it harder for the Speaker to exclude any interested members from the deliberative process.

The Rules Committee and Floor Deliberation

Since 1975 the Speaker has been authorized to nominate the majority party members of the Rules Committee, subject to Democratic caucus approval. This strengthened the Speaker's influence over the panel at the same time the Speaker gained authority over multiple referrals. The Rules Committee plays a pivotal role by fashioning special rules that resolve jurisdictional disputes and promote orderly consideration of competing provisions reported by committees in charge of the same issue. (A *rule* governs the length of general debate on the floor—when the House is sitting as Committee of the Whole specifies the extent to which the bill can be amended, and may waive possible points of order against the measure.)

According to Rules Committee practice, all committees must have reported or waived jurisdiction on a multiple-referred bill before it is considered for a rule. This policy avoids races to the Rules Committee by committees working on parallel legislation, promotes intercommittee consultation, minimizes conflict between the Rules Committee and other panels, focuses attention on resolving disputes between or among committees, and provides Rules members with wider information on the issues that evoke controversy and on the level of conflict or consensus. On occasion the policy even encourages committees to drop disputed matters from their bills to prevent their reference to other panels.

Because of the Rules Committee's unique scheduling role, it is strategically placed to act as jurisdictional arbiter. Especially potent is its authority to select the vehicle for floor amendments when competing versions of the same bill are reported by several committees. Interior Chair Morris K. Udall (D-Ariz.) explained why his panel and the Merchant Marine Committee developed a consensus or alternative version of a bill that had been extensively amended during sequential referral: "When we got to the Committee on Rules with our bill and with the [Merchant Marine] bill, we would have been hit with a barrage of [Rules] members saying, 'What's wrong with you? Why do you bring us all these amendments? It is confusing. Why can't you get down to it and consider the two bills and blend the provisions of each?'" (*Congressional Record*, 17 May 1978, 14144).

Another important function of the Rules Committee is to define the terms for debating and amending measures on the House floor. As noted earlier, multiple-referred measures are more likely than other bills to be considered under suspension of the rules or rules from the Rules Committee, but they are less likely to come up under unanimous consent procedures. The types of rules differ somewhat between single-referred and multiple-referred measures. One difference is the amount of time allowed for general debate. In contrast to the one hour normally granted for a measure (equally divided between majority and minority), a longer period is common for multiple-referred bills, with the time allocated to the several panels reporting the measure.

The Rules Committee structures the presentation of alternatives on the floor via the amendment process and protects the involved committees' rights to make changes in the legislation. (The rule itself is based in large measure on recommendations from the concerned committees.) In a majority of cases, the rule is an open one, permitting any and all germane amendments.

Increasingly, however, rules set forth complex amendment procedures for whatever vehicle is made in order for floor consideration (*Congressional Record*, 3 January 1991, H17). For example, rules may (1) require that amendments be printed in the *Congressional Record* by a certain date before they can be offered on the floor, (2) specify the member to offer an amendment, (3) set forth the exact order in which amendments are to be proposed, or (4) prohibit amendments to an amendment. One study concluded that multiple-committee bills are more likely than others to receive rules that restrict floor amendment opportunities (Bach and Smith 1988, 59).

The last word in Rules Committee artifice is undoubtedly the so-called *king-of-the-mountain* approach, which brings to the floor a series of bills or amendments and provides (in the words of one Rules Committee member) that "the last amendment adopted (in Committee of the Whole) in those specified instances shall be the one reported back to the House, even though the preceding amendments may have been adopted as well" (*Congressional Record*, 11 June 1984, H5531). Needless to say, the leadership is careful to position its preferred alternative so it is the last one considered.

Rules, too, may waive other House rules so that representatives cannot raise points of order against considering the legislation or against specific provisions or amendments. "We could not run this government without this Committee on Rules exercising that [waiver] authority in proper cases," remarked Appropriations Chair Jamie L. Whitten (D-Miss.) (*Congressional Record*, 25 May 1983, H3310).

CONCLUSIONS

The examination in this chapter of multiple referrals since 1975 yields a number of findings, not all of them apparent to observers of the legislative process.

First, since their introduction in the 1970s, multiple referrals have enjoyed spectacular growth as a portion of the House's legislative work load. This has occurred because such measures have remained relatively stable in an era of limits, which has been marked by falling total numbers of measures introduced, reported, or passed. Of the three types of multiple referrals, joint referrals are by far the most numerous while split referrals are quite rare. However, sequentially referred bills are most likely to succeed: nearly all such House bills are reported by their committees and more than three-quarters of them gain passage on the floor.

Second, multiple referrals have made an even greater impact on individual committees than the aggregate figures indicate. On average, nearly one-quarter of the legislative work load of House committees and about one-tenth of that of Senate committees consist of measures shared with one or more other panels. For some committees this figure exceeds 50 percent.

Third, multiple-referred measures enjoy growing success in being reported by their committees and considered favorably on the floor. While they are still not as apt to gain passage as single-referred measures, they have benefited from routines established among the various committees of reference. Generally, the more committees to which a measure is referred, the more difficult it is for the measure to survive in the legislative process. Success rates for multiple-referred measures vary widely according to the subject matter and the committees involved.

Fourth, relationships between pairs (or clusters) of committees vary according to the issue and the committees involved. Some relationships are relatively noncontroversial and routinized; others are marked by wariness and hostility. Although the multiple-referral procedure adds to the number of veto points that can halt or impede legislation, multiple referrals have been used to exert leverage against a recalcitrant committee. The overall level of controversy dictates the level of intercommittee conflict on a given piece of legislation. Certain committees, however, are more aggressive than others in claiming jurisdiction and initiating conflict with rival panels.

Fifth, although launched to disperse influence over policy-making, the multiple-referral device has paradoxically augmented the scheduling prerogatives of House leaders. Speaker O'Neill increasingly employed the procedure to manage high-priority, multititled measures. The use of time limits in sequential referrals, moreover, places in the Speaker's hands a potent tool for coordinating deliberations at the committee stage.

Sixth, priority measures today are unlikely to die because arbitrary chairs or the Rules Committee pigeonhole them. Instead, the multiple-referral environment creates wide opportunities for protracted jurisdictional turf struggles. Sometimes bills fall prey to intercommittee disputes. Party leaders are increasingly involved in mediating these clashes.

Seventh, following passage of multiple-referred legislation, the Speaker and committee leaders are involved in selecting conferees from the various committees (see Oleszek, this volume, Chapter 10). This can be an extraordinarily time-consuming and difficult negotiating process. For instance, a month of negotiations ensued before about 140 conferees were appointed from seven House committees to iron out bicameral differences on the 1990 Clear Air Act. Speaker Foley, Energy Chair Dingell, and Henry Waxman (D-Calif.), chair of Energy's Health Subcommittee, waged a "prickly battle" over the composition of the conference committee (*Congressional Quarterly Weekly Report*, 30 June 1990, 2044). No doubt it was the complexities of conferee selection in multiple-committee situations that prompted Speaker Foley to declare that he intended "to develop and implement a policy that would enable [him] to the fullest extent feasible to simplify the appointment of conferees" (*Congressional Record*, 3 January 1991, H31).

Such a momentous development in processing legislation cannot help but transform the legislative process, especially in the House—for example, the Speaker's prerogatives, the work of the Rules Committee, floor proceedings, and relations with the executive branch and interest groups. The multiple-referral device was part of the 1970s trend toward diffusion of power; in this case, permitting members and committees another procedural window for influencing particular measures. At the same time the procedure has augmented the powers of the Speaker and the Rules Committee, strengthening their roles as centralizing and coordinating agents in managing the House's work load. The multiple referral's implicit mandate for intercommittee coordination encourages lawmakers, committees, and staff aides to negotiate with one another, rather than act separately according to traditional practice. In other words, it promotes that mode characterized by Smith as "collegial": encouraging lawmakers to "broaden their interest and collaborate with colleagues to solve policy problems" (1985, 206).

8 / Fighting Fire with Fire: Amending Activity and Institutional Change in the Postreform Congress

BARRY R. WEINGAST

The decade of reforms (1970s) transformed the House of Representatives from one of committee government into one with stronger subcommittees and stronger, more centralized party leaders.[1] Subcommittees and their members now hold many of the key rights formerly associated with committees, such as policy jurisdiction, staff members, access to the floor, and seniority. In the last decade and especially the past few years, scholars of the reforms have traced the changing nature of congressional politics. Recent findings call into question whether some of the central features of the "textbook" Congress—that is, the Congress of strong committees of the 1950s–mid-1960s still described in textbooks—still apply to the postreform Congress.[2] Among the principal changes in congressional politics are:

1. A substantial rise in amending activity and an apparent decline of committee success and influence on the floor (Bach 1986; Smith 1986, 1989; Sullivan 1987).
2. A decline of the open rule from the lion's share of all rules to just over half of all rules. Restrictive rules now account for over a third of all rules (Bach and Smith 1988; Weingast 1991).
3. An increasing use of multiple referrals—bills referred to more than one committee—ended the monopoly jurisdictions of committees (Collie and Cooper 1989; Davidson and Oleszek 1987; Bach and Smith 1988).
4. An increasing leadership power, notably with regard to the Rules Committee, apparently placing new constraints on committees and their members (Davidson 1988b; Oppenheimer 1981; Rohde 1990; Sinclair 1989b; Smith 1989).

While it is clear that elements of the earlier congressional system have broken down, the larger questions remain elusive: Why did the new patterns emerge? What role do they play? One view holds that the patterns reflect a weakened committee system. That is, the increased amending activity suggests that bills are now substantially altered on the floor, thereby weakening the influence of the committee or subcommittee over the contents of

142

legislation within its jurisdiction. Similarly, the rise of multiple referrals may have weakened the jurisdictional hold of committees and subcommittees over their turfs. The increasing importance of the leadership and the Rules Committee, and the rise in the number of restrictive rules and multiple referrals, suggest that the central leadership now takes a far more active role in the legislative process, possibly at the expense of the subcommittees and their members (Davidson 1988b).

Another view holds that the changes in congressional politics are the result of adaptive responses to the new circumstances of the postreform period (see, especially, Collie and Cooper's 1989 discussion of multiple referrals). According to this view, restrictive rules, multiple referrals, and the new role of the leadership represent an effort to control the uncertainty associated with floor politics immediately following the reforms (Bach and Smith 1988; Smith 1989).

This chapter is intended to contribute to the latter view by providing a new perspective on the issues surrounding the postreform Congress. The chapter's thesis is threefold. First, subcommittees remain the locus of bargaining over legislation within their jurisdiction and are more successful at the floor stage than others have suggested. However, this does not imply that subcommittees remain as powerful as their committee predecessors. Rather, it suggests that a viable system of specialization (on subcommittees) remains in place, though the subcommittees relevant to a given issue may be scattered across two or more committees instead of within a single committee. The leadership plays a far more active role, both by helping maintain bargains on the floor and by participating in negotiating the bargains. Second, the subcommittees and their members have altered their behavior in the face of increasing opposition on the floor under the open rule. When the proponents of legislation anticipate challenging amendments from the opposition, they come to the floor prepared to *fight fire with fire;* that is, to defend their bills with amendments of their own and, especially, to counter amendments of opponents with second-degree amendments that mitigate the effects of the opposition's amendment. Third, all four of the changes in congressional politics listed earlier reflect in part the mechanisms used to enforce bargains among members of different subcommittees.

FLOOR BEHAVIOR UNDER THE OPEN RULE

Any explanation of committee influence over legislation must address how committees succeed on the floor. The apparent ease with which most committees prevailed on the floor during the prereform period does not imply that this is a trivial problem. Whenever a bill is brought to the floor, it is nearly always possible to "roll the committee"—that is, to defeat the committee's attempt to pass its legislation with an amendment that not only passes but leaves the committee worse off (Shepsle and Weingast 1987). Because the success of such amendments is clearly incompatible with strong committees, a successful committee system must have some mechanisms for preventing or combating them.

The literature on legislative institutions provides a starting point for explaining committee success on the floor. Scholars have shown that different institutional constraints over the *agenda*—who gets to make motions and in what order—lead to different outcomes (Shepsle and Weingast 1981, 1987; Baron and Ferejohn 1989). Understanding agenda formation in the House requires an examination of the institutions and practices that comprise the open rule, which has traditionally governed the flow of amendments on the floor.

The *open rule* is a not a free-for-all that allows anything to happen;[3] rather, it is a highly managed process that provides important advantages to the proponents of legislation. The open rule embodies a large number of constraints, including restrictions on the number of motions in order on the floor at any one time and, critically, rules governing the order of recognition. A key strategic feature of the open rule is that when an amendment is made from the floor, the next person entitled to be recognized is a member of the majority party of the relevant committee—typically the floor manager, a proponent of the legislation. This recognition right allows the proponents to counter an opposition amendment with an "amendment to the amendment." The order of voting then becomes the amendment to the amendment against the amendment, or winner against the bill. This feature of the open rule potentially allows the proponents of the legislation to weaken or emasculate the opposition's amendment (Weingast 1989). While this does not mean that proponents counter every amendment, the strategy does help to blunt the force of amendments that have a good chance of succeeding.

Preventing Opposition Amendments

During the prereform period, the House was dominated by a small number of powerful, senior committee chairmen, making it possible to negotiate bargains across committees prior to going to the floor (see Dyson and Soule 1970; Fenno 1973). The long tenure of the chairs provided a substantial incentive to go along with agreements because of the expectation of future interaction (Weingast 1989). The chairs also possessed sanctions with which they could keep members of their committees in line (for example, subcommittee assignments, assignment of bills to subcommittees, bottling up specific legislation, and access to staff). Because of the stability and potential use of sanctions against those that might renege on bargains, it was possible to gain the support of a potentially opposed "swing" group by agreeing to alter the bill before coming to the floor (Weingast 1989). In particular, the swing group would agree to forego a floor challenge (amendments) in exchange for desired provisions in the bill.

What made these agreements credible—that is, what made the parties adhere to them—was a combination of the powers noted earlier and the "shadow of the future." While reneging might yield greater short-run benefits than adhering to the bargain, it might also cause other members of Congress to view the reneger as untrustworthy and thereby foreclose potential future deals. The long-run incentives to adhere to agreements thus worked against short-run incentives to renege.[4] Prior to the reforms, these incentives played a significant role in maintaining bargains, and an informal system of norms came to support these bargains and prevent most committees from being rolled on the floor (Weingast 1989). Indeed, the behavior that followed from this equilibrium gave rise to precisely the norms reported in the literature as underpinning committee success: specialization, reciprocity, and apprenticeship (Fenno 1962, 1966; Hinckley 1978; Polsby 1988).

The decade of reforms resulted in the passage of four key rights from committees and their chairs to subcommittees and their chairs: (1) jurisdiction, (2) access to the floor, (3) staff and other resources, and (4) seniority on subcommittees (Rieselbach 1978, 1986; Davidson and Oleszek 1977). These institutional changes transformed the House from a regularized and stable institution of about 18–20 committees to a much more fluid one of 125–150 subcommittees. The reforms made the legislative process far less predictable (Bach and Smith 1988; Smith 1989). Subcommittee membership and leadership exhibited far more turnover and their leaders were on average less experienced than their committee counterparts (Smith 1989). Further, in contrast to committee leaders of the previous era, postreform subcommittee leaders did not possess sanctions over members of other subcommittees of the same committee.

The passage of power from committees to subcommittees and the removal of sanctions held by chairs were intended effects of the reforms. An important and largely unintended effect was the undermining of the informal negotiation process as a means of protecting bills on the floor under the open rule. Subcommittee leaders, as a result, no longer expected the absence of serious amendment attempts on the floor. Yet this does not imply that subcommittees necessarily became substantially weaker than their predecessors were. Rather, as the informal norms supporting prior negotiation broke down, subcommittees began to pursue more aggressive strategies on the floor.[5] Instead of passively standing by and lamenting the increase in opposition amending activity, subcommittees reacted by coming to the floor prepared to fight threatening amendments with counteramendments—to fight fire with fire. In many cases, aggressive defense of legislation on the floor does not leave the proponents much worse off than it did under the earlier and now unavailable system of informal negotiation prior to floor consideration.

Another reason subcommittees are not necessarily worse off involves institutional evolution and adaptation. Insofar as the system of specialization remained valuable to members of Congress after the reforms, they searched for new methods to protect their legislation on the floor. When the older methods proved insufficient in the postreform period, subcommittee members and party leaders sought, experimented with, and selected new institutional mechanisms and practices to help protect bargains from becoming unglued on the floor.

Some Predictions

Several predictions follow from this approach. First, in addition to the postreform increase in amendments from both proponents and opponents, we should observe a pattern of related amendments: If committees or subcommittees aggressively defend their legislation by fighting fire with fire, potentially successful opposition amendments are themselves the target of second-degree amendments from the proponents who seek to weaken or emasculate the opposition's amendment. The model predicts that the proponents of legislation should regularly succeed at this defense (Weingast 1989). Moreover, to the extent that proponents can accurately gauge an opposed amendment's chance of success, the proponents should be observed to counter those opposed amendments with successful second-degree amendments of their own.

The second prediction concerns institutional change. To the extent that, even with fighting fire with fire, committee floor success declined from the earlier prereform period, we should observe a set of institutional reactions in the form of mechanisms to improve floor success in the new environment. Moreover, because fighting fire with fire is likely to be less reliable when there are many sources of opposition, we are especially likely to see new institutions arise for the more controversial measures. Amendment consideration for such measures should take place under more restrictive rules.

THE PHENOMENA TO BE EXPLAINED

Recent scholarship has revealed a clear pattern of change in congressional amending activity over the past thirty years. During the prereform period, committees brought their legislation to the floor expecting to win. Case studies and statistical evidence support this contention. Dyson and Soule (1970) studied roll-call votes from 1955 to 1964 and calculated the percentage of times that the majority of the relevant committee was on the winning side of a roll-call vote. During this period, a majority of the committee was on the winning side almost 90 percent of the time. Their data also support conclusions in the literature. For example, when committees were well integrated (Fenno 1962, 1966) and consequently came to the floor united, they were far more likely to succeed and won about 95 percent of the time. Disunity markedly dropped the committee success rate to 83 per-

Table 8-1 / Success Rates of Amendments to Appropriations Legislation, 1975–1882[a]

	Number Passed	Number Failed	Percentage Passed
Accepted	289	57	84%
Opposed	118	306	28%

[a] $n = 770$.
Source: Bach 1986, Tables 1–3.

cent.[6] In terms of the perspective developed here, committees that came to the floor after successful prior negotiations (that is, integrated committees) usually succeeded.

Amending activity in the postreform period contrasts sharply with the earlier pattern (Bach 1986; Hall and Evans 1989; Smith 1986, 1989; and Sullivan 1987). Smith (1989) reports that during the postreform period, amendments increased severalfold the number of amendments by proponents increased by a factor of two and a half, and successful amendments by noncommittee members increased by a factor of three. Thus not only has amending activity been on the rise, but so too apparently the opposition success.

More specifically, Bach's (1986) study of amendments to appropriations legislation shows that all aspects of amending activity have increased: total numbers, numbers per bill, and the percentage winning. Importantly, the number of amendments opposed by subcommittee chairs and the percentage of those that win have also increased. Table 8-1 outlines the success rates of amendments for 1975–82. Two categories of amendments are shown: amendments supported by the relevant subcommittee chairs and those opposed by the chairs. As the table indicates, there was a large number of amendments, including a substantial fraction that passed (407 out of 770). Amendments supported by the subcommittee chair were clearly more likely to succeed (84 percent of the time) than those opposed by the chair (28 percent). The number of successful opposition amendments in the postreform era thus appears substantial and notably larger than in the past. Moreover, when the figures are computed in a way comparable to that of Dyson and Soule (1970), we see that the percentage of the time that the subcommittee chair was on the winning side dropped to 77 percent.

The conclusion drawn by most scholars of the postreform period is that the norms of specialization, reciprocity, and apprenticeship have broken down. One hypothesis tentatively advanced is that the increase in amending activity implies that the floor stage has become far more important than before.[7] This led Smith (1986) to ask the appropriate question: Did the increase in amending activity imply that bills were being rewritten on the floor?[8]

AN IN-DEPTH LOOK AT AMENDING ACTIVITY

The hypothesis that subcommittees defend their legislation by fighting fire with fire suggests a somewhat different interpretation of the rise in floor activity than provided in the literature. The analyses discussed thus far do not distinguish between successful opposition amendments that pass intact and those that pass after being altered by a successful second-degree amendment offered by the proponents. The prevalence of the latter scenario, representing a less substantial victory for the opposition than the former, cannot be determined from existing analyses. This chapter provides a new sample of floor consideration from the postreform period.[9] The sample consists of all eighty measures from the Ninety-eighth Congress (1983–84) that came to the floor under an open rule. For each bill, all amendments listed in the *Congressional Record* were collected. Each amendment was categorized according to (1) whether it was supported or opposed by the bill manager, (2) whether it passed or failed, and (3) if the amendment was opposed, whether the proponents responded to the amendment with a second-degree amendment.

The initial evidence concerns how proponents view the end result of floor consideration after the amending process. If opponents regularly forced committees to accept onerous provisions, there should have been instances when committees opposed a bill as amended.[10] The data suggest this was rarely the case in the Ninety-eighth Congress. Ignoring complications presented by multiple referrals, for seventy-three of seventy-five measures, the measure as amended was supported by its committee, subcommittee (when relevant), and bill manager (see Table 8-2). For the two remaining measures, the reasons that the manager or subcommittee did not support the measure appear unrelated to floor events.[11] This provides only weak evidence that floor events were not beyond the control of the proponents. However, if committees were regularly being "rolled" on the floor, this proportion would be much higher.

The Data

In the sample of 80 bills in the Ninety-eighth Congress, 608 first-degree amendments were offered, of which 475 (or 75 percent) passed.[12] This translates to 6.9 amendments offered per bill, of which 5.1 passed. These amendments are analyzed here in two ways: in terms of (1) the success rates of amendments and (2) contested amendments.

Table 8-2 / Committee Support for Measures as Amended, Ninety-eighth Congress[a]

Recorded vote; manager and a majority of committee voted yes[b]	52
Manager voted no, but a majority of committee voted yes[c]	1
Manager did not vote and only a plurality of committee voted yes[d]	1
Measure passed by a voice vote	21
Divided multiple referrals	
One manager voted no, the other(s) yes; both committees and subcommittees voted yes	3
Majority of one committee voted no, but managers and a majority of the other committees voted yes	1

[a] $n = 79$; one measure was not voted on.
[b] *Committee* here refers to committee (for example, an authorization bill) or subcommittee as relevant.
[c] The Military Construction bill for FY 1985 (H.R. 5604) in which Ronald V. Dellums (D-Calif.) acted as manager and worked to pass the bill but was on record as opposing it and voted against it. No opposed amendments passed.
[d] National Science Foundation Authorization (H.R. 2587): no opposed amendments passed. Hence opposition to (or lack of enthusiasm for) the bill by committee appears unrelated to floor events.
Source: Congressional Record, Ninety-eighth Congress.

Table 8-3 / Success Rates of Amendments, All Measures Considered under an Open Rule, Ninety-eighth Congress[a]

	Number Passed	Number Failed	Percentage Passed
Accepted	369	4	99%
Opposed	40	135	23%

[a] $n = 548$.
Source: Congressional Record, Ninety-eighth Congress.

Success Rates of Amendments The amendments are divided into those supported and those opposed by the bill manager (Table 8-3 based on the manager's statements during the debate (as reported in the *Congressional Record*) or vote, when recorded.[13] The new data appear remarkably similar to Bach's (1986). Both proponents and opponents offered large numbers of amendments and both met with some success. Amendments supported by the subcommittee chair nearly always passed, while those opposed passed a little less than one in four. The latter resulted in forty successful opposition amendments, or one per every other bill.

To assess the hypothesis that subcommittees fight fire with fire, we need

Table 8-4 / Countering Opposed Amendments: Adjusted Opposition Success Rate, Ninety-eighth Congress

	Successfully Countered	Unsuccessfully Countered	Not Countered	Percentage Countered
Opposed amendment				
Passed	23	4	13	58%
Failed	2	10	123	2%

Source: *Congressional Record*, Ninety-eighth Congress.

to examine the fate of opposition amendments by investigating whether an (ultimately) successful opposition amendment is itself successfully amended by the proponents. Data on the proponents' responses to opposition amendments are reported in Table 8-4, which calculates the adjusted opposition success rate. This reveals a striking pattern: most successful opposition amendments (twenty-three out of forty) were successfully amended by the proponents. This leaves the opponents' adjusted success rate at 10 percent (seventeen successes out of 175 amendments). Of the 548 amendments, only seventeen successful opposition amendments passed unamended, or less than one for every four bills.[14]

To put the opposition success in perspective, the distribution of successful opposition amendments by bill needs to be computed. Two remarkable facts emerge. First, most bills (74 percent, or fifty-nine of eighty) had no successful opposition amendments; second, one bill (House Joint Resolution 13, the Nuclear Freeze Resolution of 1983) accounted for 25 percent (ten of forty) of all successful opposition amendments. The analysis also reveals that thirteen bills had one opposition amendment and three had two such amendments. Only five measures had three or more successful opposition amendments.

Further evidence is provided by the contrast between the counterattempts by opponents and countering attempts by proponents. Proponents attempted to counter 68 percent of all successful opposition amendments (twenty-seven of forty), and were usually successful (twenty-three of twenty-seven). In contrast, the opposition attempted to counter only eleven times, or 3 percent of all amendments accepted by the proponents (11 of 369). They succeeded only twice, revealing a striking contrast between the proponents' frequent, successful attempts to counter opposition amendments and the opponents' infrequent, relatively futile attempts to counter amendments accepted by the proponents.

A final observation concerns the interaction of amendments for all first-degree amendments to measures considered under an open rule. A bill's *amendment-tree* type is called *complex* if the amendment was subject to a

Table 8-5 / Frequency of Proponents' Response, by Amendment Type, Ninety-eighth Congress

Amendment Type	Tree Type	
	SIMPLE	COMPLEX
Opposed, passed ($n = 40$)[a]	13 (32.5%)	27 (67.5%)
Opposed, failed ($n = 135$)	123 (91.1%)	12 (8.9%)
All other amendments ($n = 434$)	403 (92.9%)	31 (7.2%)
Total ($n = 609$)	539 (88.5%)	70 (11.5%)

[a] n refer to categories of all floor amendments presented in the House.
Source: Congressional Record, Ninety-eighth Congress.

second-degree or substitute amendment, and *simple* if no second-degree or substitute amendment occurred. Table 8-5 shows the proportions of amendments in the Ninety-eighth that were complex and simple. Complex amendments were relatively rare, occurring only a little over 10 percent of the time in the entire sample. However, marked differences appear after disaggregating the first-degree amendments. For the set of opposed, passed amendments, over two-thirds (or 67.5 percent) had complex amendment trees, indicating considerable interaction on the floor for amendments of this type. In contrast, for all other amendments the frequency was less than one in ten. While second-degree amendments may have been relatively rare, they were strongly targeted to amendments that posed floor challenges.

Analysis of Contested Amendments The lion's share of the amendments in the sample were those accepted by the proponents, nearly of all of which passed. Because this category is likely to include many minor amendments, the discussion follows Smith (1986, 1989) and focuses on *contested amendments,* those for which there was some controversy. These amendments are characterized by a recorded vote for which the margin of success was less than 60 to 40. This excludes minor amendments and provides a sense of how many controversial amendments lurked behind the various categories.

Table 8-6 (see p. 152) presents the data and reveals an important contrast: Most contested amendments were opposed by the bill's manager.[15] While accepted amendments comprised 68 percent of amendments in the entire sample, they comprised only 16 percent (or ten of sixty-three) of contested amendments. Further, while only 23 percent of all opposed amendments passed, 40 percent (or twenty-one of fifty-three) of opposed, contested amendments did. Nonetheless, on average this translates to only one in every four bills having a successful opposed and contested amendment.

Table 8-6 / Success Rates of Contested Amendments, Ninety-eighth Congress

	Number Passed	Number Failed	Percentage Passed
Accepted	8	2	80%
Opposed	21	32	40%
Divided	7	2	78%

Source: Congressional Record, Ninety-eighth Congress.

Table 8-7 / Countering Opposed, Contested Amendments, Ninety-eighth Congress

	Attempted Counter	Successfully Countered	Not Countered	Percentage Countered
Passed	17	13	8	62%
Failed	0	0	32	0%

Source: Congressional Record, Ninety-eighth Congress.

The data on amending activity (Table 8-7) also suggest somewhat higher levels of activity by the proponents who offered counterattempts to 81 percent of all opposed, contested amendments (versus 68 percent of all opposed amendments). They were successful in over three-quarters of their attempts (thirteen of seventeen counterattempts succeeded), yielding 62 percent of contested opposed amendments passed as amended. Proponents made no effort to counter opposed amendments that failed.

Summary of the Data

The data analyzed here tell a somewhat different story from that in the literature. Two factors emerge as critical for any interpretation of the increase in amendments. First, when second-degree amendments are examined, the proponents of legislation appear more successful than when only the aggregate number of amendments are considered. In the sample of measures for the Ninety-eighth Congress, there were only forty successful opposition amendments, or about one to every other measure. Moreover, in twenty-seven cases the proponents made attempts to counter opposition amendments, of which twenty-three succeeded. Proponents thus appear both willing and able to fight fire with fire. In other words, subcommittees remain fundamental for bargaining over what provisions are contained in a bill and play a key role in assembling a majority to support their legislation on the floor. Most changes proposed on the floor that are opposed by a bill manager fail; and of those opposed that eventually pass, more than half are amended by proponents. This does not mean that proponents can pass anything they want. While it implies that they have enough power to remain part of the majority that prefers a bill to the status quo, it says little about how much power or latitude proponents have in determining a bill's content or, equivalently, which majority forms to support the bill.[16]

Second, any argument about the rise in amending activity must explain the role of the large number of successful amendments accepted by the bill manager. The analysis here implies that this category is composed largely of two types of amendments: (1) those that are innocuous and (2) those that represent changes necessary to gain support of a majority agreed on prior to the floor. The latter type provides an explanation for why proponents accept amendments that represent important changes. Many of these changes are agreed on in advance and should not be considered hostile threats seeking to rewrite legislation on the floor.[17] Evidence from the Ninety-eighth Congress supports this interpretation. While most amendments in the entire sample were accepted (68 percent), the analysis of contested amendments shows that only a small proportion were accepted (16 percent). Further, as the case study of the Military Authorization bill later in the chapter reveals, the largest subset of amendments in this category—those accepted and passed by a voice vote—were relatively innocuous.

TWO CASE STUDIES

The data presented thus far mask a large variety of behavior that is difficult to quantify. In an effort to suggest the range of these effects, two case studies of amending activity are considered: the Nuclear Freeze Resolution of 1983 and the Military Authorization for the fiscal year 1985. Because behavior varied considerably over the eighty bills in the sample, the two cases are not meant to be representative; rather, they are intended to suggest something of the range of variation. Both cases studied here were sources of a large number of opposition amendments.

Nuclear Freeze Resolution (1983)

The Nuclear Freeze Resolution (House Joint Resolution 13) concerned possible negotiations with the Soviet Union over nuclear weapons. President Ronald Reagan called for both a freeze on additional nuclear weapons and a "build-down" or reduction in the stock of existing weapons. The Democrats viewed this as a strategic ploy: by asking for too much, the president ensured that the negotiations would fail. The strategy of the proponents of the resolution was to drop the build-down, calling solely for a freeze. The

Table 8-8 / First-degree Amendments to the Nuclear Freeze Resolution, 1983

	Number Passed	Number Failed	Percentage Passed
Accepted	2	0	100%
Opposed	8	3	73%

Source: Congressional Record, Ninety-eighth Congress.

Table 8-9 / Adjusted Opposition Success, Nuclear Freeze Resolution, 1983

	Successfully Countered	Unsuccessfully Countered	Not Countered	Percentage Countered
Opposed Amendment				
Passed	7	1	0	88%
Failed	0	0	3	0%

Source: Congressional Record, Ninety-eighth Congress.

floor strategy of the Reagan supporters was to reestablish the link between a freeze and a build-down via amendments.

A count of all amendments offered by proponents and opponents (both first-degree and second-degree amendments) reveals that there were twenty-two amendments, eighteen of which passed.[18] As Table 8-8 indicates, most of the first-degree amendments were from the opposition (eleven of thirteen, eight of which passed). That eighteen successful amendments passed suggests that the text of the resolution, as amended, differed considerably from that brought to the floor, providing some credence to the assertion that bills are rewritten on the floor. However, the analysis presented in Table 8-9 suggests something quite different. The table, which reports the actual opposition success, shows that of the eight successful opposition amendments only one passed without being successfully countered. Of these eight amendments, moreover, the first seven were virtually emasculated by the counteramendments offered by proponents.[19]

There was one major exception to this activity: The final amendment by Elliott H. Levitas (D-Ga.) was the only opposition amendment not successfully countered. Levitas's amendment weakly linked the freeze and the build-down by adding these words to the resolution: "with such reductions to be achieved within a reasonable, specified period of time."[20] Stephen J. Solarz (D-N.Y.) made the proponents' counteramendment to restore the primacy of the freeze, and this was opposed by Levitas. In contrast to previous attempts by the proponents, this counteramendment failed (210 to

Figure 8-1 / Amendment Tree: Levitas Amendment, Nuclear Freeze Resolution (1983)

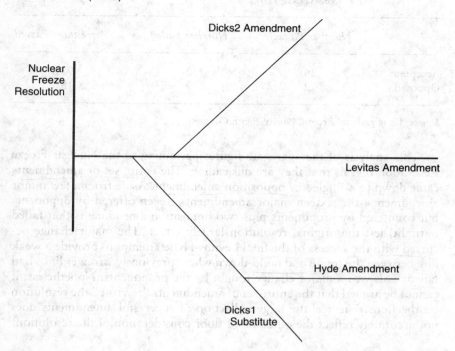

214). The proponents then attempted to counter again when Norm Dicks (D-Wash.) offered a substitute amendment—Dicks—that replaced Levitas's text with "negotiations proceeding immediately to pursuing reductions." Dicks's amendment sought to give freeze supporters a chance to vote for some language favoring reductions while retaining the substance of the original resolution. The opponents offered a counter of their own to the Dicks substitute when Illinois Republican Henry J. Hyde moved an amendment to the substitute that restored Levitas's original language. Finally, Dicks offered another second-degree amendment to the Levitas amendment— Dicks2—using the same language as in his substitute but changing "pursuing" to "pursuing and achieving" reductions. Levitas agreed to support Dicks2. The full amendment tree (minus the failed Solarz amendment to the Levitas amendment) is illustrated in Figure 8-1.

The order and outcome of the voting were as follows: Dicks2 passed by a voice vote, thus amending Levitas's original amendment. Next Hyde's amendment passed (221 to 203), amending the substitute, Dicks1. Then the substitute, as amended by Hyde, was voted against the amendment as amended (Levitas as amended by Dicks2), and won (225 to 191). Finally, the Levitas amendment, as amended by Dicks1 amended by Hyde, passed on a voice vote.

Table 8-10 / Success Rates of Amendments to the Military Authorization Bill, FY 1985 (H.R. 5167)

	Number Passed	Number Failed	Percentage Passed
Accepted	26	2	93%
Opposed	2	9	18%

Source: Congressional Record, Ninety-eighth Congress.

This analysis of the aggregate figures pertaining to the Nuclear Freeze Resolution reveals that they are misleading. The entire set of amendments came down to a single key opposition amendment. Aside from a few minor amendments, the sixteen major amendments (seven offered by opponents but countered by proponents plus two opposition amendments that failed outright) left the original resolution largely intact. The major change occurred with the success of the final Levitas-Hyde attempt to provide a weak link between the freeze and build-down where previously stronger links had failed. This was a major change fought by the proponents. Nonetheless, it cannot be argued that the entire set of amendments "rewrote" the resolution on the floor. Further, the large collection of successful amendments does not accurately reflect the outcome of floor consideration of the resolution.

Military Authorization Bill (FY 1985)

The two military authorization bills from the Ninety-eighth Congress were the target of 17 percent of all amendments in our sample of eighty bills. An in-depth look at H.R. 5167, the more controversial of the two bills, provides a much different picture than the Nuclear Freeze Resolution. H.R. 5167 was a strategic instrument and did not represent what the proponents thought they could defend on the floor. The floor activity, with one important qualification, reveals that the floor manager was able to engineer the fate of the final bill, passing the compromise amendments the manager sought and defeating most of those sought by opponents. The one exception concerned the intervention of the leadership on behalf of the opposition at the very end of the process.

H.R. 5167 was the target of fifty amendments, of which thirty-nine were clearly accepted or opposed by the floor manager. Opponents offered plenty of amendments, though not quite as many as were accepted, and the frequency with which these passed was roughly that of the larger sample (see Table 8-10). A close examination of the opponents' success reveals that, of the two opposed amendments that passed, both were the target of proponents' counterattempts, of which one was successful; of the fifty amendments, only one opposed amendment passed as offered.

The aggregate analysis fails to portray floor contests accurately because not all of the amendments in question were equally important. Table 8-11 (see p. 158) lists the more important amendments: those that were discussed by the *Congressional Quarterly* or subject to a recorded vote. Of these, the three most controversial amendments—the two Bennett amendments and the Brown amendment—are most relevant to our analysis.

As Table 8-11 shows, most attempts to scale back or delete a major program failed if opposed, including one to delete the Trident II missile, one to block deployment of the Pershing II missile, and one to cut $4.5 billion from weapons acquisition. The only opposed amendments that passed were the two offered by Charles E. Bennett (D-Fla.) as part of the MX missile controversy, one of which was effectively countered (for the other, the counterattempt failed). In contrast, all cuts or limitations proposed or accepted by the proponents passed. The most controversial amendment, offered by George E. Brown, Jr. (D-Calif.) in cooperation with Les Aspin (D-Wis.), the bill manager, sought to ban tests of antisatellite (ASAT) missiles.

The key floor controversies involved two issues whose fate became interrelated: The fight over the MX missile and the proposed ban of ASATs. The pro-defense forces favored a strong commitment to both programs, whereas the antidefense forces sought to halt both. In between stood the moderates, with floor leader Aspin seeking to steer a middle ground. This case is especially relevant to an investigation of the ability of committee leaders to engineer bargains and defend them on the floor because there was the potential for many outcomes to receive a majority of support. The compromise arranged prior to floor consideration involved two issues. For the strong supporters, the compromise seems to have authorized the largest number of MX missiles that would command a majority. In exchange for the support of some moderates for this provision, Aspin and his colleagues formulated an amendment banning ASATs, which was opposed by a majority of the committee.

The MX Missile Controversy   The floor fight over continued deployment of the MX missile was announced by the *Congressional Quarterly's Weekly Report* several weeks in advance. The antinuclear group sought to halt further deployment, whereas President Reagan asked for forty new MX missiles. The bill that came to the floor authorized thirty new MX missiles, though it is not clear whether proponents thought they could get these. In an attempt to build a reputation as a moderate, Aspin sought a middle ground between the large-scale effort called for by Reagan and the halt in deployment called for by opponents. Aspin fashioned a compromise in advance of floor consideration that authorized fifteen MX missiles along with some constraints. According to the *Congressional Quarterly*, Aspin came to the floor expecting a close victory with the compromise because it seemed to be the best they could hope for.

Table 8-11 / Success of Attempts to Delete or Scale Back Programs of the Military Authorization Bill, FY 1985 (H.R. 5167)[a]

Amender	Program	Disposition	Contested	Tree Type
Opposed Amendments				
Bennett	Eliminate MX missile	Countered	Yes	Complex
Bennett[b]	Spend on MX missile only after congressional vote	Passed/counter failed	Yes	Complex
Weiss	Delete Trident II missile	Failed	No	Simple
Lowry	Block deployment of Pershing II missile	Failed	No	Simple
Schroeder	Cut $4.5 billion from weapons acquisition	Failed	Yes	Simple
Hartnett	No troops in West Europe	Failed	No	Simple
Dellums	Ban Pershing II missile	Failed	No	Complex
Hunter	Condition on putting troops in Central America[c]	Failed	No	Simple
Accepted Amendments				
Bethune	Moratorium on nerve gas	Passed	Yes	Simple
Brown	Ban testing of ASAT missiles	Passed/opposition counter failed	Yes	Complex
Foley	No troops in Nicaragua or El Salvador	Passed	No	Simple
Nichols	Spare parts contracting[d]	Passed	No	Complex
Amendments with No Statement				
Campbell	No troops in Central America[e]	Passed	No	Complex

[a] With one exception, the table includes *all* amendments discussed by the *Congressional Quarterly Almanac* and the *Congressional Quarterly Weekly Report*, and *all* amendments with a recorded vote. The *Congressional Quarterly Almanac* mentioned an amendment by Stratton that "appeared to block deployment . . . of nuclear armed cruise missiles, or SLCMs, aboard warships . . . unless the Soviet Union had deployed its own nuclear SLCMs." But Stratton also "insisted [that] Soviet missiles were already deployed." Thus, the "political significance of [this amendment] was unclear." This amendment is categorized as "accepted, passed by voice vote" (1984, 43).

[b] A perfecting amendment to Dickinson's amendment (as amended by Price). Dickinson, Price, and Aspin all tried to fend off this opposition amendment. Here the counterattempt was offered prior to the opposed amendment, itself offered as an amendment to the previously passed Foley and Campbell amendments. The counterattempt failed.

[c] While a separate amendment, this was clearly offered as a qualification to the previously passed Foley and Campbell amendments.

[d] Called a "great emphasis on completion," the amendment included parts of a bill from the Committee on Small Business, banning the Pentagon from using lists from which to select contractors for certain contracts (presumably giving small businesses a greater chance).

[e] As amended by Foley to exempt Panama.

Source: Congressional Record.

The major attempt by opponents to eliminate the MX missile was offered by Bennett (D-Fla.) on 16 May 1984. The debate over the MX missile lasted throughout the day and into the evening. In response to Bennett's amendment, the proponents offered a compromise authorizing fifteen missiles.[21] There were three other amendments and counteramendments as the proponents and opponents jockeyed for position, the result being success by the proponents, 218 to 212. Such a close margin of victory suggests that proponents got the most they could, and that the initial authorization of thirty missiles (without any qualifications) was not feasible.

The Ban on ASATs   Aspin sought to ban the use of funds for testing ASAT missiles. Antidefense members supported this move; pro-defense forces, including majority of the committee, opposed it. Here, too, Aspin was successful. Offered by Brown, the amendment prohibited testing of ASATs unless the Soviets had tested a "dedicated" ASAT system after enactment of the legislation. The pro-defense forces countered by offering a substitute that would allow tests only if the president certified that talks with the Soviets about limiting ASATs would resume. In addition, the pro-defense amendment limited the number of ASAT tests to that made by the Soviets. Ultimately, the Brown amendment passed unchanged by a close vote of 228 to 186.

Other Amendments   Most of the amendments to the military authorization bill, like those of the entire sample, were accepted and passed. Nearly all of these amendments passed without much opposition and without a recorded vote (twenty-three of the twenty-six amendments were accepted and passed). Of these, only two were mentioned by the *Congressional Quarterly*. To indicate the content of the remaining twenty-one amendments, a random sample of one-third of the amendments was examined and found to contain only minor or innocuous provisions. One amendment, for example, directed the secretary of defense to reimburse Temistocles Ramirez for the confiscation of his farm in Honduras for use as the Region Military Training Center. Another required that the president release to Congress an existing report on Soviet compliance to arms control treaties.[22]

Summary of Cases

In the two cases studied here, the proponents usually succeeded in floor confrontations and most opposition amendments failed or were successfully countered. For the Nuclear Freeze Resolution, the twenty-two total and eighteen successful amendments were shown to overstate the amount of change resulting from floor consideration. These amendments amounted to just one change in the measure, not a wholesale revision in the resolution's contents. For the military authorization bill, the major compromise with the antidefense forces by Aspin resulted in cuts in the MX missile and a ban on testing ASATs. The closeness of the vote on the MX contest suggests that it was the best proponents could hope for. Further, the sample of accepted, passed amendments not mentioned by the *Congressional Quarterly* revealed these to be largely innocuous.

The discussion of the ASAT ban reveals something of the limits of committee power in the postreform House. While Aspin successfully defended his compromise on the floor, opponents within the Democratic party were able to modify this in cooperation with the leadership.[23] Further, the ASAT ban proposed in conjunction with Aspin was opposed by a majority of the committee, reminding us that committees do not speak with one voice. As suggested earlier, this reflected Aspin's goal—to steer a middle ground between defense proponents and opponents, thus gaining the support of the moderates within the Democratic party. The balance was a delicate one, and the moderates and party leaders were able to alter the bill on the floor.

INSTITUTIONAL CHANGE IN THE POSTREFORM CONGRESS

The perspective on institutions developed thus far provides a new interpretation of the postreform House. The transition from eighteen to twenty powerful committee chairs to 125 less powerful subcommittee chairs significantly weakened the ability of the new committee and subcommittee leaders to protect their bills on the floor. Prior to the reforms, long-term stability combined with sanctions allowed a system of informal norms to support cooperation on the floor. But with the institutional changes accomplished by the reforms, informal means were no longer adequate to prevent breakdown on the floor.

The preceding analysis has emphasized the aggressive floor participation of subcommittee leaders. Since this is an imperfect and less efficacious substitute for previous methods (Weingast 1989), the theory of institutions predicts that members of Congress will search for and adopt other mechanisms and institutions that help bridge the gap (Collie and Cooper 1989; Weingast 1991). This is unlikely to occur all at once. In the face of significant uncertainty about what strategies, conventions, or rules will succeed, considerable experimentation and dead ends can be expected. As successful strategies emerge, however, they will be repeated so that selection and survival eventually yield a new collection of methods that promote floor success.

This analysis advances the thesis that the four major behavioral and institutional practices listed at the start of the chapter as central changes in the postreform Congress play a role in promoting floor success. That is, they constitute a counterrevolution, mitigating some of the unintended effects of the reforms (Smith 1989). The role of aggressive participation in amending activity has already been shown. Our focus now turns to how the other three major developments in Congress also play the role of promoting floor success: (1) the decline of the open rule and the concomitant rise of restrictive rules; (2) the increased use of multiple referrals; and (3) the increased role of the leadership, especially its control over the Rules Committee. It must be noted that promoting floor success only partly explains these phenomena; it is not necessarily the sole explanation. Nonetheless, floor success is an essential component of such an explanation.

The Rise of Restrictive Rules

Restrictive rules allow greater control over floor events by limiting the number and content of amendments to those agreed on beforehand (and hence specified in the rule). They therefore restrict negotiation over a bill's contents to the prefloor stage. Because restrictive rules often completely control the motions allowed on the floor, they greatly enhance the enforcement of logrolls and other bargains (Weingast 1990). In particular, they deter another faction from tempting one of the parties to the original bargain to defect and support a new amendment.

Research on the substitution of restrictive rules for the open rule in recent congresses reveals a profound change. Bach and Smith (1988) report that in the Ninety-ninth Congress, the open rule declined to barely over a half (55 percent) of all rules governing floor consideration, whereas ten years earlier it governed 84 percent (see Table 8-12, p. 162). Restrictive rules often specify all amendments that will be voted on and the order in which they will be considered. Just over a half of all restrictive rules for the Ninety-seventh to Ninety-ninth Congresses allowed only one or two amendments. These, plus those bills considered under a closed rule (allowing no amendments or only committee amendments) averaged 34 percent of all rules for the Ninety-seventh to Ninety-ninth Congresses.

The greater the degree of controversy, the more likely are the players to obtain restrictive rules. Bach and Smith (1988) collected the rules governing the votes deemed by the *Congressional Quarterly* as "key votes," presumably those votes drawing the greatest controversy. In comparison with all bills obtaining rules, controversial issues as reflected in key votes were far more likely to be considered under a restrictive rule. For the Ninety-fourth Congress, 37 percent of all key votes and only 15 percent of all other bills were considered under a restrictive rule (see Table 8-12). By the Ninety-ninth Congress, 86 percent of all key votes and only 45 percent of all bills received restrictive or closed rules.

A study of amendments under restrictive rules that parallels this chapter's study of amendments under open rules shows that restrictive rules are quite successful in reducing amendments (Weingast 1991). When the restrictive rule specifies the entire set of amendments to be offered, fewer amendments and opposed amendments pass than under less restrictive or open rules.

Table 8-12 / The Rise of Restrictive Rules, Ninety-fourth to Ninety-ninth
Congresses, 1975–1986

	Congress			
	94TH	96TH	98TH	99TH
All Measures[a]				
Open rules	84%	69%	64%	55%
Restrictive rules	11	20	22	34
Closed rules	4	11	14	11
(*n* =)	(248)	(180)	(125)	(101)
Key Votes[b]				
Open rules	64%	52%	32%	14%
Restrictive rules	32	40	64	73
Closed rules	5	8	5	14
(*n* =)	(22)	(25)	(22)	(22)

[a] *All measures* are all measures reaching the House floor under a special rule during a given
Congress.
[b] Key vote measures are those involving at least one *key vote* as identified by *Congressional
Quarterly*.
Source: Bach and Smith 1988, table 3-3.

This discussion of restrictive rules leads to several conclusions. First,
since the mid-1970s the open rule has declined as the major vehicle governing floor consideration. Second, more controversial measures tend to
receive restrictive rules. Third, the evidence suggests that restrictive rules
strongly reduce amendment possibilities and occurrences. Finally, taken together, these conclusions imply that restrictive rules are an effective mechanism for managing floor consideration and passing legislation. They avoid
the uncertainty of floor consideration under the open rule (as noted by Bach
and Smith 1988) and allow committee and party leaders to engineer agreements over legislation that can be enforced on the floor.

Multiple Referrals

Multiple referrals have attracted considerable attention in the recent literature (Bawn 1990; Collie and Cooper 1989; Davidson and Oleszek 1987;
and Bach and Smith 1988). These scholars stress the role of increasing
jurisdictional fragmentation of the last two decades. Many policy issues
now cut across committees; for example, energy, the environment, and national security (see Collie and Cooper 1989). The resulting jurisdictional
fragmentation implies an increase in the demand for coordination of legislation across committees.

One key feature of multiple referrals is that they help members of sub-committees of different committees negotiate an agreement and then enforce it on the floor.[24] In the postreform House, members of a particular sub-committee may have more in common with members of a subcommittee on another committee than with other members of their own committee. Specialization in these policy areas therefore requires regular relations with other subcommittees. As Collie and Cooper (1989, 262-63) emphasize, mul-tiple referrals are an "adaptive response" to this new situation that "relieves strains 'in' the operational effectiveness of its committee and party sys-tems."[25] Multiple referrals thus make coordination of new legislation across committees far easier, especially at the crucial stage of floor consideration.

In contrast, during the earlier period, when most issues were the concern of a single committee, an exchange of support across subcommittees within a single committee was relatively easy to enforce: two subcommittees of a single committee could always bring their legislation to the floor in a single omnibus bill. A powerful and stable set of committee chairs could typically enforce exchange across committees when called for.

To illustrate the potential problems of enforcing legislative bargains on the floor, suppose that two subcommittees from different committees want to form a logroll between one another's measures. If the exchange involves two separate bills considered on the floor at different times, it leaves the bargaining partners in an asymmetric position. After having obtained their piece of legislation, the subcommittee whose measure is voted on first has an incentive to renege by withdrawing its support for the second bill. By contrast, the incentives to renege are significantly reduced if the two sub-committees can bring their measures to the floor in a single bill.[26]

One advantage of multiple referrals is that they extend this method of enforceability beyond committees by providing a means to combine com-ponents of legislation from two or more committees, allowing a single up or down vote on the package. Multiple referrals thus become a flexible tool of the leadership for protecting certain exchanges across subcommittees from falling apart on the floor.[27]

The Leadership

The party leadership has been known for its role in coalition maintenance and its close cooperation with committee leaders for success on the floor (Ripley 1967; Sinclair 1983). More recently, this has involved cooperation with subcommittee leaders (Deering and Smith 1981; Oppenheimer 1981) and the majority in the Democratic party (Sinclair 1989b; Cox and McCubbins 1990; Rohde 1990).

The leadership clearly must play a part in the situation developed earlier, for it takes part in the necessary negotiations among players that lead to restrictive rules and the decision about whether a bill obtains a multiple referral.[28] Similarly, the role of the Rules Committee, in cooperation with the leadership, is to "arbitrate [disputes among committees] in an effort to keep jurisdictional fights from reaching the floor," and "to keep the amending process and debate within boundaries and to prevent floor obstruction and the unraveling of legislation" (Oppenheimer 1981, 216, 220). Multiple referrals and restrictive rules are key tools in this effort.[29]

Party leaders work closely with committee and subcommittee leaders to help the latter succeed on the floor. This is not to suggest that the leadership helps subcommittees impose their will on the rest of the House. Rather, the leadership helps subcommittee leaders negotiate an agreement for support by a majority and then to maintain this agreement on the floor. In the postreform period, this negotiation implies that the price for a restrictive rule is a greater role by the majority party in the contents of the legislation. Moreover, for controversial measures, bargaining for support on the floor must include a wider range of individuals because they must agree to support a restrictive rule that removes their ability to offer amendments (Weingast 1991).

Not only does the party leadership decide which measures will be governed by multiple referrals and restrictive rules, but it also plays a role in determining the balance between the interests represented on the committee and those of the rest of the majority party. The case of the FY 1985 military authorization bill illustrates the fine balance between these contending groups. In the postreform House, this balance is no longer left up to the proponents of legislation and their committees, and intervention by the leadership can affect the balance. The new environment of the late 1980s and early 1990s provides a trade-off in the balance of power. From the standpoint of committee members, the advantage of the powerful new tools is that they promote greater floor success of measures on the floor. The disadvantage is that they institutionalize the influence of the majority party via the leadership over the legislation's contents. Whether this has shifted the balance of power away from committees to party majorities—and if so, by how much—cannot be evaluated without further research. It is fair to say, however, that as long as majority party members prefer a viable system of specialization, the leadership will use multiple referrals and restrictive rules to support specialization and to give committees an important influence over their legislation.

CONCLUSION

The view of institutions taken in this chapter derives from the literature following Coase (1937, 1960), known as the "new economics of organization." The key idea is that institutions place constraints on action or behavior in particular ways. Two fundamental insights of this literature include (1) not all exchanges or bargains can be enforced and (2) when problems are anticipated, parties will either avoid the bargain or attempt to devise institutions and constraints that mitigate the source of the problem.[30]

This chapter has focused on the evolving patterns of interaction on the floor in the postreform Congress. The reforms weakened the older, relatively centralized committee power centers, leading to more decentralized and larger subcommittee power centers. The older techniques for maintaining bargains on the floor—that is, to ensure committee success on the floor—began to break down. Scholars have examined the erosion of the well-known norms underpinning the committee system of the prereform era: specialization, reciprocity, and apprenticeship (Smith 1989). However, this erosion does not in itself imply that the system of specialization via committees has broken down. Rather, members have adopted new strategies and devised new institutions and practices that are more appropriate for the new circumstances (Collie and Cooper 1989; Smith 1989). As long as the gains from exchange among different members of Congress persist, the theory of institutions predicts that members will search for means of capturing them (Weingast 1990).

This analysis uses the approach to institutions noted earlier to interpret the major phenomena observed in Congress as a new underpinning of success on the floor. Because the opportunities to break apart any coalition supporting a bill during floor consideration are ubiquitous, a strong committee system requires a means to prevent coalitions from falling apart on the floor. As the older, informal means for maintaining support on the floor began to erode, challenges in the form of amendments increased. In response, proponents began substituting more aggressive floor defense of their bills, resulting in a rise in amending activity. An in-depth investigation of amending activity shows that while the number of amendments per bill is much larger in the postreform period, for the Ninety-eighth Congress this reflects neither chaos nor the rewriting of bills that were being rewritten on the floor. Proponents seem able to defend their legislation on the floor and, when necessary, to fight fire with fire. Major threatening amendments by opponents are usually met with counteramendments that also succeed, and often these are wholly emasculating. Another finding concerns the largest category of amendments—those accepted by the bill manager and that typically pass. The interpretation provided earlier suggests that these amendments are not attempts to rewrite legislation on the floor; rather, they are either innocuous (especially if passed by a voice vote) or represent changes negotiated prior to the floor stage in order to build majority support.

The institutional perspective suggests that fighting fire with fire alone was insufficient for proponents to defend successfully their legislation on the floor in the early postreform period. Thus along with a rise in amending emerged new institutions and practices—restrictive rules, multiple referrals, and a larger role for the leadership and Rules Committee. These institutions and practices evolved in part to promote floor success of agreements forged prior to the floor. Restrictive rules, for example, are a mechanism for directly managing floor consideration and hence are used to protect agreements to pass the most controversial legislation (Weingast 1991). Similarly, this accounts in part for the increased power of the leadership, especially its close working relationship with the Rules Committee. This relationship is a necessary component of any system to manage floor controversies via specialized rules.

Finally, this interpretation suggests that the adaptive strategies are succeeding in their role, providing mechanisms for enforcing agreement on the floor. While it appears that the number of amendments and resulting problems of success on the floor declined in the late 1980s (Smith 1989), further research is needed to support this conclusion.

The data and analysis in this chapter do not provide a complete picture of floor activity under the open rule in the postreform House. Many questions remain unanswered. For example, inasmuch as the data here are from 1983–84, how much of the ability of proponents to control floor fates of legislation is due to the shift from open to restrictive rules? Would similar results be found for the earlier postreform Congresses? How much power have subcommittees lost in comparison with their full committee predecessors? That is, how much has the balance shifted between the centralized leadership and party majorities on the one hand and committees and their subcommittees on the other? The analysis presented here sheds only modest light on these important issues.

Despite the open-ended nature of this investigation, two implications of congressional change can be suggested. First, strategies adapted to new circumstances are important. Second, these strategies emerge from behavioral change—fighting fire with fire—and institutional evolution—restrictive rules and multiple referrals.

Acknowledgments

The author gratefully acknowledges the helpful comments of Stanley Bach, Randy Calvert, Joseph Cooper, Roger Davidson, John Ferejohn, Morris Fiorina, Keith Krehbiel, John Kingdom, Mathew McCubbins, Kenneth Shepsle, and Steven Smith; and the research assistance of Mike Caldwell. The National Science Foundation provided funds for partial support (SES-8617516).

Notes

1. See for example, Davidson and Oleszek (1977); Rieselbach (1978, 1986), Shepsle (1988); and Sundquist (1981). This does not imply that committees have lost all their powers.
2. Analyses of institutional change in the reform era can be found in Davidson and Oleszek (1977); Rieselbach (1978, 1986); and Shepsle (1988). See the latter for further development of the "textbook" Congress.
3. This discussion is based on the development in Weingast (1989). See also Bach (1988); Oleszek (1989); and Deschler and Brown (1984).
4. As is well known, whether the long-run incentives are sufficient to outweigh short-run ones depends on how heavily individuals discount future benefits, among other things.
5. Smith (1986) emphasizes the breakdown of older norms, such as specialization by committee, reciprocity across committees, and the like.

6. Further evidence about this phenomenon is contained in Fenno (1973). Fenno's (1966, 449–53) study of the appropriations process also provides evidence of the committee success in defending legislation against amendments.

7. Bach concludes, "it appears that the committee's ability to protect its bills against being changed on the floor has weakened considerably in the years since the mid-1970s." Further, Appropriations subcommittee chairs have "clearly" had "increasing difficulty in convincing their colleagues to vote against the floor amendments that the chair(s) oppose." (1986, 48).

8. Moreover, some evidence suggests that the rise of amendments may have peaked in 1980 (Smith 1989, chaps. 1, 2).

9. Many of the conventions used to define relevant categories are taken from previous studies, esp. the work of Bach and Smith (1989).

10. Of course, since a necessary condition for being included in the conference committee was that members support the measure, committee members might vote for a measure as amended even though they oppose it because they want to participate in the conference delegation.

11. Only two of the seventy-five cases present some doubt. For H.R. 5604, the bill manager, Ronald V. Dellums (D-Calif.) worked to pass his subcommittee's bill, though he stated personally he was against it and later voted against it. For the cases of multiple referrals with divided responsibility, not all subcommittees are equal partners; some are forced to accept bills they would rather reject. Without a more extensive investigation, then, these cases cannot be separated from those in which a desired bill was transformed on the floor into an undesired one.

12. Following Bach (1986) this excludes substitute amendments.

13. This procedure closely follows Bach (1986) and allowed 548 of the 608 amendments to be classified. Of the remaining sixty amendments, forty-nine were unclear because the bill manager made no statement and the amendments were considered by a voice vote. This category is likely to be composed primarily of innocuous amendments because (a) the bill manager did not deem them worthy of a statement of support or opposition and (b) no one called for a recorded vote. Following Bach (1986) these are excluded. Most of the other eleven concerned bills were multiple referrals in which the two managers from different committees were divided on the amendment.

14. The recent work of Smith (1989, chap. 6) on second-degree amendments corroborates these findings.

15. The calculations that follow ignore those amendments classified as "divided," typically a multiple referral in which the two managers from different committees disagreed about an amendment.

16. Two additional hypotheses follow from this perspective. First, the computation of actual opposition success (Tables 8-6 and 8-10) reveals that proponents by and large do not attempt to counter those opposition amendments that fail. This suggests that they know with a high degree of confidence which amendments are threats (see also Smith 1989, 185–86). Second, since proponents can predict which opposition amendments will fail, and since countering is always feasible and usually successful, when we observe no attempt by proponents to counter, it is because the amendment does not pose a serious threat to the bill. Only further research can determine the validity of these hypotheses.

17. A further hypothesis about this category of amendments is the following. During the "textbook" period, changes in legislation needed to garner majority support were incorporated into the bill prior to coming to the floor. In the postreform period, these changes are made via a floor amendment agreed on in advance. The advantage of the latter strategy is that it enhances the amender's credit-claiming ability.

18. Not including two unsuccessful opposition motions—one to "strike the enacting clause" and the other to recommit.

19. For example, Hank Brown (R-Colo.) "proposed an amendment that would have given equal priority to a freeze and to Reagan's goal of nuclear arms reduction as the twin goals of arms negotiations" (Congressional Quarterly Almanac 1983, 208). However, to this amendment, Jim Leach (R-Iowa) offered a counteramendment "restoring the primacy of the freeze" (Congressional Quarterly Almanac 1983, 208). Another opposition amendment called for the freeze resolution to expire in eighteen months unless a build-down negotiation was completed in that period. The proponents countered by replacing the text of the amendment with "proceed to negotiating a build-down as soon as is practicable." Furthermore, in two cases amendments

to establish a build-down were outright—offered by Mark D. Siljaner (R-Mich.) and Levitas (D-Ga.). With one exception, other amendments were relatively minor.

20. The Elliott H. Levitas amendment is labeled as weak in comparison with, for example, one specifying a rigid, eighteen-month time limit. Because of its weak form, it was not immediately classified by the resolution's floor manager, Clement J. Zablocki (Chairman of the Foreign Affairs Committee) as opposed; instead, he considered it "worthy of consideration." However, the amendment was eventually defended as defusing the resolution's intended criticism of the administration, and hence the proponents attempted to counter.

21. Along with some qualifications, notably that the funds could not be spent during the first six months of the fiscal year and, after that date, only if the president had not certified that the Soviets had returned to the bargaining table to negotiate the elimination of the missiles.

22. A similar analysis of one-third of the nine amendments reveals that the amendments receiving no statement from the managers appear equally innocuous. One amendment limited the involvement of the secretary of defense in the study of nuclear winter, the climatic consequences of nuclear war; another prohibited the use of live animals in training medics to treat bullet wounds.

23. After Aspin's apparent floor success, the issue was raised again, two weeks later on May 31. While the proponents expected the opponents to reoffer their ban, the latter took a different tack: they sought to add the qualification that Congress must vote to approve spending six months later; that is, the issue must be reopened at that time. The vote was close (198 to 197) and the opposition succeeded only with concerted leadership aid. (*Congressional Quarterly Weekly Report*, June 2, 1984, 1291–93). (*Congressional Quarterly* also reported that in a rare move, Speaker O'Neill voted with the opposition.)

24. This is not the only use of multiple referrals. See Collie and Cooper (1989) for the different forms of multiple referrals.

25. Further, "multiple referral has enhanced the House's ability for building majority coalitions and passing laws" (Cooper and Collie 1989, 264–65).

26. This situation is analyzed in detail in Weingast and Marshall (1988). To give a further indication of why the package is less vulnerable, notice that if the group whose measure was considered first (now as the first title of a single package) attempts to act opportunistically by supporting an amendment that deleted the second group's measure, the second group can withdraw its support from the entire package (now, as amended), thereby defeating both parts. Combining measures in a single package provides the second group with a credible threat over the first group, thereby mitigating the latter's incentive to renege.

27. Because multiple referrals play a key role in enforcing agreements across committees, the approach used here suggests that several types of conventions will emerge that will limit the leadership's discretion over their use and provide the basis for members' expectations over their use. The first set of conventions concerns the circumstances in which the conventions will be used; the second, the emergence of relatively stable agreements among subcommittees about how to split the jurisdiction on a complex issue. Further research is called for on these issues.

28. Multiple referrals and restrictive rules thus necessarily change the locus of bargaining. Similarly, autonomy of subcommittee is not the same as that of the (older) committees. On this aspect, and the modern leadership more generally, see Sinclair (1989b).

29. Undoubtedly, the level of leadership discretion is higher in the postreform period than during the textbook phase, if only because it cannot manage all bills and hence must choose which bills to devote its effort. See Sinclair (1989) on the role of the leadership in choosing a national agenda for the Democratic party.

30. This principle is surprisingly powerful and underlies a wide range of work in the social sciences. While its main applications are to the theory of the firm (see, for example, Williamson 1985; Milgrom and Roberts 1990), it has been successfully applied to economic history (North 1981, 1987) and political science (Cox and McCubbins 1990; Kieweit and McCubbins 1991; Moe 1984, 1989; Shepsle and Weingast 1987; Weingast 1984; and Weingast and Marshall 1988).

9 / The Senate in the Postreform Era

STEVEN S. SMITH

Is there a *postreform Senate*? We know that the House of Representatives of recent years did not turn out as predicted.[1] In the years immediately following the reforms of the early 1970s, most congressional observers agreed that the House had an unsuppressible urge for decentralization. In fact, the urge proved suppressible, at least temporarily, making it reasonable to label the House of recent years a *postreform House*. The House has become more partisan, more centralized, even more dependent on flexible special rules; it is also less individualistic and more efficient. Furthermore, the autonomy of House committees has declined and the policy contributions of the minority party are more limited.

The idea of a postreform Senate also has some appeal. After all, the Senate shared with the House many of the reforms comprising the Legislative Reorganization Act of 1970, adopted further reforms of its own in the 1970s, and has been influenced by many of the same forces that led to further change in House politics since the reforms were enacted. But are the features of the postreform House found in the Senate as well?

CONDITIONS SHAPING DECISION-MAKING PROCESSES IN CONGRESS

To begin, we need to examine some general propositions about the forces that shape decision making in Congress. These considerations will lead us to expect certain similarities and differences between the House and Senate. They will also lead us to expect that some but not all features of the postreform House can be found in the Senate.

Both chambers have three major institutional features: a committee system, a party system, and a parent chamber. The interaction among committees, parties, and chamber defines the decision-making processes of the House and Senate. Because the Constitution is silent on how Congress should organize itself, each chamber is left to its own devices; that is, each chamber's decision-making process is the product of collective choice. And because preferences about process often are influenced by preferences about policy, the chambers' decision-making processes are in flux. Change occurs in response to the character of policy problems facing Congress, the alignment of policy preferences among members, and the degree of conflict

169

among the House, Senate, and White House. In addition, change is influenced by structures and procedures inherited from the past.

Policy Agenda

Generally, the larger the agenda, the more separable the issues are and the more frequently issues recur; the less salient the issues, the more a chamber relies on committees to make public policy choices. Large agendas composed of many disconnected issues require a division of labor that committees provide. If the issues recur year after year, then committee members have an incentive to specialize and develop expertise, which enhances efficiency. And if most members' political interests are unaffected by most issues, then deferring to the members of a committee is quite natural. Conversely, more focused or changing agendas, particularly those affecting the interests of most members, are less likely to yield deference to committees and more likely to foster active parties and parent chambers.

Alignment of Policy Preferences

The national policy agenda and election results are the major forces shaping the voting alignments in Congress. But whatever the source, the alignment of policy preferences influences how each chamber makes policy decisions. When many issues are salient and the majority party is highly cohesive, the leadership of the majority party tends to assert itself and decision making is more centralized. However, when the majority party lacks cohesiveness and many issues are salient, effective decision making tends to drift to the chamber floor, where rank-and-file members of both parties, regardless of their committee assignments, can seek to contribute to public policy.

Strategic Context

Legislating is typically a three-player game involving the House, the Senate, and the president. Therefore, the ease with which legislators can achieve their policy objectives depends not only on the distribution of preferences within their chamber but also on the preferences of the other chamber and the president. The more disadvantaged a majority coalition is by the preferences of the other chamber and the president, the more important it is for the coalition to use its organizational and procedural resources effectively and efficiently. In general, a majority coalition facing an opposing chamber or president tends to focus and streamline its own decision-making processes. When the majority coalition coincides with the majority party, party leaders' powers and discretion are strengthened in the face of strong opponents in the other chamber or the White House.

Institutional Context

The ability to delegate decision-making responsibility to committees or party leaders depends on chamber rules and the difficulty of changing those rules. For example, past decisions about rules governing structure and procedure may limit the extent to which changes in agendas and policy alignments reshape decision-making processes. Further, the more robust are individual and minority rights in chamber rules, the more difficult it is to decentralize power in the committee system or to centralize power in the party leadership.

House-Senate Differences

In each case—the agenda, policy alignment, strategic context, and institutional context—there are important differences between the House and Senate. Underlying many of these differences are some fundamental elements: the Senate's smaller size; the larger, more diverse character of senators' constituencies; and senators' staggered and longer terms of office (Baker 1989; Fenno 1982).

Consider the policy agenda. Broadly speaking, the House and Senate agendas are quite similar. The president's legislative program plays a prominent role in both chambers and, beyond that, the policy problems that trouble members of the House generally trouble members of the Senate as well. Thus, in the aggregate, the characteristics of the issues are likely to be similar in the two chambers.

Yet there are also subtle and not-so-subtle differences between the House and Senate agendas. Most obviously, the Senate carries the burden of presidential nominations and treaties, many of which are given priority by the president. Controversial appointments and treaties often force the Senate to set aside other business to create time to debate and vote on them. And those that do not interest the entire Senate require the attention of selected senators or their staffs. Thus, the Senate is more enmeshed than the House in foreign policy questions, though in recent decades the House has emerged as a more equal partner in foreign affairs.

Moreover, senators' larger and more heterogeneous constituencies— which tend to make Senate elections more competitive—lead senators to interest themselves in a broader range of issues than is true of most representatives of the House (Fenno 1982, 103). Issues of only moderate importance are likely to interest a larger proportion of the Senate than of the House. In addition, heterogeneous constituencies may at times lead senators to see connections between issues that representatives can safely ignore. Thus, we expect senators to be less willing to defer to committees and more insistent on their individual right to contribute to policy outcomes.

The alignment of policy preferences in the Senate and House is likely to differ as well. While the partisanship reflected in policy alignments within Congress is the result of many factors, its most important source is the electoral constituencies of members in the two parties (Rohde, this volume, Chapter 2). Here, too, the House and Senate differ to a measurable degree. Different bases of representation (states versus districts), terms of office (staggered six-year terms for senators versus two-year terms for representatives), and constituency characteristics (size, heterogeneity) are likely to produce a somewhat different mix of constituency demands and different party and ideological balances in the two chambers. The degree of cohesion within the parties and polarization between the parties are likely to differ.

Strategic context is, in part, a product of policy alignments. If the alignment of policy preferences in the two chambers differs, so too will their strategic contexts. This was most obvious in 1981–86, when Republicans controlled the Senate and White House and Democrats maintained control of the House. House Democrats were thrown into a defensive position after the 1980 election, having been in a position earlier to take the initiative on a number of matters during the Carter administration.

Finally, institutional context clearly differs in the two chambers. Senate rules protect individuals' and the minority's right to participate far more than do House rules. The rights to filibuster and to offer nongermane amendments on the Senate floor give senators leverage with committees and party leaders that representatives of the House do not have. This difference is critical in several respects: the Senate's agenda is not as readily manipulated by majority party leaders; individuals and minorities can more easily obstruct the consideration of legislation, including measures to modify the Senate's formal rules; and changes in the policy position of a simple majority are less likely to produce changes in policy in the Senate.

There is an important implication of these interchamber differences in terms of the notion of a postreform Senate: The forces that tend to produce greater centralization (that is, a more focused and salient agenda, greater partisanship, and strategic weakness) are more likely to produce change in House decision-making processes than in Senate decision-making processes. Oscillations in decision-making style are likely to occur within a narrower range in the Senate than in the House. To be sure, the Senate is not insulated from change. Indeed, it has changed in important ways since the 1950s (Fenno 1989b; Sinclair 1989c). However, for good institutional reasons, less distinctive eras of change are apparent in the Senate.

THE CONGRESSIONAL ENVIRONMENT

Four features of the congressional environment have contributed to the distinctive postreform character of House politics: the predominance of budget issues on the policy agenda, Republican control of the White House, the divergence of the electoral bases of the two parties, and pressures associated with gaining reelection. On all four counts there are great similarities between the House and the Senate as well as important differences.

Policy Agenda

Budget issues share an equally prominent place on the agendas of both chambers—and with similar effects. Budget measures associated with efforts to control deficits had top priority in both chambers during the 1980s and early 1990s. Many legislative initiatives with spending or taxing consequences were quashed because of fiscal constraints; many policies were altered with the deficit in mind. And many measures—particularly appropriations bills and other measures with direct fiscal implications—were delayed, considered on an emergency basis late in sessions, or rolled up into catch-all spending and deficit-reduction bills. Separate measures considered and passed fell in number, while the average length of measures increased greatly. In both chambers, then, the deficit issues had the effect of consolidating the agenda and increasing the salience of measures with deficit implications. The deficit and the political conflict over budgets increased the importance and size of large, omnibus measures such as continuing resolutions and reconciliation bills.

Associated with the budget politics of the 1980s and early 1990s was a decline in the number of policy innovations pushed by the administration or by members of Congress. A tight budget limited new initiatives, as did conservative presidents and their congressional allies who favored restraining federal activity. Even after the election of George Bush in 1988, few major federal programs were proposed. Increasingly, the agenda consisted of reauthorizing and modifying established programs.

In both chambers, then, the policy agenda contracted, issues became more interconnected, and budgeting gained importance.

Strategic Context

The strategic context in both chambers changed dramatically after the 1980 elections. The majority party Democrats in the House found themselves in a defensive posture. Their task was to preserve their favored programs from the new Republican president and Senate. Their precarious position in the early 1980s—it has been argued—is associated with the distinctive postreform character of the House. The Democrats' need to act more effectively as a party eventually stimulated more assertive leadership on the part of Speakers Thomas "Tip" O'Neill and James Wright and, to a lesser extent, Thomas S. Foley (Sinclair 1989a). The surge in partisan activity was reflected in greater use of the formal tools of majority party leadership—committee assignments, bill referral, special rules, scheduling—and more active party committees and task forces under leaders' direction. The minority House Republicans relied on the White House to lead their party and exerted little influence over the contours of House decision-making processes.

The 1980 change in party control in the Senate mirrored that of the

White House. During the early Reagan years, the Republicans looked to the White House for an agenda and leadership; the minority Democrats were in no position to adjust the Senate's decision-making processes to their needs. There was less pressure to alter decision-making patterns in the Senate in the early 1980s than there was in the House. The open question is whether or not the Democrats, once they regained majority party status in the 1986 elections but continued to face popular Republican presidents, were sufficiently motivated to alter their traditional ways of running their party and the Senate.

Electoral Environment and Policy Preferences

Observers of the postreform House emphasize changes in the electoral environment. Yet the Senate's electoral environment is also distinctive, in part because of the Senate's equal representation of the states, staggered six-year terms, more heterogeneous constituencies, and greater appeal to ambitious politicians (Jacobson 1986, 93–95). The party balance is the most conspicuous manifestation of differences in the chambers' electoral environments. In the Senate of the 1980s neither party controlled more than 55 percent of the seats; both parties averaged almost exactly fifty seats each and both managed to achieve majority status. In the House, however, Democrats controlled no less than 55.9 percent of the seats (1981–82), gained as much as 61.8 percent (1983–84), and averaged 58.9 percent during the 1980s.

Underlying the Senate's partisan balance are more competitive election contests. In the 1946–88 period, about 75 percent of senators who sought reelection were successful compared to 91.6 percent of House members (Ornstein, Mann, and Malbin 1990, 56–57). However, this does not mean turnover was greater in the Senate than in the House. If House incumbents' success rate is calculated over a six-year period—the length of a Senate term—it is not much higher than the rate for Senate incumbents. During the 1946–88 period, House incumbents' success rate for the average six-year period was 76.9 percent. Nevertheless, in a typical election, Senate incumbents seeking reelection cannot be as confident about the outcome as can House incumbents. In recent decades, fewer than half of Senate incumbents won with 60 percent or more of the vote, while more than two-thirds of House incumbents won by that margin. The percentage of such "safe" incumbents has increased in both chambers since World War II, though House incumbents have improved their track records far more than have Senate incumbents. In 1988, for instance, 88.5 percent of House incumbents and 54.5 percent of Senate incumbents won with 60 percent or more of the vote (Ornstein, Mann, and Malbin 1990, 59–60).

A changing regional balance between the two parties is reflected similarly in the two chambers. Among Democrats, the North–South split has been critical to defining the party's ideological balance. Since the 1950s the

Democratic party in both chambers has become less southern, while Republicans have become more southern. For two decades before the 1958 election, about two out of every five Democrats in both chambers were elected from the eleven states of the old Confederacy. With only a few exceptions, these southern Democrats were conservative. After 1958 Democratic gains in northern states and Republican gains in southern states changed the regional balance of both parties. By the early 1970s only about one of every three congressional Democrats was from the South.

Among Republicans, southern representation grew from virtually nothing in the 1950s to about one of every five congressional Republicans in the 1970s, with southern Republicans among the most conservative in both chambers (Ornstein, Mann, and Malbin 1990, 11, 15). After the 1980 election that created a Republican majority in the Senate, only half of southern senators were Democratic, though they again became about two-thirds Democratic by 1990, roughly the same as in the early 1970s. In the House, Democratic representation has maintained a more stable level of about two-thirds of southern seats since the late 1960s.

In both chambers, then, Democrats have become somewhat less southern and Republicans more southern since the 1950s. At the same time, southern politics changed—due in large part to the civil rights movement of the 1960s and 1970s—yielding a number of southern Democratic liberals in both chambers. These developments represented an ideological divergence of the electoral bases of the two parties. The critical question is whether electoral divergence was greater in one of the chambers.

Direct measurement of the ideological proclivities of congressional constituencies is a problem that has plagued studies of Congress for many years. Survey data either are not structured by states and districts, include only a sample of states and districts, or do not include responses to similar questions over a period of time. A substitute measure that has been used effectively is the presidential vote in members' states and districts.[2] Table 9-1 (see p. 176) shows how support for Democratic presidential candidates was distributed between states and districts in 1956–88.

One striking feature of presidential voting among states and districts is the distinctiveness of House Democrats. The districts of House Democrats show considerably greater variation than those of House Republicans or of either Senate party.[3] The variation among states represented by Senate Democrats (with the important exceptions of 1964 and 1968) is in the same range as the constituencies of House and Senate Republicans.

Table 9-1 also indicates an important change over time. Both House Democrats' districts and Senate Democrats' states showed the greatest variation in support for Democratic presidential candidates in the 1964–72 period than in the surrounding elections. In 1968 George Wallace's third-party effort attracted substantial support in the South. Differences among Democrats over civil rights and law and order peaked in that election and led to Richard Nixon's election over Hubert Humphrey. The North–South

Table 9-1 / Variation in Percent Support for Democratic Presidential Candidates in Districts and States, by Members' Party (in standard deviations), 1956–1988

	House		Senate[a]	
Year	DEMOCRATS	REPUBLICANS	DEMOCRATS	REPUBLICANS
1956	10.8%	5.9%	6.7%	4.4%
1960	10.9	5.9	5.4	5.1
1964	13.0	10.1	12.4	7.6
1968	15.4[b]	7.4[b]	11.8[b]	8.3[b]
1972	13.9	6.9	7.4	6.0
1976	10.5	6.3	6.3	6.0
1980	12.9	7.1	7.2	8.2
1984	12.6	6.5	4.6	6.5
1988	12.1	7.3	5.0	6.3

[a] The Senate columns do not represent mutually exclusive sets of states because a state may be represented by a senator from each party.
[b] No adjustment is made for George Wallace, so the 1968 figures are the standard deviations in votes for Hubert Humphrey.
Sources: Compiled by the author from the *Almanac of American Politics, Congressional Quarterly Almanac,* and *Congressional Quarterly Weekly Report.*

split remained important until 1972. In 1976 and 1980 southern states represented by Democrats provided more support, on average, for the Democratic presidential candidate, Jimmy Carter, than did northern states represented by Democrats. And even when the South gave somewhat more support for Republican presidential candidates in 1984 and 1988, there was less variation among states of Senate Democrats than among states of Senate Republicans.

Thus, this crude indicator suggests that the political orientations of Senate Democrats' constituencies were most varied in the late 1960s and early 1970s, after which they became somewhat more alike. This pattern parallels that in the House. Republicans in neither chamber exhibited much change in the diversity of their constituencies.

DECISION-MAKING PROCESSES

The environmental developments of the 1980s clearly influenced decision-making processes in the House. Changes in the electoral bases of the parties and in the agenda produced policy preferences that were more homogeneous within the parties. Majority party leaders were in a stronger position to rely on the party organization to consider and develop policy, to employ their enhanced parliamentary tools on behalf of party causes, and to push partisan issues with less concern about alienating party members and their constituents. Thus House politics have become more partisan: majority party leaders are more influential while committees and individual members are less influential; majority party members collaborate in party organs to design public policy, insulate themselves by employing more unofficial or closed meetings, and flexibly arrange floor action and even the stages of decision making within their chamber to suit their partisan needs. The House has become more majoritarian and efficient.

The similarities in the changes in House and Senate environments suggest that a similar pattern of change occurred in the Senate. Does the description of the postreform House fit the Senate as well?

Partisanship: Floor Voting

The level of partisanship has increased less in the Senate than in the House during the past decade. This is most obvious in floor voting alignments, but it is also visible in the policy-making role of party organizations.

A commonly used measure of partisanship in voting alignments is the percentage of roll-call votes in which a majority of Democrats are aligned against a majority of Republicans (party votes).[4] David Rohde (this volume, Chapter 2) demonstrates that the changes in the percentage of party votes are less extreme in the Senate than in the House.[5] Party votes in the Senate did not fall as much as they did in the House during the early 1970s, and they did not increase as much as they did in the House during the 1980s. The moderating influences of the Senate's electoral and institutional features may be showing their force here.[6] Nevertheless, the House and Senate patterns are broadly similar, which may reflect the changes in the political environment that affected both chambers and the absence, in the Senate, of magnifying influences from changes in electoral bases or strengthened party leadership.

Figure 9-1 (see p. 178) shows the percentage of party votes among those few important votes that the *Congressional Quarterly* identifies as "key votes." The figure also indicates the average difference between the parties on key votes, as represented by the Rice Index of Party Likeness measure.[7] It has the advantage of measuring party differences even when the party majorities are not opposed to each other. For both measures, the same basic pattern arises: partisanship dropped in the late 1960s and early 1970s, then increased thereafter.

Party votes do not reveal much about the degree to which the parties are internally cohesive, so it is useful to examine the loyalty of party members. After suffering declining loyalty during the 1970s, Senate Republicans recovered in the first Reagan Congress of the 1980s, and retained a high level of loyalty until recent Congresses (Rohde, this volume, Chapter 2).

Figure 9-1 / Senate Partisanship on Key Votes, 1953–1989

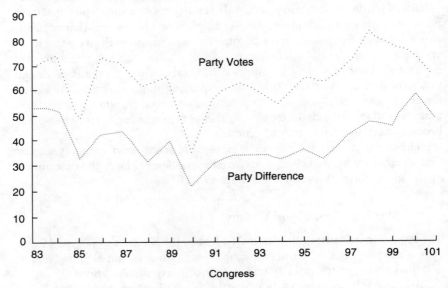

The vertical axis for party votes represents the percentage of key votes that are party votes; for party differences it is the Rice Index of Party Likeness (see note 8). (From the *Congressional Quarterly Almanac*, 1953–89.)

The abrupt change in 1981 suggests that factors other than the homogeneity of Republican constituencies were at work. No doubt these included Reagan's landslide presidential victory and popularity, the focused agenda, new majority status, and the leadership skills of the majority leader, Howard H. Baker, Jr. (R-Tenn.). Indeed, other research indicates that Senate parties' cohesiveness is sensitive to control of the White House (Patterson and Caldeira 1988).

In contrast, Senate Democrats demonstrated somewhat greater loyalty in the late 1970s—more even than Republicans—and have maintained a fairly stable level of loyalty since then.[8] The pattern of increasing party support among southerners during the 1970s and 1980s was similar in the two chambers (Rohde, this volume, Chapter 2). Although Senate Democrats have not achieved the cohesiveness of their House counterparts in recent Congresses, they have reached levels notably higher than those of the early 1970s.

Broadly speaking, the pattern of Democratic cohesiveness within the Senate parallels the changes in the regional composition of the party and the variation in support for Democratic presidential candidates found in Senate Democrats' states. The same cannot be said of Senate Republicans. Their states' variation in presidential voting is relatively stable over time and so it cannot account for the substantial and sometimes sharp variation in party loyalty.

Partisanship: Decision-making Process

There is more to partisanship than voting alignments, of course. The processes for setting the agenda and crafting legislation also may have a partisan cast. For example, reliance on party leaders and organizations to initiate and structure the consideration of legislation may vary between the chambers and over time.

The two Senate parties have a parallel set of official bodies: the conference of all party members, a policy committee, and a committee on committees (called the *Steering Committee* by Democrats).[9] The conferences and policy committees have the potential of playing a critical role in policy-making. Policy proposals can originate within the conferences and their policy committees, expert staff can be housed in these units, and the units' chairs can use them to promote their own political interests. In practice, though, the conferences and policy committees play only a limited role. Some floor leaders prefer not to share their power with others and so avoid meetings that might end up reducing their discretion. At other times, intraparty divisions may be exacerbated by efforts to force agreement in party councils. Often, too, senators serving on committees with the relevant jurisdiction object to outsiders intruding in their spheres of activity.

Party positions usually are not articulated in the Senate, even for major legislation. Of course, Senate observers still ascribe party positions to the policy proposals supported by party and committee leaders. And Senate leaders frequently appeal to party loyalty on behalf of proposals viewed as dividing the two parties. But senators take great pride in their independence, which limits the pressure leaders can apply to rank-and-file members without antagonizing members. Senate individualism is grounded in formal rules and informal practices. Senate leaders have relatively weak formal powers, limiting the leverage they can gain by extending or withholding favors to members. And because some fellow partisans and members of the opposite party resent official party policy positions, party endorsements often are counterproductive.

A cohesive majority party can impose its will in the House but generally not in the Senate. A Senate minority party can circumvent committees with floor amendments and obstruct action on the floor with amendments and filibusters. Thus, Senate majority leaders must work with minority party leaders (or at least faction leaders within the minority party) to pass legislation. Indeed, initiating legislation within majority party councils may alienate minority party members who might otherwise have supported the legislation on its merits. And such efforts have a further risk. If the minority comes to view the majority leader as being excessively partisan, the leader might lose the minority cooperation necessary to operating the Senate on an endless series of unanimous-consent agreements.

Both Senate rules and Senate individualism, then, reduce the role of party organizations in the policy process. Little has occurred in recent Congresses—even heightened partisanship in voting alignments—that changes the conclusion that Senate party conferences and party committees play only a small direct role in shaping public policy.

The Republicans Since World War II and until only recently, Republican party units of the Senate have been more active than Democratic units.[10] In the early 1950s the Republican conference met weekly, as did the Republican Policy Committee. Weekly luncheon meetings of all Republicans were initiated in 1956 under the auspices of the Policy Committee. At first, the weekly luncheons were in addition to the regular meetings of the Policy Committee. However, regular meetings of the Policy Committee were discontinued after Everett Dirksen (Ill.) became the party's floor leader in 1958. The luncheons rapidly substituted for conference meetings because they, too, provided an opportunity for the leadership to raise policy, strategy, and scheduling issues with the membership and usually provided an open forum for discussing issues of concern to rank-and-file Republicans. But with few exceptions neither the conference nor the Policy Committee established party policy positions to which the adherence of Republican senators was expected (Bone 1956, 1958; Canon 1990; Galloway 1953; Jones 1970, 1976; Matthews 1960; Oleszek 1985; Peabody 1981; Ripley 1969a, 1969b; Tolchin 1982; Torcom 1973; Whalen and Whalen 1985; White 1957).

Senate Republican floor leaders' personal styles and strategies and their relationship with the White House have had some influence on the role of their party organization. Dirksen's strong-willed control over party affairs left little room for meaningful policy activity in party councils, but most of Dirksen's service as minority leader occurred when Democrats controlled the White House. His successor, Hugh Scott (Pa.), served during the Republican Nixon and Ford administrations, which took the lead on most Republican policy initiatives. Not until Howard Baker became Republican leader in 1976—the same year that Democrat Jimmy Carter was elected to the White House—did Republican party organs gain new life. Baker supported further expansion of the whip organization and encouraged the efforts of the Policy Committee chair, John Tower (Tex.), to formulate more policy proposals.[11] However, the minority status of Senate Republicans meant that the Republican conference and its Policy Committee had little direct influence on policy outcomes (Hildenbrand 1985; Malbin 1977; Peabody 1981).

Winning majority status in the 1980 elections, along with Ronald Reagan's presidential victory, dramatically altered Republican circumstances in the Senate. The regional whip system was disbanded, apparently because floor coverage was no longer a problem—the leader or his designee and the presiding officer would provide continuous floor coverage for the majority party Republicans.[12] Baker had all full committee chairs appointed to the Policy Committee and held regular meetings with the group before the weekly luncheon of all Republicans to plan and push the Republican agenda. The meetings of committee chairs and all Republicans did not set policy—that was left to the administration and individual chairs and their committees. But the meetings were sometimes important for generating party cohesiveness and coordinating Senate business. The party conference met somewhat more frequently in the 1980s (Ornstein, Peabody, and Rohde 1985; Canon 1990; Tolchin 1982).

Little change occurred in the function of Republican party organs when Bob Dole (Kan.) became floor leader after the 1984 election. Both the Policy Committee and conference staffs continued to elaborate the information and telecommunication services they provided for senators. Today, these activities are supervised by the Policy Committee and conference chairs and play little direct role in policy-making. Dole makes greater use of informally appointed task forces to negotiate with Democrats than did his predecessors, but Senate individualism prevents such task forces from being very exclusive or autonomous (Patterson 1990).

The Democrats   Senate Democrats' record is different in several respects. As leader in the 1950s, Lyndon Johnson called no conference meetings to discuss policy. He used the Policy Committee, whose meetings were closed to nonmembers, as an advisory cabinet on scheduling matters. As Policy Committee chair, Johnson appointed staff to serve his leadership needs, a practice that continued until recently. Under intense pressure from liberals, whose ranks had swelled after the 1958 elections, Johnson in 1960 promised to call conference meetings at the request of any senator, but after only a few meetings in January he refused to call any more (Baker 1978; Matthews 1960; Ripley 1969a; Steinberg 1968; Stewart 1975).

Mike Mansfield (Mont.), who became floor leader after Johnson was elected vice president in 1960, made greater use of party organs but, at least initially, their effect on policy was minimal. The conference met only occasionally to discuss policy, but never to establish an official party position. The Policy Committee became more representative of the conference, continued to meet regularly, and held more substantive policy discussions. At least at first, its substantive role in policy-making did not change much, although it infrequently issued statements on policy. While some Democrats complained that the use of the party organs had not changed enough since the Johnson days, most did not object. The presence of legislatively active Democratic presidents in the 1960s meant that liberals' favorite programs were given attention in standing committees and on the floor. The few conference meetings that were held in the 1960s generally were poorly attended (Ripley 1969b; Stewart 1975).

Not until Mansfield faced a Republican president after the 1968 election did Democrats again turn to their own party apparatus for setting an agenda and promoting their policies. Mansfield began to ask the Policy Committee to approve policy resolutions that would then go to the full conference for endorsement, and such action was pursued in a wide range of policy areas. The Policy Committee was particularly active in 1973 when, responding to colleagues frustrated by the 1972 election results, Mansfield sought to rally the party behind a series of policy initiatives. In 1975 Mansfield appointed a special task force on energy and economic policy that produced a policy proposal approved by the conference. However, the standing committees with jurisdiction failed to act on the party recommendation and the proposal was not offered as a whole program on the Senate floor (Jones 1976; Robinson 1976; Stewart 1975; Oleszek 1985).

Robert C. Byrd (W. Va.) took over as Democratic leader when Jimmy Carter was elected president in late 1976. Byrd reverted to Johnson's practice of calling few conferences for other than organizational purposes and he ignored the Policy Committee, even for scheduling matters. Byrd preferred to meet with the committee chairs, which he did regularly to discuss matters of general interest to the party and to apprise himself of the status of important legislation (Peabody 1981; Baumer 1990). But Byrd used the party apparatus more after Reagan was elected president in 1980, and the Senate Democrats lost their majority status. Several task forces were appointed to develop policy alternatives and the Policy Committee was used to build a consensus within the party on a few important issues.

After Byrd regained majority leader status following the 1986 elections, his party was reinvigorated and more cohesive. President Reagan seemed to have given up his legislative agenda, Senate Republicans were quite restive, and the initiative shifted to Capitol Hill. In this context, and in the face of demands for a more active party, Byrd instituted regular weekly conference meetings—the first such regular meetings of Democrats in many years. But the function of the Policy Committee did not change; in fact, it still did not meet.

The next floor leader, George J. Mitchell (Me.), campaigned for his post on a platform of making more meaningful use of the party organization and was ultimately responsible for some notable changes in party organization activity. Under Mitchell's direction, the conference continued to meet weekly to discuss matters currently before the Senate. Mitchell also appointed a Policy Committee cochair and began, in January 1989, to hold Policy Committee meetings for the first time in twelve years. In 1990 the Policy Committee sponsored weekly luncheons usually open to all Democrats, as Republicans had been doing since the 1950s. Most Thursday luncheons were devoted to prospective issues and policy problems. Under the direction of the new cochair, the Policy Committee approved an agenda for Congress and held several issue seminars. With Mitchell's support, a larger, more active whip organization was created; it meets regularly and conducts head counts. Mitchell occasionally employed informally appointed task forces of Democrats to work on Democratic policy proposals and strategy, most of which involved matters that crossed committee jurisdictional lines. In each respect, Mitchell was more inclusive than his predecessor (Baumer 1990; Cohen 1989).

Since the 1950s, then, the policy-making functions of both parties' conferences and policy committees has been limited by internal party divisions, individualism, resistance from standing committees, and some leaders' interest in maintaining personal control over party strategy. Although party activity appears contingent on floor leaders' strategies, party organs have played policy-related roles in two types of situations.[13] First, opposition presidents sometimes have stimulated party activity. Second, prospective and new party leaders sometimes have found it advantageous to promise a more collective leadership and greater consultation with the rank and file by calling more conference and policy committee meetings. But as the record demonstrates, neither an opposition president nor a new leader can always produce more party activity. And the use of party organs for policy-related purposes has been short-lived. Even in recent congresses, neither Senate party relies on its organizational apparatus to design policy and strategy nearly as much as the House parties do.

Nevertheless, rank-and-file senators, particularly Democrats, now have more regular contact with party and committees leaders, as well as with each other, in their weekly meetings. This may be tolerable for leaders because of the greater like-mindedness of party members and the common interest in responding effectively to presidents. It also is a response of leaders to the demands of the rank and file for a more active voice in setting the agenda and party strategy. In this sense, it is as much an expression of Senate individualism as it is an expansion of party-structured decision making. And it certainly represents a decline in the autonomy of committees and their leaders. But, by itself, it does not represent a greater centralization of power.

Majority Party Leadership and Centralized Decision Making

The now conventional argument about the power of congressional leadership is that it arises when the constituency bases of the two parties are polarized, which in turn yields polarized congressional parties (Cooper and Brady 1981; Sinclair 1989a; Rohde 1988). In such circumstances, members of the cohesive majority party are willing to empower their leaders to act on their behalf, confident that leadership power will be exercised in their interest. A cohesive majority party can even alter the formal rules to enhance its leaders' ability to pursue the party's policy agenda. Thus, the formal powers of central leaders are linked directly to the levels of party polarization and intraparty cohesiveness. In the postreform House, partisan conflict and Democratic cohesiveness licensed majority party leaders to employ procedural tools in a way that created a centrally directed decision-making process. More initiative and direction came from the majority party leadership; the leadership was no longer relegated to a role of brokering the demands of factions and the decentralized locations of power.

In the Senate, the relationships among electoral alignments, party polarization and cohesiveness, strength of majority party leadership, and centralization of decision making are weak. Consider this post–World War II record: the strongest leaders have not always emerged at times of party polarization and intraparty cohesiveness; majority party cohesiveness has not produced efforts to strengthen leaders' formal powers and the efforts that were made have not succeeded; and majority party leaders considered to be strong have not produced a more centralized decision-making process in the Senate.

First, partisan polarization and intraparty cohesiveness are not strongly correlated with strong majority party leadership in the Senate during the post–World War II period.[14] Lyndon Johnson, arguably the strongest Senate leader of the period, presided over the most evenly split majority party— the Democrats of the mid-1950s. Neither conservatives nor moderates nor liberals were strong enough to impose their will on the party, let alone the Senate, but with the help of a few Republicans both factions usually were strong enough to block legislation. Johnson vigorously employed his few formal roles and privileges to block floor consideration of issues that divided his party and to promote issues that could unite the party. One result was that southern Democrats maintained a level of support on party votes, when they occurred, similar to the level among other Democrats. Thanks in part to Johnson's effectiveness, the depth of conflict within his party was not accurately depicted in aggregate voting statistics. Clearly, party voting and leadership strategies are entangled, and political scientists have much to do to disentangle them.

In the broader view of Senate history, party polarization and strong leadership are clearly linked. At the turn of the twentieth century, polarized parties created conditions favorable to the emergence of strong, centralized majority party leadership (Brady, Brody, and Epstein 1989; Rothman 1966). One reasonable proposition is that the threshold of party polarization for the emergence of centralized leadership is higher in the Senate than in the House. Another is that Senate individualism—supported by long-standing rules but reinforced by greater careerism and a wider distribution of resources—has increased the threshold since the turn of the twentieth century.

Second, to strengthen the formal powers of leaders in the Senate, the majority party must be larger and more cohesive than is required in the House. In the post–World War II period, the majority party was largest in the 1960s, an era of declining cohesiveness among Democrats. Rules changes were blocked consistently by the conservative faction within the Democratic party. Thus, within the range of party polarization and intraparty cohesiveness experienced in recent decades, formal Senate leadership powers and their uses have not been as responsive to changes in the partisan alignment as they appear to have been in the House.

The most serious consideration of expanding the formal powers of Senate leaders occurred in 1986, when the Senate considered a resolution providing for televised floor sessions. Senator Byrd, then minority leader, hoped to use the prospect of televised sessions to motivate his colleagues to support a set of reforms intended to streamline and organize floor action on legislation. The proposals would have allowed the Senate to impose germaneness and time restrictions more easily and required section-by-section consideration of legislation. While the leaders would not be able to impose restrictions single-handedly, they would have initiated such efforts with fewer supporters than under current rules. But the package of reforms was blocked by a threatened filibuster on the part of senators who feared that minority and individual rights would be undermined.

Finally, the correlation between strong leaders and centralization is attenuated in the Senate by obstacles to centralization. Strong Senate majority leaders have emerged, whether by force of personality or the grant of discretion on the part of party members to their leader. But strong party leaders cannot create the kind of centralized decision-making process that is possible in the House. Lacking the authority to set the Senate agenda by the vote of simple majorities, the majority party leader must rely on minority support and, on a day-to-day basis, on unanimous consent to bring legislation to the floor. Lacking a general germaneness rule, the Senate leader cannot keep issues off the Senate floor for long. Consequently, agenda setting in the Senate is a process of negotiation, compromise, and mediation to a degree that would seem exotic in the House. And lacking strong agenda-setting powers, the Senate leader is less able to take the initiative and set a policy direction for the chamber.

Nevertheless, a Senate majority leader is in a stronger position to block and push legislation than other senators. The majority leader's right of recognition, a precedent reflecting senators' understanding that some minimal direction is required, ensures that the leader is the first to gain the floor to bring up a bill, amendment, or motion. Yet the standing rules give the leader little help in acquiring cooperation, attracting support, or achieving legislative objectives. Therefore, the Senate leader's personal skills, resources, and strategies—sometimes summed up as "style"—are more critical to the leader's success, and to evaluations thereof, than is true of House leaders. The success of various leadership styles, however, is contingent on circumstances like the size and cohesiveness of the party and control of the White House—which tend to change more frequently than do Senate leaders themselves.

A recent experience may call into question the conclusion that Senate decision making has not become more centralized. Conditions seemed ripe for a more centralized process in 1990: a constricted agenda, a strongly partisan alignment of preferences on that agenda, and a strong president of the party opposite to the House and Senate majorities. The prospect of a continuing stalemate with disastrous budget consequences led President George Bush to call for a summit of top congressional and executive leaders. Congressional leaders, not wanting to spurn a presidential appeal for co-operation and consensus building, agreed to the request. The budget summit and construction of a massive budget-reconciliation bill that followed in-volved negotiations between a handful of party and budget leaders in each chamber and a few top White House aides. Rank-and-file senators seemed to give their leaders more leeway than usual. Should the 1990 budget ex-perience be taken as evidence that the Senate moved into a more centralized decision-making process despite the institutional obstacles to doing so? And, if so, does this indicate that the Senate has indeed moved into an era with features similar to those of the House?

The answer is a qualified "yes" to the first question and "no" to the second. In both chambers, the initiative for policy change—indeed, dozens of important policy changes—rested with the summiteers in 1990. In both chambers, political circumstances limited the degree to which the chambers could alter the format of the summiteers' deficit-reduction package, reducing the role of committees and individual senators. And in both chambers, policy choices reflected in other legislation were constrained by budget consider-ations. Many senators exercised greater self-restraint in pursuing narrow amendments and criticizing their leaders than in most other situations.

But there were also important differences between the House and Senate. Unlike their House counterparts, Senate Democratic leaders could not insist that committees adhere to the details of the original summit agreement, so the issue never arose in the Senate as it did in the House. Nor could Senate leaders pass the Senate reconciliation bill without the support of minority-party Republicans. Furthermore, Senate Democratic leaders could not pre-vent disabling amendments from being offered on the Senate floor, as their House counterparts could. Thus, Senate majority party leaders were not in a position to initiate and sustain agreements among fellow Democrats as House majority party leaders could and did. Cooperation between Dem-ocratic and Republican leaders was essential. So, while the initiative clearly had shifted to central leaders in the 1990 budget debate, the ability of Senate leaders to enforce a summit agreement was much weaker than that of House leaders.

Quite apart from budget summitry, Senate decision making in the 1980s and early 1990s looked a bit more centralized than it had for some time. It was the product of a particular blend of leadership styles in the two parties. By the end of the 1980s, both floor leaders had strong, policy-oriented leaders, a situation not seen since Johnson and Dirksen in 1959 and 1960. Today, Mitchell and Dole both take a more active, personal role in nego-tiating legislation than did their predecessors. Dole's approach has been labeled "*quorum* call government" to reflect his tendency to ask for a time-out in floor action in order to give himself time to press for the compromises necessary to bring legislation to the floor and see it through to final action (Deering 1986). Though not nearly as belligerent as Dole, Mitchell plays a substantive role in as wide a range of issues. Of course, negotiations at the floor stage are hardly new to the Senate. What was different in the 101st Congress was how often both leaders chose to join the negotiations rather than leave them to committee leaders.

The assertiveness of the current leaders, however, should not be mistaken for a new centralization of power in the Senate. To the contrary, the assertiveness of leaders reflects the weakness of their formal powers; for the most part, it is assertiveness devoted to diverting disaster. They must work incessantly to overcome obstacles to Senate action erected by colleagues of both parties. And, contrary to the impression that power was more centralized, Mitchell actually began his leadership service by giving away some of his formal sources of power by sharing the chairship of the Policy Committee and granting the Steering Committee chairship to another senator. The primary roles of Senate leaders remain mediation, brokerage, and damage control.

Finally, it should be noted that leaders' central role in budgeting may be substantially smaller in coming years because of provisions in the 1990 reconciliation bill. The bill eliminated the October sequester mechanism known as the Gramm-Rudman Act. In its place are spending ceilings for four separate categories of programs and automatic sequesters when the ceilings are exceeded. This is intended to force Congress and the president to find new sources of revenue every time spending increases are enacted. The self-enforcing character of this new process virtually eliminates the need for a summit of party and budget leaders, previously necessary to avoid deep, across-the-board cuts. If the 1990 package produces a few years of budget peace between Congress and the White House and between Democrats and Republicans, party leaders will play a less central role in policy-making in the future.

Committee Autonomy

The autonomy of Senate committees has declined since the 1970s (Smith and Deering 1990, chap. 5). The recent activity of the parties was noted earlier. More importantly, though, stringent budget constraints, sometimes enforced by reconciliation instructions and spending caps, have limited the discretion of committees to pursue policies of their own choosing. These constraints were most severe in 1990, when severe budget cuts compelled committees to accept policy changes they otherwise would not have approved. The initiative for policy change shifted to party and budget leaders and away from the committee and subcommittee leaders accustomed to shepherding legislation through the process. In this important respect, the decision-making processes of the two chambers were affected in a similar way.

Of course, House committees had more to lose than Senate committees. For several decades Senate committees have been more permeable to outside influences and their recommendations granted less deference than House committees'. Unlimited debate and nongermane amendments have long been tools for challenging Senate committees that are not available in the House. Moreover, House committees suffered losses of autonomy from sources that have not proved to be important in the Senate, such as multiple referrals, conference appointment practices, and active party caucuses and task forces.

Nevertheless, the loss of flexibility due to budget strictures has been substantial in the Senate. And the continuing force of the 1990 budget package constraints into the mid-1990s suggests that committees will suffer substantially reduced discretion for at least another three years. But note that the constraint is really a constraint on all budget players, not just committees. The new sequester mechanism—sometimes called a *rolling sequester*—limits the ability of the president, the two chambers of Congress, and the committees to increase spending or cut taxes for several years.[15]

Structuring Floor Debate

A central element of the postreform House was more creative uses of special rules to structure floor debate and especially to limit floor amendments (Bach and Smith 1988; Sinclair 1983). In contrast, little has changed in how the Senate schedules and structures floor action on legislation. The majority leader works continuously to schedule debate and votes in order to dispose of legislation expeditiously and lend some predictability to floor action. Limiting debate and amendments normally requires unanimous consent, for which the leader must negotiate with bill managers, leaders, and rank-and-file members of both parties. This severely limits the majority leader's discretion and gives all senators a source of leverage with which to exact concessions from party leaders.

Managing floor business has required creativity on the part of majority leaders. The use of holds and filibusters has expanded greatly since the 1960s (Oppenheimer 1985; Smith 1989), compelling floor leaders to work harder to devise means of bringing legislation to the floor and to a vote. Among other things, floor leaders have become more dependent on unanimous-consent agreements—orders that supplement or substitute for the standing rules that can be adopted only if no senator objects—to limit debate and amendments. Unanimous-consent agreements have become more complex, increasingly tailored to individual members and amendments, and more likely to involve multiple measures (Smith and Flathman 1989). Any change over the last decade, however, is a matter of degree and not of kind. Consent to limit debate or amendments has not become easier to obtain and the majority leader has not gained any power to call up measures and bring them to a vote. Indeed, the increasing complexity of, and detail, in unanimous-consent agreements reflects the difficulty of meeting the demands of senators who threaten to object. The Senate looks different than the postreform House on this count.

In one policy area, budgeting, the Senate has imposed special limits on debate and amendments. In 1974 the Senate accepted a prohibition of nongermane floor amendments to budget resolutions and limited debate on budget resolutions and reconciliation bills to twenty hours. When the Congress set deficit-reduction targets in 1985 as part of the Gramm-Rudman procedure, the Senate barred floor amendments that had the effect of increasing the deficit beyond the specified levels. The Senate allowed points of order to be raised against ineligible amendments and required a sixty-vote majority to adopt ineligible amendments that are ruled out of order.

More stringent limits were set in the 1990 reconciliation bill that embodied the budget agreement between Congress and the president. Previous limits on amendments and debate were extended and tightened. For example, debate on special, year-end reconciliation bills is limited to ten hours. Furthermore, any amendment that is not deficit neutral, or any measure or amendment not consistent with the specified spending ceilings, is subject to a point of order and the sixty-vote rule. And special limits on Senate debate and amendments were adopted for resolutions that suspend or modify the spending limits in certain situations or demand that the president modify sequestration orders. Significantly, in most places where the 1990 bill set explicit limits for the Senate it did not do so for the House, where it was assumed that the standing rules and special rules designed by the majority leadership would set the necessary constraints on floor debate and amendments.

The self-imposed limits on debate and amendments seem out of character for the Senate. After all, the Senate has rejected more general restrictions on debate and amendments. But in each case—1974, 1985, and 1990—institutional ineffectiveness was particularly acute. Senators, not trusting each other to exercise voluntary restraint, accepted leaders' recommendations that they impose limits for matters affecting the deficit. Including the limits in large budget packages that promised some hope for correcting the budget policy problems made them easier for senators to accept.

The Senate's efforts to limit floor debate and amendments have taken a different form than House efforts. The Senate still lacks a general limit on debate or germaneness and it has nothing comparable to House special rules with which to structure floor action on a tactical, bill-by-bill basis. Instead, the Senate limits were adopted for budget-related matters and apply to all senators. The limits can be manipulated by the majority party of its leaders only by unanimous consent or by using special procedures that require extraordinary majorities to endorse. Therefore, even cohesive Senate majority parties would have to be very large to set aside the limits without support from a substantial number of minority party senators. Simple majoritarian mechanisms are thought to be unworkable.

THE POLICY-MAKING ROLE OF THE SENATE

The Senate of the early 1990s is much as we would expect. A more narrowly focused agenda that divides the parties and a Democratic Senate pitted against a Republican president heightens partisanship and places more responsibility for strategy and policy in the hands of the majority party floor leaders. But Senate individualism, reinforced by formal rules, limits the degree to which party organizations can engage in meaningful policy-making and the degree to which party leaders can direct Senate action on important legislation. Senate partisanship is in fact somewhat more intense and the parties are slightly more active. Committees are less powerful, but power hasn't gravitated to the party organizations. Individual and minority rights are well preserved and the majority leader's ability to manipulate procedure or policy choices remains limited. The inefficiency of the Senate persists. In these respects, the Senate looks different than the postreform House.

The most important changes in Senate decision-making processes since the 1970s are related to budget policy. Budget procedures have reduced the power of committees. On a few occasions, budget negotiations have forced central party and budget leaders into a more prominent position, but large deficits have constrained senators, the parties, and committees. Frustration about deficits has led the Senate to agree to procedures that severely limit its own policy discretion, at least for a few years. And complaints abound about how a policy is being made. In these respects, the Senate looks more like the House than it did in the late 1970s.

These developments have affected the function of the Senate in national policy-making. A traditional strength of the Senate has been its role as a policy incubator (Polsby 1970). Senators are ideally suited to the task of promoting new policy ideas and keeping them alive until the time is ripe to enact them. Senators have several advantages over representatives: greater national visibility, easier access to the media, multiple committee assignments, larger staffs, and better access to the chamber floor. Therefore, senators are preferred over representatives by groups seeking champions for their causes. Furthermore, senators seeking influence over a range of issues and those with more than a passing interest in the presidency are motivated to develop a national constituency, and so seek policy ideas that attract national attention.

But since the early 1980s, budget constraints severely limited policy initiatives that cost money. Today, fewer new policy ideas are percolating among organized interest groups and senators. Policy activists spend much of their time fighting rearguard actions to protect past policy achievements rather than promoting new proposals. Media attention has drifted to central party and budget leaders. Building national constituencies in the pursuit of higher office is more difficult. Moreover, the burden of raising larger sums of money for reelection distracts more senators from their legislative activities and makes them somewhat more cautious in setting their own priorities.

As its recent history demonstrates, the Senate is less able than the House to resolve the tensions inherent in a collective decision-making body. Most senators want a viable system of committees to handle the Senate's large work load and provide a platform for attracting media attention. At the same time, senators applaud assertive but consultative party leaders—at least when those senators find leaders acting in their interest. But the powers of both committees and party leaders are checked by the unwillingness of senators to sacrifice individual prerogatives in order to grant committees and leaders formal powers similar to those that have been bestowed on House committees and leaders. In the post–World War II Senate, even surges in partisanship and changes in party control did not spawn new chamber or party rules that reduced the formal power in individual senators. Conditions sufficient to motivate significant concessions on individual prerogatives have arisen only in budget politics.

Thus the *postreform* label that fits the House so well is only awkwardly applied to the Senate. Indeed, the close association of the alterations of Senate decision-making practices to budget making in recent years suggests that the changes may have little lasting effect. The Senate remains a collegial body biased against both the centralization of power to leaders and the decentralization of power to committees. The decision-making processes of the Senate are congenitally unsettled.

Notes

1. Regarding the postreform House see, for example, Davidson (1988, 1989b); Sinclair (1989a); and Smith (1989).
2. The major weakness of the presidential vote as a measure of ideological balance is that a party's presidential candidates do not attract the same mix of voters from election to election, so some variation is due more to the candidates than to the constituencies. Nevertheless, the presidential vote is one of the few reliable indicators of political preferences available for states and districts.
3. Moreover, the variation among House Democrats' districts is not due to regional North–South differences. Rather, most of the variance is in the very large number of northern districts.
4. For a review of the literature and a longer perspective on partisanship in congressional voting alignments, see Patterson and Caldeira (1988); and Hurley and Wilson (1989).
5. In the House the proportion of party-unity votes has increased since the mid-1970s, especially in recent Congresses. As Rohde (this volume, Chapter 2) has demonstrated, the House trend is related to a declining number of southern Democrats and increasing party support among the remaining southerners.
6. Patterson and Caldeira (1988), however, point out that party voting in the House and Senate have nearly identical standard deviations for the 1949–84 period. And yet their multivariate analysis leads them to conclude that the level of party voting in the Senate is less sensitive to environmental changes than is House party voting.

7. This is the mean absolute difference between the percentage of Democrats voting yea and the percentage of Republicans voting yea.

8. The pattern is just the reverse in the House. For the House, the figure indicates that the Republicans became more cohesive during the course of the 1970s but did not change greatly in the 1980s, while the increase in Democratic party unity occurred in the 1980s. These differences between the chambers should caution us further about the importance of distinguishing the chambers from each other.

9. In both parties, *ad hoc* task forces, usually named by the floor leader, occasionally have supplemented or complemented the regular party units, as have many less formally identified groups.

10. The difference is due to the minority status that Republicans suffered in most Congresses. The Democrats, by virtue of their majority party status during most of the period, have controlled the standing committees and their staffs and enjoyed floor scheduling prerogatives. As a result, Republicans have required alternative means for devising policy proposals, meeting the electoral needs of members, and providing outlets for members to express their views and frustrations.

11. Several subcommittees or task forces were created to pursue a variety of issues, two of which produced substantial legislative proposals that attracted broad Republican support (see Oleszek 1985; and Peabody 1981).

12. The assistant whips were not involved in head counts (this task was handled by a staff member supervised by the floor leader), and much of the head-counting responsibility could be shared with the president's congressional liaison team on most important matters.

13. See a somewhat different conclusion in Oleszek (1985).

14. For a similar argument and a more systematic test, see Hurley and Wilson (1989).

15. The spending limits adopted in 1990 also allow discretionary spending to increase by the rate of inflation, giving the appropriations committees more room to maneuver than in previous years.

10 / House-Senate Relations: A Perspective on Bicameralism

WALTER J. OLESZEK

"The House with 435 members did this in four hours. We only have 100 [members] but it is taking us twenty hours," noted Senate GOP Leader Bob Dole (Kan.). "I guess that says there is a difference in the two bodies" (*Congressional Record*, 17 October 1990, p. S15525). As Dole noted, the Senate usually takes far longer than the House to pass similar legislation. A major reason is *bicameral* differences in the philosophy of each chamber's rules. House rules permit a determined majority to achieve policy or partisan objectives with some dispatch. For example, the House Rules Committee, which is an arm of the majority leadership, can structure floor decision making to limit debate and restrict amendments.

Senate rules, by contrast, emphasize minority rights: one senator, a group of senators, or the minority party. Senators' rights of extended debate—the so-called *filibuster*—perhaps the world's most famous parliamentary practice, epitomizes the Senate's deference to individual prerogatives. To shut down senatorial talkathons requires unanimous consent, accommodations to the filibustering senators, or invocation of cloture (Senate Rule XXII), which requires a sixty-vote supermajority. As Illinois Democratic Senator Paul Simon, a former House member, once said: in the House "no single member can tie the body in knots; in the Senate, any member can" (Simon 1985, 150; see also Baker 1989; Carmines and Lawrence 1985). No wonder bills often take longer to complete in the smaller Senate compared to the larger House.

Another factor that explains lengthier Senate deliberations is legislative work load. Both chambers have approximately the same schedule of business and deadline pressures, but the House has more members than the Senate to do the work. "You have 100 people doing the same work as 435 in the House," observed Senator Wyche Fowler (D-Ga.). "By its very nature, we have more balls in the air at any given time" (Gramarekian 1988). Part of senators' broad responsibility involves the heterogeneity of states versus districts. Every senator, for instance, represents some farmers but not all representatives do. There are, in brief, more constituency demands on senators compared to House members.

Textbooks on Congress usually discuss bicameralism in the context of interchamber differences, conflicts, and rivalries or examine the House and

Senate as separate institutions. There is little analysis of House-Senate interactions—how the two chambers influence each other across a whole range of policy, political, or procedural dimensions. For example, House members are sometimes present on the Senate floor (or vice versa) to lobby wavering senators to support bills. Neglected, too, in textbooks is discussion of a crucial arena of bicameralism—the conference committee—where House and Senate members meet to reconcile their disagreements on some of the nation's most important and controversial legislation.

To broaden our understanding of why and how Congress makes decisions, this chapter explores an often-neglected topic: House-Senate relations and changes during the postreform era. Our objective is to underscore that the House and Senate, like the legislative and executive branches, are interlocked rather than isolated institutions. Their relationships, often simply one chamber's "presence," affect the other's activities and decisions. More specifically, the chapter examines two fairly recent bicameral developments that seem likely to continue as important policy-making initiatives for the foreseeable future: (1) House-Senate changes in the tax and foreign policy arenas and (2) the huge size and diverse composition of many conference committees.

TRANSFORMATION OF HOUSE-SENATE ROLES

Our national political structure, it is said, consists of separate institutions sharing power. This principle applies also to the House and Senate—even in areas that, formally or informally, are perceived as the exclusive preserve of one chamber or the other. The blurring of constitutional-institutional boundaries between the House and Senate highlights how changing circumstances or intrachamber developments can challenge long-held assumptions about either chamber's legislative role.

Initiation of Revenue-raising Measures

Under Article I, section 7 of the Constitution, the so-called *origination clause*, "all bills for raising revenue shall originate in the House of Representatives; but the Senate may propose or concur with amendments as on other bills." The Founders granted this exclusive right to the House because it was then the only legislative chamber directly elected by the people. With two-year terms, representatives can be held accountable rather quickly at the polls for their revenue-raising decisions. Senators—who serve six-year terms—were indirectly elected until 1913, when the Seventeenth Amendment was ratified.

The House's authority to initiate revenue measures has often been a source of bicameral conflict. Controversies usually involve such questions as the scope of the Senate's authority to amend House-passed revenue bills or the proper definition of a revenue-raising measure. These disputes have reaffirmed that only the House may originate tax measures; the Senate has no right to act initially on such legislation. This prerogative is jealously and vigorously guarded by House members.

Important recent exceptions, however, highlight the Senate's ability under the right circumstances to take the tax-initiating lead from the House. One such instance occurred in the early 1980s. When Ronald Reagan won the White House, his electoral coattails produced GOP gains in the Democratically controlled House and GOP control of the Senate for the first time in twenty-six years. Reagan's agenda was clear: slash domestic spending, increase defense expenditures, and cut taxes. Senate Republicans acted with unity and alacrity to advance the administration's agenda and to pressure the House in 1981 to enact a massive three-year tax cut.

In an unusual move the Senate Finance Committee marked up and sent to the floor the tax-reduction package even before the House Ways and Means Committee had concluded its deliberations. Senate Majority Leader Howard H. Baker, Jr. (R-Tenn.) argued that there is "no legal or constitutional reason why the Senate cannot act," because the Senate's tax bill was added as an amendment to a House-passed joint resolution raising the national debt ceiling (Cowan 1981). There ensued an argument between the chambers as to whether debt-ceiling legislation is, constitutionally, revenue-raising legislation. In the end, the Senate waited to receive the tax package from the House. Nonetheless, the Senate's strategy helped prod the House to meet President Reagan's timetable for action and provided another policy alternative for House Republicans and their Democratic allies.

In 1982 the Senate again took the tax initiative. This time, however, it was plain that the House preferred it that way. On 28 July the House voted to go directly to conference with the Senate on a tax increase measure developed solely by the Senate and considered by neither the House membership nor the House Ways and Means Committee. Technically, the Constitution was complied with. The Senate attached its tax increase bill to an obscure House-passed revenue measure.

Several factors account for this role reversal. First, the expected economic stimulus from the 1981 tax cut failed to materialize. Instead, the nation sank deeper into recession. Then came President Reagan's admission that his goal of a balanced federal budget by 1984 could not be achieved. Indeed, his budget for Fiscal Year (FY) 1983 contained record-breaking, soaring deficits. Lawmakers were shocked by projections of mushrooming deficits. Pressures mounted quickly in both chambers to reduce the deficit through tax increases (or revenue enhancements), further spending cuts, or other means.

Now came the reversal from 1981: House Democrats wanted Senate Republicans to originate and take the expected negative electoral consequences of raising voters' taxes in an election year and during a period of economic distress. The political concerns of House Democrats were clear. As the chief deputy Democratic whip said, "I don't want my tracks on this" (Houston 1982). Asked why the tax increase did not originate in the House, the Senate Finance chair responded: "Well, I'll be very honest, because the House didn't want to originate it. And I think the Democrats said, 'Well, they control the Senate and they control the White House and if they can't pass it in the Senate why should we mess with it?'" (Lofton 1982).

House Ways and Means Committee Chair Dan Rostenkowski (D-Ill.) supported the strategy of sending the Senate-initiated tax plan to conference as a way to avoid deadlock in his committee and on the House floor. Before he formally proposed this unusual procedure, Rostenkowski insisted that some Ways and Means Republicans support the approach. "Obviously," said a Republican committee member, "the chairman didn't want a party-line vote on whether we should abdicate our constitutional responsibilities" (Merry 1982; see also Fessler 1982). After intervention from the White House, which did not mind the Republican-controlled Senate taking the policy lead from the Democratic House, four of the twelve committee Republicans voted with Rostenkowski to request an immediate conference with the Senate. As Rostenkowski said during floor debate: "This is an unusual procedural step to take . . . [but the] severe economic distress and volatile political environment at this moment . . . dictate that we travel this route" (*Congressional Record*, 28 July 1982, p. H4777).[1]

Thus the House went directly to conference with the Senate without writing a bill of its own. Many House Republicans objected to this procedure, which amounted to bypassing the Constitution's intent. Representative John Rousselot (R-Calif.), for example, twice offered privileged resolutions to return the tax amendments to the Senate on the ground that they violated the origination clause. Each time the House voted to table (kill) the resolution. The Senate brought a tax bill of some 758 pages to conference while the House brought none. The only time the House formally considered the policy to raise federal taxes by nearly $100 billion was when it debated and agreed to the conference report.[2]

Summary Points

Several observations flow from these cases of tax initiation by the Senate. First, the immediate situation instigated the role reversal. The action required majority concurrence by the House buttressed by presidential support and Senate willingness to produce a tax bill on its own.

Second, the changing political and economic context, especially the rise of huge deficits and sharp partisan conflict, made the issue of taxes difficult to address in either chamber. From Reagan's preference for tax cuts and President George Bush's "read my lips" policy (his no-new-taxes pledge in the 1988 campaign) to demonstrated voter antipathy to higher taxes, politicians in both houses are reluctant to advocate tax hikes. Speaker Thomas

"Tip" O'Neill (D-Mass.) said he supported a tax increase, but added that "it's going to originate in the White House" (Dewar and Walsh 1986).

When President Bush at last agreed publicly to support tax revenue increases as a way to reduce the fiscal deficit, he aroused the consternation of many congressional Republicans and shifted the terms of national debate from whether to raise taxes to whose taxes should be raised. His change of heart led eventually, after arduous House-Senate-White House negotiations in October 1990, to passage of a five-year budget package that contained significant revenue increases and spending cuts. This budget process also produced interesting bicameral dynamics.

House Democrats wanted their negotiating leaders (Speaker Thomas Foley [Wash.] and Majority Leader Richard Gephardt [Mo.]) to craft a Democratic budget plan that highlighted differences between the two parties. Senate Democrats, even with their fifty-five-seat control, simply did not have the votes to pass a partisan budget. Senate Republicans could stymie action on a Democratic budget by filibustering it to death, or at least long enough to win changes in such a budget's content and character. (Recall that sixty votes are required in the Senate to break a filibuster.) Our leadership, said Representative Charles Schumer (D-N.Y.), "was prepared to go with a Democratic budget, but the Senate did not have the votes" (Cohen 1990, 2416).

Third, interchamber shifts on taxes seemed to create opportunities for change in another budget arena: the traditional prerogative of the House to originate appropriation measures. From its beginning the House has asserted the right to originate appropriation measures (relying on its constitutional authority to initiate revenue bills). With a few notable exceptions, the Senate has acquiesced to the House's position, customarily waiting for the House to act first before taking up the appropriation bills (see Pressman 1966). Yet several reversals of this practice occurred during the postreform period.

In 1981 House Appropriations Chair Jamie Whitten (D-Miss.) observed that "for the first time in history the [continuing appropriations] bill was originated by the Senate and not the House" (*Congressional Record*, 23 November 1981, p. H8824). During debate on this bill, House GOP Leader Robert Michel (Ill.) suggested that a plan be devised to permit half the appropriation bills to be originated in the House and the other half in the Senate. Chair Whitten said, "I would not want to surrender to the six-year term on the other side" what ought to rest exclusively with "the people's branch" (*Congressional Record*, 23 November 1981, H8825).

The Senate even devised a way of originating appropriation bills while still observing House prerogatives. The Senate may proceed under a unanimous-consent agreement to initiate an appropriations bill, which is then debated and amended on the floor. Then the Senate-originated measure is incorporated into the House-passed appropriations bill. Procedurally, the Senate's provisions are embodied in an "H.R." bill. As Senator Daniel Inouye (D-Hawaii), chair of the Defense Appropriations Subcommittee, explained, this "somewhat unusual, but not unprecedented, consideration of defense appropriations" enables the Senate to expedite action on this legislation (*Congressional Record*, 15 October 1990, S15232).

Fourth, it bears repeating that, despite the 1981 and 1982 cases, the House is watchful of its tax-initiating prerogative. This reality affects Senate deliberations on scores of bills. For instance, when the Senate debated the Clean Air Act of 1990 (which President Bush signed into law), Ways and Means Chair Rostenkowski wrote the Senate Finance chair that he was reviewing senators' floor amendments to determine if they violated the Constitution's origination clause by raising revenues in the guise of fees. Armed with this letter, Finance Chair Lloyd Bentsen (D-Tex.) objected to certain floor amendments on the ground that the House would never accept them and that their adoption might jeopardize congressional enactment of the legislation (*Congressional Record*, 28 March 1990, pp. S3340–41).

Finally, the 1982 case spotlighted an ongoing bicameral issue that will likely continue throughout and beyond the postreform era. The Senate took a House-passed miscellaneous tax bill and substituted for it (keeping the H.R. number) a major tax increase proposal. While the origination clause permits the Senate to "propose or concur with amendments as on other Bills," it remains unclear to what extent the Senate can initiate revenue measures in the form of nongermane substitutes to House-passed tax bills. (Unlike the House, the Senate has no general germaneness or relevancy rule covering floor amendments to pending legislation.)

A long history of bicameral controversy and court suits surround this issue, but with no definitive resolution (see Hoffer 1984). Sometimes the House returns Senate-added amendments to the other body on the ground that they violate the origination clause. Other times, as in 1982, political and economic circumstances encourage House acceptance of Senate revenue initiatives. This arena, in short, is the bicameral equivalent of the "invitation to struggle" between Congress and the White House over the direction of the nation's foreign policy. Needless to say, the foreign policy arena is another place that has witnessed House-Senate changes during the postreform period.

A Bicameral Shift in International Policy-making

Throughout much of Congress's history, the Senate rather than the House was closely involved with foreign affairs. The Framers expected this bicameral imbalance because they granted an executive role to the Senate: providing "advice and consent" to treaties and diplomatic appointments. The Senate also possessed certain qualities that the House did not that were viewed as important to diplomacy. Its longer terms promoted stability and continuity; its smaller size (twenty-six senators in 1789 compared to sixty-five representatives) promoted secrecy, debate, and dispatch. As John Jay wrote in *The Federalist* (Ford 1898, 428), "They who wish to commit the [treaty-ratifying] power under consideration to a popular assembly, composed of members constantly coming and going in quick succession, seem not to recollect that such a body must necessarily be inadequate to the attainment of those great objects which require to be steadily contemplated in all their relations and circumstances." The passage of time has negated some of the qualities highlighted by Jay. Senators are now popularly elected, the Senate has grown from twenty-six to one hundred members, and House members enjoy even more stability and continuity in office-holding than senators do.[3] Moreover, since the post–World War II period, the foreign and defense obligations of the United States have increasingly required huge sums of money. Because the House traditionally originates tax and appropriation measures, the House can frame much of the debate on international issues. Further, presidents have increasingly resorted to executive agreements with foreign nations rather than treaties. Implementation of such agreements usually requires bicameral action. For example, in 1956, of the 260 international agreements about 95 percent were under legislative enactment, and only five were treaties (Griffith 1967, 183). In short, the House is as much a partner in international decision making as the Senate.

This House-Senate pattern accelerated as each chamber moved toward greater parity with the executive branch in foreign and defense policymaking. Journalist David S. Broder has even suggested that "initiative and, one is tempted to say, control have passed from the executive to the legislative branch, in which Congress is on the offensive and the president is responding as best he can" (Broder 1975). Both chambers equipped themselves with new processes and procedures, especially specialized staff and information resources, enabling them not only to analyze and evaluate executive initiatives more effectively but also to formulate and refine proposals of their own.

Throughout this period, the House became more than just an active partner with the Senate—it became a full-fledged partner. Foreign policy activities by the House, for which there are many precedents in the post–World War II years, intensified in scale and scope during the subsequent decades. Indicators abound: world leaders now visit the Senate *and* House when they journey to Washington, D.C.; more House delegations than ever before travel abroad to meet with foreign leaders, such as Speaker Jim Wright's April 1987 meeting in Moscow with Soviet President Mikhail Gorbachev; and the Senate and House each appointed a group of lawmakers to monitor the SALT II (Strategic Arms Limitation Talks) discussions in Geneva. House Foreign Affairs Chair Dante Fascell (D-Fla.) reported in August 1987 that members of his panel have "monitored the United States-Soviet Geneva arms control talks since they began in March 1985" (Whelan 1988, 553). A senator and a House member are, respectively, chair and cochair, on an alternating basis, of the U.S. Commission on Security and

Cooperation in Europe, established to monitor human rights compliance in various nations.

There has been a surge in the number of informal, bicameral caucuses (groups of interested House and Senate members) that are concerned exclusively with foreign and defense policy. Of the twenty-one informal caucuses created during the 1980s, fourteen addressed international issues (for example, the Congressional Task Force on Afghanistan and the Congressional Coalition for Soviet Jews). During the previous decade, only five of fourteen bicameral caucuses dealt with international topics (see Richardson 1989).

However, this does not suggest that the Senate now plays less of a role in the foreign policy arena; rather that the House has achieved full—not junior—partnership with the Senate in international relations. Two seemingly unique developments of the postreform era, however, merit discussion. Each has the potential for reshaping Congress's policy-making activities. The first concerns Speaker Jim Wright's role as diplomat extraordinaire. The second involves global changes that appear likely to require all senators and representatives to monitor developments in their "international constituency."

The Speaker's Role Transformed

The contemporary speakership has been transformed in at least three important ways. First, television has highlighted the Speaker's national visibility and role in legislative decision making. Speaker O'Neill (1977–87) ushered in the era of heightened public notice as well as its concomitant byproduct: the Speaker can function in a "bully pulpit" role to articulate an agenda for the House. The current House Speaker, Thomas S. Foley, captured this turn of events when he remarked that the legendary Speaker Sam Rayburn (D-Tex.), who served in that role at various times from 1940 to 1961, could walk down the streets of any city "without anybody noticing him." Today, "it is very unlikely that any . . . Speaker will be anonymous to the country" (Byrd 1986). In short, the Speaker's national visibility enables him or her as never before to communicate party and legislative views to the nation.

Second, largely during the decade of the 1970s, the House witnessed a change in its internal power structure (as did the Senate). The era of powerful, even autocratic, committee chairs came to a close with changes in the seniority system. Chairs, for instance, are now subject to approval by secret ballot within the confines of the party caucus. Three committee chairs in the mid-1970s, and several more since then, were ousted from their posts. Along with far less powerful chairs came the diffusion of power to subcommittee leaders, *ad hoc* groups, staff aides, and individual lawmakers. "Juniority" replaced seniority as newcomers quickly exercised initiative in lawmaking without the necessity, as before, of serving in an apprenticeship capacity. "You don't have to wait around to have influence," said Representative Schumer, who began his House service in 1981. "Entrepreneurs do very well" (Birnbaum 1987).[4]

Ironically, the advent of participatory democracy with its attendant fragmentation and diffusion of power created the need for strong leadership. The Speaker has been the beneficiary of this tendency. Not since the heyday of Speaker Joseph Cannon (R-Ill., 1903–11), who saw his power clipped by the 1910 House "revolt," have so many prerogatives been accorded the speakership. The Speaker, for instance, chairs the Democratic committee-on-committees and names the chair and Democratic members of the Rules Committee. In brief, while power is spread more widely in the House than ever before, committee leaders and individual members require more assistance from the Speaker in mobilizing support for their proposals and in creating outside, grass-roots backing for policy initiatives.

Finally, a newfound potential may inhere in the contemporary speakership—an expansion of the leader's role in shaping international policymaking. Speaker Jim Wright (D-Tex., 1987–June 1989), an acknowledged power like his predecessors in shaping domestic policy, became for a while in 1987 a leading shaper of national policy toward Nicaragua. In a 1988 editorial, the *Washington Post* headlined "Superdiplomat Jim Wright."

For much of the 1980s, Congress and the Reagan administration battled bitterly over military aid to the contras—a guerrilla force fighting against the Nicaraguan government led by its Sandinista leader Daniel Ortega. (The Sandinistas, a popular front movement, had fought for nearly twenty years to topple from power dictator Anastasio Somoza; this occurred in the summer of 1979. Subsequently, the Ortega-led government instituted authoritarian rule, took aid from the Soviet Union, and fomented unrest in neighboring nations.) The Reagan administration believed military force was required to get Ortega's government to adopt democratic reforms. Many in Congress, including Speaker Wright, supported diplomatic initiatives rather than armed conflict to bring peace to Central America. They argued that U.S.-funded contras gave Ortega an excuse to curtail political freedom in his country. Wright, fluent in Spanish and with strong ties to many Latin American leaders, wanted the Sandinistas and contras to engage in peaceful negotiations and strived to encourage Central American leaders to facilitate this process.

In 1987 the Reagan administration invited Speaker Wright to join in sponsoring a new Central American peace initiative. With the White House weakened by the Iran-contra scandal, the loss of the Senate to the Democrats, and doubts about its sincerity in seeking an end to the contra-Sandinista conflict, the president recognized that he needed Wright's assistance to bring about a negotiated settlement of the armed conflict. Speaker Wright thus became a dominant player, encouraging a negotiated settlement. The joint peace settlement that Reagan and Wright sponsored was largely written by the Speaker. The Speaker "transformed his office into an independent embassy" meeting with Central American officials, dispatching aides to Central America, consulting widely with the region's leaders, and almost daily calling "friends throughout the region, including President José Napoleon Duarte of El Salvador" (Roberts 1988, 34; see also Barry 1989, chaps. 12–13). The joint peace plan, which was announced on 5 August 1987, was followed two days later by a peace agreement signed in Guatemala by five Central American presidents. (The Costa Rican president, Oscar Arias, won the Nobel Peace Prize for his efforts.) Speaker Wright's efforts paved the way for the Central American accord.

Not since Henry Clay's role in the War of 1812 had any Speaker assumed such a powerful position in foreign policy-making. Speaker Wright's actions provoked outcries from many in the State Department and elsewhere as an infringement on the president's diplomatic responsibilities. Wright noted, however, that Congress and the president are "equal partners" in government policy-making. However one views Speaker Wright's Central American role, it is evident that the House, the Senate, and all lawmakers will be engaged in international issues as never before. "Everybody in Congress is a foreign policy expert—it's just part of the game," noted House Foreign Affairs Chair Dante Fascell (D-Fla.) (qtd. in Stanfield 1990, 2919).[5] The game, in short, is no longer local but global.

All Politics Is Global

Speaker O'Neill was fond of saying, "All politics is local." It is axiomatic that lawmakers must attend to the needs and concerns of their constituents or else they might not be returned to Congress. O'Neill's prescription, while encouraging accountability and responsiveness on the part of lawmakers, also understandably promotes localistic perspectives. As Richard Neuberger of Oregon, senator from 1955 to 1960, said, "If there is one maxim which seems to prevail among many members of our national legislature, it is that local matters must come first and global problems a poor second—that is, if the member of Congress is to survive politically" (qtd. in Huntington 1965, 15). This general attitude no longer applies with the force that it once did; subsequent decades have witnessed an expansion of transnational perspectives in the Congress. Today, virtually all senators and representatives are generally cognizant of global developments and their impact on the folks back home. This trend accelerated during the postreform era in response to developments significantly different even from previous decades: among them the end of the cold war, new trade interdependencies and imbalances, the reunification of Germany, the economic integration of the European Community, and the multilateral diplomacy in the Persian Gulf crisis. Members, in short, cannot avoid the mutual linkages among nations that directly affect their constituencies. One scholar even coined a new word—*intermestic* (the first part of "*inter*national" and the last part of "do*mestic*")—to underscore the growing irrelevancy of distinctions between domestic and international affairs (Manning 1977).

New challenges and threats fill Congress's agenda—global warming, trade imbalances, nuclear and chemical weapons proliferation in the Third World, drug trafficking, terrorism, deforestation, the exchange value of the dollar, and our growing dependence on foreign investment. The globalization of nearly every aspect of the economy diminishes the nation's ability to control unilaterally its economic well-being. Even U.S. tax rates are shaped by international forces as much as by domestic political circumstances. "The world of the 1990s is one big integrated capital market," wrote an economic analyst, "with investment funds ready to move at the speed of light and at the cost of a phone call to countries with the most hospitable tax climates" (McKenzie 1990).

Many of the challenges that confront today's lawmakers are beyond the control of any single nation. They require international cooperation and shared decision making. While senators and representatives will continue to focus on domestic concerns—inflation, unemployment, health care, transportation, and the like—they will do so with heightened appreciation of their international dimensions. Simply put, no member can politically afford to remain insulated from global developments because no district or state is isolated from their effects.

The new global politics require broader forms of representation and communication. In May 1990, for instance, Representative Sander Levin (D-Mich.) invited a Japanese Diet member to visit his Detroit-area district to explain his nation's trade policies and to hear from American automobile workers. Subsequently, Levin visited Japan at the Diet member's invitation to talk with Japanese businesspeople and to outline the concerns of Detroit's workers (Jones 1990). Today's members, in brief, must communicate and consult not only with blocs of voters back home but often with an array of international constituents as well. These dual responsibilities—promoting the basic needs of constituents and accommodating global issues—broaden the representational role of lawmakers in the postreform Congress.

Indeed, a major challenge of the 1990s is how to reconcile divergent tendencies. Economically, the world is rapidly moving toward greater global integration. Politically, the electoral imperative compels lawmakers to represent local interests. Economic internationalization and political localism are parallel phenomena that can be difficult to accommodate easily.

Summary Points

Far-reaching global developments have changed the agenda and political discourse on Capitol Hill. Both chambers as never before are heavily involved in debating a plethora of intermestic issues because the post–cold war world is so different from anything in the past. A major issue for lawmakers is how to reconcile, politically and economically, citizens' diverse and often competing expectations with the global cooperation that is increasingly required to achieve national objectives.

The international overlay to domestic issues is often evident in conference committees—a bicameral forum that has seen significant change in the postreform Congress. In an era of divided party control between Congress and the White House and scarce fiscal resources, it is often in conference that laws take their final form. For instance, because of Egypt's strong support of President Bush in the Persian Gulf War, the administration wanted to forgive Egypt's nearly $7 billion debt to the United States for military aid. During the conference Representative David Obey (D-Wis.) said, "The American people don't understand how we can afford to forgive all this debt when we can't do it for our farmers" (Stanfield 1990, 2917). The result: The conference reached an artful accommodation that muted popular resentment against debt-forgiveness for Egypt. Conflict and cooperation are themes common to conference committees and the interdependence of nations.

CONFERENCE COMMITTEES IN THE POSTREFORM CONGRESS

The conference committee is a critical juncture in the legislative process. Bills must pass both chambers with identical language before they can be forwarded to the president for his consideration. Three methods are used to achieve bicameral agreement: (1) one chamber adopts the other's legislation verbatim; (2) the House and Senate may send measures back and forth several times, amending each other's amendments, before they agree to identical language; or (3) the two chambers agree to go to conference when they pass dissimilar versions of the same bill. It is usually the most controversial, significant, and well-publicized issues of the day that reach the conference committee stage.

Historically, these bicameral bargaining units always met secretly. The 1970s witnessed the opening of conference committee deliberations to public observation. (Scores of private, during-the-conference discussions still characterize these sessions, however.) During the 1970s the House amended its rules to address a long-standing interchamber controversy: how to deal with nongermane (not relevant) Senate amendments added to House-passed bills and included in the conference report. The House adopted a procedure to delete nongermane matter from conference reports. Interestingly, in the mid-1980s the Senate imitated the House by adopting rules to delete extraneous matter in conference reports dealing with certain budget measures.

A variety of other formal and informal changes occurred during the past two decades that reshaped conference committee activity. Two interrelated developments that emerged from this period are unique and appear certain to continue into the foreseeable future. The two developments concern the size and composition of conference committees.

Size and Composition

In 1981 the largest conference in history—over 250 conferees from both chambers—met on the omnibus reconciliation bill to resolve over three hundred matters in disagreement between the two houses. That size record still stands, but big conferences are fairly commonplace today. (Before, conference delegations typically ranged from five to twelve conferees from each house.) Two phenomena treated elsewhere in this volume—multiple referrals and megabills—largely account for the increase in size and change in composition (Davidson and Oleszek, this volume, Chapter 7).

Composition refers to the diversity of conferees who serve on these *ad hoc* joint panels. Prior to the mid-1970s conferees nearly always were the most senior lawmakers from the committees that reported the legislation. Today conferees are commonly chosen from scores of panels and reflect complex selection arrangements. Conferees are appointed with relatively little seniority; their place on a subcommittee may influence their appointment more than their rank on the full committee; they may be named to negotiate only specific items in bicameral disagreement rather than all the matters in dispute; and they may come from committees that did not report the legislation. Just as extensive negotiations characterize conference deliberations, they now frequently characterize the appointment of each chamber's conference delegation.[6] Multiple committee consideration of megabills is the driving force behind these developments.

Ever since 1975, when the House changed its rules, there has been an increase in the referral of legislation to several committees for simultaneous or sequential consideration. A 1975 House rules change permitted the Speaker to refer measures to several committees. The Senate permits multiple referrals by the unanimous consent of the membership. With more committees claiming jurisdiction for the same bill, it means that more members are selected as conferees. The number of conferees per committee is commonly worked out informally by the respective panel leaders with input from the elective party leadership and generally reflects each committee's proportionate involvement with the legislation. Large and diverse conference delegations often complicate the compromise-making process.

Multiple committee representation also affects the mechanics of conference decision making. The conference may subdivide into smaller groups called *subconferences*. There may be general conferees to coordinate the activities of the special conferees assigned to various subconferences. During the omnibus trade conference of the 100th Congress (1987–89), for instance, conferees were chosen from twenty-three House and Senate committees. No less than 155 House and forty-four Senate conferees convened in seventeen subconferences, with some subconferences even forming subgroups ("sub-subconferences") of their own. Interestingly, House conferees were selected to consider only issues that fell within their committee's jurisdiction. As a result, the decisions reached by any House subconference were binding on all House conferees. The Senate conferees, however, operated under informal procedures that permitted the entire group to review and override decisions reached by their senatorial colleagues on the respective subconferences.

Increasing use of megabills during the past decade also accounts for wider use of multiple referrals and larger conference delegations. These omnibus measures, or packages, typically affect the jurisdictions of several standing committees. Drug, trade, clean air, crime, spending, tax, and Social Security legislation are recent and prominent examples of megabills, which run for hundreds and sometimes thousands of pages in length.

Various factors account for the recent surge in the use of megabills. They are employed to overcome institutional inertia and to protect members from the importunings of special interest groups. By bundling scores of issues into one massive bill, lawmakers can argue that they had to support the comprehensive measure both because of party leadership pressure and because any change in the package could cause it to unravel. "As long as special interests dominate the political scene in Washington, D.C.," said Representative Mike Synar (D-Okla.), "the only way to fight them off is by packaging the legislation" (Tolchin 1983).

Megabills are sometimes moved through the House and Senate under procedures that restrict opportunities for floor amendments. Huge amendments may be added in one chamber without any opportunity for the other to consider them in committee or on the floor. Instead, the House-passed bill and massive Senate amendment to it, for example, are sent directly to conference. In such circumstances the authority of the conference is plainly enhanced; it not only adjusts interchamber differences but also crafts the final legislation.

Conference committees do not operate in a vacuum but reflect changes and developments in Congress itself. During the era of powerful standing committee chairs (roughly from 1920 through the early 1970s), House and Senate conference negotiations were controlled by these committee leaders. During the 1960s, for instance, the respective chairs of the two armed services committees—Representative Carl Vinson (D-Ga.) and Senator Richard Russell (D-Ga.)—dominated the closed-door proceedings. Representative Otis Pike (D-N.Y.), who served as a conferee on military issues, characterized the conferences as "two gentlemen from Georgia, talking, arguing, laughing, and whispering in each other's ears" (*Washington Star*, 12 March 1964, A2). Today, given multiple referrals, megabills, open conference sessions, and the broad diffusion of influence throughout the contemporary House and Senate, participatory democracy now permeates many of these bicameral negotiating sessions, even those involving defense issues.

Summary Points

Policy-making is an interconnected process. What happens in the House affects decisions in the Senate (or vice versa) and later in conference. No wonder lawmakers try to shape and direct legislative outcomes during the preconference stages so as to augment their bargaining influence in conference should the legislation reach that bicameral forum. As President Reagan said about Senator Russell Long (D-La.), "He was the one legislator who had his mind on the conference . . . when the others were worrying about the floor debate" (qtd. in *Weekly Compilation of Presidential Documents*, 17 October 1985, 1261).

Policy interrelatedness is also evident in the increasing overlap of domestic and international issues. This development affects conference deliberations. Scores of House and Senate committees are involved in considering international issues—even panels that are usually regarded as domestic committees. The House Public Works and Transportation Committee, for example, reviews international aviation policy. Not surprisingly, conference size and composition has changed significantly during the postreform era. Many more committees than before have a legitimate claim to review measures that previously were referred to only one panel. Further, if the legislation is a megabill, the chances are even greater that several panels will consider the measure and then select conferees to meet with counterparts from the other body.

Needless to say, large conference delegations invariably require more time to iron out bicameral differences. The diversity of views that need to be harmonized affects the pace of deliberations. Large conferences also promote access to the negotiations by lawmakers who are not conferees, interest groups, and executive officials. If large conferences become unwieldy even if they divide into subconferences, they often break down into smaller and smaller groups. This process was followed in the 101st Congress on the huge savings and loan conference, which embraced nearly one-quarter of the House. As one House conferee said:

> One hundred two conferees were appointed and no progress was made until the four principals went behind closed doors. And I'm not complaining. If [House Banking] Chair [Henry] Gonzalez had not reduced the conference from 102 members to four, we would still be there arguing over this bill. He should get an oscar for his starring role in, "Honey, I shrunk the conference." (*Congressional Record*, 3 August 1989, H5003)

Lawmakers, in short, adjust unwieldy bicameral circumstances to reach necessary compromises.

CONCLUSION

A consistent pattern of national decision making is separate institutions sharing power. When commentators evaluate this pattern, they commonly assess legislative-executive relations. House-Senate interactions, too, merit attention for two main reasons: they establish the framework for all our laws and they influence the within-chamber decisions of each house. Our national policies, in short, are shaped by the interchamber connection as well as by the electoral or legislative-executive connection.

Change, an iron law of politics, is certainly evident in bicameralism. New interchamber relations and tendencies have evolved during the postreform Congress. Our focus on three—House-Senate changes involving the initiation of tax legislation, the impact of intermestic issues, and the configuration of conference committees—highlights the themes of adaptability, participation, and innovation that characterize bicameralism today.

Notes

1. For a general article, see Strahan 1988.
2. A bipartisan group of House members later brought a federal court suit challenging the constitutionality of the Tax Equity and Fiscal Responsibility Act of 1982. The court, however, dismissed the case on the ground that it preferred to exercise judicial restraint on questions involving the separation of powers.
3. Recent elections have seen as high as a 98 percent rate of return for House incumbents seeking reelection. In November 1990 the rate of return was over 96 percent. Senate incumbents, by contrast, are more vulnerable to electoral defeat.
4. In December 1990 the House Democratic caucus ousted two incumbent chairs from their positions (Public Works and Transportation and the House Administration committees).
5. For an earlier perspective see Carroll 1966.
6. Conferees are named from the committee or committees that reported the legislation. Congressional rules state that the Speaker and Senate presiding officer formally select conferees; actually, the decision is made by the respective committee chairs and ranking minority members (see Longley and Oleszek 1989). Because conferee selection has gotten so complex, Speaker Thomas Foley announced at the start of the 102nd Congress that he intended "to the fullest extent feasible to simplify the appointment of conferees" (*Congressional Record*, 3 January 1991, p. H31).

PART · V

Policy-making in an Age of Stalemate

11 / The President and the Postreform Congress

JAMES P. PFIFFNER

In 1976 it appeared that Congress had decisively reversed the inroads on its constitutional prerogatives effected by the "imperial" presidencies of Lyndon Johnson (1963–69) and Richard Nixon (1969–74). Congress had established a new budgetary process that would give it the capacity to formulate a congressional budget, and it used its new tools to substitute congressional budget priorities for President Gerald Ford's in 1975. Many also hoped that the new budget process would bring fiscal discipline and rein in the huge budget deficits of more than $50 billion that appeared in the mid-1970s.

Congress had also passed in 1973, over President Nixon's veto, the War Powers Resolution, which set distinct limits and conditions on the president's right to send troops into hostile military situations. With the election of Jimmy Carter in 1976, the nation again had unified government, with both Congress and the president controlled by the same party, a situation that had prevailed for most of the history of the Republic.

By the early 1990s, however, the high expectations of the proponents of congressional reassertion had been disappointed. The nation suffered record deficits of over $300 billion, and the national debt had risen to over $3 trillion. The second concurrent resolution of the new budget process had been abandoned and the budget committees had lost important parts of their functions. The budget process had broken down and Congress was not able to create comprehensive alternatives to the president's budget. Deficit limits had been adopted and abandoned, and presidents continued to blame federal spending on Congress.

No president had admitted to the constitutionality of the War Powers Resolution. Even in most instances when it would have been applicable, presidents had ignored its provisions. When the issue concerning a sixty-day limit on troop deployments had been raised, Congress was unable to forge the consensus to start the clock ticking. In other areas of national security policy, however, Congress was much more assertive, sometimes delving into the details of defense management in intrusive ways.

Divided government came to be the expected state of affairs, with the unified government of the Carter administration a brief interlude between Republican domination of the White House and Democratic control of Congress. The imperial presidency had not reemerged (with the possible exception of the Iran-contra affair). There was no major reversal of the

211

constitutional balance; the claim made by some members of the Bush administration that congressional approval was not needed to initiate war with Iraq was never tested. Both branches continued to assert their constitutional prerogatives, but with the added overlay of partisan differences reinforcing institutional rivalry.

This chapter traces the contemporary roots of confrontation between the president and Congress in order to examine in some detail the two main areas of confrontation between the two branches: (1) the constitutional power of the purse, or budgeting; and (2) the constitutional power of the sword, or national security. The chapter will then address the increasing incidence of divided government and how it affects interbranch relations. These considerations lead us to some conclusions about how personality and historical circumstance affect the presidency.

CONFRONTATION AND REFORM: 1965–1980

The contemporary roots of confrontation between the president and Congress lie in the breakdown of consensus over the war in Vietnam and in partisan disputes over domestic policy priorities. U.S. military involvement in Vietnam was supported in Congress by the Gulf of Tonkin resolution (1964) and general public acceptance of President Johnson's decision the following year to escalate military activity. But as U.S. casualties in Vietnam increased, public opinion began to change and congressional opposition to the war grew. Eventually, opposition to the war became so great that Johnson decided not to seek reelection in 1968.

Congressional opposition to the war continued after Richard Nixon became president in 1969. When Nixon was not able to obtain the terms he wanted for ending U.S. involvement in Vietnam, Congress forced his hand by threatening to cut off funds for the war. Yet Nixon's efforts failed not only to sustain congressional support for the war but also to take domestic policies in new directions. The failures led the president to seek his goals through administrative means in order to control the executive branch and confrontation with the Democratic-controlled Congresses (Nathan 1983).

Nixon refused to spend large amounts of money provided by Congress for programs of which he did not approve. Claiming to have the constitutional power to impound funds, the president tried to eliminate many programs unilaterally through impoundment (Pfiffner 1979). He attempted to politicize the civil service and to stretch the pocket veto further than any other president before had attempted. Nixon proposed a major reorganization of the executive branch that would have given him unprecedented control of its agencies, and he engaged in the cover-up of Watergate that eventually led to his resignation under the threat of impeachment in the House.

Congress's reaction to Nixon's assertions of presidential power was to pass a series of laws intended to reassert congressional prerogatives. Congress passed the War Powers Resolution over Nixon's veto in 1973; the Budget Act of 1974, which imposed severe limits on presidential impoundment proposals; the Case Act of 1972, which required that all executive agreements be reported to the House and Senate; and the Hughes-Ryan amendment of 1974, which prohibited the Central Intelligence Agency (CIA) from conducting peacetime covert operations abroad unless the president issued a finding that they were important to the national security and reported them to committees in Congress.

At the same time, Congress decided to put its own house in order through a series of reforms that had far-reaching effects on the budget process, committee chairs' powers, and conduct of committee business. Congress also increased significantly personal, committee, and support staff. One result of these reforms was to disperse power that had been previously held by committee chairs, making Congress more democratic but more fragmented. Decentralization led to a more disjointed and pluralistic decision-making process (Smith 1985). New tools were given to party leaders, though initially they were not enough to counterbalance the fragmenting thrust of the reforms (Mezey 1989, 125).

The postreform trends were accompanied by a new breed of legislator in Washington, symbolized by the "Watergate class" of the 1974 elections (Loomis 1988). Because of the decline of political parties, the new candidates had to raise their own campaign money; once in Congress, they sought individual recognition rather than identification with their party. They exhibited much less patience than their predecessors, asserting themselves from the back benches, initiating legislation, offering floor amendments, and seeking media coverage. The new legislators had few incentives to defer to the president or even their own party leaders, and they had the resources to pursue their own objectives. This new context of changed rules and individual members thwarted strong leadership of Congress by the president or even congressional leaders (Smith 1985).

The new type of legislator and a more assertive Congress made life more difficult for presidents. In 1975 President Ford failed to get passed his fiscally conservative economic policies, as the liberal-controlled Congress used new budgetary tools to develop its own fiscal policy. Ford reacted to his weakened position by vetoing a large number of bills in his short time in office (1974–77). Even President Carter, with large Democratic majorities in both houses, faced difficulties getting his legislative priorities enacted. No longer were there "whales" in Congress who could bring along the rank-and-file "minnows" once the president made a deal with the leaders. President Dwight Eisenhower, for example, could bargain with House Speaker Sam Rayburn and Senate Majority Leader Lyndon Johnson with the assurance that they could enforce the terms of the deal on their respective houses. Later presidents had to undertake "retail" selling of their positions with individual lawmakers. According to Kenneth Duberstein, President Carter was "blindsided constantly by people he would have paid no attention to twenty years ago because then they were not factors in the congressional power equation" (Hunter et al. 1986, 242).

By the late 1970s scholars began to question whether the new array of political power in the national government had made it impossible for presidents to be successful leaders. Between 1961 and 1981, all five presidents had left office without a full second term; people thus began to speak of the "no-win presidency." The first year of the Reagan presidency (1981) however, seemed to prove them wrong. Reagan restored public confidence in the office by winning impressive legislative victories in 1981 and by changing the direction of U.S. public policy priorities. His main achievement was a budget package that included large increases in defense spending, significant cuts in domestic spending, and the largest tax cuts in history. In his first year as president Reagan seemed unstoppable (Pfiffner 1986b).

The Reagan administration signaled the end of the initial period of the congressional reforms of the 1970s and the beginning of a new era of interbranch relations characterized as the postreform era. The two main changes in the constitutional conflict between the president and Congress will be considered: the power of the purse—budgeting—and the power of the sword—national security.

POSTREFORM RELATIONS: THE PURSE

The 1980s saw major reversals of the budget process from earlier years: from bottom-up budgeting to top-down budgeting, and from an incremental process to dependence on leadership summits. The 1980s also saw the United States change from the world's largest creditor nation to the largest debtor nation, unprecedented budget deficits of 5–6 percent of the gross national product (GNP), and a national debt that tripled from $1 trillion to $3 trillion.

The Traditional Budget Process and Reform

In the 1950s and 1960s the federal budget process was marked by relatively predictable incremental changes—each year Congress slightly modified the president's proposed spending but kept all major programs operating at roughly their existing levels. In the executive branch the process was begun by budget justifications and proposals that worked their way up from agency to department to the Bureau of the Budget and back down in a series of refinements around a generally agreed-on spending base (Wildavsky 1988). The congressional process was dominated by the thirteen House Appropriations subcommittees that jealously guarded their prerogatives and earned a reputation for hard work and diligence. Norms of reciprocity and specialization predominated and seldom were floor amendments offered to appropriations bills (Fenno 1966). The Senate Appropriations Committee often acted like a court of appeals in restoring some of the cuts made in the House. Congress almost always made some cuts in the president's proposals, but it also provided the money to keep programs funded at their current levels plus an increment.

Changing economic circumstances soon upset this established process, however. Beginning with the guns-and-butter policies of the late 1960s—that is, the United States was paying for both the Great Society and the Vietnam War without significant tax increases—inflation began to build. The creation of the Organization of Petroleum Exporting Countries (OPEC) and an increase in oil prices shocked the U.S. economy and increased inflation. The combination of inflation and recession in the mid-1970s produced stagflation and increasing deficits. The post–World War II economic boom ended and a period of slower growth and reduced productivity began. Federal spending, however, did not respond accordingly. The federal budget had become increasingly locked into higher entitlement spending programs that were indexed to inflation. When inflation went up, so did spending, regardless of whether production was increasing (Schick 1990). By the end of the 1970s the inflation rate was over 10 percent and interest rates approached 20 percent.

Although the reformed budgetary process generally worked from 1974 to 1980—in the same sense that deadlines were met and budget resolutions were passed—the new process could not handle the pressures created by inflation and large deficits. The breakdown of the process and the resort to budget summits were foreshadowed in 1980 when President Carter met with congressional leaders to reduce the deficit after it became clear that his initial budget proposal and a changing economy would not produce a politically acceptable deficit. The summit meeting produced significant cuts and relied on the reconciliation process to force congressional committees to adhere to them.

The Reagan administration's budget victories of 1981 made unprecedented changes in policy and were accomplished by impressive political tactics. The reconciliation process was again used to force one up or down vote on the whole package of cuts. It was a major display of presidential leadership and shrewd political tactics (Pfiffner 1986b). But Reagan's victories in 1981 did not lead to further budget success. He continued to send budget proposals to Congress that asked for more cuts in domestic spending and larger increases in defense spending than bipartisan majorities in Congress were willing to accept. The president's budget proposals became opening gambits in a process of negotiations rather than a statement of where he wanted to end up (Schick 1990, 162).

The congressional reaction to Reagan's ploys was "dead on arrival."

The result was budget stalemate. Reagan refused to consider any cuts in defense or any congressionally-imposed tax increases. He challenged Congress to "make my day" by passing what he considered excessive appropriations that he could veto. The Democrats in Congress would not consider cuts in Social Security benefits or further cuts in already slashed social programs. The Democrats were so successful in fighting potential cuts in Social Security that their efforts became known as the "third rail" of budget politics—that is, touching the electrically charged third rail made political death virtually certain. Politicians were thus unable either to reduce spending significantly or to increase taxes—which, along with the 1982 recession, produced unprecedented deficits over $200 billion, amounting to 5–6 percent of GNP.

Centralization in Both Branches

The normal institutions of the budget process could not handle the pressure. To meet such huge deficits, large spending cuts or equally large tax increases were needed. Rising budgetary and political stakes led to the "fiscalization of the policy process"; that is, most domestic and military budget issues were swept up in deficit-reduction politics and programmatic concerns were subordinated to the bottom line of the size of the deficit. From 1980 to 1988 congressional votes on budget issues compromised more than half of all roll-call votes (Thurber 1991, 148).

With the political stakes so high, the locus of decision making rose to higher levels in both branches. After 1981 Congress continued to rely on the reconciliation process, which put most of the budget into one large set of instructions for other committees to implement. Power over the budget in Congress thus shifted from the relevant committees (authorization, appropriation, and budget) to the floor and thereby increased the importance of the leadership. Floor consideration of budget packages, however, was not controlled by any single coalition during the mid-1980s (Gilmour 1990b).

Just as budget control in Congress became centralized at the floor and leadership levels, so was budgeting centralized in the executive branch. The emphasis on deficit reduction and budget aggregates in the 1980s led to top-down control by the Office of Management and Budget (OMB). And with the volatility of changing economic projections and shifting deals with Congress, OMB Director David Stockman demanded immediate answers to questions about the effect of changed economic assumptions on budget aggregates. The OMB's staff and computer capacity were developed to respond to Stockman's concerns.

Stockman also reoriented the OMB. Staffers spent more time tracing the status of legislation than in program oversight in the executive branch. Agencies found themselves at the receiving end of changing budget deals that were negotiated by Stockman with Congress. The concerns of OMB staffers shifted away from program performance and toward negotiation with Congress over the bottom line (Heclo 1984).

The OMB also significantly centralized presidential control over the issuance of executive branch regulations. Executive orders 12,291 and 12,498 now permit the OMB to review all potential executive branch regulations to assure that they are in accord with the president's priorities. During the 1980s the OMB used this power to prevent many regulations from being proposed or implemented. At times this power was used to delay or impede the implementation of laws by executive branch agencies. For example, some members of Congress felt that the EPA was being prevented from carrying out its legal duties by the refusal of the OMB to permit the agency to issue regulations called for by law.

The Resort to Budget Summitry

The high stakes involved and the rigid positions of the president and some Democratic leaders led to budget summits to try to break the impasse. When in 1983 the Social Security Trust Fund was about to run out of money, President Reagan appointed a commission to examine ways to reestablish its solvency. Chair Alan Greenspan and the commission proposed a combination of tax increases and benefit cuts to solve the short-term problem. The plan succeeded only because President Reagan and House Speaker Thomas P. O'Neill agreed to back it. The commission's approach produced a solution to a very difficult problem (Light 1985; Neustadt and May 1986).

In 1985 the Republican Senate leadership proposed a package of spending freezes, cuts, and tax increases that would have made a significant dent in the deficit. But the same two key actors who had made the Social Security summit successful doomed this proposal as well. President Reagan refused to go along with the proposed tax increases and Speaker O'Neill opposed the cuts in benefits. As a result, the Gramm-Rudman-Hollings (GRH) deficit-reduction law was passed later that year. It provided that if fixed deficit levels were not reached, across-the-board budget cuts (or sequestration) would be made equally in domestic and military programs (many entitlement programs were exempted). Across-the-board cuts are, in general, irrational because they cut essential programs along with the less important and the efficient along with the wasteful. Thus GRH amounted to a doomsday machine intended to force the president and Congress to reach some agreement on reducing the deficit.

The stalemate and thus the threat of sequestration led the leaders of the two branches in 1987 to negotiate a two-year deficit-reduction pact. The summit agreement did not flow from the normal budgetary process but from the mutual need of the president and congressional leaders to avoid sequestration.

In the election year of 1988 Congress created a bipartisan National Economic Commission to draft a set of options to reduce the deficit. The

Commission was meant to provide political "cover" for the new president so that he could endorse a combination of spending reductions and tax increases shortly after the election that would put the economy on the path of deficit reduction (Mathiasen 1990). During the presidential campaign, however, Bush decried what he called the "tax increase commission" and ignored its proposals after he was elected in 1988.

The Politics of Blame Avoidance

Reducing the deficit was virtually impossible during a decade of blame-avoidance politics practiced by both political parties (Weaver 1988). Whenever Republicans suggested any cuts in Social Security benefits, some Democratic politicians would exploit the issue to accuse the Republicans of trying to destroy the Social Security system. Similarly, whenever Democrats proposed any tax increase some Republican politicians would exploit the issue to blame Democrats for high tax burdens. Neither side compromised for fear that it would be blamed by the voters for doing something distasteful. As economist Charles Schultze put it:

> Democrats will not put forward a plan that includes a tax increase because, with good cause, they know that apparatchiks and ideologues of the Republican party will tar them with that position in the coming elections. And Republicans, with equally good reason, are afraid that if they propose the slightest cut in Social Security benefits, some rabble-rousing Democrats will try to repeat their electoral success of 1982 by accusing them of taking away the birthright of the nation's senior citizens. Each side's more disreputable partisans are blackmailing the other side. And both sides are locked into frozen positions. . . . (1990, A27)

In other words, the nation wanted government benefits without having to pay for them.

Republican presidential candidates benefited from this arrangement, winning three presidential elections with promises of no tax increases. Congressional Democrats benefited by posing as protectors of benefit programs cherished by voters. The 1988 presidential election was influenced by Bush's promise: "Read my lips, no new taxes." His pledge helped him beat Bob Dole (D-Kan.) in the New Hampshire primary and Michael Dukakis (D-Mass.) in the general election.

The Budget Summit of 1990

President Bush's first budget proposal to Congress was based on his pledge of no new taxes coupled with an optimistic set of economic assumptions. Although he reached an agreement with Congress, it relied on a number of gimmicks that did not produce real or lasting deficit reduction (for example, part of the savings and loan bailout was off budget, the U.S. Postal Service was taken off budget, and asset sales as well as increases in tax collections were assumed). Both the president and Congress went along with the assumption that the $100 billion deficit target mandated by GRH would be met. The actual fiscal year (FY) 1990 deficit, however, exceeded $160 billion.

Taking a similarly optimistic approach in his FY 1991 budget proposed to Congress in 1990, Bush projected a deficit of $63 billion. But the economic situation deteriorated in the spring of 1990: a recession was looming and, in July, the OMB's estimate of the probable deficit rose to $168 billion. In addition, the savings and loan bailout turned out to be far larger than previously admitted, swelling the deficit even further.

President Bush called a budget summit with the congressional leadership in May 1990, and after a period of negotiation abandoned his pledge of no new taxes by admitting that so-called tax revenue increases would be needed to shrink the deficit. In September of that year the budget summit negotiators, including congressional leaders and presidential aides, met in special secluded sessions at Andrews Air Force Base to try to break the impasse. The summit was based on the expectation that behind closed doors leaders of both sides could reach compromises not possible if each side's concessions were open to political attack prior to a final agreement. This type of process had worked in the 1983 Social Security Commission.

By 30 September 1990, the eve of the new fiscal year, the summit negotiators announced a budget agreement. Then, on 2 October, President Bush, calling the deficit a cancer threatening U.S. economic health, appealed to the nation and Congress to support the compromise. Senate Majority Leader George Mitchell, speaking for the Democrats, also endorsed the budget compromise. The problem was that the deal did not have the necessary support in the back benches of Congress. House Republican Whip Newt Gingrich (Ga.) defected from the budget summit and led conservative House Republicans to vote against the president's proposal because it involved tax increases. Liberal Democrats also voted against the package because they felt that the wealthy were spared from their share of the burden and that the cuts in Medicare were excessive. The strategy of using summit meetings of leadership of the two branches was not able to hold together the set of compromises they proposed.

It was a major defeat for President Bush after his direct appeal to the nation, as well as for the leadership of Congress on both sides of the aisle. The result was an outcome of the fragmenting trends in Congress described earlier. It was also the result of a national fiscal policy that amounted to what Stockman (1986, 8) called "free-lunch economics," in which tax cuts on a large scale were believed to result in increased tax revenues.

Some argued that President Bush's political operatives did not adequately prepare their supporters to inundate Congress with messages of support for the budget package immediately after his speech, as the Reagan administration had done in 1981. But the strategic problem that led to the lack of public and congressional support for the budget deal was that presidential leadership over the previous decade had argued that no tax increases were necessary to deal with the deficit.

The two sides went back to the drawing boards, and after three weeks of negotiations, including several continuing resolutions and a shutdown of the government, reached an agreement. The new deal was only marginally different from the previous agreement, with further increases in taxes partially offsetting a reduction in the proposed cuts in Medicare benefits. The final package was expected to cut the FY 1991 deficit by $40 billion and a total of $490 billion from the next five years of deficits. The reductions came from a combination of cuts in discretionary spending and entitlements along with increases in taxes and user fees; they were calculated from a baseline of projected spending under current law plus expected increases for inflation.

In procedural changes, Congress made the decision to shift the focus on future savings from controlling the size of the deficit, which was the trigger for sequestration under GRH, to controlling increases in spending. Any new spending in three separate categories of discretionary spending—defense, international, and domestic programs—would now have to be offset by decreases elsewhere within a category. Violations of these strictures would lead to across-the-board sequestration within the affected categories. The deficit targets for the 1990s previously established by GRH were drastically revised upward—to over $300 billion in the next two fiscal years.

The new procedures, however, gave the president the authority to adjust the new deficit targets in order to take into account changing economic and technical assumptions. These provisions gave the president considerably more budgetary power, and the law effectively, if not formally, repealed the GRH legislation (Shuman 1991). The surplus in Social Security receipts was taken off budget, increasing the nominal deficit by about $60 billion per year. Military expenditures for the Persian Gulf War were not counted against the budget allocation for defense. The vulnerabilities of the new budget procedures were that the several sequestrations could be too cumbersome to implement or that the deficits could rise to politically unacceptable levels and lead to new budgetary crises and further changes.

The 1990 budget changes significantly affected some major goals of the 1974 Budget Act. The act was intended to give Congress more control of overall budget priorities. But by segregating the budget into three separate categories, the new law effectively precluded Congress from shifting budget priorities across the categories (such as from defense to domestic spending). It also locked in spending totals for five years, depriving the Budget committees that were created in 1974 of most of their functions. The overall impact of the 1990 changes was to shift budgetary power marginally toward the president, but the continuing fiscal crisis of huge deficits was by no means solved. Robert Reischauer, director of the Congressional Budget Office, pointed out the irony: "Congress just enacted the largest deficit-reduction package in the nation's history and now we will be treated to the largest deficit in the nation's history" (*Washington Post*, 8 January 1990).

POSTREFORM RELATIONS: THE SWORD

The president and Congress have always vied for control of foreign and national security policy. The Framers gave the president operational control of the armed forces through the commander in chief role and the right to conduct diplomacy. Congress was given the duty to provide for an army and navy and declare war as well as the power of the purse. While the president has usually dominated U.S. foreign policy, Congress has occasionally asserted itself and determined the direction of foreign relations.

An exception to the usual state of conflict between the two branches was the post–World War II, or cold war, era. Both the executive branch and Congress agreed on containing Communism and opposing the Soviet Union.

Congressional support of the president after World War II was so consistent that Aaron Wildavsky, in his "two presidencies" thesis, argued that Congress was willing to defer to the president in foreign affairs while in the domestic arena it asserted its own priorities (1966). Since this pattern of deference did not continue into the 1970s, George Edwards (1989) argues that congressional support of the president was due to agreement with policy goals, not to any deference to the office.

The war in Vietnam, however, shattered the cold war consensus about U.S. foreign policy. Congressional liberals succeeded in bringing the war to an end by cutting off funds from Congress, and they continued to be skeptical of U.S. involvement in foreign military actions. Conservatives, generally hostile to the Soviet Union, were willing to commit military forces to support anti-Communist efforts throughout the world (Mann 1990b). This schism in the U.S. public reinforced the breakdown in comity between the branches resulting from U.S. military actions in Southeast Asia (Destler et al. 1984).

The ability of the president and Congress to agree on foreign policy priorities was also undermined by an opening and politicizing of the policy process. Think tanks were established to house foreign policy professionals and scholars, who sometimes constituted a virtual shadow government in the national security arena. New interest groups in business, trade, and ethnic policies were more aggressive in gaining access to the policy process. The policy arena was enlarged; it became more fragmented in the executive branch as well as in Congress.

New Congressional Activism

The result of the changes was a Congress much more willing to assert itself in foreign policy-making, not merely in questions of policy direction but also in the details of defense management. For instance, congressional involvement in arms control issues in the 1980s was unprecedented. In some instances Congress forced the Reagan administration to adopt specific positions in negotiations and pushed it toward a more conciliatory stance with the Soviet Union (Blechman 1990). Members of Congress in the 1980s also were more involved in diplomatic initiatives that sometimes cut against the executive branch's priorities. House Speaker Jim Wright (Tex.) and Senator Jesse Helms (N.C.), from opposite sides of the political spectrum, at times invoked the fury of the Reagan administration for their forays into diplomacy. Congress also occasionally insisted on having congressional representatives at international negotiating conferences.

As for covert operations, Congress did not engage in tight oversight of the executive branch from the end of World War II to the mid-1970s, but it became much more involved in intelligence activities as a result of abuses by the CIA. After passage of the Intelligence Oversight Act of 1980 and the creation of the Intelligence committees in Congress, the two branches developed workable relationships concerning oversight (Treverton 1990; Blechman 1990). (Revelations about the Iran-contra affair, however, badly damaged comity and trust between the two branches.) In addition, Congress became more assertive in delving into the details of defense management. Between 1960 and 1984 the Armed Services committees extended their control over defense budgeting by requiring annual authorizations for increasing portions of the defense budget. In 1961 only 2 percent of the defense budget had to be authorized annually; in 1971 it was 31 percent; by 1983 it was 100 percent (Blechman 1990).

Congressional oversight activities, especially hearings, have increased considerably. The days of hearings by the Armed Services committees increased from an average of about sixty days annually in the 1960s to an annual average of one hundred days per year in the 1980s (Blechman 1990, 40). Annual reports of the committees (which often contain detailed instructions for the Defense Department) increased from approximately 100 pages to more than 1,000 pages, and reports of the defense appropriations subcommittees increased from 130 pages to more than 700 pages (Blechman 1990, 40). Mandated budget justification books prepared by the Defense Department for Congress increased in volume from 12,350 pages in 1977 to 30,114 pages in 1988 (U.S. Dept. of Defense, 1990, 7).

Another indicator of increased congressional involvement in defense policy is the number of reports and studies required to be submitted to Congress. In 1970 Congress required 36 reports from DOD; by 1985 the total was 458 reports and studies; in 1988 the total was 719 (Blechman 1990, 41). Perhaps the most striking and most disruptive aspect of congressional involvement in the defense budget was an increase in the number of programs whose budgets were changed each year by request of the president. In 1970 some 180 programs were changed in the authorization process and 650 in appropriations; by 1988 the changes totaled 1,184 in authorization and 1,579 in appropriation (Blechman 1990, 41).

Executive branch officials often complain about the "micromanagement" by Congress of what they consider to be presidential turf. Members of Congress, in turn, cite the right of Congress to decide how funds are to be spent; they point to former abuses of discretion by the executive branch to justify their involvement in the details of policy implementation. While some of these interventions by Congress are justifiable reactions to executive branch abuses of discretion, others are motivated by the political desire to protect constituent interests regardless of what is in the public interest. In addition, the 535 members of Congress are seldom united in opinion, so some faction in Congress is likely to oppose the priorities of any presidential administration. Therefore, what constitutes intrusive congressional micromanagement, and what is an appropriate assertion of congressional prerogatives, are matters of ongoing debate between the two branches (Fisher 1991).

War Powers

One irony of congressional assertions of prerogatives in national security affairs since the 1970s reforms is that the most highly visible action, the War Powers Resolution, passed over President Nixon's veto in 1973, has had the least effect in practice. The resolution requires that the president consult with Congress before introducing armed forces into situations where hostilities are imminent. It also requires that presidents report their actions to Congress. After the report is submitted, a sixty-day period begins; if Congress has not by the end of that period either declared war or given a time extension, the president must withdraw the troops. The president can extend the period by thirty days by declaring that it is necessary to protect U.S. lives, and Congress can force withdrawal of troops before the end of sixty days by a concurrent resolution.

Presidents, arguing that the resolution unconstitutionally infringes on their prerogatives as commander in chief, have refused to report military actions to Congress as provided in the law. Most members of Congress consider the resolution an important assertion of the institutional right of Congress to participate in committing the United States to war. Ironically, when presidents refused to report deployment of troops and start the sixty-day clock ticking, Congress was unable to forge the consensus to begin the clock itself. For instance, in 1987 President Reagan decided to have the navy protect Kuwaiti oil tankers in the Persian Gulf by letting them sail under the U.S. flag. U.S. naval forces were deployed to the Persian Gulf in what was generally recognized to be danger from possible hostilities. Reagan refused to report the deployment to Congress under the War Powers Resolution (section 4) requirement because, like other presidents, he did not want to admit to the legitimacy of the law. There were a number of initiatives in Congress to declare the sixty-day clock started, but all of them foundered and Congress took no decisive action. Members of Congress clearly did not want to take responsibility for undermining the president in the Gulf, yet neither were they willing to legitimize his actions. They wanted to have the option of criticizing Reagan's actions if things went wrong without being implicated in actions that they could not control (Blechman 1990; Katzmann 1990).

A similar situation developed when President Bush moved two hundred thousand U.S. troops to Saudi Arabia to deal with the Iraqi invasion of Kuwait in 1990. Members of Congress generally supported the president's initial deployment of troops to prevent the possible invasion of Saudi Arabia by Iraqi forces. But Congress refused, at least initially, to endorse strongly Bush's military intentions, especially after the president doubled the number of troops, giving U.S. forces an offensive capability. Bush did not report to Congress the deployment of troops to the Gulf. Congress made no move to invoke the War Powers Resolution, though members were still haunted by the specter of the Gulf of Tonkin resolution that Johnson used to legitimize his prosecution of the Vietnam War even after public and congressional attitudes toward the war had shifted.

Because of the congressional Democrats' unwillingness to endorse fully his evident intention to initiate hostilities against Iraq, President Bush was hesitant to ask for congressional authorization. However, by early January 1991 the administration concluded that it could win a vote in Congress to authorize the use of force against Iraq. In a dramatic series of debates, opponents of the administration argued that the president's initial strategy—the blockade—should be given more time to force Iraq to leave Kuwait. However, the resolution supporting the administration passed in both houses, and U.S. forces attacked Iraq on 16 January 1991. Once hostilities began, congressional support of the president's conduct of the war was virtually unanimous.

In terms of the constitutional issue, the congressional vote was tantamount to a declaration of war. After the vote, no one challenged the constitutional legitimacy of the president's decision to attack and invade Iraq. Some members of the administration, however, felt the president could have begun the war *without* congressional approval. According to Secretary of Defense Richard Cheney, "The president has the authority to undertake this kind of operation without the approval of Congress" (qtd. in *U.S. News & World Report*, 15 April 1991, 31). While presidents had previously engaged U.S. armed forces in hostilities without congressional approval, an invasion the size of the Gulf War might have provoked a constitutional confrontation if it had been undertaken without congressional authorization.

A compelling argument can be made that the Framers intended that Congress have a voice in committing the nation to war, but it is evident from the history of military actions since 1973 that the War Powers Resolution is not an effective vehicle for Congress to assert that prerogative.

After the Gulf War, it is unlikely that the resolution will be effectively involved in the future.

Postreform National Security Relations

The changes introduced during the reform period have greatly affected relations between the branches of Congress in national security matters. Congress has used some laws to extend its purview over executive actions, but more importantly members of Congress have changed their attitudes. Members now expect to play a serious role in national security policy. This expectation was fostered by divided government, Democratic congressional opposition to Reagan's strongly held values and personal style, and perceived overreaching by the executive branch.

The Reagan administration and Congress were often in conflict during the 1980s over the appropriate stance toward the Soviet Union, with the administration arguing a hard line. But the major breech of comity was the Iran-contra affair. The Reagan administration pursued an "opening" to Iran by selling it missiles and other military equipment. The hope was to obtain the release of a number of U.S. hostages held by terrorists in the Middle East. However, the arms sales to Iran were conducted without notifying Congress as provided by law. Even Secretary of State George Shultz was not informed after he and Defense Secretary Caspar Weinberger objected to the plan.

Even more destructive to comity and constitutional balance was the decision to divert some of the funds that Iran paid for the arms to the contra rebels in Nicaragua. Such aid was prohibited by law at that time. Aid to the contras was the focus of a major policy debate between the president and Congress during Reagan's first term. When the administration failed to achieve its foreign policy goals through the constitutional process, some members of the National Security Council staff decided to pursue their objective of aid to the contras in secret. The congressional investigating committee concluded, "Officials [involved] viewed the law not as setting boundaries for their actions, but raising impediments to their goals. When the goals and the law collided, the law gave way" (U.S. Congress, 1987, 18).

Another confrontation that marred relations between the branches in the 1980s was the Reagan administration's reinterpretation of the 1972 ABM Treaty with the Soviet Union limiting antiballistic missile (ABM) systems. In October 1985 the administration revealed that it would break with the previous three administrations' interpretation of the treaty so that it could develop and test new types of antiballistic missile systems (the Strategic Defense Initiative). Members of the Senate challenged the administration's interpretation and argued that the executive branch could not unilaterally change the understanding of treaty terms that had been the basis for initial Senate ratification of the treaty. After about a year of confrontation and argument, the administration abandoned its attempt, but not before relations between the branches were damaged by the administration's unprecedented actions.

When the Bush administration came to office in 1989, conflict over national security issues was reduced considerably, partly because of the collapse of the Soviet economy and the reversal of decades of Soviet foreign policy by Mikhail Gorbachev begun in the latter years of the Reagan administration. But conflict over national security also decreased because of the Bush administration's choice not to pursue aid to the contras in Nicaragua without congressional approval. Early in the administration a compromise between the two branches was worked out by Secretary of State James Baker in which limited aid would continue until the scheduled elections. When President Bush sent forces to Panama in 1989 and to the Middle East in 1990, there was no major dissent from Congress (though there was considerable disagreement as to whether U.S. forces should pursue an offensive strategy in Saudi). President Bush's decision to go to war in the Middle East in 1991—over the objection of some members of Congress—and its swift and successful conclusion created an important political precedent favoring presidential prerogative regarding the war power.

DIVIDED GOVERNMENT AND THE NEW TOOLS OF GOVERNMENT

The Constitution's design ensures that there will be conflict between the president and Congress. Different constituencies, different terms of office, and different institutional interests foster a rivalry that the Framers argued would preclude the excessive concentration of power. But this inherent tension between the president and Congress is exacerbated when control of the two branches is divided between the two major political parties, a situation called *divided government.*

Throughout U.S. history, the control of the presidency by one party accompanied by the control of one or both houses of Congress by the other party has not been an unusual situation. From 1832 to 1990, thirty elections resulted in divided government whereas forty-nine produced unified government (Fiorina 1989a, 3). In the late twentieth century, however, divided government occurred more often and constituted an important departure from traditional political divisions.

From 1897 to 1954 divided government occurred in only eight years (or 14 percent of the time), from 1955 to 1990 it occurred in twenty-four years (or 67 percent of the time), and since 1968 it has occurred 80 percent of the time. Divided government in the nineteenth century resulted primarily from midterm elections, when the president's party usually loses seats. However, recent incidence of divided government occurred as often from presidential election years as from midterm elections (Fiorina 1989a). In presidential election years the president's party failed to win both houses of Congress only four times in the nineteenth century and not in the twentieth century until 1956. In the last twenty years, this has happened in six of nine election years.

The proximate cause of divided government is ticket splitting, when voters opt for candidates of one party for president and another party for Congress. The percentage of congressional districts in which this occurred increased from less than 10 percent in the first decade of the 1900s to 44 percent in the 1972 and 1984 elections. The percentage of individual voters who split their tickets increased from 12 percent of the electorate in 1952 to 25 percent in 1988 (Fiorina 1981).

Ticket splitting has been encouraged in recent years by the breakdown of political parties (in terms of party identification and control of resources) and the rise of the personalized candidate. Candidates for political office are no longer dependent on their parties to get elected. They raise their own money and run on their own records, rather than emphasizing their party connections and positions. Incumbents run on service to their districts. Thus voters pay less attention to party cues in deciding on their vote.

In addition, contemporary presidents tend to have shorter coattails than did past presidents. That is, the election of a popular president is less likely to result in more votes for the congressional candidate. Further, any increase in the number of votes for a congressional candidate is less likely to result in the change of a seat in Congress because of the increasingly large margins of wins by incumbents (Brady and Fiorina 1990).

Some observers argue the divided government that results from split tickets is due to conscious choices on the part of voters (Jacobson 1990). Voters are said to want Democrats in Congress to protect them from cuts in benefits and Republicans in the presidency to keep taxes down. Voters seek to contribute to the constitutional checks and balances by dividing control of the government. While the results of opinion polls show the electorate divided in these ways, there is insufficient evidence to demonstrate that individual voters who split their tickets do so for these reasons (Fiorina 1989a, 28). Ticket splitting does assure, however, that contemporary presidents are much less likely to have a majority in Congress and that those members who are of their party are less likely to feel beholden to the president (Brady and Fiorina 1990).

Others argue that divided government is good because it is what the electorate desires. Further, the Constitution ensures that making major changes in public policy will be difficult (Pfiffner 1991a). Still others argue that divided government makes a government already structurally biased against change move toward stalemate. Michael Mezey defines *stalemate* as a situation in which "neither the executive nor the Congress is capable of acting on its own and each is capable of stopping the other from acting" (1989, 125).

In the 1980s observers pointed to the seeming deadlock between President Reagan and the congressional Democrats over the foreign policy issues of the nation's strategic stance toward the Soviet Union and involvement in Nicaragua. These issues became much less contentious after the elections in Nicaragua and the breakup of the Soviet Empire. After Reagan's budget victories in 1981, the budget conflicts between the president and Congress were undoubtedly aggravated by divided government. While it is impossible to prove that these conflicts were not due to the nature of the times rather than divided government, it is highly likely that divided government made them worse.

In contrast, David Mayhew (1989) argues that since 1948 there has been no evidence to suggest that divided government itself prevented major legislation from being passed or congressional investigations of the executive from being carried out. Legislation passed during periods of divided government, however, may not be as coherent as during unified government (Porter 1988; Pfiffner 1991a). Divided government also may lead to a bidding-up phenomenon in which Democrats and Republicans do not want to let the other party take credit for legislation enacted and so go overboard in support for laws. In some important cases, Gilmour (1990a) argues, this has led to laws that are worse than their original formulations (for example, the Social Security amendments of 1972, the Clean Water and Clean Air acts, and the 1981 tax cut). However, competition for credit taking may enhance the chance for passage of good legislation, such as the 1986 tax reform (Conlan, Wrightson, and Beam 1990).

The frustrations of policy stalemate, due in part to divided government, have led to the use of special mechanisms designed to achieve agreement in spite of major differences between the parties. These devices include budget summits between the two branches, special commissions, and automatic legislative devices. While sometimes useful, these mechanisms have achieved mixed results.

One example of a successful bipartisan commission is the Greenspan Commission, created by President Reagan in 1983 to deal with the crisis in the Social Security Trust Fund. The commission was able to prepare the ground for Reagan and House Speaker O'Neill to agree on a package of benefit cuts and tax increases. The commission itself did not create the compromise, but it did provide political cover for the president and Democratic leaders to make compromises in their positions without being as vulnerable to political attack (Light 1985).

President Reagan also used the commission device to make some progress, though no breakthrough, on two national security issues. The Scowcroft Commission arrived at a temporary compromise for strategic forces by advocating that Congress fund both the MX and "Midgetman" missiles. The Kissinger Commission recommended compromise actions of the United States in Nicaragua and Latin America. One notable commission failure was the congressionally created National Economic Commission, intended to provide political cover to enable the winning presidential candidate in 1988 to attack the budget deficit with a combination of spending cuts and tax increases. The commission became irrelevant when Bush derided it as the "tax increase commission" and ignored it after his election.

Another mechanism to force action in the contentious atmosphere of divided government is an automatic device that, once set in motion, makes changes without further agreement between the branches. The most notorious of these is the Gramm-Rudman-Hollings (1985) deficit-reduction legislation, in which the budget would be cut automatically in an across-the-board fashion if the president and Congress could not achieve certain fixed levels of deficit reduction. The distasteful prospect of across-the-board cuts was intended to force agreement between the two branches. According to Senator Warren Rudman (R-N.H.), "We had reached the point in divided government where you have to have some mechanism out there to force it to get its act together" (*Washington Post*, 15 October 1990). But even though it may have created pressure to arrive at a compromise, the attempt to avoid its strictures led to irresponsible gimmicks.

The War Powers Resolution also contains an automatic device to force the president to remove troops from hostilities if Congress takes no action to approve of their presence. As noted earlier, however, the law has thus far been unworkable. An automatic device was also included in pay legislation—the president can accept the recommendation of the Quadrennial Commission on executive, legislative, and judicial salaries to raise pay for Congress and the executive branch. If the president forwards the recommendation to Congress, pay levels increase automatically without any vote in Congress. In 1989, when President Bush recommended increases of almost 50 percent in congressional pay, there was such a political backlash from voters that the proposal was abandoned.

Presidents in the postreform years also tried to lock in their political preferences with constitutional amendments. President Reagan proposed to amend the Constitution to balance the budget, to prevent abortions, and to allow prayers in public schools. President Bush advocated those same amendments as well as proposed amendments to outlaw flag desecration and to set limits on congressional terms. Bush and Reagan also argued for the item veto, which would give presidents the power to veto individual items in appropriations laws, rather than having to accept or reject the whole bill.

The failures of the National Economic Commission in 1988 and of the budget summit in 1990 demonstrate the limits of these types of devices in overcoming the tensions inherent in a period of divided government. Not enough political support exists for the various constitutional amendments that have been proposed to mitigate the effects of divided government or increase presidential power. While strong political leadership may solve some public policy problems, it is not clear that the American electorate is unified enough to support coherent policy agendas.

CONCLUSION

This chapter has focused on recent developments in interbranch relations, with an emphasis on changes since the reform period of the mid-1970s. We have seen that budgetary politics were transformed and today consume a much larger chunk of the domestic policy debate. Deficit politics drives much of the public policy agenda and constrains options available to presidents and Congresses. The importance of aggregates—top-line totals and bottom-line deficits—raises the political stakes and tends to centralize power in both branches. The budgetary process now operates much more in a top-down fashion than a bottom-up mode.

In recent years Congress has delved much more deeply into the details of national security policy than it has in the past. But at the same time the president has continued to dominate the broad contours of national security policy, especially the use of military force and questions of war and peace. The fragmentation of power in Congress and the increasing presence of divided government have made life more difficult for presidents. Leadership summits and special commissions only occasionally lead to effective compromises.

It is also important to note that, despite high public expectations for presidential performance (Peterson 1990), the president is not in a position of strength with respect to getting legislation through Congress (Bond and Fleisher 1990; Edwards 1989). It is unusual in American history for the president and Congress to have a sustained and productive legislative relationship. The major modern exceptions were the initial years in office after presidents Franklin Roosevelt, Lyndon Johnson, and Ronald Reagan were elected. But even these brief periods of cooperation were not sustained after the initial outbursts of activity (Pfiffner 1988b).

The main component of presidential legislative success is the partisan balance in Congress, over which presidents have little influence. But even within their parties presidents can count on supporting votes only about two-thirds of the time (Edwards 1989, 40). Besides party, legislators' own policy preferences and perceived constituent desires dominate their voting. Popularity in the polls can help presidents when it is high and undermine presidents when it is low, but by itself popularity cannot guarantee legislative success. While presidential skills in dealing with Congress may be helpful, they cannot overcome other major factors. "Presidential legislative skills are not closely related to presidential support in Congress. . . . [A] president's legislative skills operate in an environment largely beyond the president's control. In most instances presidents exercise them at the margins of coalition building, not at the core" (Edwards 1989, 211).

However, the presidency is a very personal office, and the impact of personality can be crucial to presidential success, failure, and historical perception. Richard Nixon's personal intelligence led to much of his success in foreign policy, but his psychological makeup strongly influenced his reaction to the Watergate break-in. Jimmy Carter's perseverance and character made possible the breakthrough in the Camp David accords, but his self-righteous attitude toward Congress hurt his legislative relations. Ronald Reagan's ideological convictions made possible the budget victories of 1981, but his values and management style combined allowed the Iran-contra affair to occur. George Bush, as Reagan's vice president, accepted the Reagan agenda, but once Bush became president his personal style changed executive relations with Congress and U.S. relations with the rest of the world.

The impact of personality and style is well illustrated by contrasting Reagan and Bush with respect to "going public"; that is, appealing for public support for specific policies rather than engaging in bargaining with other elites in Washington, especially Congress. This tactic is intended to bring public and constituent pressure to bear as a means of getting congressional support for presidential initiatives. Samuel Kernell (1986) has traced the increasing use of this approach in the contemporary presidency, especially its masterful use by Reagan.

Armed with the same technological tools and a similar policy agenda, President Bush did not go public to the extent that Reagan did. As president, Bush approached politics much more as the insider he had been for most of his career. His experience and personal style lent themselves much more to bargaining than to going public. Bush's television presence and speaking abilities were not as suited to public appeals as were Reagan's, which was reflected in Bush's decision to hold ninety-one press conferences but only five television addresses in his first two years in office (Thomas 1991, 34).

The strengths and weaknesses of Bush's style were evident in his handling of the 1990 budget summit and the Iraqi invasion of Kuwait. Behind the closed doors of Andrews Air Force Base, Bush aides were able to hammer out a budget compromise with Congress that the public posturing of his first year and a half in office could not create. But his public appeal to the American people and to the rest of Congress for the deal was unsuccessful. After the invasion of Kuwait, Bush brilliantly put together a worldwide coalition against Iraq by using his personal relationships with world leaders. His firm conviction that the U.S. offensive against Iraq was the best policy paid off handsomely when U.S. forces were victorious and suffered very few casualties. Bush's public popularity hit historically high levels in the immediate aftermath of the war, but criticisms of his domestic agenda, or purported lack of one, returned to plague him after the Gulf War.

Besides the idiosyncracies of individual personality, historical circumstance plays an unpredictable and sometimes determining role in presidential success and relations with Congress. We need only to reflect on the impact of the U.S. hostages in Iran on Carter's presidency, or the influence of Soviet President Gorbachev on Reagan's, or the impact of the Iraqi invasion of Kuwait on Bush's, to realize that historical circumstance often plays a determining role in a presidency. U.S. politics and history are often played out in reaction to world forces beyond anyone's control.

Thus when we consider the postreform developments of budget politics and congressional activism in national security policy, we need to keep in mind the short-term unpredictables of personality and historical circumstance. These short-term factors operate in the longer-term context of the relatively weak legislative position of the president in the U.S. system of separated powers.

12 / Summits and Stalemates: Bipartisan Negotiations in the Postreform Era

JOHN B. GILMOUR

The relationship between Congress and the president is commonly described as one of bargaining and negotiations, and this can hardly be more true than under divided party government. However, the negotiations that occur often fail to conform to standard bargaining theory. Normally we expect the parties to a negotiation to move closer together in their bargaining positions, or not to move at all. Even though we do not expect the parties to move farther apart over the course of discussions, this can and does happen in American national politics, as the two case studies examined in this chapter will show.

In 1983 the Social Security system went to the brink of insolvency while Congress and the president blamed each other for its demise. Democrats who had initially proposed moderate, balanced solutions to the problem later took increasingly extreme positions. Similarly, in 1987 a Gramm-Rudman-Hollings sequestration order, which would have mandated substantial across-the-board budget cuts, was very nearly implemented. Instead of taking action to prevent this occurrence, Democrats and Republicans consoled themselves with the knowledge that they could blame each other for the consequences of the sequester. Democrats proposed tax increases as a means of cutting the deficit. Meanwhile, President Reagan denounced all talk of raising taxes, vowing to veto any tax increase, despite having previously proposed a variety of tax increases in his budget submission.

In both cases, political stalemate nearly led to disaster. In both, resolution of the problem at hand was made either much harder or impossible by the efforts of the two parties to extract partisan political advantage from the situation. And in both, the problem was ultimately resolved by means of direct, bipartisan negotiations between the parties and between the legislative and executive branches of government.

The inability of ordinary institutional arrangements to cope with these problems is perplexing in at least two respects. First, the solution to the problem is often quite obvious from the start: the two sides must compromise. Second, the urgency of reaching an agreement often fails to produce a spirit of accommodation. The participants in the negotiations studied here all professed deep concern over the issue at hand, and all had to know that only a reasonable compromise could produce an agreement and end the crisis. But they did not accede to it because it would have been politically damaging.

This chapter argues that the quest for partisan political advantage created an environment in which normal interbranch negotiations could not proceed. Bipartisan commissions (one formally constituted, the other informal) helped ease the stalemate by relieving either party of the onus of initiating the compromise and allowed politicians to do what they probably knew had to be done while suffering only minimal political damage. To explain the failure of politicians to reach an obvious solution, and to show how the commission made a difference, it is argued that the efforts of politicians to maintain the loyalty of constituency groups often foreclose the possibility of achieving success in elite negotiations.

The success of bipartisan negotiations, particularly the Social Security Commission's, has generated optimism about the capacity of high-level bipartisan bodies to fashion solutions to seemingly intractable problems. Optimism should be restrained, however, for bipartisan commissions are useful only under a limited set of circumstances. In 1988 and 1989 another bipartisan body, the National Economic Commission, was launched with high hopes and intended to chart the way out of the deficit swamp, but it failed miserably to produce a consensus on reducing the deficit. In the area of health care, the Pepper Commission—named for its instigator and original chair, Representative Claude Pepper (D-Fla.)—was created to develop a consensus on controversial health care issues. Despite early optimism, the Pepper Commission did not produce a consensus and issued a report supported only by its Democratic members. In a 1990 summit negotiation, however, leaders of Congress and from the White House were able to agree on a major deficit-reduction package. Even though that agreement was not implemented, one very close to it was.

Sometimes summit negotiations work and sometimes they do not. How can we account for these successes and failures? In the case of the successful negotiations, partisans ceased to pillory each other and entered into serious negotiations only when it became apparent that the alternative was immediate, total disaster. This is the crucial factor. Merely having negotiations does not produce agreement. Only when politicians desire an agreement can summit negotiations help to overcome impediments in the political process.

Deadlock, stalemate, and inaction are possibly the most persistent pathologies of American politics. Within the discipline of political science, the traditional answer to this problem has been stronger, more disciplined political parties. At one time it may have been reasonable to view political parties as a means of bridging constitutional separation of powers. The past two decades have made it clear, however, that divided party government today is the rule rather than the exception. Under these circumstances, we should cease looking to the party as the unifier of government and begin a more intensive study of divided party government.

This chapter examines interbranch and interparty bargaining, as well as the conditions that lead to stalemate. It also focuses on the use of high-level, direct negotiations between the president and Congress as a means of escaping stalemate. It is argued that (1) in these cases, the bargain that Congress and the president should reach is relatively obvious and reachable; (2) the obvious solution is often avoided in favor of a stalemate; (3) stalemate results from problems inherent in public, sequential negotiations among parties that must both cooperate and compete with each other; and (4) commissions and summit negotiations can help to overcome the problems that impede public negotiations, but only to a limited extent.

THE OBVIOUS SOLUTION TO STALEMATE

Despite the extreme rhetoric and radical positions taken during the 1983 Social Security and 1987 Gramm-Rudman-Hollings battles, common sense and theories of bargaining suggested that the only possible way to achieve an agreement was through some sort of balanced compromise. In fact, after months of public haggling followed by private negotiations, the result in both cases was an agreement that could almost certainly have been predicted well in advance. The reason that such agreements are generally predictable is that the bargaining situation between the president and Congress is relatively symmetrical: The agreement of both the president and Congress is needed and neither has the power to compel the other to accept an agreement. The two sides prefer almost completely different solutions to the problem, with Republicans seeking benefit cuts and Democrats tax increases. A failure to reach agreement would hurt both sides nearly equally. Collapse of Social Security would have been a disaster of nearly unimaginable proportions. If squabbling between the parties had led to the bankruptcy of the Social Security system, the contempt of the public for politicians would have known no bounds. Rather than punish one party or the other, the electorate may have followed a strategy to destroy all incumbents.

These conditions imply a highly symmetrical relationship between the branches of government, in which neither side has a power or bargaining advantage over the other. It so happens that these conditions are close to those imposed by John Nash in his classic article, "The Bargaining Problem" (1950). The implication of Nash's solution to such games is that, when both sides stand to benefit equally from an agreement (or to lose equally in the event of a failure to agree), the two sides should meet each other halfway. Howard Raiffa (1982, 52) cites experimental evidence that in highly symmetric bargaining games, when the two sides know each other's preferences, there is an overwhelming tendency to settle on an equal division.

However, perfect symmetry is not often satisfied in real politics. At times public opinion favors one side or the other and this is manifested in bargaining strength. Or one side successfully asserts that it cannot make concessions while its opponent can. When the two sides are not entirely symmetric in bargaining strength, we should expect some corresponding imbalance in the agreement. When one side can credibly contend that it cannot make an equal sacrifice, that side enjoys a substantial bargaining advantage (Schelling 1960). The 1987 budget negotiations produced the less equal solution of the two cases studied here, probably because Democrats' position was strengthened by a lack of support within President Reagan's own Republican party in Congress for further deep cuts in domestic spending. In none of the cases studied here are the asymmetries substantial, which means that in all cases the agreement must be relatively balanced.

Sensible people need no fancy apparatus to understand intuitively that, when neither side has the power to compel the other and when both sides lose similarly from the failure to agree, neither can demand that the other make a grossly disproportionate sacrifice. Politicians are sophisticated players of the political game. Democrats certainly know that Republicans will not accept a deal that is seriously injurious to Republican political interests and beneficial to Democratic interests, or vice versa. Knowing this did not prevent politicians in the 1983 and 1987 cases from making offers that were blatantly self-serving and that had no chance of being enacted. In the end, though, the final agreements were close to what game theory and common sense suggested they should be—a balanced compromise.

The Social Security rescue legislation embodied a close balance between revenue increases and benefit reductions. Both parties had previously staked out extreme positions: the Reagan administration initially insisted that the entire Social Security deficit be made up through benefit cuts, whereas the Democrats in Congress demanded that no benefits be cut at all. Robert J. Myers, who was staff director of the National Commission on Social Security Reform, offers an assessment of the final rescue package. It was a complicated agreement, but Myers contends that the agreement was composed of 48 percent revenue increases and 52 percent benefit changes (1985, 287).

The 1987 budget summit agreement between the president and leaders of Congress was not as evenly balanced, but it still represented a moderate compromise. In a sense, Republican interests "paid" 64 percent of the total cost of the agreement in taxes and defense cuts, whereas Democrats paid 36 percent in the form of domestic spending reductions.[1] While not an equal division, the agreement was far more equal than anything offered by either side previous to the summit. The imbalance can be explained by the general antipathy of members of Congress—Democrats and Republicans—to further domestic spending cuts. The domestic side of the budget had borne the brunt of spending reductions over the 1980s, while the defense budget had grown substantially during those years.

NEGOTIATIONS: TWO-LEVEL GAMES

When the president and Congress seek a bargain on an issue like Social Security or deficit reduction, they should be able to reach it quickly. Politicians are sophisticated players who should be able to predict quite readily the best deal they are likely to get and then move in that direction. But they tend not to reach agreement because they have more on their minds than compromise and problem solving. Politicians are also seeking partisan political advantage at each other's expense, and this discourages compromise.

Participants in political negotiations often have two conflicting purposes. While they seek to produce solutions to problems, they look to do so without losing political support or foregoing opportunities for assaulting their opponent in quest of additional support. The instinct for partisanship is so strong that politicians are willing to subordinate their desire to promote their political prospects to the need to reach a solution only when the alternative to agreement is certain disaster.

Politicians conduct negotiations among themselves at an elite level, making offers and counteroffers to each other as they strive for a mutually satisfactory accommodation. For the president, these offers emerge in speeches, legislative recommendations to Congress, the annual budget submission, and other sources. Congress makes its offers to the president through speeches by its leaders and committees chairs and by introducing and passing legislation. Discussions can also be conducted in private.

Negotiators in American politics have relatively little latitude in making and accepting offers because they must constantly be concerned about the reactions of two external audiences—their party and constituents. They must be concerned about the political fortunes of their party in Congress, as well as whether their party will support a bill or agreement in Congress. Negotiators must also pay attention to constituency groups; even though these groups cannot vote directly against a bill or agreement, they can threaten to withdraw financial, electoral, or organizational support. Because elite negotiations are embedded in political and electoral process, offers may be directed as much to outside audiences as they are to elite audiences, intended not so much to advance negotiations as to embarrass the other side, gain media attention, or generate public support.

Elite negotiations and mass-level politics are closely linked, for what is said and done in one context can have important ramifications for the other. Agreeing to a compromise can risk the loyalty of constituents, who may fail to understand the necessity of compromise and even interpret it as betrayal. Consequently, fear of electoral repercussions can exert an important effect on the conduct of elite negotiations. Similarly, the promises that politicians make to constituents as they run for office exert a constraint on what can be agreed to in negotiations.

Negotiations between Congress and the president under divided party government can be described as *two-level games*, in which the bargain reached by a set of negotiators must be ratified or implemented by an external entity (Putnam 1988; Tsebelis 1988, 1990). In international negotiations (the focus of Putnam's discussion), the domestic politics of the countries involved often constrain negotiators and limit the range of agreements to which they can assent. The amount of constraint can vary enormously depending on the relationship between bargainers and their constituents. Under certain circumstances, presidents or congressional leaders can credibly refuse to make a particular concession on the grounds that their party in Congress will not accept it.

REASONS NOT TO COMPROMISE

The need to maintain the support of constituencies seriously constrains the legislation that politicians will agree to. First, politicians must keep their party's traditional constituencies from defecting to the other party. Second, they must keep rivals within their own party from stealing away support. Third, they seek to maintain distinctiveness of their party from the other one on issues that are beneficial to them.

For purposes of political advantage, each political party appoints itself the custodian of different public policies—such as Social Security, agriculture, defense, taxes, or any of dozens of others—and devotes itself to the care and cultivation of the constituents of those properties. The parties advertise themselves as protectors of these policies and, presumably, the constituencies that benefit reward their protectors. The two best contemporary examples of this are Republicans' efforts to cultivate voters on the basis of their antitax pledge, Democrats' to gain support by being the party that defends Social Security. We may assume that the beneficiaries of a government policy tend to equate its preservation with the greatest public good and that they do not reward politicians who defend them halfheartedly or who make compromises at their expense. These constituents are unlikely to be pleased with a budget agreement or a bill that reduces the deficit by cutting a favorite program or increasing their taxes.

The politicians who negotiate agreements understand that compromise is inevitable in politics. But they have a hard time communicating this necessity to constituents, and thus often avoid compromise. Politicians must hate to explain to constituents that "this deal is not perfect but it's the best we can get under the circumstances." Supporting such a deal often means betrayal to constituents. Explaining otherwise requires educating constituents, which can be hard to do. To Richard Fenno, educating constituents means any explanation of government activity that at least "hurts a little." During Fenno's journeys with eighteen members of Congress, he found them unwilling to expend even a little political capital on the education of constituents (1978, 162). Thus the prudent course of action for politicians is never to agree to any compromise that may harm constituent support.

The task of a politician who wants to compromise is compounded by the presence of rivals for the loyalty of a group, who explain to that group why compromise is not necessary. In the case of the 1983 Social Security rescue, the leaders of advocacy groups for the elderly attacked the summit agreement in harshly critical terms, arguing that there should have been no benefit cuts. Educating the public is especially difficult when the public receives conflicting messages.

Another reason politicians avoid compromise is that it blurs distinctions between the parties and obscures the reasons constituents should be loyal to their party. In the Social Security case, Democrats had a good issue with which to assault Republicans—agreeing to benefit cuts, however necessary to reach an agreement with the president, meant sacrificing their best political issue. Constituents who perceived politics only dimly would not be able to distinguish between Democrats and Republicans on Social Security. Republicans similarly strive for purity on taxes, their best issue. When Republicans agree to tax increases, as they did in 1987 and 1990 budget accords, they sacrifice their greatest advantage over Democrats—an identification by the public as the party of low taxes.

Negotiations that take place as a part of a political contest between the two parties can be extremely difficult to conclude successfully because the actions calculated to generate constituency loyalty tend to undermine negotiations, and vice versa. A willingness to compromise and to eschew strident language encourages success in negotiations. However, bargaining away something valued by a constituency threatens the support and trust of that constituency. The fact that such compromises must be made in order to reach agreement does not mollify a deprived and enraged constituency. To a large extent, parties to negotiations must decide whether to seek partisan advantage or to make good public policy. Further, they choose good public policy over partisan advantage only when it is necessary to avert disaster, and even then only at the last possible moment.

PROBLEMS OF SEQUENTIAL, PUBLIC BARGAINING

Much of the problem stems from the sequential nature of normal, public executive-legislative bargaining. This is a public process in which the participants appeal as much to the mass audience as to their negotiating partners. Uncertainty about the intentions of one's partner—specifically, about whether it is their intention to make good public policy or to bash their opponent—reduces the likelihood that either side will engage in serious negotiations.

In framing an offer the president or Congress has the choice of making a reasonable offer or an unreasonable offer. A *reasonable offer* is one that imposes costs on both sides in roughly similar proportions; an *unreasonable offer* imposes nearly all costs on the other side. Moreover, a reasonable offer is intended to lead to negotiations and an agreement, whereas an unreasonable one is intended to appeal to constituencies and is likely to be rejected immediately by the other side because of its inherent unfairness. If the party receiving an offer responds with a counteroffer that suggests room for compromise, then we say that the party is cooperating. If the party instead denounces the offer or responds with an unreasonable counteroffer, it is defecting.

Two hazards attend making a reasonable offer. First, because it imposes costs on one's own constituencies, it could alienate them. Second, the opposition party could refuse to view the offer as one made in good faith, and instead use it for unilateral political advancement. Rather than responding with a similar offer, the side that defects attacks the offer for the pain it imposes on its favorite constituencies. If a reasonable offer is met by a defection, the party making the offer loses doubly. Thus, the problem is no closer to being solved, and the party making the offer has indicated to possibly loyal supporters that it is willing to sacrifice them. The defecting party loses nothing and gains something. It has done nothing to alienate its constituents while the other side has. Therefore, unless a party knows in advance how the other side will respond, it is unwise to make a reasonable offer.

A similar choice faces a party in deciding how to respond to an offer. If the offer is unreasonable, the choice is rather simple—denounce it and its authors. When a party has made it clear that it is most interested in cultivating its constituency, putting forth a balanced counterproposal makes no sense—the other side would use it as an opportunity for a new attack. A reasonable offer requires a more difficult choice. A party can cooperate by responding with a reasonable reply intended to lead to further discussions and an eventual agreement. Or it can instead defect by playing to the mass audience, attacking controversial aspects of the offer as cruel or heartless and taking a firm stand as the true defender of the interests proposed for slaughter. The latter course of action secures political advantage over the opponent, but it does not solve the problem.

Figure 12-1 diagrams the offer-counteroffer process by means of a decision tree. As the figure shows, a party benefits by waiting for the other party to act first, regardless of the party's intentions. This is true when the party intends to cooperate (the other party makes an offer and shows its intentions) as well as when it intends to defect (the opponent may make a reasonable offer). The decision tree also indicates that, regardless of what the opponent does, a party should always defect. This is particularly true of the first mover. The possibility that the other party will respond to a reasonable offer with a withering attack discourages the parties from making a reasonable offer. If against all odds a reasonable offer is made, the second mover probably should defect. Cooperating helps to produce an agreement and benefits both sides equally; defecting hurts one side and

Figure 12-1 / Decision Tree of Interbranch, Sequential, Public Negotiations

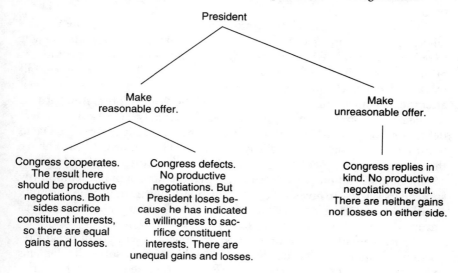

President

Make reasonable offer.

Make unreasonable offer.

Congress cooperates. The result here should be productive negotiations. Both sides sacrifice constituent interests, so there are equal gains and losses.

Congress defects. No productive negotiations. But President loses because he has indicated a willingness to sacrifice constituent interests. There are unequal gains and losses.

Congress replies in kind. No productive negotiations result. There are neither gains nor losses on either side.

benefits the other side. Therefore, defecting is preferable. This is a grim logic, but it receives ample support from the behavior of Congress and the president in recent years.

THE DEVELOPMENT OF POLITICAL STALEMATE

The politics of the 1983 Social Security rescue and the 1987 budget agreement exemplify the problems of dealing with contentious issues under divided government. In both cases, serious negotiations were driven out by the efforts of politicians to gain partisan advantage.

The Social Security Case (1983)

In 1980 it became apparent that the old-age portion of the Social Security system was heading toward financial troubles. Consequently, the Social Security Subcommittee of the House Ways and Means Committee began to write legislation to put the system on a sound financial base. In early 1981 Representative J. J. Pickle (D-Tex.), who chaired the subcommittee, prepared legislation that relied on an infusion of general revenues to get over a short-term problem,[2] some tax increases, and some benefit cuts—particularly a deferred, gradual increase in the Normal Retirement Age. This legislation proceeded through the subcommittee, where it enjoyed bipartisan support.[3]

In 1981 the Reagan administration entered the picture. While the administration was interested in keeping Social Security solvent, it also sought to reduce the overall federal deficit, which by mid-1981 had become a major problem. From the standpoint of deficit reductions, the subcommittee bill was horrendous. The bulk of its spending reductions would take place well after the Reagan administration had vacated the White House. And because it relied on general revenues, the bill would actually increase the budget deficit for some time. Office of Management and Budget Director David Stockman's reaction was extremely negative: "The moment I heard about the contents of the Pickle bill, I was determined to derail it" (Stockman 1986). Administration officials requested that the subcommittee temporarily suspend its activity to give the Social Security Administration an opportunity to produce a plan. After receiving the president's approval, this plan was unveiled on 12 May 1981.

The Reagan administration's proposals consisted entirely of benefit reductions. If implemented, the proposals would not only solve all problems of Social Security financing but, because they would reduce Social Security spending by twice the amount needed to ensure solvency, the proposals would also help to reduce the rest of the federal deficit. This seemed to many observers less a Social Security rescue than an effort to milk Social Security for budget savings to offset administration-backed tax cuts.

The reaction was immediate and harsh. Although many of the proposals were reasonable, the administration's plan ran into serious and widespread public opposition because of the suddenness with which some aspects were to take effect. The most damaging aspect of the package was the immediate reduction of benefits for persons taking early retirement benefits at ages sixty-two to sixty-four (Stockman 1986, 190–191; Myers 1985, 283). If enacted, the plan meant that people retiring in the expectation of a certain level of Social Security benefit would not receive it.

Democrats sensed an outstanding political opportunity and exploited it fully. Just days before, on 8 May, Democrats had taken a beating at the hands of the president on the budget resolution, so they were looking to even things up. Speaker Thomas P. "Tip" O'Neill called the proposal "despicable" and a "rotten thing to do." Claude Pepper called the plan "cruel and insidious." House Democrats passed a resolution calling the proposals "an unconscionable breach of faith," while Senator Daniel Patrick Moynihan (D-N.Y.) introduced a resolution denouncing the administration's proposals. The Republican leadership managed to temper Moynihan's language, but still the Senate voted unanimously for a resolution that put it on record against any proposal that would "precipitously and unfairly penalize early retirees" (qtd. in Dewar 1981). In the debate over the resolution, no Republican senators defended the administration's proposal.

Democrats' highly partisan response to the proposals was natural given their beleaguered status at the time. They had suffered a number of setbacks at the hands of Republicans and were looking to make amends. According to one Democrat: "When the White House announced that package, I couldn't believe it. It was the first crack in a solid wall of resistance. . . . If we hadn't jumped on the issue, we would have been declared politically *non compos mentis.*" A Republican remarked: "It was like a bunch of duck hunters waiting in the bushes with the ducks too high to hit. Along came this old turkey, and that was it." And as Pickle explained: "It was the only good thing that had happened all year [for the Democrats], and some couldn't resist the temptation to swing out. . . . That's as normal as breathing" (qtd. in Light 1985, 125–28). Resisting the temptation to inflame the issue, Pickle sought to bring his subcommittee's bipartisan bill to the full Ways and Means Committee. But House Democrats opposed any further action on Social Security. The Pickle bill, after all, did call for some program reductions, and Democratic leaders were now on record as opposing any cuts at all. Considering the Pickle bill would have spoiled the purity of Democrats' opposition to cuts and possibly confused the public about who was on what side.

Democrats pressed the Social Security issue with enthusiasm. Representative Tony Coehlo (D-Calif.) said: "The ball has been lofted to us. We've taken it and we're running with it. . . . We're not going to fumble it. It is without doubt our biggest issue, and there's no close second" (qtd. in Light 1985, 129). Elimination of the Social Security minimum benefit passed Congress as a part of the massive reconciliation bill enacted in the summer of 1981. After burying the administration's proposal, Democrats passed legislation restoring the minimum benefit under some circumstances.[4] This, of course, did nothing to resolve the funding problem, but it did solidify Democrats' reputation as defenders of Social Security. The Democratic party also made the Social Security issue the focus of a massive, extraordinarily successful direct-mail campaign.

Faced with the Democratic onslaught, Republicans hunkered down and made no further proposals on Social Security. The White House was hurt badly by the issue; any further maneuvering short of agreeing to no program cuts would only have opened them up to renewed criticism. Discussions in the White House about trying once again to obtain some Social Security cuts were canceled, Stockman explained, because "the Democratic campaign committee already had ten million letters ready to roll. They were preparing to unleash Claude Pepper again" (1986, 310). An aide to Senator Bob Dole (R-Kan.) explained that the Democrats "wanted us to take the bait and announce our own package. They didn't want to do anything about Social Security but wanted to give them more cannon fodder" (qtd. in Stockman 1986, 310). Unwilling to serve as cannon fodder, though, Republicans offered no new proposals. Meanwhile, Democrats continued to send out direct-mail appeals using the issue to raise money for the 1982 elections. The stalemate continued as the Social Security Trust Fund inched toward bankruptcy.

Some comparisons with the Social Security bailout in 1977 provide insight into the effect of divided party control. President Carter began the process that year by making a Social Security recommendation to Congress. It was mostly ignored by the Ways and Means Committee, which wrote and passed its own legislation. But in doing so it took no pot shots at the president. The bill was potentially controversial, especially because it called for large tax increases. Although Carter did not like the bill that Congress handed him, he did not denounce it. There was no benefit for Democrats in attacking the package, regardless of how little they liked it; delay in enacting the rescue would have reflected badly on the party. Republicans could benefit from attacking the actions of Democrats, and they did; but as the minority party in 1977, they were not well situated to stop the bill.

Thus the 1977 experience, when Democrats controlled both houses of Congress and the White House, suggests that unified party government is better suited to dealing with extremely contentious issues. In both 1977 and the 1980s, the Social Security system faced a tremendous financial challenge that could be dealt with only by means of politically unattractive measures, such as revenue increases or benefit cuts. In 1977 the problem was dealt with quickly, whereas in the 1980s it dragged on for two years. The important difference was that with Democrats controlling Congress and the presidency in 1977, there was little for either party to gain in denouncing the other.

The Budget Negotiations Case (1987)

As with the 1983 Social Security rescue, Democrats and Republicans manifested wholly incompatible preferences about how to solve the budget problem in 1987. Neither side had an entirely coherent plan for bringing the deficit to more reasonable levels, but Republicans were unified in their view that taxes should not be raised and Democrats more or less so in their view that spending should not be slashed. This was a prescription for stalemate.

Gramm-Rudman-Hollings (GRH), the budget-balancing law enacted in 1985, had its automatic enforcement mechanism disallowed by the Supreme Court in 1986; nonetheless, its deficit target remained in place. The Congressional Budget Office estimated that in order to reach the fiscal year (FY) 1988 deficit target of $108 billion, spending cuts and tax increases of $61 billion would have to be enacted (Kenworthy 1987a). However, when President Reagan's FY 1988 budget was unveiled in January 1987, it immediately became one of several earlier Reagan budgets pronounced "dead on arrival" by Congress. The FY 1988 budget relied on optimistic economic forecasts, domestic spending cuts, and revenue-raising measures such as asset sales and user fees. On paper, at least, the budget package satisfied the GRH targets without cutting defense. But it found no friends on Capitol

Hill. Numerous Democrats assailed it for its cuts in programs for the elderly, farmers, students, and others. Republicans offered only restrained defenses of Reagan's budget, but most were not pleased with the spending cuts it would require.

Achieving a significant measure of deficit reduction would require both domestic spending cuts and tax increases for two reasons: the president would not permit taxes alone to account for deficit reduction and Democrats would not allow the domestic budget to absorb all deficit reduction. Questions remained, however: Would any deficit reduction occur? And if so, how much of it would come from taxes and how much from spending? Throughout the spring and summer of 1987 there ensued a battle to resolve these issues.

In 1987 President Reagan had a significant bargaining advantage over Democrats: after their presidential candidate in 1984 had spoken of taxes and suffered a terrible defeat, Democrats in Congress had left it to Republicans to initiate tax increases. As long as tax increases were not a subject for discussion, the only way to meet the GRH requirement was through large spending reductions, a substantial part of which would have to come from domestic spending. Yet the president also had a serious handicap: his preferred solution to the deficit problem—large domestic spending reductions—had been repeatedly rejected by both parties in Congress. In 1984 a fiendish Democrat offered Reagan's budget as an amendment to the House budget resolution, and it lost by a vote of 1 to 401. Of course, if both tax increases and spending cuts were unachievable, then no deficit reduction would occur.

To unblock the stalemate, Speaker of the House Jim Wright (D-Tex.) began a campaign to reintroduce the "T-word" (*taxes*) in political discourse. Even before his election as Speaker by the Democratic caucus in December 1986, Wright spoke of the need for additional revenues. For example, he mentioned the possibility of canceling a scheduled reduction in the income tax rate (Broder 1987a) and proposed a tax on stock-market transactions (Kenworthy 1987b). Wright's enthusiastic support for taxes played into the hands of the president and earned him the nickname "tax-of-the-month man" (Broder 1987b). Nonetheless, Wright apparently hoped that by daring to raise the tax issue, and surviving, he could bolster the courage of other Democrats. "They know I am willing to say the unsayable and lightning hasn't struck me," he explained. "I haven't been smitten like St. Paul" (qtd. in Kenworthy 1987e).

Wright's tax campaign provoked attacks from Republicans and increased their dedication to resisting tax increases. President Reagan embarked on a series of speeches that denounced Wright and Democrats. In 1987 *Washington Post* reporter Tom Kenworthy wrote that "White House officials [are] convinced the best way for the president to capture the momentum he has lost in the Iran-contra affair is for him to lambaste the 'tax and spend' policies of the Democratic party . . ." (1987c). This tactic disturbed Ways and Means Chair Dan Rostenkowski (D-Ill.), who normally had reasonably good relations with the White House. He complained that Reagan "hasn't been fair to us. I'm starting to interpret this president on the stump as not only somewhat irresponsible but enjoying it" (qtd. in Kenworthy 1987b). Republicans on the House Budget Committee refused to participate in drafting the resolution, apparently so they would not be implicated in any of the revenue increases that it recommended. When the Ways and Means Committee later convened to write tax legislation, Republicans on the committee refused to consider any tax increases, even those previously supported by the president (Swardson 1987). Their purpose was to remain pure on the tax issue so that they could denounce Democrats with complete abandon.

In late June 1987 Congress gave final approval to a budget resolution that went very much against President Reagan's wishes, proposing a tax increase of $20 billion and a spending cut of $7 billion. Although the president had proposed more than $20 billion of revenue increases, nearly all of them came from nontax sources (such as asset sales) and were far less offensive to Republican sensibilities than the Democrats', which consisted of bona fide tax increases. To make tax increases less politically damaging to themselves, Democrats envisioned writing a tax law that would put the burden on the wealthy. When the president vetoed the bill, Democrats claimed he was favoring the rich.

Congress applied still more pressure on President Reagan to accept tax increases by reviving the Gramm-Rudman-Hollings budget-balancing law. This effort, spearheaded by Rostenkowski, gave GRH a new trigger to replace the one declared unconstitutional by the Supreme Court in 1986. At the same time, the deficit-reduction targets of GRH relaxed. The maximum allowable deficit was raised from $108 billion to $144 billion, decreasing the amount by which the deficit had to be reduced from about $60 billion to a more modest $23 billion. Congress also threatened the president with defense cuts of about $12 billion if the sequester took place.

By mid-October 1987 it appeared that the threats would not work: congressional Democrats continued to insist that taxes be a part of any deficit-reduction legislation and President Reagan was still equally adamant that taxes not be raised. In addition, Democrats were not forthcoming with domestic spending reductions. Indeed, it seemed that both sides preferred the onset of a sequester to a compromise, and they used the threat of a sequester to bash their opponent. The president attributed the stalemate to Democrats' insistence on tax increases, while Democrats blamed the president for his inflexibility and intransigence.

While public accusations and denunciations can sometimes function as a kind of bargaining, these represented a curious sort of bargaining. Over time, the two sides moved farther apart rather than closer together on the issue, and each side moved toward a more extreme position. Whereas in January 1987 the president proposed a budget that called for some tax increases, in October he swore to veto any tax increase. Similarly, in June 1987 Democrats proposed a budget consisting mostly of revenue increases but also of significant spending cuts; in October, however, the House and Senate revenue committees produced bills raising taxes by about $12 billion, and other committees did not produce legislation to yield the outlay savings promised earlier. Thus both sides moved from somewhat moderate (but still unbalanced) positions to absurdly extreme ones. Ultimately, there was no compromise. On 20 October the president issued the sequester order, initiating across-the-board spending reductions (Havemann 1987).

THE ROLE OF COMMISSIONS

The two cases examined here illustrate separation of powers and checks and balances at their most destructive levels. Madison's argument in *Federalist* paper 51 that "ambition must be made to counteract ambition" (1961, 322) clearly applies to both case studies. Insofar as good government can be obtained by preventing governmental action, our constitutional system is ideally framed. However, when the public well-being requires expeditious governmental action, the political competition engendered by separation of powers does not protect the public. In both cases, the use of high-level, direct, interbranch negotiations ultimately helped to overcome partisanship and allowed the emergence and implementation of compromise agreements.

Negotiations conducted through the ordinary political process are both sequential and public—characteristics not conducive to success. Temptations to make partisan use of a statement or an offer from the other side can be irresistible. Moreover, neither party will seek to initiate a reasonable offer through public channels if it believes the other party will respond in a hostile manner. Commissions can be helpful in overcoming these problems by making it possible to offer proposals in private. The logic of bipartisan commissions is that leaders of both parties, or their designated representatives, can meet to negotiate a deal without the media, the public, or interest groups present. Parties to the negotiation refrain from making inflammatory comments to the press and from revealing what has transpired during the deliberations. If and when a deal is agreed to, leaders from both sides announce and endorse it simultaneously. When deliberations are private, parties can make offers without being denounced either by their opponent or by affected constituency groups. Because the public is excluded, there is less opportunity to use an offer from the other side to curry favor with constituents.

Once leaders have condemned each other and sworn never to compromise, it can be embarrassing to change positions. After its image was damaged by the Social Security issue, the Reagan administration was reluctant to make another proposal (Light 1985, 175). While Democrats may have gotten negotiations moving again by making a serious, balanced offer, after unequivocally opposing benefit cuts it would have been difficult for them to make a public offer of benefit reductions. The commission relieved Democrats and Republicans of the painful necessity of making the next offer. They did not have to be the first to back down publicly from a previously announced position, nor did they risk being attacked by the other side.

Agreeing to summit talks and adhering to their logic are significant because they represent an implicit promise not to attack the opponent. They also mean foregoing partisan attacks and imply a strong preference for reaching an agreement. Of course, entering into negotiations does not guarantee success, nor does it necessarily indicate that the participants want an agreement. If one of the parties prefers to attack its opponent rather than to reach an agreement, that party can easily sabotage the negotiations by leaking to the media proposals from the other side.

THE NATIONAL COMMISSION ON SOCIAL SECURITY REFORM

The National Commission on Social Security Reform was first suggested by the Reagan administration in September 1981, ostensibly to propose reforms, but mostly as a way of shedding responsibility for an issue that could only harm the president. The commission was formally instituted by an executive order dated 16 December 1981. Although it was eventually a great success, its creation was not viewed auspiciously. Budget Director David Stockman dismissed the value of the commission: "Jim Baker had fobbed off Social Security to a bipartisan study commission whose instructions were to take a year to think about it" (Stockman 1986, 332).

The commission was composed of fifteen members—five were appointed by the president, five by the Senate majority leader, and five by the Speaker of the House. The congressional appointments were made in consultation with the minority leaders of each chamber. The partisan balance of the commissioners was eight to seven in favor of Republicans, although the ideological balance favored conservatives over liberals by a margin of ten to five (Light 1985, 191). More important was the inclusion on the commission of some of the most influential members of Congress—among them Bob Dole (R-Kans.), Senate Finance chair; Barber Conable (R-N.Y.), ranking minority member of the House Ways and Means Committee; Bill Archer (R-Tex.), ranking minority member of the House Social Security Subcommittee; William Armstrong (R-Colo.), chair of the Social Security Subcommittee of the Finance Committee; Claude Pepper (D-Fla.), chair of the House Rules Committee; Daniel P. Moynihan (D-N.Y.), ranking minority member of the Subcommittee on Social Security; and John Heinz (R-Pa.), chair of the Senate Special Committee on Aging. In addition, there were two former members of Congress—Martha Keys and Joe Waggonner—as well as Robert Ball, former Social Security commissioner, and Lane Kirkland, president of the AFL-CIO and an important voice for American labor, who lent great prestige to the panel. Three businesspeople appointed by President Reagan completed the membership. The chair, Alan Greenspan, was a highly respected conservative economist with substantial government experience who later became chair of the Federal Reserve System. The executive order directed the group to report its findings by 31 December 1982, though the deadline was later extended to 20 January 1983.

It was highly beneficial to the purposes of the commission that its members were so likely to command respect for any recommendations that they would produce; however, some of the members were extremists and unlikely to engage in the kind of compromise necessary to produce a substantial, bipartisan agreement. Pepper had built a nationwide reputation as a watchdog for the elderly, and it was exceedingly unlikely that he would agree to substantial program cuts. Archer and Armstrong were firmly opposed to tax increases. The commission's makeup virtually ruled out the possibility of a unanimous report; without at least near unanimity, the commission's conclusions were likely to engender more partisan bickering.

Early in the life of the commission, Heinz suggested an equally split bargain—half increased taxes and half benefit cuts. This seemingly reasonable suggestion was rejected by the extremists on both sides. The commissioners met nine times in 1982 but made no progress toward agreement. The commissioners were able to reach agreement on technical matters, especially on the size of the Social Security deficit and on maintaining the fundamental structure and principles of the program. But they did not agree on the politically charged issue of how to eliminate the deficit. The commission's staunch partisans were a problem, as were its open meetings with live C-SPAN coverage. With so many interest groups either in the room or watching on television, it was impossible even to discuss concessions without raising a storm of protest. In early December the group essentially gave up the quest for a solution.

Negotiations resumed in late December 1982 on an informal, secret basis among five of the more moderate commissioners—Moynihan, Ball, Conable, Dole, and Greenspan. They were joined by four representatives from the White House—Stockman, Ken Duberstein, Dick Darman, and Jim Baker, White House Chief of Staff. This group of members consisted of good negotiators because none was an ideologue. They were also adept at keeping their mouths shut and not leaking each day's developments to the media. Still more important, they had the tacit support of President Reagan and Speaker O'Neill.

Ball was the lead negotiator for the Democrats, speaking frequently with O'Neill; Darman and Baker negotiated for the Republicans, clearing matters with the White House. The group met throughout January 1983 and gradually crafted an agreement. The negotiations were conducted explicitly on the basis of a fifty-fifty division between cuts in benefits and increases in taxes. As one participant explained, "It became clear very early that, in-asmuch as the Republicans wanted to solve the problem entirely with benefit cuts and the Democrats entirely with revenues, an even division would be required" (personal interview). All components of the agreement were clas-sified as benefit cuts, revenue increases, or "unscored"—a category reserved for changes that were not counted in the other two categories. The major breakthrough was the decision to tax the Social Security benefits of high-income earners. This provided a substantial savings and did not annoy either side excessively. Democrats agreed to a permanent delay in the cost-of-living adjustment (COLA) and Republicans to an acceleration of already scheduled tax increases.

After assembling a complete package and privately obtaining the backing of the president and the Speaker, the group took it to the full commission for approval on 15 January 1983. For the agreement to have any force, all interested parties had to agree to it; however, none of them would commit before others had. Greenspan explained the situation: "The last thing was the tricky problem of getting everybody within an hour's time to all agree to this document, all contingent on everyone else's agreement. What we had going was that the president would agree if the Speaker would agree if the commission would agree" (Light 1985, 191). And that is how it worked. The commission endorsed the plan by a surprisingly wide margin of twelve to three; the dissenters—Waggonner, Archer, and Armstrong—did so in remarkably measured, moderate terms. The White House exerted substan-tial pressure on some of the president's appointees. And Pepper agreed—a surprise, given his previously unyielding opposition to benefit reductions. With the commission on record in favor of the plan, both the president and the Speaker endorsed it strongly and publicly.

The most contentious, partisan, and difficult issue in American politics became, almost overnight, an issue on which there was a very wide con-sensus. With the same plan drawing support from such unlikely sources as Reagan, Pepper, and leaders of both parties in the House and Senate, passing the legislation took on an aura of near inevitability. The only important challenge in implementing the agreement was in finding additional savings to provide adequate financing in the long term, which was accomplished by a gradual increase in the Normal Retirement Age.[5] The legislation mir-rored the commission's recommendations on all important points and glided easily through both the House and Senate. It received final approval from Congress on 24 March 1983, and was signed by President Reagan on 20 April.

There were a few dissenting voices. Federal workers opposed the agree-ment because it brought them into the Social Security system. The American Association of Retired People fought the agreement because it cut benefits. Though both groups were usually influential in the past, neither was effec-tive in this case despite their active lobbying campaigns against the deal. Of course, many politicians would have liked to satisfy senior citizens' and federal workers' concerns by voting against the provisions. But because they could not do so without causing the entire package to collapse, members of Congress resisted constituent pressure.

The commission succeeded largely because it avoided negotiating the Social Security bailout in public, excluding both the public and interest groups from the negotiating process. Because the audience for negotiations consisted only of elites, the participants could not submit an unreasonable offer in hopes of currying favor with a constituency group. Similarly, there was no purpose in denouncing a proposal from the other side since no interest groups were present. Moreover, virtually all interested parties lent their support simultaneously, so the risk of betrayal was minimal.

THE BUDGET SUMMIT OF 1987

By October of 1987 President Reagan and the Democratically-controlled Congress had reached what seemed like an unresolvable stalemate on the budget. There was every reason to believe that sequestration under GRH would have taken place, if not for the intervention of a five-hundred-point decline in the Dow Jones average on October 19. No one knew why the stock-market crash occurred, and no one could tell if it was just a blip or the precursor of still larger declines. In any case, the Wall Street community declared that the federal budget deficit was too large and had to be reduced to return stability to the nation's financial markets.

The stock market did what the GRH law could not do—introduce a sense of panic and desperation that made deficit reduction so high a priority that it displaced considerations of partisan advancement. To calm the markets, President Reagan declared at a press conference that he would enter into negotiations with Congress in an effort to reduce the deficit. Everything but Social Security, he declared, would be on the table. Although Democratic leaders of Congress had frequently called for a summit meeting throughout the year, Reagan declined on the grounds that Democrats intended to use the discussions for the purpose of raising taxes. When he agreed to consider taxes, negotiations could proceed.

With the financial markets in a continuing turmoil, and with Wall Street watching and waiting, the budget negotiators began their meetings under tremendous pressure to come to an agreement. "A sense of apprehension, even fear, seems to have gripped negotiators on all sides of the table," Steven Roberts of the *New York Times* reported. "With the financial markets watching their every move, lawmakers say this is not the time to play their usual political games with the budget" (1987, 29). Senator J. Bennett Johnston (D-La.) explained that among the negotiators "the feeling is that the markets are really looking at what we're doing. We're very conscious of the markets" (qtd. in Roberts 1987, 29). An unnamed Republican senator expressed hope that Wall Street would remain depressed because, he explained, "that's the only way we'll get together. We've got to keep the pressure on" (qtd. in Roberts 1987, 29). A Wall Street economist warned that a cut of only $23 billion, the minimum needed to avert sequestration, "certainly cannot help the markets" (Bennett 1987, 15).

In order to produce a deficit reduction of greater magnitude than the $23 billion sequester, the conferees continued meeting over a period of several weeks. The negotiations were not easy; Democrats and Republicans continued to try to protect their favorite programs. But the talks were promising because both sides were less interested than usual in scoring political points and more interested in reaching an agreement. The White House showed new flexibility on tax increases, while Democrats showed greater flexibility on domestic spending. By 10 November 1987, one participant could say that there were "the outlines of a plan [visible] through the mist" (qtd. in Feuerbringer 1987a, 1). Then, on 20 November, an agreement on a $30 billion deficit reduction was signed. The group had previously come close to agreement on a much larger reduction involving highly controversial limits on entitlement COLAs, "but the idea was dropped when neither administration negotiators nor congressional leaders could figure out how to limit the political damage to their colleagues' satisfaction" (Feuerbringer 1987b, 1).

Although the agreement was not as sweeping as many had hoped, it was sufficient to forestall a GRH sequester. "We are sending the right message at the right time," the president claimed as he and congressional leaders announced the plan. Reagan called the agreement "a blueprint that sends a strong signal both at home and abroad that together we can and will get our deficit under control and keep it that way" (Kenworthy 1987f). Speaker Wright defended the agreement as a reasonable compromise: "It is a demonstration that in times of stress, the administrative and executive, as well as the legislative branches of government, can work together, even when they are in the hands of different political parties" (Kenworthy 1987d). Many participants in the negotiations worried that there would be great difficulty in persuading Congress to pass the legislation, but the legislation moved easily through Congress.

WHEN AND WHY SUMMITS WORK

Summit negotiations work when both parties, especially their top leaders, want an agreement, and when the alternative is immediate disaster. Of course, one of the main reasons leaders may seek an agreement is the prospect of dire consequences in its absence. These conditions describe both cases examined here, as well as the 1990 budget summit, which also produced a bipartisan agreement. In the two failed summits—the National Economic Commission's and the Pepper Commission's—there was little desire on either side to compromise in order to reach an agreement, mostly because no dire consequences were threatening.

The National Economic Commission (NEC), set up in late 1987 to reach a consensus on how to balance the budget, was based on the successful model of the Social Security Commission. Behind the NEC lurked the hopeful notion that if reasonable people gathered in a nonpartisan atmosphere and thought hard about the budget deficit, they could come up with a solution. Of course, the solution they would arrive at, being reasonable people, would be some form of a "share-the-pain" formula of tax increases, defense cuts, and domestic spending cuts. Moderate politicians have been speaking for years of the "grand compromise"; the NEC was envisioned as the means of implementing that compromise.

The foregoing logic would have been compelling if politicians were primarily interested in reaching an agreement. Unfortunately, politicians' strategies for gaining and retaining political support doomed the NEC. George Bush ran for president with the slogan, "Read my lips—no new taxes." This promise certainly helped him defeat Bob Dole for the Republican nomination, and it probably helped him in the general election. Throughout the campaign Bush found the NEC a useful target, calling it a tax increase commission. The NEC finished its deliberations in 1989. Since this was President Bush's first year in office, it was too early for him to consider breaking his most prominent campaign pledge. There was also no room for compromise on the Democratic side. When Bob Strauss, a Democratic commissioner, discussed the possibility of Social Security cuts, he was bitterly criticized within his party and forced to retract the heresy. Ultimately, the commission majority issued a vacuous report that made virtually no substantive recommendations. The minority Democrats all dissented and the commission disbanded without having made any contribution to solving the deficit problem.

The Bipartisan Commission on Comprehensive Health Care, also known as the Pepper Commission, was established in 1988 to find solutions to the problems of providing long-term health care for the elderly and broadening access to health care for the uninsured. Like the NEC, this commission's members were highly prestigious and likely to generate legitimacy for an agreement, should one emerge. However, the commission failed to generate a bipartisan consensus on health care because there was no pressure for an immediate resolution to the problem. Lacking pressure to solve the problem, neither Democrats nor Republicans were willing to engage in the kind of compromise necessary to reach agreement.

Regarding long-term health care for the elderly, the commission agreed by a bipartisan vote of eleven to four on a government-financed plan for nursing home and in-home care. Nonetheless, the agreement was virtually meaningless because the commission did not address the crucial question of how the plan would be financed. Given the budgetary situation of 1990, an agreement on what to do but not how to pay for it would not produce action. One commissioner, Pete Stark (D-Calif.), summed up the situation: "We didn't do our job. We didn't figure out how to pay for it. There is no tax fairy out there who is going to pull it out from under a pillow." As for the reason for the failure, Stark remarked that there was not "enough pressure to bring us together" (Rovner 1990, 667).

Not even a fictional accord emerged on the issue of access to health care for the uninsured. When it became apparent that a majority of the commission favored an ambitious proposal, the Bush administration told Republican commissioners that it did not want a bipartisan recommendation to emerge. The White House wanted to avoid pressure for a new and costly program at a time when it was trying to reduce the deficit. Republican commissioners complied, and the proposal passed on an eight to seven party-line vote.

For a plan providing a comprehensive solution to either problem to be approved, taxes would have to be increased. Republicans would not agree to this. However, there was a less expensive alternative to comprehensive care—a set of piecemeal reforms that, while not a solution to the whole problem, would presumably address some of the worst symptoms of the American health-care system. Many Democrats cherished the idea of national health insurance and so wanted to use the commission as a vehicle for advancing that cause. They were not interested in meliorative reform because it would undermine support for comprehensive reform. Under divided government, a balanced proposal was the only kind that could pass; but given the political incentives of Democrats and Republicans, and the absence of a widely perceived health-care crisis, neither side found a moderate proposal attractive.

In contrast, the budget summit negotiations of 1990 did reach a bipartisan agreement. The precise deal struck by the negotiators was not implemented because of an unwillingness of Congress to follow their ostensible leaders. But the summit produced an agreement that formed the basis for subsequent deliberations, and the final legislation conformed in general outline (though not in specific detail) with the summit agreement. The development of a budget stalemate was reminiscent of 1987. The GRH law required cuts of $100 billion, an amount that could not be met by spending reductions or tax increases alone. After protracted discussions, negotiators unveiled an agreement that was the most far-reaching deficit-reduction package ever to win bipartisan endorsement. Legislation incorporating the agreement died on the floor of the House, killed by the back-bench opposition of both Democrats and Republicans. Thereafter, deficit-reduction legislation was crafted by means of the more conventional process of committees drafting legislation and presenting it to their chambers for approval. Eventually, it passed, but not before the government was shut down for a day. In one respect, the summit negotiations approach did not work in that the negotiators were unable to maintain the support of their parties in Congress. But all the legislative packages subsequently considered by the House and Senate adhered carefully to the overall framework devised by the summit, differing only in detail. Moreover, the committees in Congress almost certainly would not have passed such ambitious legislation had the summit not provided a blueprint.

CONCLUSION

Commissions and summit negotiations became a routine feature of American government in the 1980s, and we can expect that they will continue to be useful in the future. Yet a puzzle surrounds their use in resolving partisan stalemate—while deadlock has occurred with great frequency in American politics, summits were virtually unknown prior to the 1980s. Why, then, did summits come into use as a means of breaking deadlock?

Bipartisan summit negotiations are particularly helpful when action must be taken on highly distasteful legislation. Thus summit negotiations became prominent as the number of issues on which decisions had to be made quickly increased. Normally, in a democratic government, few issues must be decided by a specific date. When agreement does not exist on an issue, decision can be deferred until one emerges. This happened frequently in the presidencies of Eisenhower, Nixon, Ford, Reagan, and Bush. In the cases of successful negotiations discussed in this chapter, action was needed by a specific date, and both parties recognized this. In contrast, in the forty years prior to the 1980s, there were no cases in which these conditions existed.

Summit negotiations typically include instances of *blame avoidance*, the effort of politicians to shirk responsibility for controversial actions. Weaver (1986, 1988) argues that blame-avoidance strategies emerge in zero-sum situations, when politicians must make choices that provide benefits to some constituencies but at a cost to others. Summits allow politicians to avoid blame for controversial decisions because the summit format obscures the origin of proposals. The summit, rather than any party or individual, can be blamed for unpopular policy choices; but a summit, unlike a person, cannot be held responsible.

The manner in which a summit allows politicians to shirk responsibility makes it controversial. It is widely argued that politicians in a democratic system must be accountable for their actions, otherwise there is no democracy. But summits have no authority to implement agreements, only the capacity to negotiate them. Whatever they produce must later be voted on in Congress and signed into law by the president. Thus those who support a summit agreement must later defend their actions to their electorates.

Summits succeed when the top political leaders in the executive and legislative branches are amenable to compromise. If political leaders are intent on indulging their instinct for partisan promotion, commissions will not help and summit negotiations will not occur. Commissions cannot impose solutions on leaders unwilling to hear or implement them. The role of commissions is to help overcome the uncertainty that attends public negotiations and ease the emergence of an agreement that both sides see as advantageous. Because the temptation to seek benefit at the expense of a rival is so great, politicians seem willing to forego the pleasures of partisanship only when the alternative is complete disaster.

Acknowledgments

The author would like to acknowledge the valuable assistance, comments, and suggestions of Ann Kendrick, George Tsebelis, Julie Withers, Stephen Stedman, Jack Knight, Robert J. Myers, William Lowry, Erwin Hargrove, Mary Olson, Michael McKuen, Charles Franklin, Paul Quirk, and Rosanna Perotti. Thanks also go to Daniel Beck and Kevin Corder for their research assistance, and especially to Nick Masters for his encouragement and assistance.

Notes

1. The agreement called for a deficit reduction of $30.2 billion in fiscal year (FY) 1988 and another $45.8 billion in FY 1989—a total of $76 billion. To understand the extent to which this agreement harmed Democratic and Republican interests, close examination of the final package is necessary. First, revenues from asset sales and interest savings can be disregarded because these harm neither party. Second, revenues from IRS initiatives and user fees can be disregarded; these increase government revenue, but not in ways Republicans find particularly offensive. With these "easy" savings removed, what is left is a total "hard" deficit reduction of about $57 billion over two years. The "hard" tax increase of $23 billion and the defense cut of $13.2 billion were the painful parts of the package for Republicans; the domestic spending cuts of $20.6 billion were the part of the deal that hurt Democrats.

2. The use of general revenues had been advocated for many years by some Social Security experts, but it was impractical in an era of $100 billion annual deficits. According to Senator William Armstrong (R-Colo.), the idea of using general revenues to assist Social Security was "like asking Amtrak to bail out Conrail" (Rich 1981, A3).

3. On the Pickle legislation, see Clark (1981).

4. The reconciliation bill contained other significant benefit reductions that were not later restored, including (a) the elimination of child/student benefits with respect to retired, deceased, or disabled workers; (b) restrictions on lump-sum death benefits; and (c) the introduction of a cap on disability benefits when other disability benefits are payable.

5. The original retirement age of sixty-five will be maintained until the year 2002, after which it will rise gradually to sixty-seven by 2027.

13 / New Rules for an Old Game: Zero-Sum Budgeting in the Postreform Congress

JAMES A. THURBER

Ending months of tortuous partisan brawling and fiscal disarray, Congress approved the Omnibus Budget Reconciliation Act (OBRA) during the weekend of 27–28 October 1990, which set the fiscal year (FY) 1991 budget and established major changes in the congressional budget process. The battle over the 1991 budget began on 29 January 1990 when President George Bush submitted his spending proposals to Congress, moved to a highly contentious summit meeting between congressional leaders and representatives of the president in the fall, collapsed in a public defeat of the summit plan on the floor of the House, and finally ended in the passage of the OBRA, which included the Budget Enforcement Act (BEA) of 1990 (Title XIII of OBRA).

The president's original budget plan included modest cuts in mass transit and Medicare, an end to Amtrak subsidies, and a commitment to hold overall spending growth below the rate of inflation. A capital gains tax cut was proposed to spur growth and purportedly to increase tax revenues. The final act contained something quite different: tax increases (after President Bush abandoned his "no new taxes" pledge), major entitlement cuts ($25 billion from Medicare alone, despite electoral threats from retirees), fundamental restructuring of Gramm-Rudman-Hollings (GRH I and II), the Balanced Budget and Emergency Deficit Control Act, and changes in the Congressional Budget Act (CBA) that significantly alter the way Congress will consider the budget in the 1990s.

The new budget process rules further centralize power within Congress and force Congress to make *zero-sum* choices; that is, trading visible reductions in one program for visible increases in another, or tax cuts from some in exchange for tax breaks for others. The BEA included changes in substantive law and budgetary procedures designed to bring more control over the budget process and reduce the deficit by a total of almost $500 billion over five years. The most visible change was the elimination of fixed deficit targets as established in GRH I and II, but other innovations—such as categorical sequesters, pay-as-you-go (PAYGO) provisions on taxes and spending, and a new enhanced role for the Office of Management and Budget (OMB)—affect the budgetary powers within Congress and for the president. This chapter describes and assesses these new rules for the old game of budgeting in the context of the postreform Congress.

We begin with a brief description of the budget process, including the cast of actors who participate in the annual battles of the budget. To put the 1990 changes into context, one must understand congressional budget patterns in the postreform era, from 1974 to 1990. Next, the new BEA rules are described. Finally, the major 1990 reforms are analyzed in terms of (1) their impact on presidential and congressional budgetary power, (2) their influence on the distribution of spending power within Congress, and (3) their effect on the openness, complexity, and timeliness of the congressional budget process.

THE ANNUAL BATTLE OF THE BUDGET: PROCESS AND ACTORS

While budget processes have varied since passage of the Budget and Impoundment Control Act of 1974, the participants have remained constant. Although actors naturally seek to change the budget process to enhance their power, certain basic roles remain for the administration and Congress.

The budgeting processes generally occur in four main stages: (1) executive branch budget preparation and submission, (2) congressional passage of budget resolutions, (3) congressional authorization and appropriations, and (4) budget execution and control. Each stage has its own process and cast of characters (see Thurber 1989; Axelrod 1988; Lynch 1985; Rubin 1990; and Wildavsky 1984, 1988).

Presidents are responsible for formulating and transmitting a proposed federal budget to Congress. They set general budget policy by discussing the overall budgetary outlook with the director of the OMB and cabinet officials. Their decisions establish general guidelines and agency planning targets for the annual budget. In setting spending priorities and fiscal policy, presidents rely on their staff and advisors, the OMB, the Council of Economic Advisors, the Department of Treasury, and the government agencies that administer federal programs. The budget includes an accounting of how funds have been spent in the past along with the president's recommendations and estimates of receipts and outlays for the coming fiscal year. In reality, most of the budget is relatively "uncontrollable" from year to year (Weaver 1988). That is, previous-year commitments have made almost 85 percent of the budget difficult if not impossible to change in a single budget year.

After the president submits a budget to Congress, the congressional budget process formally begins. Although under no obligation to accept the president's budget, Congress operates within budget policy that is initially outlined by the president. Congress changes the details of that policy, but its general contours are shaped by the president's preferences, along with previous policy commitments. The final level of federal receipts and outlays is determined by Congress. Before money can be spent by the executive branch, Congress must both authorize federal programs and appropriate money for them.

The major players in the congressional budget process are the budget committees, Appropriations committees, revenue committees, authorization committees, the Congressional Budget Office (CBO), and the party leadership of the House and Senate (see Thurber 1989; Rubin 1990; Schick 1980; and Shuman 1984). The House and Senate budget committees, created in 1974, are responsible for legislation dealing with the federal budget in general and specifically with the concurrent budget resolutions. House and Senate Appropriations committees are responsible for legislation that appropriates revenue for support of the government. From the 1940s to late 1960s the Appropriations committees were key players in budgetary decision making and generally exercised fiscal constraints on other committees. The authorizing committees (nineteen in the House and fifteen in the Senate) propose the solutions to public problems by designing new federal programs, reauthorize existing programs, and advise the Appropriations committees on the necessary level of funding for programs. The Congressional Budget Office provides information and analysis on economic trends and budget requirements for the budget process (Thurber 1976). The CBO also serves as a scorekeeper in the process, comparing current authorizations and appropriations to ceilings on overall government expenditures, budget authority, and outlays set in annual budget resolutions.

Budgetary authority is granted for varying periods of time to federal agencies through appropriations that enable them to function. Most agencies are given this spending authority annually. Appropriations bills fall within the jurisdiction of both the House and Senate Appropriations committees but, like revenue bills, they are first considered in the House. Once the House has passed appropriations legislation, it is sent to the Senate. As with other forms of legislation, if the legislation passed by the Senate differs from the House version, a conference committee meets to resolve the differences. Once the differences are resolved and both houses of Congress have passed the same legislation, it is sent to the president for signing. The president can either sign or veto the legislation.

In summary, congressional budgeting is complex, there are many actors, and the types of actions are diverse. The process includes several broad activities: setting budget totals, making decisions about how much money to authorize for programs, establishing how much money to appropriate for programs, deciding who and at what level to tax, and overseeing the carrying out of the budget (budget execution). These activities were fundamentally changed in 1974 (Thurber 1989).

CONGRESSIONAL BUDGET REFORMS OF 1974

From 1966 to 1973 government spending for the Vietnam War and Great Society domestic programs grew without accompanying increases in revenues, swelling the federal deficit to an unprecedented size. During this period Congress and the president waged major battles over the conduct of the war and domestic spending priorities. Appropriations bills were passed late and the number of continuing resolutions for appropriations increased (Thurber 1989). Congress began to demand more budget information (Thurber 1989). After President Richard Nixon withheld billions of dollars for popular domestic programs that Congress had authorized and appropriated, checks were sought on the president's impoundment power. At the same time, fiscal scarcity created pressure to reduce spending, control deficits, and increase Congress's budgetary leverage over the president. Fear of the rise in spending and deficits, lack of control in the appropriations process, a need to control fiscal policy and spending priorities, a desire to have an independent source of budget information and analysis, and the demand to check presidential impoundments all led to passage of the 1974 CBA (Thurber 1989). All of these fears and reforms were fueled by sagging economic performance in the 1970s. Poor economic performance has continued to be a major shaper of the zero-sum era, necessitating incessant budgetary wars and calls for budget process reform.

Since passage of the Congressional Budget and Impoundment Control Act of 1974 (P.L. 93-344), the budget process has been organized around the budget committees and a "concurrent resolution on the budget," which sets ceilings on spending and estimates revenues. Not having the force of law, the primary purpose of the resolution is to guide and restrain Congress in its actions on various spending and revenue bills. The budget resolution is supposed to be adopted before the House and Senate consider appropriations, revenue, and entitlement legislation. In recent years, however, Congress has generally failed to pass budget resolutions on time (Thurber 1989).

The spending total in the budget resolution is divided into twenty-one functional categories and further divided among the committees with jurisdiction over various programs. Special procedural rules make it difficult for a committee to exceed its spending allocation. For example, the tax committees (House Ways and Means; Senate Finance) are not allowed to propose tax cuts that, if enacted, would cause revenues to fall short of the target set in the budget resolution.

The CBA helped to centralize decision making in Congress and enhance its budgetary power over the president and executive branch. According to Rubin (1990, 65), centralization can be characterized by two dimensions: (1) the degree to which the budget process is top-down or bottom-up, and (2) the degree to which power is dispersed among committees and subcommittees without an effective organizing device. A top-down, coordinated budget procedure is a centralized process. In principle, the CBA process integrates the fragmentation of the spending and authorizing decisions. In practice, there have been great tensions between the efforts to centralize the budget process and the desire of the Appropriations, authorization, and revenue committees to control privileged programs within their jurisdiction.

The Budget Act shifted congressional budgeting toward a top-down process. Top-down budgeting occurs during times of scarcity, a condition that was dramatically brought to the attention of Congress in the late 1970s. When spending must be tightly controlled, having a coordinated policy is essential; that policy is usually formulated by budget leaders and dictated to budget drones. This centralized decision making is driven by the need to control spending and the focus on shifting priorities (for example, Reaganomics), two key characteristics of budgeting in the postreform years.

The 1980s saw a concentration of budgetary power within the budget committees and among party leaders coupled with a reduction in the autonomy of authorization, revenue, and Appropriations committees. Before the 1974 budget reforms, the power centers operated with a fair degree of autonomy. Appropriations committees in each house set spending levels and authorization committees passed program legislation. The House Ways and Means and Senate Finance committees made revenue and some entitlement (for example, Social Security) program decisions with little outside direction. The 1974 act overlaid the budget committees on this appropriations-authorization-revenue decision-making process. These budget committees were established to estimate revenues, spending, and the deficit (or surplus). The other committees were supposed to stay within the guidelines set by the budget committee's resolution, a powerful tool to coordinate committee actions.

As the size of the deficits mushroomed in the postreform era of the late 1970s and 1980s, the power of the budget committees and party leadership also grew. By requiring Congress to establish annual expenditure and revenue levels with prescriptions for arriving at those spending and income totals, budget committees and party leaders consolidated their power over the budget. Beyond the power of the budget committees, the procedures included three important elements that fostered centralization. First, a timetable set deadlines for action on budget-related legislation so to ensure completion of the budget plan prior to the start of each fiscal year. Second, the annual adoption of budget resolutions brought more discipline to the process by setting spending ceilings. Finally, the act established the reconciliation process to conform revenue, spending, and debt legislation to the levels specified in the final budget resolution—a classic method of forcing top-down budgeting and coordination among the various congressional actors (Schick 1981).

Reconciliation is a procedure for bringing existing law into conformity with the budget resolution. Under this procedure, Congress instructs designated committees to report legislation changing existing law to adjust revenues and expenditures by certain amounts. These committees have a deadline by which they must report the laws, although they have the discretion of deciding which changes are to be made into law. The recommendations of the various committees are consolidated without change by the budget committees into an omnibus budget reconciliation bill (for example, the 1990 OBRA). Reconciliation instructions have been included in most budget resolutions since FY 1981. Reconciliation significantly reduced committee autonomy in the 1980s.

Reconciliation is the most important centralizing procedure of the CBA because it allows the budget and party leaders to direct other committees to make revenue and spending actions deemed necessary to achieve specified savings. It forces revisions in substantive law, driven by the need to make the budget numbers come out even. House and Senate committees must report legislation that will meet budget authority, outlays, and revenue targets. The budget committees control the numbers and the other committees have jurisdiction over the substantive aspects of the law, but the numbers heavily influence the substance. Because reconciliation provides a mechanism other than voluntary compliance of the budget committees to direct legislative committees to make changes in existing laws to achieve the desired budget reductions (or revenue increases), it gives the budget and party leaders an important coordinating mechanism that centralizes spending power.

The reconciliation process as contemplated in the 1974 Budget Act was to be a relatively brief and simple exercise. By most interpretations, reconciliation measures were to be in the second concurrent resolution, which was binding and applied only to appropriations. For the first five years, everyone played by these rules. In 1980, however, a sluggish economy, an unanticipated large budget deficit, and an aggressive president, Ronald Reagan (with the assistance of OMB Director David Stockman) altered congressional budget politics dramatically. The budget committees included reconciliation directions for both authorization and Appropriations committees in the first budget resolution for FY 1981, cutting deep into the authority of the other committees. The strategy of placing ceilings on the first resolution worked again for FY 1982. The Senate's GOP and a Reagan-inspired bipartisan coalition in the House backed the budget committee reconciliation and forced other standing committees to make major substantive changes in their programs. Through the reconciliation process, the budget committees were able to require several congressional committees to reduce spending by about $6.2 billion and to force the tax-writing committees to recommend revenue increases of $4.2 billion.

The FY 1981 reconciliation bill (P.L. 96-499) established an important precedent and resulted in a projected savings for fiscal years 1981–85 of more than $50 billion in outlays and $29 billion in additional revenues. As Smith and Deering observed, "by revealing how they had devised the reconciliation figure for each committee, the budget committees were indicating which programs might be cut to achieve the specified level of spending savings. Committee chairs protested this infringement on their jurisdictions, arguing that the budget committees had no business making suggestions about individual programs within the jurisdiction of authorizing committees" (1991, 201). Reconciliation, a top-down process, has been an integral part of congressional budgeting since 1980 (Sinclair 1983).

Although reconciliation shifted power away from the Appropriations, revenue, and authorizing committees and toward the budget committees and party leaders, the process fell far short of total centralization. Deficits, delay, and interbranch stalemates between 1982 and 1985 prevented the budget committees and party leaders from consolidating their power. Moreover, committees discovered that reconciliation was a good way to pass unrelated authorization bills. Reconciliation became a guaranteed method of getting authorization bills to conference that were opposed by the other chamber. The potential of a coordinated and centralized budget process that threatened committee and subcommittee autonomy was never completely realized, as committees used the reconciliation process to advance stalled legislation and to gain power inside their own chambers.

DEFICIT GROWTH AND BUDGET CONTROL

By the 1980s projected budget deficits were in the $200 billion range, far higher than ever before (Eisner 1986). After failing to pass a budget until early December 1985 and facing large deficits, Congress passed the Balanced Budget and Emergency Deficit Control Act (P.L. 99-177), sponsored by senators Phil Gramm (R-Tex.), Warren Rudman (R-N.H.), and Ernest Hollings (D-S.C.). The goal of the Gramm-Rudman-Hollings (GRH) plan was to balance the federal budget by establishing maximum levels for the federal budget deficit eventually balancing the budget in 1991 (see Table 13-1, p. 264). The legislation instituted new deadlines and procedures to bring more spending control (more top-down decision making and centralization) to congressional budgeting, to make the process more efficient, and to focus attention on reducing the deficit.

The central enforcement mechanism of GRH was a series of automatic across-the-board spending cuts (referred to as *sequestration*) that would occur if the federal budget did not meet the deficit targets. The threat of sequestration was supposed to motivate Congress and the president to make the necessary deficit reductions because the across-the-board cuts were presumably worse than the cuts devised by each of the committees. Like reconciliation, sequestration further threatened the committees' control over their own jurisdictions. If the proposed budget did not meet the annual deficit targets established in the act, the president under GRH was required to meet these targets through across-the-board spending cuts evenly divided

Table 13-1 / GRH Deficit-Reduction Targets and 1990 BEA Deficits[a]

Fiscal Year	Deficit-reduction Target (in $ billions)		Estimated Deficits, 1990 BEA	Actual Deficits
	1985 GRH LIMITS	1987 GRH LIMITS		
1986	$172	—	—	$221
1987	144	—	—	150
1988	108	$144	—	155
1989	72	136	—	152
1990	36	100	—	195
1991	0	64	$327	—
1992	—	28	317	—
1993	—	0	236	—
1994	—	—	102	—
1995	—	—	83	—

[a] The budget figures include Social Security; although an off-budget item, it is counted for the purposes of the Balanced Budget Act targets.
Sources: Adapted from Thurber 1989, 85. Estimated deficits are from Congressional Budget Office 1990a, 8; Congressional Budget Office 1990b. The 1990 deficit targets are from Title XIII, section III, "Revising and Enforcing Deficit Targets," Budget Enforcement Act of 1990, conference report, 6.

between domestic and defense programs. Most entitlement programs (approximately 43 percent of the budget) and interest payments (about 14 percent of the budget) were partially or totally exempted from the potential cuts, making the sequestration threat devastating for all nonexempt programs.

The 1985 GRH legislation gave the General Accounting Office (GAO) the responsibility for triggering the across-the-board cuts. In 1986 the Supreme Court declared that part of the legislation was unconstitutional because it gave the GAO, a legislative support agency, executive functions. The Supreme Court's decision would have prevented the implementation of GRH, but Congress responded with the passage of the Balanced Budget and Emergency Deficit Control Reaffirmation Act of 1987 (GRH II). The GRH II legislation altered the original GRH deficit-reduction plan by directing the Office of Management and Budget, an executive agency, to issue the report that would trigger sequestration if deficit-reduction targets were not met and revised the original deficit-reduction targets in accordance with more realistic economic assumptions (see Table 13-1).

Gramm-Rudman-Hollings procedures further centralized congressional budgeting by enhancing the role of the budget resolution and by forcing budget and party leaders to bargain directly with the administration over the budget resolution. Most other committees and nearly all individual members found they could wield little influence over the deficit-reduction plan set in the budget resolution (Penner and Abramson 1988). In 1989, for example, the advantages House and Senate committees gained in the reconciliation process were lost when Senate party leaders negotiated a budget bill that eliminated extraneous legislation and, in the House, only a few extraneous bills survived the conference that year.

THE FAILURE OF GRH

The Gramm-Rudman-Hollings deficit-reduction plan promised long-term progress toward lower deficits and a balanced budget, but these goals proved to be elusive and overly optimistic. Presidential and congressional attention to each budget year was increased but neither considered long-term budgetary goals. More time was spent on budgetary matters. Since 1980 more than half of all roll-call votes in Congress have been on budget-related bills, with a high of 56 percent in the House and 71 percent in the Senate (Thurber 1991b, 148). Even though GRH II revised the original deficit targets (see Table 13-1), the new targets were well out of reach as early as 1990 when Congress considered the budget of FY 1991.

Sequestration was supposed to threaten the interests of all participants in the congressional budget process enough to make them want to avoid it. However, in 1990 the threat of sequestration did not have the intended effect. Comparing the projected impacts of sequestration on their favored programs with the potential impact of cuts from regular legislation, policymakers simply decided that their interests were best served by delaying the passage of bills until after sequestration occurred.

Two other factors contributed to the failure of GRH. First, and most important, sequestration can be avoided by using optimistic economic and technical assumptions as substitutes for actual policy changes—a common practice in recent years. In the past, presidents underestimated federal outlays, largely because they tended to underestimate the current services outlays. In FY 1987, for example, the administration's current services outlay estimates were $27 billion below the CBO's ("current policy" outlay) estimates. The difference in estimates was due almost entirely to divergent economic or technical assumptions. Interest accounted for 64 percent of the difference between estimates of the current services outlays by the administration and Congress; lower OMB estimates of inflation accounted for almost all of the remaining difference. Second, enforcement of the deficit targets is not effective after the final budget "snapshot." After the snapshot is taken, indicating that the deficit target has been met, legislation can be adopted that raises the deficit in the current year and following years as well. Clearly something needed to be done to counteract these loopholes; and that was the 1990 Budget Enforcement Act.

Thus the budget reforms of the 1970s and 1980s did not: curb growth of federal spending, bring an end to the growth in uncontrollable spending, reduce the deficit, force Congress to complete budgeting on time, reorder national spending priorities, allow Congress to control fiscal policy, or eliminate the need for continuing resolutions (Thurber 1989). Congress was ready for more budget process change at the beginning of the 1990s.

THE 1990 BUDGET PROCESS REFORMS:
NEW RULES FOR AN OLD GAME

The Budget Enforcement Act of 1990 sought long-range budget control through additional top-down budgeting and more centralization of the congressional budget process. This was to be achieved by two basic means: (1) a five-year package of spending restraints and tax increases expected to reduce the deficit by an added $482 billion and (2) a reformed budget enforcement process.

The BEA replaced the GRH system of fixed deficit targets (maximum deficit amounts) with caps on appropriations and a new "pay-as-you-go" requirement on taxes and all other spending. Direct spending and new revenue legislation must balance or be deficit-neutral (that is, not increase the deficit) in each fiscal year through FY 1995.

The BEA embodied other changes in the way budgets will be considered by Congress. New discretionary spending ceilings were established. Social Security was declared an off-budget item, multiyear (five-year) budgeting was instituted, and GRH deficit targets were extended to 1995. The Office of Management and Budget's powers to estimate performance of the economy and keep score of the cost of new programs passed by Congress were expanded. Of primary concern to Congress was a requirement that the president's economic and technical assumptions must be locked in place at the time a budget is submitted each year. This was intended to eliminate the moving target or so-called "August budget surprise" which had occurred regularly in recent years.

Collectively, these changes may have a significant impact on the way Congress budgets in the next decade. The BEA set spending caps for both budget authority and outlays in discretionary appropriations for five years. Spending limits (or ceilings) and informal floors were imposed on defense, international, and domestic discretionary spending in FY 1991–93, to be followed by a single ceiling on total discretionary spending in 1994–95. Discretionary spending, severely limited in the past decade, was projected to be around 37 percent or $526 billion for FY 1991 (see Table 13-2). Appropriations bills that breach any of the three appropriation categories (defense, international, and domestic) will trigger across-the-board automatic cuts in programs within the breached category.[1] The discretionary caps on spending establish more controls and fewer degrees of freedom for

Table 13-2 / Budget Plan, Fiscal Years 1991–1996 (in $ billions)

Item	1991	1992	1993	1994	1995	1996
Total spending	$1,409.6	$1,445.9	$1,454.2	$1,427.1	$1,470.3	$1,540.8
Discretionary	526.3	532.1	536.9	538.0	542.7	554.2
Defense	307.8	300.4	293.3	287.6	289.2	293.8
International	18.7	19.6	20.4	21.5	21.8	22.0
Domestic	199.8	212.0	223.2	228.9	231.7	238.5
Mandatory	686.2	707.5	705.3	673.5	713.8	775.6
Interest	197.0	206.3	212.0	215.5	213.8	211.0
Total revenue	1,091.4	1,165.0	1,252.7	1,365.3	1,467.3	1,560.7
Deficit (surplus)	318.1	280.9	201.5	61.8	2.9	(19.9)
Deficit, excluding Social Security	378.6	343.3	274.9	151.1	106.8	101.9
Deficit, excluding deposit insurance	206.6	192.8	157.3	99.9	45.3	10.0
Deficit, excluding Society Security and deposit insurance	267.1	255.2	230.7	189.2	149.1	131.8

Source: Office of Management and Budget, 1991.

members and committees, especially the appropriators, by not allowing funds from one category to be used to offset spending that breaks the caps in another category. For example, shifts from defense to domestic will not be allowed for at least the first three years of the agreement.

The 1990 budget reforms attempt to impose overall expenditure control. Categorical sequestration will be triggered whenever projected spending due to legislation enacted prior to July 1 exceeds the ceiling (caps) on program spending set in OBRA. If a category cap is breached by a post-July 1 appropriation, the required offsetting savings will be achieved by lowering the next year's (FY 1992) cap by the amount of the FY 1991 breach. This so-called "look-back" provision is an attempt to stop a popular congressional budgeting trick of the past few years: overspending in the current fiscal year and not charging it to the next fiscal year.

All tax and direct spending legislation must be deficit-neutral in each year through FY 1995. This PAYGO provision requires that the total of each year's legislation increasing entitlement spending or reducing receipts must be within the caps or must be offset by entitlement cuts or tax increases, thus establishing a zero-sum game. The PAYGO procedure will cut entitlement spending automatically to make up for any increase in the deficit due to the passage of new entitlement or revenue reductions. Increases in direct spending or reductions in revenues not paid for by other spending reductions or revenue increases will be subject to a special reconciliation to eliminate any net revenue loss and a sequester to eliminate any deficit increase. Although each bill need not be deficit-neutral, the net of all bills must be deficit-neutral. In a major shift of budget rules, if the PAYGO requirement is breached, the deficit amount will be sequestered from all entitlement programs that have not been exempted from GRH. In other words, either an entitlement liberalization or a tax cut, if not offset, will generate a sequester of entitlement. If PAYGO is violated after the sequester date for a fiscal year, the look-back provision is used to produce the necessary offset.

Collectively, these changes establish more budget control, expand the power of the budget committees and party leaders, and narrow other committees' scope of influence by establishing a tight zero-sum budget game. At the same time, the congressional budget process is made more accessible and accountable to the public, interest groups, and the administration by publicly revealing the trade-offs that must be made in discretionary and entitlement program spending. A zero-sum game with controls on the number of behind-the-scenes budget tricks that can be played makes the budget process more visible to everyone. The combination of an open and more accountable zero-sum budget game has the potential for more conflict over the budget. The 1990 budget agreement assures that the president and Congress will not fight over the size of the deficit, but they will continue to battle over domestic discretionary and entitlement spending priorities in a controlled zero-sum budget game.

As part of the BEA, Social Security receipts and disbursements are removed from the GRH law; they will be completely off-budget. If more Social Security monies are collected than dispersed, these excess revenues may not be used to reduce the real size of the deficit, as was the case under GRH. The Social Security Trust Fund was placed behind a protective fire wall: points of order in the House and Senate to guard against legislation that would reduce fund balances.

House and Senate points of order against budget-busting provisions are another enforcement mechanism. Under the 1990 act, legislation is subject to a point of order for breaching either the budget-year levels or the sum of the five-year levels set in a budget resolution (the five-year enforcement mechanisms apply to all budget resolutions through the 1995–99 resolutions, after which the requirement sunsets). To prevent temporary savings and timing shifts (such as military pay delays), budget resolutions in each year through FY 1995 would be for five years, with five-year discretionary spending allocations, revenue floors, and reconciliation.

The multiyear pact led the House and Senate to create different procedures for the appropriators. House appropriations will be allowed to proceed on 15 May even in the absence of a budget resolution. The House Appropriations Committee must use the statutory caps in making their allocations. Senate committees other than Appropriations will be allowed to proceed in the absence of a new budget resolution if their bills conform to the out-year allocations in the most recent budget resolution. This establishes more spending control over members and committees, but allows the House and Senate to move bills even if the budget resolution is late.

The GRH deficit targets were extended through 1995, with new FY 1991–95 deficit targets to reflect current economic and technical assumptions. The targets will be adjusted if economic and technical assumptions change. Only categorical sequesters, based on policy violations, could occur in FY 1991–93. Later, the GRH system would return to fixed deficit targets enforced by the current sequestration rules unless the president exercises an option to adjust the targets on the basis of later economic and technical estimates. The new deficit targets for FY 1991–95 are shown in Table 13-1. Under the 1990 reforms, however, the targets may be adjusted for changes in economic assumptions, estimating caps, and emergencies that increase direct spending or appropriations. Therefore, they may have little real enforcement value.

The economic and technical assumptions used in estimating the president's budget will be locked in for the sequestration projection, which will be made later in the year. Congress will have stable targets because presidents will be prevented from altering their estimating assumptions as the year progresses.

Budget categories are frustratingly complicated and inconsistent. The twenty-one functional categories in the budget resolutions do not neatly fit the thirteen separate appropriations bills or the three categories of spending in the 1990 BEA. There is no one-to-one correlation between line items and functional categories of the budget. So Appropriations committees are required to translate the functional allocations into appropriations allocations and report the result. Scorekeeping is the process of accounting for the cost of authorizations and appropriations bills and determining whether they are consistent with the budget resolution. The 1990 BEA shifted this function from the Congressional Budget Office to the Office of Management and Budget. This was temporarily a major coup for President Bush, and would have greatly enhanced his power. Subsequently, however, the House Democratic Caucus revised the 1990 budget agreement by requiring the Congressional Budget Office and the Joint Committee on Taxation (JCT) to do the scoring of spending and tax actions. President Bush immediately objected: "This rule would change the new pay-as-you-go enforcement mechanism by overturning a specifically negotiated and agreed scoring provision. More important, if the proposed rule is adopted, the House of Representatives will have begun the 102d Congress by undercutting the credibility of the entire budget agreement."[2] Despite these harsh words the revision held, retaining within the legislative branch the key power of scorekeeping.

The 1990 budget agreement also requires that all new revenues go to reduce the deficit, putting further limits on members and committees. This means that even if the economy grows faster than anticipated and revenues exceed projections, the increased revenues would not be available to pay for increased spending.

POTENTIAL IMPACT OF THE 1990 BUDGET REFORMS

What are the consequences of the recent reforms on the budget process, the internal workings of Congress, and congressional-presidential relations? The potential impact can be evaluated in terms of (1) the degree of centralization (that is, the extent of top-down versus bottom-up budget making and dispersal of the process), (2) the control by the president versus Congress over the budget, (3) the amount of openness in the decision-making process, (4) the extent of complexity in decision-making rules, and (5) the impact of BEA revisions on the timeliness of the process (Thurber 1986, 1989; Thurber and Durst 1991).

When members of Congress dislike budget outcomes or process reforms, they simply make more revisions in the process (examples of this include the 1974 Budget Act, reconciliation in 1981, GRH I and II, and the 1990 BEA). The changes have led to ever-increasing centralization and control as well as a better grasp of the scope of budget problems by the budget makers and those affected by their work. The 1990 reforms changed the process once more in response to the goal of congressional actors and the president—to gain control over budget outcomes and ultimately the deficit.

The president and Capitol Hill budget and party leaders looked to the 1990 reforms to provide them with more control over spending through new categorical sequesters, pay-as-you-go provisions, and a five-year budget. Committees fought to regain some control over their programs, pushing the institution to disperse power among the committees and subcommittees. For their part, the budget and party leaders worked to consolidate their budgetary power. Those who see their power enhanced by reform usually support change, whereas those who will lose power oppose reform.

The 1990 BEA changes clearly show that when budget outcomes are perceived to be unacceptable, and the causes of the outcomes cannot be easily influenced, there is pressure to reform the budget process to favor new outcomes (Rubin 1990, 63). Although the coalition of BEA supporters had a wide variety of policy goals, they supported change out of fear of the projected massive negative impact of a FY 1991 GRH sequestration to reduce the budget deficit, as well as a perception that the underlying causes were complex and uncontrollable in the short term.

Table 13-3 outlines the predicted impact of several major BEA reforms. The types of impact displayed are presidential power versus congressional power; the distribution of power within Congress (for party leadership and

Table 13-3 / Predicted Impacts of the 1990 Congressional Budget Reforms

			Types of Impacts			
Reforms	PRESIDENTIAL/ EXECUTIVE BRANCH POWER	CONGRESSIONAL LEADERSHIP POWER	BUDGET COMMITTEE POWER	BUDGET PROCESS COMPLEXITY	BUDGET PROCESS OPENNESS	TIMELINESS OF BUDGET DECISION MAKING
Categorial Sequestration	−[a]	+	+	+	+	+
Social Security off-Budget	+[b]	−	−	−	+	−
PAYGO	+	+	+	+	+	+
OMB assumptions fixed	+	−	−	−	+	+
OMB scorekeeping	+	−	−	−	+	+
Five-year budget	+	+	+	−	+	−

[a] Decrease
[b] Increase

committees); and the openness, complexity, and timeliness of the budget process.

Presidential Budgetary Power

"A balance of power between the executive and the legislature, so one actor can catch the other at bad practice," Rubin argues, "is probably more sound over the long run than the weakening of one and the continual strengthening of the other" (1990, 234). Most of the 1990 reforms increased the budget power of the president relative to Congress. However, the reforms have affected presidential and executive branch power in different ways. The battle between the president and Congress between 1991 and 1995 will not be over how much money should be spent, as it has been in the past. Theoretically, that was settled in the five-year budget pact. Instead, the conflict between the president and Congress will be over how that money should be spent. The reforms that impose new deficit targets, set the Social Security surplus off budget, and establish PAYGO do not have a direct impact on the president's power to act directly in the budget process. But they do increase the president's resources to negotiate budget policies and priorities with Congress. The OBRA also sets limits on total spending, something that Republican members of Congress, President Bush, and conservative Democrats wanted. Those structural and policy changes could indirectly increase the president's power.

Several of the 1990 changes increase the power of the president in the budget process relative to the power of Congress. Such an increase in presidential power may be unacceptable to those in Congress who want to protect their constitutional "power of the purse." Senate Appropriations Committee Chair Robert C. Byrd (D-W.Va.) described it this way: "If you turn over control of those purse strings to the man downtown [the president], whether he is a Democrat or Republican, you eliminate the need for a Congress. . . . The president will not only be the chief executive, he will be the chief legislator" (Thurber and Durst 1991, 148).

The history of budget reform since 1974 reveals an effort by Congress to gain more budget power and create an improved balance between itself and the president. The potential impact of the 1990 reforms on congressional power over the budget process is substantial.

Currently, Congress has substantial flexibility in budget decision making, in spite of the self-imposed limitations by the Congressional Budget Act and GRH I and II. New or enhanced deficit targets, taking Social Security Trust Fund surpluses off budget, pay-as-you-go provisions, and categorical sequestration all decrease the ability of Congress to appropriate the level of funding it might wish to. Although raising taxes to pay for expanding existing programs or establishing new programs is unpopular, President Bush and congressional leaders agreed in the OBRA to increase revenues to do just that. The five-year budget agreement made new tax increases more public and painful, thus limiting new spending by Congress. The pay-as-you-go proposals especially limit the prospects for new programs because they require funding for new programs to be taken from existing programs or new taxes. The separate spending limits set for military, domestic, and international programs mean that military savings cannot be used by Congress to finance domestic programs. Instead, domestic programs must compete with one another for funding. This zero-sum game gives more power to conservatives and a president that want to limit domestic spending.

Power Inside Congress

The 1990 reforms may have mixed consequences for the distribution of power within Congress (see Table 13-2). The pay-as-you-go, zero-sum reforms have a centralizing impact: The reforms discourage individual members from initiating their own budget proposals because cuts and revenue enhancements would have to be instituted in other programs in order to save their proposals. However, stricter enforcement of categorical sequestration, PAYGO provisions, and taking the Social Security Trust Fund surplus off budget raise the visibility and public understanding of spending priorities and the specter of heavy lobbying, intensifying pressure on members and committees to protect their favorite programs and to make cuts in other programs. Such controls also centralize more of Congress's budget decision making around the leadership and the budget committees, institutions with the power to negotiate trade-offs in the zero-sum game. Reconciliation, CBA 302(b) constraints, and now the 1990 BEA categorical sequestration all tend to centralize power by calling for more top-down budgeting.

The more rigid constraints set by the 1990 BEA may have further reduced the autonomy of the Appropriations committees, but most budget participants argue that the committees were the big winners in the 1990 pact. The new budget process rules diminish the role of the House and Senate budget committees by giving more degrees of freedom to the Appropriations panels. One budget observer summarized this shift: "Since the pot of money the Appropriations committees will have to work with has already been decided, they needn't wait for a spending outline from the budget committees before divvying it up" (Yang 1991, A12).

Appropriators will be more able to determine the legislative details within the 1990 constraints than through the old reconciliation process and sequestration under GRH. A budget summit observer concluded that, "As chairman of the Senate Appropriations Committee, a panel whose control of spending has been enhanced by the current budget pact, Robert C. Byrd is again squarely at the center of power" (Haas 1991, 316). Appropriators have more control over backdoor spending by the authorizers in reconciliation bills. The budget process reforms also encourage appropriators to favor slow spending programs over fast spending programs in order to reduce the projected spending for the next year. The reforms give the Appropriations committees more control over their own policy preferences. The big losers are the authorizing committees that have little freedom under the new controls.

Openness of the Budget Process

The BEA reforms have made the congressional budget process more visible to the public. The discretionary spending limits and PAYGO controls over entitlement spending for five years are visible and well known to all the players. The new rules reduce degrees of freedom for the actors while revealing the budget decisions to interest groups and the administration.

According to Rubin, "closing the budget process is often considered one way to help control increases in expenditures; opening it is usually a way of increasing expenditures" (1990, 66). The BEA attempts to do the opposite: it opens up the process and places more controls on the players. The reforms open the process and reveal the trade-offs within mandatory spending, and the three discretionary spending categories thus put tough spending and taxing decisions in full public view. As a consequence of these changes, constituents, lobbyists, and the administration will continue to turn to the appropriators for discretionary spending and the revenue committees for entitlement and tax decisions, while watching the budget committees with special care.

Budgetary Complexity and Timeliness

The five-year budget may simplify the process, but only if members abide by the agreement—which, according to Leon E. Panetta, chair of the House Budget Committee, is not likely (interview, 26 February 1991). Hence the innovations may work at cross-purposes when it comes to timeliness. A five-year budget agreement theoretically should make it easier to pass budget resolutions on time. If the resolutions are not passed on time, the appropriators may still pass money bills.

In many other ways, however, complexity, conflict, and delays have been highlighted. Several BEA reforms increase the complexity of Capitol Hill budget making. Steps in the process have multiplied, as have the decision-making rules. The more complex the process, the more time consuming it is. Categorical sequestration and PAYGO provisions will slow the process down by increasing the number of confrontations within Congress and between Congress and the president. Alternatively, confrontations increase complexity and delay in the process as more cuts (or tax increases) are made to meet the caps. Already difficult budget decisions may be made more difficult because of the 1990 process changes, but it will depend on the will of the members and the pressure of their constituents to do something about limiting spending or increasing revenues.

The Future of Budget Process Reform

Members of Congress agreed to the 1990 package because of the failure of the Gramm-Rudman-Hollings system and its threat of a massive sequestration. Yet the players remain restive, and further "fixes" are advocated. President Bush, for example, proposed several reforms that have little support in Congress, including a joint budget resolution that would be submitted to presidents for their signature or veto, a biennial budget, an enhanced rescission authority, a presidential line-item veto, and a balanced budget constitutional amendment. While the 1974 CBA, the 1985 GRH, and the 1990 reforms were attempts to improve the budget process, they have not been able to prevent budgetary delay, deadlocks, growth in uncontrollable spending, or unprecedented deficits. Senate Budget Committee Chair Jim Sasser (D-Tenn.) recently suggested that further reform is not necessary: "The problem is not the process. . . . The problem is that revenues do not match outlays" (Yang 1991, A12). In other words, the problem is the problem. Increasingly, a common response on Capitol Hill is that the problem is the process. House Budget Committee Chair Leon E. Panetta (D-Calif.) revealed this by stating, "We knew there was trouble on the horizon. To some extent the budget agreement was designed to slow down the catastrophe" (Yang 1991, A12).

No budget process is policy-neutral. Policy outcomes and budget process reforms cannot be separated politically, as the 1990 budget negotiations demonstrated. The BEA controls have a conservative bias; they are intended to control spending. Like earlier reforms, they centralize budget power, reinforce top-down budget control, open up the process, and encourage more discipline over congressional spending and taxing. The budget process continues to require budget and party leadership in order for Congress to do its work.

Budget process reform does not work by itself; it must have the support of the actors. Members of Congress create the budget process reforms and try to abide by them, but if the policy outcomes do not comply with the preferences of the members, they will change the process again. The budget process rules are important but the preferences of the major budget actors are much more important in determining the policy outcomes in the battle over the budget. Congress must demonstrate that it has the political will to abide by the 1990 BEA reforms or it will simply create new rules for the old game of budgeting.

Further change in budget making will come, if at all, from the American electorate. If voters wanted a balanced budget, Congress would pass a balanced budget without new procedures. At present American voters and interest groups seem to want to go to heaven without dying: they support spending for desired programs but resist increased taxes—thus mandating deficit financing. Process reforms cannot make up for the lack of political will. Neither the American electorate nor their elected officials in the White

House or on Capitol Hill have displayed the political will necessary to make revenues match outlays. The 1990 budget summit clearly showed that when Congress was faced with the hard reality of a massive sequester under GRH, the deficit targets were dropped. The BEA puts more controls on the budget process, which limits new spending, but the overall policy preferences embodied in the budget will hardly change under the new procedures. It would be wise to remember what House Budget Committee Chair Panetta said in early 1991: "The instincts of this institution are not to accept constraints" (Yang 1991, A12).

The responsibility for current budgetary problems lies with both the American electorate and their elected officials. The American electorate demands domestic and defense spending without the burden of higher taxes. Voters want social problems solved and have turned to government to solve them. The federal government has stepped in to meet the needs and demands of the people. By the same token, elected officials are torn among their genuine desire to serve the needs of their constituents (potential benefactors from federal programs and higher federal spending), their own desire to win reelection by sending federal dollars back to their districts, and their need to legislate in the best economic and political interests of the country. The result of all of this has been larger budgets, higher deficits, and repeated changes in the budget process over the last fifteen years.

If the electorate really wanted to cut back government programs they desired or needed, the means for directing and controlling Congress have always been at their disposal. If they wanted to maintain those programs *and* pay for them, their elected representatives would surely get the message. Most importantly, the electorate has always been able to vote for candidates who support greater fiscal responsibility or to vote out of office an elected official who fails to make sound budgetary decisions. Perhaps this kind of commitment and display of political action will become more evident as the BEA controls are fully instituted. A survey taken by the *New York Times* before the 1990 budget agreement indicated that Americans overwhelmingly expected their federal taxes to go up to reduce the budget deficit, and they were willing to accept some new taxes (and new taxes did go up in the 1990 budget pact).

CONCLUSION

What generalizations can be made about the postreform era of congressional budgeting, especially its most recent version?

Specific policy outcomes are not likely to change dramatically as a result of the BEA. The constraints of previous budget decisions, especially deficits and mandatory entitlement spending in social welfare, will continue. Congress is attempting to be more honest about budget deficits by showing the "real" number for each of the next five years rather than playing tricks (see

Table 13-1), but it will be impossible to say who is to blame for the increasing deficits under the 1990 rules. Blame avoidance to help insure reelection will be played by all the budget actors, as in the past decade. The BEA has further diffused the target of responsibility for the deficit. One budget observer remarked that: "the new budget agreement has acted as a kind of fiscal neutron bomb, leaving the deficit standing but for the time being eliminating the fighting over it" (Yang 1991, A12). Who will be blamed for the deficit? Not the budget committees, the tax committees, the Appropriations committees, the party leadership, or the president. Budgetary politics will continue to be the center stage in Congress, but the responsibility for macrobudget decisions will be diffused.

Budget and party leaders will continue to build coalitions in the formulation of the budget and to negotiate with the president about spending priorities. The major impact of the 1990 pact is more controlled, top-down, centralized budgeting by the budget leaders and a tighter zero-sum budget game. The trade-offs between program reductions and increases are more visible, as are tax reductions and increases. The emphasis of the 1990 budget agreement is on spending and taxing, not on deficits. The budget battles will be struggles over spending priorities within zero-sum limits defined by the 1990 reforms. The process will continue to show the American public the inside of the democratic process and the difficult decisions that must be made, which is not a pretty sight.

The BEA procedures are new tools of integration that give more power to the core budget actors in the face of normal congressional tendencies toward fragmentation. Integration and centralization of the budget process run contrary to congressional preference for making it appear that everyone wins or does well simultaneously in the allocation of resources. The BEA makes the spending trade-offs more visible as it imposes more controls over the process. The BEA has added more complexity to budget making (for example, categorical caps on discretionary spending and PAYGO) while simplifying some aspects of the process (such as the five-year budget), which imply larger roles for budget and party leaders. Ultimately, the conflict over further centralization of budget power is inevitable, but there is little consensus as to how the ever-more-complex set of procedural rules will turn out.

Acknowledgments

This chapter is based on interviews with House and Senate members, staff, and informed observers. The author is grateful to them for offering their time and observations about the congressional budget process. Thanks go also to Samantha Durst, graduate research assistant with the Center for Congressional and Presidential Studies at the American University, for her assistance in evaluating the impact of potential budget reforms on Congress. I am especially grateful to Dr. Nicholas Masters, Senior Staff, House Budget Committee, and Dr. Joe White, Brookings Institution, for sharing their wisdom and attending to my continuing education about congressional budgeting. Special thanks go to Roger Davidson for his valuable comments and careful editing of the manuscript.

Notes

1. The BEA provides that the caps can be adjusted for several factors: changes in inflation; revision of concepts and definitions; credit reestimates; specified IRS, IMF, and debt-forgiveness costs; appropriations for emergency needs; and an estimating cushion. In early 1991 the definition of what constitutes an emergency was still being discussed by budget leaders, which some considered a major loophole in the budget agreement.

2. Letter, President George Bush to the Speaker of the House, White House, Office of the Press Secretary, press release, 21 Dec. 1990.

14 / Congress and the Intelligence Community: Taking the Road Less Traveled

FREDERICK M. KAISER

This chapter examines why, when choosing between "two roads [that] diverged in a wood . . . [Congress] took the one less traveled" and whether or not "that has made all the difference" (with apologies to poet Robert Frost). The metaphor has two meanings here. First, the choice Congress made signaled a new direction: from minimal and sporadic oversight of intelligence, Congress moved to a measurably higher and more consistent level, where it is even accused of "micromanagement" by administration officials and supporters (Bush 1987; Crovitz 1990). Second, the choice reflected a new approach: from a fragmented and isolated subcommittee system, involving only a few legislators who met infrequently and had a tiny staff, Congress moved to a more routine, regularized, and institutionalized process featuring committees on intelligence with comprehensive jurisdiction and involving a larger number of legislators and professional staff. (For background, see Crabb and Holt 1989, 163–92; Jeffreys-Jones 1989, 194–247; Johnson 1989, 207–67; Smist 1990; and Treverton 1990).

These newly traveled roads paralleled other broad trends and developments affecting Congress during the postreform era (Davidson, 1988, 351–62). These include: reinvigorated partisanship, particularly in the House; strengthened party and institution-wide leadership; assaults on the jurisdiction and power of established standing committees, sometimes to the benefit of new select or ad hoc panels; and weakened committee leadership. Other changes are evident, such as a concentration of policy-making arenas and shifts in congressional workload and activities, for instance, from lawmaking to oversight and from enacting new programs to modifying and fine-tuning existing ones.

These developments, of course, are only trends; they are neither absolute nor guaranteed indefinitely. This is because the bicameral legislature is far from uniform or monolithic and because other competing forces and pressures, both inside and outside the institution, influence its structure and organization (Oleszek 1983; Davidson and Oleszek 1976).

In 1956 the Senate debated—and defeated—a proposal to create a joint committee on intelligence as a means of increasing oversight of the Central Intelligence Agency (CIA). Senator Leverett Saltonstall (R-Mass.), who

279

served on the two CIA oversight panels at the time, argued that the agency's twice-a-year briefings to an Armed Services subcommittee and its once-a-year report to an Appropriations subcommittee were sufficient. His remarks reveal the then-fundamental assumption of minimal oversight: "It is not a question of reluctance on the part of CIA officials to speak to us. Instead, it is a question of our reluctance, if you will, to seek information and knowledge on subjects which I personally, as a member of Congress and as a citizen, would rather not have . . ." (*Congressional Record* 1956, 5924).

Thirty-one years later, CIA Deputy Director Robert Gates described a much different scene. Writing in 1987, Gates contended that major developments in congressional oversight of intelligence—particularly "the obtaining, by Congress in the mid-1970s, of access to intelligence information essentially equal to that of the executive branch"—ranked alongside of Watergate and the Vietnam War in shifting the "balance of power between the executive and Congress on national security matters" (1987, 224). While Gates's contention goes too far—the Iran-contra affair demonstrated that Congress can be not only deceived but also closed out of important policy decisions, at least in the short run—it is generally applicable to the postreform Congress.

As a result, important variations remain in the way oversight is conducted, its organizational and structural characteristics, and proposals for change. There is variability between the House and Senate, among different time periods, and among the policies, programs, and agencies. The differences arose in part from changing political conditions, such as the persistence of divided party government, inherent contrasts between the Senate and House, and the turnover of legislators and executive officials. They also developed because of rival views on general policies and particular projects, executive branch officials' actions and reputations, and Congress's role in national security policy-making.

PRECURSORS AND PRECEDENTS

Highly visible political developments in the executive branch indirectly advanced the cause for increased oversight of intelligence in the mid-1970s. Most importantly, the executive branch was in turmoil during this period. Individual officeholders were discredited and the presidency was severely weakened by the abuse of office and other serious wrongdoings. The result was numerous forced resignations and firings, which along with the normal course of events produced an unusually high turnover in positions connected with the presidency and intelligence community.

Even without these wounds, the political executives—the president, vice president, and political appointees—alone could not realistically control the intelligence community. Indeed, they had long been unable or unwilling to do so, as the Watergate and intelligence agency investigations discovered.

The intelligence community, moreover, grew dramatically during the cold war era, expanding its range and scope of activities to include covert operations abroad and sophisticated intelligence gathering. It operated under a degree of secrecy unmatched by any other part of government. Further, because of its capabilities in intelligence collection and assessment as well as in covert action, the intelligence community amassed influence in a wide range of national security matters and grew accustomed to its independence and autonomy. This autonomy and lack of accountability allowed the earlier abuses to occur.

The 1976–77 move toward greater consolidation and concentration for overseeing intelligence emerged, somewhat ironically, from the increasingly fragmented, decentralized, and dispersed system of the early to mid-1970s. Congressional investigations at that time uncovered serious abuses in the intelligence community and attempts to manipulate it. Also disclosed was a defective congressional oversight system—one that led either to neglect or to a protective symbiotic relationship between intelligence agencies and their traditional overseers on Capitol Hill. These inquiries proved to be catalysts for the precedent-setting legislative changes—in law, chamber rules, organization, and structure—of the postreform Congress.

Congressional investigations of the Watergate scandal, conducted in 1973 and 1974, revealed extensive illegalities and abuses by the White House, including attempts to manipulate intelligence agencies—particularly the CIA and Federal Bureau of Investigation (FBI)—for political purposes (Watergate Committee 1973, 1–45; U.S. Congress, House Judiciary Committee 1974, 1–4). At about the same time, a House Judiciary subcommittee launched the first major investigation of the FBI in its history, focusing on the bureau's counterintelligence program. The results of this investigation led to regular annual oversight hearings and new statutory controls, which enhanced Congress's oversight powers by requiring annual authorizations for the FBI and limiting the bureau's director to a single ten-year term.

Also at this time the House made a concerted effort to realign committee jurisdictions, resulting in the Committee Reform Amendments of 1974 (Davidson and Oleszek 1976). The Foreign Affairs Committee acquired special oversight for intelligence activities relating to foreign policy. This was part of a *quid pro quo* with the Armed Services Committee, which previously had exclusive dominion over CIA organization and operations among the authorizing committees (*Congressional Record* 1974, 34409–10; Kaiser 1977, 262). Shortly after this change in House rules came passage of the Hughes-Ryan amendment (P.L. 93-559). It set unprecedented guidelines for CIA covert operations abroad, requiring the president to prove that the operations are essential to national security. For the first time, the president was required to report "in a timely fashion, a description and scope of such operation to the appropriate committees of the Congress," with the Senate Foreign Relations and House Foreign Affairs committees specifically identified in the amendment. The following year, 1975, Congress halted a covert operation for the first time, cutting off funds for military and paramilitary operations in Angola. The ban was extended in 1976 and remained in force for a decade.

In 1975 congressional oversight of intelligence was consolidated into a single panel in each chamber. The House and Senate each created a select committee—the Pike Committee and the Church Committee, respectively—to investigate charges of intelligence agency illegalities and improper activities (see Freeman 1977; Johnson 1985; and Smist 1990, 25–82, 134–214). The committees found numerous long-standing, widespread, and serious abuses. The FBI, for example, had engaged in a counterintelligence program to "neutralize" civil rights leaders; it included wiretapping Dr. Martin Luther King, Jr., to gain information that could be used to discredit him. The National Security Agency had conducted electronic surveillance of U.S. citizens on "watch lists" supplied by law-enforcement and other intelligence agencies, even when no illegal conduct was charged. The CIA and FBI had covertly and illegally operated mail-opening programs. The CIA had infiltrated domestic dissident groups, despite a statutory ban on domestic security activities, and had tested drugs on unwitting subjects, several of whom later committed suicide. The CIA, relying in part on organized-crime figures, had engaged in bizarre attempts to embarrass foreign leaders and in assassination plots against them, including Fidel Castro of Cuba. (This vital information was kept from the Warren Commission when it investigated the assassination of President John F. Kennedy in 1963.) The CIA also had engaged in various other covert operations abroad; some of these were successfully directed against democratically elected governments (such as the regime of Salvador Allende in Chile) while others proved ineffective (such as the one against Castro).

In some cases the abuses were compounded by White House pressure. Other cases of abuse were marked by negligence—on the part of the intelligence community or the presidency—in insisting on accountability or in providing proper controls over the agencies and activities (U.S. Congress, Church Committee 1976).

Congress, too, was not without blame. Its fragmented, isolated system of overseeing intelligence was at times ineffective, insufficient, or nonexistent (U.S. Congress, Church Committee 1976). As a result, the Church and Pike committees urged the formation of a permanent intelligence committee in each chamber to expand, regularize, and improve congressional oversight (U.S. Congress, Church Committee 1976; U.S. Congress, Pike Committee 1976). Two temporary investigative bodies—the Church and Pike committees—were created and granted nearly identical jurisdictions, mandates, and authority. Such twin creations are extremely rare in the contemporary Congress, occurring only twice—in the 1970s with these two panels, and in the 1980s with the creation of select committees on the Iran-contra affair. The mirror approach of creating parallel, consolidated panels reflected the seriousness and jurisdictional breadth of the problems. And given the media's coverage of massive abuses, these efforts were classic "fire-alarm" approaches to oversight; that is, reactions to problems that are raised first by the media or by criticisms from adversely affected parties (McCubbins and Schwartz 1984).

Intense controversy and conflict—between Congress and the executive branch, Republicans and Democrats, and factions within the majority Democrats in Congress—followed, especially in the House. The House had to re-create its select committee when the first one failed, after five months, to "get off dead center," as one legislator described its terminal condition (*Congressional Record* 1975, 22623). Both the House and Senate select committees encountered numerous obstacles in securing information from the Ford administration and affected agencies. And an early draft of the Pike Committee report was leaked to the press by an undetermined source, violating both a plea from the White House and a pledge by the full House.

Congress's new efforts challenged the traditional oversight orientation and the hegemony of powerful standing committees. The initial thrust, however, followed the prevailing tendencies of the era of subcommittee government—additional (oversight) units, fragmented authority and jurisdictions, and increasingly dispersed power (Davidson 1988b, 350–51). But by 1975 each chamber consolidated jurisdiction in one panel. This and other legislative changes set the stage for new roles and actors to ascend.

THE ESTABLISHMENT AND EVOLUTION OF SELECT COMMITTEES ON INTELLIGENCE

A number of complementary causes and conditions merged to determine the establishment of a select committee on intelligence in the Senate in 1976 (the Senate Select Committee on Intelligence) and in the House in 1977 (the House Permanent Select Committee on Intelligence). While the committees' essential features remain largely intact and still govern their general orientation, they differ in ways that affect their behavior, activities, and influence.

Developments and Conflicts in Congress

In the 1970s the consensus was that Congress needed to take responsibility for control of the intelligence community, especially if Congress was to gain parity with the president over national security policy. Moreover, earlier developments inside Congress contributed to the creation of the new select committees on intelligence by laying the foundation that they would eventually copy, adapt, or rely on. That foundation embraced new structures and orientations, including intense adversarial oversight for intelligence, new organizational options, and new types of authority like the Hughes-Ryan amendment and annual authorizations.

Other trends, many of which would become prominent features of the postreform era, were evident during Congress's restructuring of intelligence oversight. Party leaders, particularly House Democrats, became more active and assertive, and partisanship, especially in the House, was heightened. One by-product of the restructuring was that certain standing committees and their seniority leaders suffered a further loss of exclusive control over their jurisdictions. In addition, a change in congressional priorities—from lawmaking to oversight—was implicit in the establishment of the new panels.

Even though the House and Senate Intelligence committees became the locus of power in Congress over intelligence matters, their establishment and essential features were not guaranteed given the highly charged political atmosphere and conflicts that surrounded them; nor was their stability entirely predictable. Furthermore, over time, each committee grew more distinct from the other in several respects (for overviews, see Johnson 1985, 253–65; Johnson 1989, 207–34; and Smist 1990, 82–133, 214–51).

When the Intelligence committees were established, general agreement existed on the need for Congress to restructure its oversight of intelligence—as an alternative to the fragmented, isolated system—through panels with consolidated jurisdiction. The consensus on this central precept, however, belied differences over other governing principles and pragmatic concerns. Conflicts arose over the panels' jurisdiction, status (as a select or standing committee), power (to report legislation or to conduct oversight), authority (to disclose classified information), membership size, partisan composition, selection criteria, length of term, and leadership structure. The stakes involved in these debates were significant and conflictual. Most obvious were the vested interests of established standing committees, which would lose varying amounts of jurisdiction and authority. The parties' influence would differ, depending on whether a partisan or bipartisan structure was adopted. Congress's operating norms and procedures also would be affected if the new committees were given authority to report legislation and treated like other authorizing committees. And the oversight process and performance would hinge on the jurisdiction, power, and structure of the new panels.

The conflict surrounding these difficult choices was evident in both chambers. The Senate acted first, airing its differences openly and voluminously; House majority party leaders scripted the discussion and action narrowly. However, the House's abbreviated consideration did not reflect overwhelming agreement with the proposal drafted by Democratic leaders; rather, the leaders imposed artificial limitations on the debate and the vote because of deep differences on several major issues.

Establishment of the Senate Intelligence Committee (1976)

On 19 May 1976 the Senate agreed to create the Select Committee on Intelligence by a seventy-two to twenty-two majority. The vote climaxed a long and involved process of committee deliberation and Senate debate on the floor. The resolution—Senate Resolution 400—and companion proposals generated hearings and meetings by five standing committees, reports or recommendations from four standing committees and one select committee, five distinct versions of the basic resolution, and floor debate spanning ten days and thirteen proposed amendments, ten of which were ultimately adopted.

Disputes and Their Resolution   The extensive and extended Senate debate occurred for several reasons, including the many issues that needed to be resolved, the controversy surrounding the choices, the high stakes involved, and the uniqueness of the venture. Divided government also played a role, with a Republican president and a Democratic Senate (and House) at odds.

Eventually, though, the disputes were resolved in a final compromise version arranged by Rules Committee Chair Howard Cannon (D-Nev.) and Majority Leader Mike Mansfield (D-Mont.) in consultation with a large number of senators and representatives of the Ford administration. The process itself enlisted support, or reduced some opposition, by incorporating a wide spectrum of viewpoints without arbitrarily excluding any of them. Mansfield, whose attempts to enhance oversight of intelligence began in the 1950s, was strongly committed to creating a potent new committee. Yet he also realized the need for restraint in order to gain Senate GOP and executive branch acceptance in an atmosphere of divided government and executive-legislative conflicts over intelligence matters. Mansfield was not an aggressive partisan; his moderate style was conducive to the development of a compromise. In addition, despite its conflicts with the executive branch, the Church Committee's own organization and recommendations supported several of the basic arrangements adopted for the new panel (such as its bipartisan structure).

The compromise succeeded in lessening the concerns of several important rival camps. One raised the prospect that a new panel would not be strong enough to oversee and control intelligence activities adequately if it lacked independence and important bill-reporting power. Another raised the prospect that a committee granted too much power and independence would handicap intelligence activities and operations. Some administration supporters and opponents of the intelligence panel, particularly senior Republicans on Armed Services, argued that a new panel might jeopardize classified national security information and legitimate intelligence activities—an especially glaring charge in light of the highly visible clashes with the executive branch over such access and the allegations of leaks involving the Church and Pike committees.

Balancing these competing forces, the compromise version created an improved system for overseeing and controlling intelligence through far-reaching authority, including legislative power, authorizing power, and far-ranging jurisdictions. The executive was directed to keep the new panel "fully and currently informed, with respect to intelligence activities, including any significant anticipated activities," a reference to advance notice for covert operations. Although only a nonbinding directive, this provision carried weight because it was endorsed by a sizeable bipartisan majority.

However, the compromise version also imposed a number of checks on the new committee. Among other things, these set limits on:

— its powers, by circumscribing its ability to disclose classified information through an elaborate set of procedures, which formally involved the president, and through required investigations of suspected leaks by the Ethics Committee;
— its independence as a congressional committee, by specifying that a representative of the president may attend its closed meetings, subject to the panel's agreement;
— its autonomy within the chamber, by designating seats for standing committees with overlapping jurisdiction and sharing jurisdiction over most of the intelligence community;
— its members' independence and power, by limiting their terms (to eight years) and staggering rotation; and
— its potential partisanship, by erecting a bipartisan structure for its membership and leadership.

The success of the compromise is reflected not only in its approval by a wide majority in 1976 but also in the continuation of the Senate Intelligence Committee's basic characteristics since that time.

Evolution of the Senate Intelligence Committee

The essential features of Senate Resolution 400 remain intact today. And although the Senate Intelligence Committee is not a standing committee under the rules of the Senate, it effectively attained permanent status early in its history.

The first jurisdictional test grew out of the nomination for the deputy director of Central Intelligence, which had been submitted to the Armed Services Committee before the Intelligence Committee was created in 1976. Conflict was averted, however, when Armed Services asked to be discharged from further consideration of the nomination and the Intelligence Committee instead reported the nomination (*Congressional Record* 1976, 22017). The chairs of the two panels issued a memorandum of understanding to deal with matters of "joint concern," which "will be promptly made a matter of consultation and resolution" (*Congressional Record* 1976, 22017). Signed by the chair of the Armed Services Committee, which lost the most to the new Senate Intelligence Committee, the memorandum cited Senate Resolution 400 and thus affirmed the committee's legitimacy and institutional integrity.

The Senate Intelligence Committee's institutional integrity and stability were further enhanced when, in early 1977, the Senate realigned its committee jurisdictions but left the Intelligence panel undisturbed (*Congressional Record* 1977, 3692, 3694). The Stevenson Committee, which had initially studied committee realignment, was skeptical about the continuing need for a permanent committee to oversee intelligence activities (U.S. Congress, Stevenson Committee 1976, 96). But the Senate Rules Committee, which reported the committee reorganization proposal to the Senate floor, was headed by Howard Cannon, who had played a key role in the creation of the Intelligence panel. Thus, the Rules Committee urged that the Intelligence Committee "should be able to carry out its important work without any question as to its future" (U.S. Congress, Senate Committee on Rules 1977, 5).

Establishment of the House Intelligence Committee (1977)

More than a year after the Senate had acted to establish its new Intelligence panel, the House created its own version in House Resolution 658: the Permanent Select Committee on Intelligence. *Permanent* confirms the panel's status; unlike its Senate counterpart, the House committee is a permanent body under the rules of the chamber (House Rule XLVII).

On 14 July 1977 by a vote of 227 to 171, the House established the new panel, which is similar but not identical to the Senate Select Intelligence Committee (*Congressional Record* 1977, 22932–34). The two committees were granted almost identical jurisdiction and authority—exclusive control over authorizations and legislation affecting the CIA and Director of Central Intelligence (DCI) and consolidated jurisdiction over the remainder of the intelligence community. The House panel, however, differed from its counterpart in its size, partisan composition, leadership structure, number of seats reserved for other committees, and authority to disclose classified information.

Disputes and Their Resolution   The creation of an independent oversight panel occasioned more conflict in the House than in the Senate. This is reflected in the delay in creating a House committee, the restrictions placed on it, the closed process governing the debate and vote, and the narrower margin of victory. Only 57 percent of the voting representatives agreed to the resolution, compared to 75 percent of voting senators. A distinctive set of conditions—alliances, forces, and strategies—surrounded the House panel's creation.

More than a year had passed since the Senate launched its effort, allowing the controversy and acrimony surrounding the Pike Committee to subside. In part to alleviate concerns raised by the Pike Committee's experience, however, the new House panel was given less authority and less autonomy than its Senate counterpart. Intelligence agencies, for instance, were not directed to keep the committee fully and currently informed. More importantly, the House Intelligence Committee was prohibited from disclosing classified information on its own; this power was reserved for the full House and then only under elaborate procedures, including referral to the president and a vote of the chamber. Suspected leaks of classified information from the House Intelligence Committee were also required to be investigated by the Ethics Committee.

Further, House Resolution 658 qualified the requirement that the Intelligence Committee "shall" make any information available to other members or committees and permit any member to attend its closed hearings. The new committee was ordered to prescribe regulations governing the availability and accessibility of information in its custody and was directed to keep a written record of what information was made available and to whom. Both supporters and opponents of this provision recognized that it could restrict and even prohibit access by other representatives to the committee's information. Such restraints were contrary to House Rule XI: committee "records are the property of the House and all Members of the House shall have access thereto. . . ." However, the procedures were viewed as necessary to prevent unauthorized disclosures and to secure cooperation from the intelligence community. Rules Committee Chair Richard Bolling (D-Mo.), floor manager for the resolution, admitted that members could be denied access: "It is not, in my judgment, sensible for the House of Representatives to say that election to Congress automatically gives any member the right to see the most secret matters in the security establishment" (*Congressional Record* 1977, 22936). Liberal critics of the intelligence community vehemently disagreed. Representative Ted Weiss (D-N.Y.) stated that "when my constituents elected me . . . they did not expect and I did not expect that I would become a second-class member of Congress, subject to thirteen other members telling me what I could say and what I could read and what I could talk about" (*Congressional Record* 1977, 22946). Representative Robert Giaimo (D-Conn.), a member of the Pike Committee, viewed the provision as a step backward because it allowed the new panel to write rules that "are going to limit and infringe on those rights which we now have" (*Congressional Record* 1977, 22946).

Another distinguishing characteristic of the House Intelligence Committee was its partisan composition compared to the more bipartisan Senate panel. This brought intense criticism from the Republican minority. The nine-to-four majority-minority ratio was the same for other House committees with the authority to report authorization bills to the floor in the Ninety-fifth Congress (when House Democrats held a better than two-to-one advantage in the number of seats). Republicans urged a bipartisan composition of the House panel because of the sensitive nature of intelligence activities, the need to gain cooperation and acceptance from a wary executive, and the perceived advantages for consensus building and continuity in national security policy.

Moreover, the House's delay in establishing the new panel worked to its advantage; by 1977 split-party government was no longer an obstacle. In that year Democrat Jimmy Carter, a proponent of reform of the intelligence community, became president, and Thomas P. "Tip" O'Neill (D-Mass.) became Speaker of the House. O'Neill was a more accomplished leader than his predecessor and his accession opened the majority leader position to Jim Wright (D-Tex.) (see Davidson and Oleszek 1990, 163). To some, the new team recalled (in reverse order) the post–World War II "Austin-Boston" connection when Sam Rayburn (D-Tex.) was Speaker and John McCormack (D.-Mass.) was majority leader.

The alliance between the Democratic president and House was made clear during the debate on the Intelligence Committee when Wright stated bluntly that "it [the committee] was requested by the president of the United States" (*Congressional Record* 1977, 22936). Rules Committee Chair Bolling added that "not only is the Democratic leadership in support of the resolution but it also has the approval of the president"; indeed, the Intelligence panel was expected to be "a committee run, in effect, by the leadership" (*Congressional Record* 1977, 22934). To help accomplish this goal, the Rules Committee reported House Resolution 658 under a closed rule, which limited debate and prohibited amendments from the floor.

The proposed House Intelligence Committee thus relied on strong Democratic leadership and partisan appeals to the party's overwhelming majority. This majority proved significant because a number of liberal Democrats defected (they suspected that the new panel would become isolated and co-opted by the intelligence community and that critical overseers like themselves would be closed out of the oversight process).

Evolution of the House Intelligence Committee

Most current features of the House Intelligence Committee have remained in place since its inception in 1977. In part the committee's stability can be credited to its first chair, Edward Boland (D-Mass.), who led it for nearly eight years. A senior member of the Appropriations Committee, Boland was a longtime friend of Speaker O'Neill and a trusted ally of the leadership.

The only significant changes in the committee have been in its size and party ratio, from thirteen seats (9-4) to nineteen seats (12-7). The number of members was increased on four separate occasions, thereby altering interparty ratios. These increases occurred in response to demands for membership on the Intelligence Committee, reflecting its heightened prestige, and for increased minority party representation.

In addition, a 1989 amendment to the House rules gave the Speaker direct access to any information held by the Intelligence Committee (*Congressional Record* 1989, H8575–80). This change arose in the aftermath of an alleged leak or inadvertent disclosure of classified information from the committee by then-Speaker Jim Wright (Koh 1990, 61). The Speaker was not granted any special status under House Resolution 658 but had access to committee information by custom and practice. Among the leadership positions, only the majority and minority leaders, not the Speaker, are *ex officio* members of the Intelligence Committee. The Speaker, however, has an interest in and a need for direct access. The Speaker appoints committee members and, under the 1980 Intelligence Oversight Act, is one of the so-called "gang of eight"—the bipartisan leaders of the House, Senate, and the two Intelligence committees—who receive reports of covert operations when they are not made to the full Intelligence panels.

THE HOUSE AND SENATE INTELLIGENCE COMMITTEES: A COMPARISON

The Senate and House Select Committees on Intelligence, although named *Select*, are actually hybrids of contemporary select and standing committees. Like other select committees, the Intelligence panels lack exclusive control over much of their jurisdictions, instead sharing it with authorizing committees not dealing with the military, foreign policy, and judiciary. Also like other select committees, the Intelligence committees' membership is temporary, resulting in a high degree of turnover. Membership is also nonexclusive, with positions earmarked for members from standing committees with overlapping jurisdiction.

In other respects, however, the Intelligence committees are identical to standing committees. They have relative permanency, broad and stable jurisdictions, and, most critically, the authority to report authorizing and funding bills directly to the floor of their respective chamber. They hold this exclusively for the CIA and DCI, the key components of the intelligence community.

Despite their similarities, the House and Senate Intelligence committees diverge in important respects. Table 14-1 outlines some of the differences between the two committees' membership size, composition, leadership structure, and other characteristics. In particular, because the Senate is a much smaller body than the House is, a larger proportion of senators serves on the Senate Intelligence committee (15 percent) than do representatives on the House Intelligence panel (4 percent). As a result, a substantially larger number (and percentage) of representatives are on the outside looking in; for this and other reasons, the House Intelligence Committee has adopted

Table 14-1 / Characteristics of the House and Senate Select Committees on Intelligence

Characteristic	House	Senate
Total number of voting members	Nineteen (an increase over the original thirteen)	Fifteen (same as the original complement)
Number of *ex officio* members	Two (majority and minority leaders)	Two (majority and minority leaders)
Party ratio of voting members	Twelve majority:seven minority (changed)	Eight majority:seven minority (fixed)
Other committees represented	At least one member from each of four committees: Appropriations, Armed Services, Foreign Affairs, and Judiciary	Two members (one majority and one minority party) from each of four committees: Appropriations, Armed Services, Foreign Relations, and Judiciary
Number of at-large members	No provision	Seven selected at large (four majority and three minority party)
Length of term	Six years of continuous service with staggered rotation	Eight years of continuous service with staggered rotation
Leadership structure	Standard (majority party chairman, when absent, is replaced by the next ranking majority party member)	Chairman/vice chairman (majority party chairman, when absent, is replaced by the minority party vice chairman)

Sources: H. Res. 658, 95th Congress, 1st Session (1977), codified as Rule XLVIII; and S. Res. 400, 94th Congress, 2d Session (1976), as amended through the 101st Congress.

more elaborate and exacting rules governing access to its holdings (Kaiser 1988b, 70).

Institutionwide representation on the Intelligence committees is broader in the Senate than in the House. Not only is the Senate a smaller body, but also it guarantees the four committees that share jurisdiction two seats each (a majority and a minority member) on the Senate committee, compared to only one seat apiece on the House panel. In addition, nearly half of the Senate seats are reserved for at-large members, whereas the House has no comparable requirement. Thus the Senate Intelligence Committee, which operates in a smaller chamber and more collegial atmosphere than does the House panel, enjoys greater deference in the full chamber and among other committees for its policy stands and its internal activities.

In addition, the Senate Intelligence Committee has bipartisanship built into its organization. This has been achieved through several arrangements unique to a single-chamber panel empowered to report substantive legislation and authorizations for executive programs. A nearly even party ratio generally gives disproportionate weight to the minority on the Senate Committee unless, of course, the parties are evenly divided (or nearly so) in the full chamber. Both the majority and minority parties, moreover, are represented equally among the members assigned from the four standing committees with shared jurisdiction. Finally, the Senate Committee vice chair— "who shall act in the place and stead of the chairman in the absence of the chairman"—must be a member of the minority party (S. Res. 400, sec. 2c, Ninety-fourth Congress).

In contrast, the House Intelligence Committee's leadership structure follows the standard practice of the chair being replaced by the next ranking majority party member. And there is no provision for both a majority and minority party member from each of the four represented committees, in part because there are fewer minority seats overall. Changing party strengths in the chamber have improved the minority's proportion of the House Committee membership, from about 31 percent in the Ninety-fifth Congress to about 37 percent in the 101st Congress. But the ratio still gives a slightly disproportionate weight to the majority.

The two committees' degree of partisanship is shaped by other chamber and membership characteristics, including less partisanship, weaker party leadership controls, and greater institutional loyalty (in defense of congressional prerogatives in foreign policy) in the Senate than in the House. The effects of the different structures are manifold and important. For instance, the Senate Committee's reports on proposed legislation or oversight findings are not just bipartisan, they are usually unanimous as well. By contrast, the House Committee's reports are often split along party lines, sometimes signed only by the majority or with dissenting minority views appended.

The Senate's bipartisan structure and resulting internal committee agreement enhance its influence with other committees to which its bills are referred, on the floor, and with the executive. The Senate Committee, for example, had a greater impact than the House Committee did in the development of the executive orders on intelligence issued by presidents Carter and Reagan. The bipartisan structure of the Senate panel also allows it to exert more independence from the executive branch on legislation, especially during divided or split-party government. Bipartisanship and the resulting unanimity give credibility to the Senate panel's views and make it impossible for the executive branch to cast those views in a partisan light. The Senate Committee took the lead, for instance, on Iran-contra reform legislation (to create a statutory Inspector General for the CIA and to modify covert action notice requirements).

Term limits—six years of continuous service on the House Committee and eight on the Senate—also play a role in committee behavior and influence. Overall, high turnover for chairs has been the rule—each panel has had five chairs since its establishment. But the differences between them—and the disadvantages for the House Intelligence Committee leadership—are evident when we consider that the Senate has changed party control twice, helping to account for the new chairs. Recently, the shorter-term limit has dramatically affected the House Committee. After 1985 there were four new House chairs over four Congresses (99th–102d); one, Anthony C. Beilenson, D-Calif., had to have his term extended to serve for the full two-year Congress. Proposals to lengthen the term of all House committee members to eight years, however, failed at the end of the 101st Congress.

In addition to its impact on continuity in leadership positions, the shorter-term limit affects individual members. Representatives cannot develop as much experience or as many contacts as senators can, and the internal committee coalitions on the House side undergo more frequent alterations than on the Senate side. Thus the advantages that representatives normally have over senators—through their greater ability to build expertise and alliances in a certain field (because they have fewer committee assignments)—are neutralized when the field is shortened by a term limit in general and, especially, by a limit that is shorter than senators'.

Further, term limits benefit the party leadership, which selects the committee members. By comparison with the Senate, House leaders have more selections available to them because vacancies occur more frequently. House leaders also have greater discretion in making those choices for two reasons: there are no requirements for at-large selections and there is only one seat reserved for each of four standing committees.

INTELLIGENCE COMMITTEE ACTIVITIES AND INFLUENCE

The work of the House and Senate Intelligence committees, despite their specialized jurisdiction, runs the gamut of committee functions and responsibilities. Much of their effort, though, is involved directly or indirectly with oversight; that is, the review, monitoring, and supervision of executive agencies and their activities (Ogul 1976, 11; Johnson 1980, 478; and Kaiser 1988a, 80–81). Oversight takes place in special investigations as well as in regular meetings (such as meetings designed to review executive reports on covert operations). Oversight also occurs in other contexts and activities, including work on budget authorizations, legislative initiatives, and, in the case of the Senate, presidential nominations and proposed treaties.

Effective Jurisdiction

The efforts and activities of the House and Senate Intelligence committees reveal changes in their power and effective jurisdiction. Change is not only dependent on the official list of agencies or units in each committee's domain, which remains relatively constant; it is also dependent on the size, scope, and range of intelligence activities, operations, and capabilities as well as their impact on various policy areas. These have grown in the recent past, in part because of a substantial increase in national security spending during the 1980s. This, together with their authorizing power, in turn, added to the prestige and importance of the Intelligence committees. In light of the estimated annual intelligence community budget of about $30 billion, for instance, the Senate Intelligence Committee can no longer be viewed as the poor version of the Foreign Relations Committee, as it was in 1976. The effective range of both committees' influence has also increased as foreign intelligence ventured into new fields like counternarcotics.

The escalation of covert operations during the Reagan years augmented the importance of the committees; they became the focal point for opponents in some cases (for example, Angola and Nicaragua) and for proponents in others (Afghanistan). Yet the heightened significance of covert action has been a two-edged sword for the committees. Public exposure of certain controversies, most notably those involving Angola and Nicaragua, expanded the scope of conflict inside and outside of Congress. These issues thus slipped away from the Intelligence committees and into different arenas—Appropriations, other authorizing committees (especially House Foreign Affairs and Senate Foreign Relations), the full chambers and the floor amendment process, and temporary investigative committees (as in the Iran-contra affair) (see Smist 1990, 252–81; and Koh 1990).

Secrecy

A built-in power base for the Intelligence committees is the extraordinarily high degree of secrecy under which they operate. Both panels control access to classified information in their custody. The control over access by other members and committees, unmatched by any other panel, allows the Intelligence committees to determine the debate over issues in its jurisdiction. Moreover, when information is made available by the committees, the recipients must abide by certain guidelines concerning its use, which clearly infringes on other committees' autonomy (Kaiser 1988b, 49–50, 66–68).

Authority

Authorizing the Intelligence Budget The power to authorize the consolidated intelligence community budget was given to both Intelligence committees. The authority was seen as crucial for Congress to exert controls over the agencies and their activities. Recently, the Intelligence committees have used the authorization act, the accompanying report, and hearings on it to prod the intelligence agencies away from their primary focus of the past four decades—countering the Soviet threat—into other priorities—economic intelligence and counternarcotics efforts (U.S. Congress, House Intelligence Committee 1990, 2–3). Such a change in direction expands the Intelligence committees' effective jurisdiction into new policy areas.

The authorizing power is also used to affect specific policies and programs, again enlarging the Intelligence committees' range of influence. The Senate Intelligence Committee, for instance, played a role in the 1988 strategic arms reduction talks (START) because of its support for new surveillance satellites to monitor Soviet compliance with treaties that might emerge. President Reagan reportedly endorsed the satellite package when the committee chair and other senators threatened to oppose the United States–Soviet treaty banning intermediate-range nuclear missiles (*Congressional Quarterly Weekly* 1989, 2129). The Bush administration, which sought to reduce spending for the new satellites, initially retained the satellite package because of the same pressure. In the meantime, House Appropriations members questioned the cost benefit of the expensive satellite program, especially in light of the growing deficit when Bush entered office. (Funding was later cut, in 1990, because of changes in the Soviet Union and the reduced threat from it and Warsaw Pact nations.) This episode presents an intriguing example of the sometimes convoluted way bipartisanship and continuity in public policy are put into effect. Here, the Democratic-led Senate Intelligence Committee came to an agreement with one Republican administration, which the successor Republican administration wanted to abort but instead was forced to adopt (at least temporarily). The effort, moreover, put the Democratic-led Senate Intelligence Committee at odds with the Democratic House Appropriations panel, which, in effect, sided with the new Republican administration against the old one.

The Intelligence committees are linked to other panels in their chamber by shared jurisdiction over authorizations and other legislation for most of the intelligence agencies. This means that most of their bills are referred to other panels (Davidson 1989, 383; and Davidson, Oleszek, and Kephart 1988, 10–11). A recent study of House committees found that the Intelligence Committee was "champion" among them, with 77 percent of its bills referred to other panels (Davidson, Oleszek, and Kephart 1988, 10–11, 26). The multiple-referral process, which came into being in 1975, shortly before the House Intelligence Committee was established, provides yet another avenue for influence by the Speaker and Rules Committee.

Generic Legislation in Authorizing Bills   In addition to its immediate purpose of funding the intelligence community, the authorization bill is used as a vehicle for generic legislation that sets broad guidelines on intelligence activities, establishes offices, and enhances congressional oversight power.

For instance, the annual authorization act—rather than separate legislation—was used in 1980 to establish new reporting requirements. It was also used in 1989, this time to erect a statutory office of inspector general in the CIA; in fact, this bill was recommitted to the Senate Intelligence panel (the first time this had occurred) so that the inspector general provision could be attached to it. Separate legislation for such broad institutional and procedural changes would have exposed the legislation to the prospect of being amended or defeated on the floor and being vetoed by the president. In contrast, an authorization bill can be an exercise in logrolling, in that it contains a variety of provisions that together help to build a majority coalition in support of the entire package. It also reduces the likelihood of a veto based on objections to a particular section, since this would jeopardize other provisions that the White House and intelligence agencies favor. The strategy did not work in 1990, however, when an intelligence authorization bill was vetoed, for the first time, because of the president's objections to new reporting requirements (Bush 1990).

Leverage through the Authorization Power The Intelligence committees are intended to have leverage over the agencies under their jurisdiction. The agencies and their officials are more prone to comply with requests for information and pay attention to directives or proposals from the committees (in reports and at meetings and hearings) when the committees hold the purse strings. Bobby Inman, former Director of the National Security Agency and former deputy DCI, referred to the tangible incentive to complying with congressional demands and even "onerous constraints" when he recognized that "some measure of oversight is absolutely essential for ongoing public support and flow of dollars" (1987, 2). This leverage was used in 1983 by the Senate Intelligence Committee to force the Reagan administration to scale back and clarify its covert action program in Nicaragua (*Congressional Record* 1983, 30620–21).

Oversight Authority and Reporting Requirements Since their creation, the House and Senate Intelligence committees have received new oversight authority on several occasions and at the expense of other committees. The Intelligence panels were made the exclusive recipients of new or expanded executive reporting in three areas: domestic surveillance for foreign intelligence purposes, intelligence activities including covert operations, and audits and investigations conducted by the inspector general at the CIA.

In 1978 the Foreign Intelligence Surveillance Act (P.L. 95-511) was passed to establish guidelines and controls over domestic electronic surveillance, usually conducted by the FBI, for foreign intelligence purposes. The follow-up reports of the Attorney General are sent exclusively to the House and Senate Intelligence committees. However, had this legislation been enacted before the Intelligence committees were created, the reports would have gone to the Judiciary committees.

In late 1980, at the end of the Carter administration, the Hughes-Ryan amendment was itself amended. The 1980 Intelligence Oversight Act (P.L. 96-450) imposed new reporting obligations on the executive branch, expanding the scope, volume, and timeliness of information about intelligence activities including covert operations. The act directed intelligence agencies to keep both Select Committees on Intelligence "fully and currently informed of all intelligence activities . . . including any significant anticipated intelligence activity" (a reference to advance notice for covert operations). An exception is granted only when "the President determines it is essential to limit prior notice to meet extraordinary circumstances affecting the vital interests of the United States." Even then, notice is to be given to eight leaders in Congress, the so-called "gang of eight"—the Speaker and minority leader in the House, the majority and minority leaders in the Senate, and the chairs and ranking minority members on the House and Senate Intelligence committees. If prior notice is not given to the Intelligence committees, the president should notify them "in a timely fashion" of the reasons for same. The 1980 act also requires the agencies "to furnish any information or material concerning intelligence . . . which is requested by either of the Intelligence committees." These provisions were violated during Iran-contra, when neither the Intelligence committees nor the "gang of eight" were notified.

The advance-notice provision was designed to correct a defect in the Hughes-Ryan amendment, which called for notice about CIA covert operations only "in a timely fashion." This was part of a *quid pro quo* between Congress, which wanted advance notice, and the executive branch, which sought a reduction in the number of committees receiving the reports. The eight committees under the Hughes-Ryan amendment were reduced to the two Intelligence committees. The consolidation benefited the Intelligence panels at the expense of the six other former recipients—the House and Senate standing committees on appropriations, armed services, and foreign policy.

Attempts to clarify and tighten the reporting provisions in law since the Iran-contra affair (through the 101st Congress) have been surrounded by conflict between the branches. A veto was threatened by President Bush against a specific-time notice requirement and delivered against new procedural and informational requirements (Bush 1990).

Reports from the Inspector General (IG) at the CIA were affected in 1988 and again in 1989, when a statutory IG office was created there. In 1988 Congress called for semiannual reports from the administrative IG office (P.L. 100-453). Continuing controversy and conflict over the reports, especially which ones Congress could request, resulted in a more far-reaching change the next year. Based in part on a recommendation from the Iran-contra committees (1987, 425), and over the objections of the agency, Congress in 1989 established a statutory office of Inspector General at the CIA. The IG is required to submit (1) semiannual reports and (2) special reports about issues particularly serious and flagrant to the DCI, who must transmit them, along with any comments deemed appropriate, to the Intelligence committees within thirty days and seven days, respectively. The IG is also to report directly to the Intelligence committees when encountering any serious problems in carrying out statutory duties or when the director is the subject of an investigation.

Confirmation   The Senate's power to confirm presidential nominations has been important to its Intelligence Committee. Two presidents—Carter and Reagan—submitted a total of five DCI nominations to the Senate Select Committee since its establishment in 1976. Three were confirmed, but two were withdrawn because of Senate objections.

Confirmation approval, of course, is no guarantee of continued confidence. The Senate Intelligence Committee, for instance, conducted an investigation of DCI William Casey only six months after he was confirmed. The panel examined his activities as director, his hiring of an inexperienced acquaintance as director of operations, and his financial dealings. Although Casey was not forced to resign, the committee's conclusion—that "no basis has been found for concluding that Mr. Casey is unfit to hold office"— was hardly a ringing endorsement (U.S. Congress, Senate Intelligence Committee 1983, 29).

IRAN-CONTRA AFFAIR

The greatest threat to the House and Senate Intelligence committees' stability and survival was the Iran-contra affair—the secret sale of arms to Iran and the illegal diversion of profits to the contras in Nicaragua in 1985–86 (Iran-Contra Committees 1987, 11–22; Smist 1990, 258–67). The House and Senate Intelligence committees looked into the matter through specialized investigations, confirmation proceedings (for a DCI nomination), and hearings on corrective legislation.

Yet the House and Senate committees' efforts were not enough. As the vice chair of the Senate Intelligence Committee recognized, "when the relationship between [the CIA and] the Oversight Committee breaks down by virtue of the non-notification such as it did here, then it breaks the credibility of this committee. . . . Every other committee now wants to investigate the Central Intelligence Agency and related activities" (U.S. Congress, Senate Intelligence Committee 1987, 101). Indeed, the centerpieces of the Iran-contra investigation did not exist in the Intelligence committees but in specially created investigative panels (though there was a significant overlap of members, including some former and current chairs). Following the 1975 precedent of the Pike and Church committees, each chamber set up a new select committee to look into the Iran-contra charges.

Unlike the earlier episode, though, no permanent change in congressional organization resulted from the Iran-contra investigations. The Intelligence committees remained intact, indicating how institutionalized they had become. In addition, the findings of the Iran-contra panels pointed to a set of underlying problems quite different from the earlier intelligence agency abuses. In the earlier episode, Congress found its own oversight efforts deficient and its oversight structure defective. In the Iran-contra affair, however, Congress was not at fault; rather, the Intelligence committees (along with executive officials) had been deceived by the project operators and the established reporting requirements had been evaded. Consequently, the recommendations from the Iran-contra committees for congressional oversight of intelligence were modest, calling for improved audit capabilities and examination of sole-source contracting for possible abuse. The bipartisan majority also explicitly rejected the minority's recommendation to create a joint committee on intelligence, concluding that it "would inevitably erode Congress' ability to perform its oversight function in connection with intelligence and covert operations" (Iran-Contra Committees 1987, 427).

CONCLUSION

In the mid-1970s Congress took the road less traveled, one that made all the difference for increasing legislative oversight and controls over the intelligence community. Congress changed both its direction and approach. It rejected the minimal and often protective relationship between the agencies and their traditional overseers, and it replaced an isolated, fragmented system with a consolidated approach and a new perspective. These changes led to permanent Senate and House Select Committees on Intelligence. The committees became integral parts of each chamber during the postreform era, surviving the Iran-contra affair, which harmed their credibility, and its aftermath, which included proposals to replace them with a joint committee. The Intelligence committees have prospered since their creation, gaining power at the expense of other authorizing committees (as with the 1980 Intelligence Oversight Act).

Today the Intelligence committees are heirs to long-standing tendencies as well as beneficiaries of more recent developments in the postreform era. Most important among these is executive-legislative conflict, which grew out of the Vietnam War and Watergate scandal and then expanded as a result of the disclosure of intelligence agency abuses in 1975. Congressional investigations laid the groundwork for new organizations, authority, and structures to review, monitor, supervise, and check executive action. And underlying this were increased congressional independence and assertiveness reinforced by developments in the postreform era. Yet these developments occurred not only in intelligence but also in other national defense and foreign affairs matters, including war powers, human rights requirements in foreign assistance programs, use of the military in drug-interdiction efforts, restrictions on foreign arms sales, Defense Department reorganization, and new institutional controls over defense procurement and departmental operations (Crabb and Holt 1989; Franck and Weisband 1979).

The major tendencies of the postreform era were evident in the Intelligence committees at the time they were established (particularly the House panel). The committees' key characteristics, except for the House committee's size and interparty ratio, have remained constant ever since. However, there are important differences between the two panels, particularly in terms of their influence and orientation. Whereas the Senate Intelligence Committee has a bipartisan structure (unusual for a bill-reporting committee in either chamber), restrictive selection criteria (such as required at-large seats), and a comparatively large size, the House Intelligence Committee has a partisan structure similar to other authorizing panels in its chamber, few selection criteria, and a comparatively small size. These committee features were largely determined by the markedly different interbranch, chamber, and leadership characteristics that existed at the time each committee was created, even though only one year apart.

Moreover, the differences between the House and Senate Intelligence committees were reinforced by intervening political developments, especially the truncated party government during the first six years of the Reagan administration (1981–87), when the House was the only democratically controlled institution. And the differences were intensified by partisan and chamber characteristics that separated House Republicans—who represented a seemingly perpetual (and often frustrated) minority—from Senate Republicans—who were less partisan and more institutionally loyal in national security matters.

Strengthened party leadership, especially in the House, continues to exert itself on the Intelligence committees. The Speaker's powers, on the ascendancy in the postreform era, include the appointment of committee members with few constraints on the selections, which are made regularly and frequently because of the six-year term limit. The Speaker is also a member of the "gang of eight" and has direct access to the classified holdings of the Intelligence Committee (initially by practice and later by a change in House rules). Finally, most of the House committee's bills—77 percent, more than any other panel's—are multiple-referred ones, giving added discretionary power to the Speaker and Rules Committee. Implied in the strengthened party and institutionwide leadership is weakened committee leadership. Because of the term limits, for instance, the turnover of the chairs for both committees is high, especially on the House panel.

The House and Senate Intelligence committees illustrate two important shifts in congressional work load and activities—from lawmaking to oversight, a long-term and institutionwide trend (Aberbach 1990, 34–46), and from the passage of new programs to the fine-tuning of existing ones.

PART · VI

Conclusion

15 / Structures and Performance: An Evaluation

PAUL J. QUIRK

For two decades the structures of Congress have been in almost constant flux. The many changes led commentators to announce, first, a *reform* Congress and, more recently, a *postreform* Congress. There is no generally accepted view, however, about the effects of these changes on Congress's capacity as a policy-making institution—that is, on its ability to respond to the needs of the country.

Indeed, there has been little serious effort to evaluate the new arrangements in the postreform Congress. With few exceptions (see, in this volume, Kaiser, Chapter 14; Gilmour, Chapter 12; Thurber, Chapter 13; and Pfiffner, Chapter 11), political scientists have been content to describe the changes in Congress and explain why they occurred (Rieselbach 1978, 1986). Members of Congress usually do not worry much about the condition of the institution; they are not, in any case, disinterested observers. Nor has there been a broad public debate about the merits of the institutional developments in Congress. Public discussion rarely goes beyond generalized expressions of frustration with congressional pay increases, disorderly budget processes, and the like. The lack of evaluation of major changes in congressional structure is unfortunate. It leaves members of Congress free, by default, to promote changes merely to serve their personal convenience, to give them advantages over other members, or to enhance their prospects for reelection.

Several major obstacles stand in the way of any objective evaluation of Congress's structure. First, there are no clear, agreed-on criteria for assessing policy outcomes or institutional performance. Yet an evaluation of congressional structures will be of little use if it merely reflects the policy preferences of the evaluator. Second, it is extremely difficult to distinguish the effects of institutional structures from other influences on congressional performance—such as the energy and inflation crises of the 1970s, the budget deficits of the Reagan and Bush years, and the prevalence of divided party control of government during most of the reform and postreform periods. Thus any attempt to identify the independent effects of structural change will be subject to challenge.

Rather than retreat in the face of analytic adversity, this chapter undertakes an admittedly speculative and highly preliminary inquiry into the effects of recent structural changes on congressional performance. It is intended to frame some central issues for subsequent discussion. To do so it first suggests some criteria for evaluating the performance of Congress (or any other public policy-making institution). Then the chapter discusses the probable effects of the major reform and postreform developments on each dimension of performance and examines some casual evidence about policy outcomes. The analysis shows that, in general, these developments enhanced certain aspects of congressional performance but also created or exacerbated some serious deficiencies.

AN EVALUATIVE FRAMEWORK: THREE DIMENSIONS OF POLICY-MAKING

To evaluate congressional structure, we need a simple normative notion of how Congress's policy decisions should relate to the values and preferences of the public. Presumably, Congress should adopt policies that to some satisfactory degree approximate the policies that the public would adopt if it made decisions directly and under ideal conditions. Setting aside some thorny issues of democratic theory, this analysis proposes the following as a serviceable, bare-bones list of those ideal conditions:

1. that all members of the public have equal power;
2. that they all make fully informed decisions in light of their values and preferences; and
3. that where the values and preferences of different individuals conflict, they reach balanced and efficient agreements by unanimous consent.[1]

It is plausible to stipulate that the policies adopted under these conditions would be ideal democratic outcomes, given the public's values and preferences.

To arrive at an approximation of the same policies, Congress must approximate the corresponding ideal conditions for a representative institution. Each of the ideal conditions for direct democracy thus points to a central dimension of Congress's performance and suggests criteria for evaluating that performance. The dimensions of performance, therefore, are the *representation of interests, deliberation,* and the *resolution of conflict.*

The Representation of Interests

The dimension of performance most prominent in discussion of political institutions is the representation of interests.[2] To approximate the standard of equality of power among citizens, Congress must give proportionate weight to the competing interests at stake in policy conflicts. To begin with, it must take into account the number of citizens who have various interests. It should also consider the magnitude of their stakes. For example, Congress should be willing to impose certain costs on majorities to serve more important interests of minorities—not only underprivileged ones, such as racial minorities or the disabled, but sometimes privileged ones as well, like wealthy individuals or the exceptionally talented. The magnitude of a group's stakes is not to be equated with the amount of pressure it generates or the loudness of its demands; certain kinds of groups have huge advantages in organization and mobilization. Ideally, Congress should minimize the disproportionate influence that results from those advantages.

To support this proportionate weighing of interests, congressional structures should prevent or reduce three common kinds of distortion of representation. First, Congress should not randomly give disproportionate influence to some interests over others.[3] For example, wheat growers should not dominate corn growers, farm groups should not dominate labor unions, and the Northeast should not dominate the Southwest. Second, Congress should not give undue weight to narrowly based or well-organized interests over broadly based or unorganized ones. It should serve general social interests—such as aggregate economic welfare or widely shared ethical concerns—and not merely functional or geographic interests. In all likelihood, of course, some advantage for concentrated interests is inevitable. Congressional institutions should keep that advantage to a minimum. Third, Congress should not give disproportionate consideration to one broad social class or ideological grouping for a substantial period; both Democratic and Republican constituencies should sometimes get their way. In a seeming contradiction of this view, advocates of party government argue essentially that domination by a single party and its constituencies is required for effective decision making (Sundquist 1989). Whether or not this claim is valid, it concerns the requirements for effective deliberation or conflict resolution. Purely from the standpoint of representation, the notion that a roughly proportionate balance between class or ideological groupings is desirable follows from the ideal of equal influence among citizens.[4]

Some of the structural features that help to minimize distortions of representation are readily defined. To avoid giving random advantages to certain groups, power should be widely distributed among legislators or concentrated in leaders who are accountable to the others. There should not be exceptionally powerful legislators with free reign to favor their own interest group or geographic constituencies. To avoid excessive imbalance along partisan or ideological lines, there should be barriers to action on the part of a narrow majority. These may include structural divisions (like separation of powers), requirements for extraordinary majorities, and procedures for legislative minorities to force delay.

The effects of two other important structural features, however, are more difficult to specify. One is the openness of decision making; that is, the degree to which decision-making processes are exposed to public view. On the one hand, reform groups like Common Cause advocate "government in the sunshine"—open committee meetings, recorded votes, public access to official documents—to reduce the influence of narrow interests. They argue that legislators will more readily stand up to those interests if the public can observe their actions. On the other hand, some analysts have more confidence in closed processes as means to achieve the same ends (Destler 1986; Arnold 1990). They point out that it is mostly organized groups that take advantage of opportunities to observe congressional decision making and that use those opportunities to exert pressure on legislators.

The ambiguity about the effect of openness exists because there are two very different sources of governmental resistance to interest group demands, each with different implications for the effect of open processes. The first source is countervailing demands of broadly based constituencies; these demands are strengthened by open processes. The other source is autonomous action by politicians; such action is encouraged by closed processes. It is unclear which kind of resistance to interest groups is generally more important.[5]

What is more clear is that the effect of openness depends on the issue at hand and the kind of general interest at stake. Some general interests such as reducing environmental pollution are salient to mass constituencies. These interests gain strength from open decision-making processes. Other general interests like the economic efficiency of a simple tax code are recognized mainly by elites. These interests fare better under closed decision-making processes. An exception to this pattern is that broadly based interests can only benefit from measures that permit wider observation of processes that are already accessible to interest groups (for example, the televising of floor debate).

The other structural feature with ambiguous effects for representation is the degree of centralization or decentralization—that is, the relative power of party leaders as opposed to committees, subcommittees, or individual members. In this case, the effects on representation differ between the initiation stage and the decision stage of the legislative process. To some degree, party leaders are more reliable allies for general interests than are committee chairs or rank-and-file legislators when they are forced to decide in an active conflict. The general public is more aware of leaders' actions and more prone to hold them responsible for national conditions.[6] However, committees, subcommittees, and individual members are more likely than party leaders to initiate general interest-oriented policy change. Because these actors are numerous and compete with each other to put significant issues on the agenda, they try their luck with many issues. The effect of their efforts is to expand the agenda. In contrast, because party leaders are automatically associated with the major issues on the agenda, they seek to limit those issues to a modest number carefully selected for their political advantage. The effect of their efforts is to contract the agenda. This difference is often apparent. In the deregulation of airline and trucking industries in the late 1970s, for example, committee-based entrepreneurs had difficulty eliciting presidential and party support for general interest-oriented reforms (Derthick and Quirk 1985).

For these reasons, decentralization should promote the initiation of general interest-oriented policy change while centralization should facilitate the adoption of such proposals once they have been initiated. This makes it unclear which structural condition will better serve general interests overall.

Deliberation

The second dimension of performance, largely neglected in the political science literature, is deliberation.[7] To approximate the ideal of informed decision making, Congress must be reasonably thorough, accurate, and unbiased in identifying and weighing information relevant to decisions. It must invest appropriate effort in gathering information and then use that information without undue distortion in making decisions.

It is important not to oversell this dimension. When Congress ignores information relevant to a policy choice, the reason may have nothing to do with any difficulty obtaining or evaluating that information. Rather, it may be simply a lack of concern for the interests to which the information pertains. Congress may overlook economic evidence about the effects of milk price supports, for example, because dairy farmers are well organized and make large campaign contributions while consumers are oblivious to small increases in the price of milk. The fundamental failure in such a case is one of representation. A failure of deliberation occurs when some inadequacy in the gathering or use of information prevents Congress from serving interests that it genuinely wants to serve.

Commentary on Congress is sometimes based on simplistic notions about legislative deliberation. One such notion is that deliberation occurs or could occur largely on the House and Senate floor. Thus some have charged that the contemporary Senate is no longer a deliberative body because floor debate is dominated by action on procedural issues instead of on substantive discussion of legislation (Kassebaum 1988). But most of the consideration of any bill takes place before the floor debate—in committee hearings, markup sessions, and presentations by lobbyists to individual legislators. It would be worrisome if legislators often arrived for floor debate without knowing how they would vote: Floor debate is too late and too short for responsible deliberation.[8]

Another simplistic notion is that legislative deliberation is mainly a matter of direct dialogue among legislators. Critics sometimes point out that there is little of this dialogue in Congress—attendance at committee hearings and floor debates is usually sparse; members rarely spend time together apart from these sessions; most of the communication within the institution is handled by staff (Malbin 1980). This situation, however, is appropriate to the volume of business that Congress handles. There is no apparent reason why members must take the lead role in developing arguments or presenting information to each other. In the contemporary Congress, lobbyists, executive officials, and other advocates from outside the institution supply most of the information. Staff collate and summarize it. The role of the legislator is mostly, in effect, to judge the debate.

Effective legislative deliberation requires successful performance of two tasks.[9] The first is managing the flow of information—the legislature must get the relevant information to the right people at the right time. This is often difficult because some policy issues are highly technical, because policies on different subjects are often interdependent, and because Congress must act on an extraordinary number and variety of issues. Although Congress can sometimes simply rely on the administration for advice, it cannot do so when it does not fully share the administration's goals. The capacity for information management depends on several aspects of legislative structure. To perform this task effectively, a legislature should have routines that elicit extensive information about policy choices; for example, hearings on a major issue should include witnesses on all sides of the debate. It should reward legislators who specialize in a legislative subject by giving them special influence over it. The legislature should have staff resources that can handle a large volume of information. For maximum effect, they should be divided between staffs that play partisan, advocacy roles and those that maintain a politically neutral, objective posture (Muir 1986). This combination ensures that competing positions are both stated vigorously and tested for their credibility. Finally, the legislature should have effective liaison among committees or other units with related jurisdiction.

The second task in deliberation is weighing information to reach decisions—the legislature must induce members to pay attention, keep an open mind, and think carefully. In short, it must maintain a deliberative disposition. There are several obstacles to success in this task. The political sensitivity of certain subjects may inhibit discussion. Political demands or strategic opportunities for quick action may tempt Congress to decide hastily. The most important threat to open-minded deliberation is undoubtedly the pressure on legislators to adopt the beliefs and prejudices of important constituencies, especially the general public.

Of course, no structures or resources can force legislators to think carefully. One useful feature for encouraging them to do so, however, is the presence of barriers to rapid action. With bicameralism, the committee system, and other sources of delay, Congress has a number of such barriers. Unfortunately, what is probably the most important feature for preserving a deliberative disposition may be costly in other respects. Deliberation is enhanced by structures that insulate decision making from public view. If legislators can reach decisions in private, they are relatively resistant to the influence of stereotyped or uninformed constituency opinion. The problem is that in many circumstances this insulation also allows legislators to neglect broadly based interests. To this extent, the conditions that support deliberation and those that strengthen representation are in conflict.

Conflict Resolution

Another dimension of Congress's performance is its capacity for cooperative resolution of policy conflict. This capacity is needed to approximate the stable, balanced, and efficient agreements of an ideal direct democracy. It is often difficult to achieve cooperative outcomes in high-level policy conflict (Quirk 1989).[10] In principle, there is opportunity for cooperation when the competing factions in a policy dispute have both complementary and conflicting interests. The question is whether they will actually reach agreement and adopt policies designed to produce joint gains: Can liberals and conservatives work out a budget package that substantially reduces federal deficits? Can pro-environment and pro-industry factions agree on ways to improve the efficiency of environmental controls? Very often they fail to do so. The result may be stalemate, a one-sided outcome (usually with distributive gains for the victorious faction), or a lowest-common-denominator agreement that merely minimizes concessions without achieving substantial joint gains.[11]

To promote cooperative outcomes, legislative structures should erect barriers to one-sided victories, provide an environment conducive to negotiation, and facilitate the actual implementation of negotiated solutions. More specifically, the following features are relevant:

1. Structures that level off power differences between factions, such as the privilege of filibustering in the Senate, encourage negotiation by undermining conflictual strategies.
2. A large and skilled staff can help perform the labor-intensive activity of working out detailed agreements.
3. Procedures that permit negotiation to be confined to small groups and conducted in private reduce the constraints of constituency pressures on the participants and help them to develop interpersonal trust.
4. Flexible practices in the selection of negotiators (as opposed, for example, to rigid reliance on standing committees) can improve the match between the legislators who participate in negotiations and those whose support is critical to a measure's enactment.
5. Devices that facilitate making linkages between unrelated issues (for example, by coordinating their consideration in different committees) can sometimes enhance opportunities for cooperative outcomes. The most promising opportunities for joint gain sometimes require an exchange of concessions across issues in different committee jurisdictions; in the absence of some coordinating device, it is difficult to establish the necessary linkage.
6. Skilled mediators with significant power can facilitate the exchange of information, provide sanctions to encourage cooperative behavior, and help legitimize difficult concessions. Various officials may play mediating roles—including presidents, party leaders, committee

chairs, and other legislators—provided that they have the incentives to do so.[12]

EVALUATING THE POSTREFORM CONGRESS

What were the effects on performance, then, of the structural changes of the reform and the postreform Congress? To answer this question is necessarily a hazardous exercise. But there are grounds for a tentative conclusion that the changes improved some aspects of congressional capacity while also creating some serious deficiencies.

Representation of Interests

Among the three dimensions of performance discussed earlier, the changes in Congress probably had the most favorable effects on the representation of interests. The reforms of the 1970s had mixed but predominantly beneficial effects on representation. The developments of the postreform period further improved the situation by preserving most of the benefits of the reforms while mitigating some of their disadvantages.

Decentralization and Recentralization As several earlier chapters describe, Congress underwent a sweeping decentralization of power in the 1970s and then, especially in the House, a significant "new centralization" in the 1980s (see also Davidson 1988b). The latter did not simply cancel out the former. Taken together, these changes reduced random biases of representation and probably enhanced representation of general interests.

In the reform years, Congress shifted power from committees to subcommittees, gave committee members more control of committee chairs, and made it easier for individual legislators to take issues to the floor. These changes reduced the centralization of power in the committee chairs. Instead, as Steven Smith (1989) has noted, they increased the roles of decentralized decision making (in subcommittees) and collegial decision making (on the House and Senate floor). They reduced the propensity toward random bias by diminishing the power of committee chairs to bestow favors on their own geographic or interest group constituencies. A contemporary chair of the Senate Finance Committee, for example, does not have the ability that Russell Long had in the early 1970s to design tax policies for the benefit of his state or to trade influence over taxes for favorable provisions in other legislation.

Decentralization had mixed effects on the representation of broadly based interests. In one respect, it may have been a disadvantage. To the extent that chairs were more deferential than other legislators to party leaders and those leaders were motivated by the parties' collective responsibility for national conditions, the weakening of the chairs should have diminished congressional response to general interests. Instead, though, committee chairs were notoriously independent. Moreover, the party leaders' concern with the parties' collective responsibility was probably less important as a distinctive incentive than some analysts have supposed (Quirk 1990). In the end, it is not clear whether this loss of general interest representation was substantial.

In other respects, moreover, decentralization was advantageous for general interests. It increased entrepreneurial promotion of policy change by subcommittees and individual legislators. The increased scope for entrepreneurship should tend to advance broadly based interests. Policy entrepreneurs often direct their appeals to such interests, and some of their principal resources (like the ability to publicize a cause) are mainly useful for that purpose. They in any case cannot act alone. To enact legislation, they must obtain the consent of the House and Senate floor as well as the president. The requirement for broad support should block particularistic initiatives by entrepreneurs more often than general interest-oriented ones.

There is also an indirect gain for general interests in the reduced power of interests associated with committee chairs. To the extent that particularistic benefits cannot be reserved to a few narrow groups favored by a chair but rather must be shared among a large number of such groups, their political appeal is reduced. The reason is simple: If a few narrow groups can capture all the benefits of an expenditure of tax revenues, they will almost certainly expect a net gain from the expenditure, even if the total benefits are much smaller than the total costs. In contrast, if the benefits must be shared by a large number of groups, they may all be better off avoiding the taxes. Thus the need to share particularistic benefits among more groups will sometimes lead to their abandonment.

In the postreform period, a new centralization sharply restricted direct participation in certain decisions. The congressional agenda was actively shaped by party leaders (Sinclair, this volume, Chapter 5), budgets were put together in closely held summit negotiations (Thurber, this volume, Chapter 13), and large packages of taxing, spending, and policy decisions were disposed of in leadership-sponsored omnibus bills (Pfiffner, this volume, Chapter 11). These developments excluded most legislators and even the standing committees from crucial stages in the decision process.

Nevertheless, most of the positive effects of the reform-era decentralization probably remain intact because the new centralization left committees, subcommittees, and individual legislators with generous resources for indirect participation. As Barry Weingast (this volume, Chapter 8) points out, the postreform Congress accommodated and did not reverse the diffusion of power of the reform era. In the long run, individual legislators could hold elected party leaders accountable for their actions. In the short run, they could veto the procedures that leaders employ to orchestrate legislation. Any senator, for example, can block the unanimous-consent agreement necessary to limit floor amendments to an omnibus bill; any majority of representatives can defeat a restrictive rule for the same purpose. As party leaders learned in 1990, when the full House voted down the budget that emerged from arduous summit negotiations, legislators can also reject the products of leadership-dominated negotiations (Gilmour, this volume, Chapter 12). Thus individual legislators and any cohesive committees, subcommittees, or other legislative groups have bargaining power over both the use of centralized procedures and the policies that emerge from them. They remain in a strong position to block arbitrary distribution of particularistic benefits and to initiate general interest-oriented policy change.

Moreover, one aspect of the new centralization improved representation of general interests in many circumstances. A major reason for resorting to omnibus bills has been to escape interest group pressures and give greater weight to general interests, especially the national interest in reducing budget deficits. It is a clever device for that purpose (Arnold 1990): Leaders put together an omnibus bill that includes essential provisions, like an increase in the debt limit or continuation of funding for existing programs, and that cuts benefits or raises taxes for a number of well-organized groups. The bill is brought to the floor under procedures that restrict amendments. Rank-and-file legislators vote for it and explain to disappointed interest groups that the bill as a whole was too important to defeat. Of course, members go along with the omnibus procedure only because they share the goal of defeating the interest groups and know that they would be hard-pressed to do so without this device.

Open and Closed Procedures   In much the same way as it reversed direction on decentralization, Congress opened its decision-making processes to public observation in the 1970s and then partially closed them up again in the 1980s. The net effect was to give Congress procedural flexibility that probably worked to the advantage of broadly based interests.

One of the goals of congressional reformers in the 1970s was to bring decision making into the "sunshine." Two kinds of measures sought that objective. First, Congress required most committee markups and conference committee meetings to be open to the public. Second, the House and Senate both adopted procedures that permitted virtually routine recording of votes on floor amendments. This made floor votes visible to the public, gave legislators incentive to overturn committee recommendations, and led to a dramatic increase in the frequency of floor amendments and the importance of floor action in congressional policy-making (Smith 1989).

As noted earlier, the effects of greater openness on the representation of general interests vary with the issue—it generally strengthens broadly based interests that are salient to mass constituencies but weakens those that depend mainly on autonomous action by politicians.

It is therefore significant that the postreform Congress adjusted both the use of open meetings and the role of floor amendments in ways that provided greater procedural flexibility. To get around the requirements for open meetings, committees made generous use of the statutory exemptions; committee members worked out agreements during informal, private sessions and even, in public sessions, huddled together and conducted negotiations in whispers too low for the audience to hear. In some cases, like the 1990 Senate Clean Air bill, legislation was drafted in private meetings convened by party leaders outside the committee structure. To bring floor politics under control, both chambers found ways to reduce amending activity. The House Rules Committee did so by expanding the use of restrictive special rules (Bach and Smith 1988; Weingast, this volume, Chapter 8). Though with less success, the Senate sought to accomplish the same thing with restrictive time agreements adopted under unanimous-consent procedures. As a result, many bills in each chamber come to the floor today subject to few or no amendments.

The postreform Congress operates under a rebuttable presumption of open procedures; it has a general policy of openness but makes frequent exceptions to the policy. The effect of this situation depends on what interests—narrow ones or broad ones—Congress seeks to serve when it decides how to handle particular cases. Arnold (1990) argues that because legislators rarely have significant electoral stakes in procedural decisions, they reach those decisions on the basis of their policy preferences and their understanding of how procedures affect outcomes. But more often than not, in decisions free of electoral pressures, legislators prefer to serve broadly based interests. Moreover, legislators find it easier to justify departures from openness the more clear the purpose is to promote general interests. As a broad tendency, then, the rebuttable presumption of openness should lead to the use of open procedures when they favor general interests and to the use of closed procedures when they do not favor those interests.

Partisanship Another change—one that began in the reform Congress and intensified in the postreform period—was increased party control of the legislative process. Although in principle such control could produce an imbalance of representation along class and ideological lines, the trend did not go far enough to have that effect.

Several earlier chapters detail the development of more cohesive, organized, and assertive parties in the postreform Congress. The House party leadership sought more actively to shape the congressional agenda (Sinclair, Chapter 5; Palazzolo, Chapter 6). Through its control of the Rules Committee, the House majority leadership increasingly defined the agenda for floor debate (Weingast, Chapter 8). A variety of party committees became more prominent in policy development and the determination of political strategy (Herrnson, Chapter 3). Finally, there was a marked increase in party unity and partisan voting in both chambers (Rohde, Chapter 2).

Taken to the extreme, a party-dominated legislative process could deprive minority party constituencies of effective representation. But that situation has not existed and is unlikely to develop in the contemporary Congress; despite recent trends, formidable barriers to single-party domination remain. To begin with, Republicans usually occupied the White House. The Democratic congressional majority was on the defensive—struggling just to block or modify the president's initiatives and to prevent the president from shaping the terms of debate. The increased cohesion and assertiveness of that majority in the postreform period at most shifted the overall balance of power from one of Republican advantage to one of rough party equality.

Moreover, regardless of which party controls the presidency, the Senate remains a secure bastion of minority party influence. The rules of the Senate give elaborate prerogatives to individual senators—including largely unlimited rights to offer amendments, carry on debate, and delay action on the Senate floor. These prerogatives prevent the majority party from running roughshod over any significant Senate faction, much less the entire minority party. This situation discourages Senate Democratic leaders from attempting to define and push party positions, an approach that would merely elicit Republican obstruction (Smith, this volume, Chapter 9). If Democrats were to regain the presidency, therefore, Republicans would still have a secure base in the Senate from which to protect their constituencies.

However, one postreform procedural development—the rise of omnibus legislation—can allow the Democratic majority to avoid accommodating the Republican minority. While one reason for putting together large packages of legislation, as we have seen, is to evade pressure from narrow groups, another reason is to protect purely partisan items from obstruction or veto. Regardless of their procedural opportunities, Republicans cannot afford to block, say, a continuing authorization just to kill a handful of Democratic pet projects. This partisan use of omnibus legislation cannot give majority party constituencies major windfalls, but it can give them a steady stream of small victories.

Performance Generally, the pattern of major policy outcomes of the past two decades seems consistent with the expectations outlined earlier regarding the character of representation in the postreform Congress. In particular, there seems to have been a reduction in the advantages that particular groups or localities can derive from association with powerful committees or committee leaders. In the mid-1970s Congress rebelled against arrangements under which members of the military committees were specially protected from base closings in their states and districts. The immediate result was that for several years Congress permitted no base closings at all. But as one can expect when inefficient spending is spread too widely, Congress eventually got tired of the waste and established new procedures that expedited base closings in all districts (Arnold 1990). More generally, spending directed toward geographic constituencies, which is the spending most conducive to random bias, declined substantially as a proportion of the federal budget (Arnold 1983).

More important, Congress in this period by and large cut back regulatory and subsidy policies that benefit organized groups at the expense of the general public. Two traditionally egregious forms of special interest policy—anticompetitive economic regulation and preferential tax provisions—were objects of monumental reforms. From the mid-1970s to the early 1980s federal regulation that protected industries from competition was eliminated or drastically reduced in telecommunications (equipment and long-distance service), financial services (stock brokerage and banking), and transportation (airlines, intercity buses, trucking, and railroads).[13] In a number of cases, deregulation represented clear-cut defeats for the most directly affected organized interests—the regulated industries and their labor unions (Derthick and Quirk 1985; Quirk 1988, 1990). The 1986 Tax Reform Act abolished or diluted numerous special tax privileges that had accumulated over decades and benefited hundreds of well-organized groups. A thoughtful study of previous reform efforts (Witte 1985) concluded that substantial reduction of tax preferences was virtually impossible. The interests that stood to lose from such a measure were inevitably more clearly defined and better organized than those that stood to gain from rate reductions and improved economic efficiency. Accordingly, the 1986 reform bill elicited lukewarm public support and intense opposition from organized groups, especially the real estate industry (Conlon, Wrightson, and Beam 1990; Strahan 1990). But after a tortuous debate, Congress passed it. The act cut tax expenditures sharply, reduced tax rates substantially, and eliminated much of the economic distortion embodied in the tax code.

To be sure, progress on the special interest front has not been uniform. Contrary to the trend, the United States in recent years was backsliding on trade policy—with a rapidly growing catalogue of import quotas and other trade barriers protecting American industries from foreign competition (Destler 1986). Moreover, this new protectionism was largely a congressional policy (Destler 1986; Nivola 1990). Although the executive branch actually imposed or negotiated most of the barriers, Congress demanded these actions, adopted legislation to encourage them, and threatened more severe measures if the executive failed to act.

It is important not to overstate the significance of protectionism in an evaluation of Congress, however. Because of the unprecedented, enormous trade deficits that the United States experienced in the 1980s, the political pressure for trade protection became extraordinarily intense, far out of proportion to any previous outbreak of protectionist sentiment (Destler 1986). In fact, protectionist pressures rose well beyond the level of mere interest group politics. There was widespread public strong support for trade barriers designed to retaliate against alleged unfair trade practices of other nations. Even some presidential candidates made a get-tough trade policy a prominent feature of their campaigns. Thus the new protectionism, however regrettable, does not suggest a diminution of Congress's capacity to resist narrow interests. The shift in policy had broad support, and Congress arguably did well to avoid imposing more restraints.

Further, congressional policy-making during the reform and postreform periods demonstrated balanced representation of opposing class and ideological interests. Even in the brief time of unified party control of government during the Carter administration, policy did not respond exclusively to majority party constituencies. For example, Carter and organized labor sponsored a major revision of labor law that would have given labor major advantages over management in strikes and organizing campaigns, but business groups and congressional conservatives were able to block it. The only sweeping defeat for a broad ideological grouping in the reform and post-reform era was the adoption of the Reagan administration's 1981 tax and budget program. That outcome was largely the result of transient circumstances that magnified the president's influence in Congress—an atmosphere of economic crisis, Reagan's landslide election victory, and public sympathy after the president was seriously wounded by an assassin. Within a few months, Democratic groups and legislators became more unified and assertive, and President Reagan was unable to sustain the pace or direction of policy change.

Deliberation

The consequences of the reform and postreform changes for deliberation have been more mixed and, on balance, probably less salutory. In general, Congress increased its capacity to obtain and manage information. But it ended up with less ability to weigh information and made careful judgments on issues that are salient to mass constituencies.

Structures   The improvements in deliberative capacity came from several sources. Congress in the reform era increased its capabilities by expanding all forms of its staff resources. Through the expansion of committee staffs and the staff agencies, Congress became much less dependent on the executive branch for information. Indeed, the Congressional Budget Office's economic forecasts had more credibility in Washington than did the administration's. Partly because of the new staff capacity, congressional debates are now punctuated with references to voluminous and often highly sophisticated analytic information. With the expansion of their individual office staffs, the legislators now have considerable ability to digest this information and bring it to bear in making decisions.

In addition, structural changes improved Congress's ability to identify and address the major issues in two critical areas of policy. To deal more effectively with questions of intelligence and national security, each chamber established a Select Intelligence Committee and reached agreement with the executive branch on procedures to ensure the committees' access to information and their opportunity for consultation on important decisions (such as the authorization of major covert operations). As Frederick Kaiser (this volume, Chapter 14) argues, these arrangements helped make Congress an effective partner of the executive branch in intelligence and national security policy. Congress not only gained the necessary competence and credibility needed to challenge the executive, but also became less prone to reflexive criticism of executive policies.

There were also major changes in the area of budgeting: the establishment of the budget committees, the concurrent budget resolution, the reconciliation process under the 1974 Budget Reform Act; and the adoption of deficit-reduction targets, automatic spending cuts, and functional-category spending limits under the Gramm-Rudman-Hollings Act of 1985, as amended in 1987 and 1990 (Thurber, this volume, Chapter 13). The main effect of these changes was to force Congress to recognize the connections among decisions about revenues, expenditures, and deficits and among those about different categories of expenditure. The recognition of these connections did not lead Congress to sharply reduce budget deficits. But it did ensure that Congress would at least make conscious choices about the budget.

The improvements in Congress's deliberative capacity were offset by adverse effects of other changes. The main source of difficulty was the same opening of decision processes that sometimes enhances representation of general interests. Unfortunately, the more open processes also exposed Congress to intense pressure from mass constituencies and, ironically, made it hard for Congress to deliberate about the genuine interests of those constituencies. Furthermore, the partial retreat from openness in the postreform era provided little relief from this pressure. Any attempt to use closed procedures to avoid pressure from public opinion was likely to be attacked and defeated by legislators eager to champion a popular cause.

In addition, the difficulties of deliberating on salient issues were magnified by trends in electoral politics. The recent prominence of negative, issue-oriented advertising in election campaigns made casting a potentially unpopular vote increasingly dangerous. In short, although the contemporary Congress is today quite responsive to widely held interests, it is often compelled to adopt whatever perception of those interests—however simplistic or misinformed—prevails among the mass public.

The contemporary Congress may also have difficulties in deliberation because of the number of decisions taken on the floor or the complexity of individual bills. At the height of floor-amending activity in the late 1970s, the House and Senate were each holding around fifteen hundred roll-call votes per year (Smith 1989). Even if legislators relied on staff for advice or took cues from other members, they were likely overloaded by that number of votes. Moreover, many of these amendments undoubtedly underwent little scrutiny prior to the floor debate. In some cases, there was little protection against reckless or haphazard decision making. As noted earlier, the postreform House and Senate both developed means of controlling floor amendments. As a result, the number of roll calls was cut almost in half.

The risk of Congress acting hastily on ill-considered floor amendments therefore diminished but did not disappear.

However, the postreform trend toward omnibus legislation often forces legislators to deal with enormously complex bills and decide a multitude of issues simultaneously. Sometimes an omnibus bill is virtually an operating plan for the entire government. Rank-and-file legislators can hardly grasp the contents of such legislation, much less have informed opinions about every important item. Nevertheless, it is unclear whether omnibus bills lead to ill-considered policy choices. In contrast to some floor amendments, leadership-sponsored omnibus bills may undergo adequately thorough consideration prior to floor debate.

Performance In the actual performance of the deliberative function during the reform and postreform periods, Congress showed the strengths and weaknesses that the changes in its structures would lead us to expect. There was virtually no limit to the volume and complexity of information Congress was able to incorporate into decision making. In formulating the 1990 income tax increase, for example, Congress employed sophisticated computer models of tax incidence to estimate the impacts of possible changes on different segments of the population. It was able to make relatively precise decisions about the overall distributive effects of the entire bill. In the debate over the 1990 Clean Air Act, Congress took into account voluminous evidence on topics ranging from the severity of the greenhouse effect and the sources and consequences of acid rain to the health effects of numerous pollutants and the economic consequences of environmental regulation for numerous industries and geographic areas.

At the same time, though, Congress showed only limited ability to deliberate carefully and reach responsible decisions on issues that are salient to mass constituencies. Responding to blatantly contradictory public attitudes about fiscal policy—support for spending combined with opposition to taxes—Congress tolerated budget deficits so large that they today threaten long-term economic growth. Partly because the public perceives the Social Security retirement program, incorrectly, as a contributory insurance program, Congress has been unable to control the largest single item of federal domestic expenditure.[14] Public fears about hazardous wastes led Congress to impose extraordinarily expensive control requirements for the sake of marginal health benefits (Landy, Roberts, and Thomas 1990). In short, some of the most costly policy mistakes of recent years resulted from undue congressional deference to uninformed public opinion.

Conflict Resolution

Changes in Congress also had mixed consequences for conflict resolution. The postreform Congress gained considerable ability to bring appropriate groups of legislators together for negotiation, to work out complex deals, and to implement agreements. Unfortunately, however, the contemporary congressional environment often encourages posturing and rigidity and militates against constructive negotiation.

Structures A number of structural developments in the reform and postreform periods facilitated cooperative policy-making. For instance, a condition of divided party control of government became routine, if not normal. As Pfiffner shows (this volume, Chapter 11), Congress and the president developed reasonably effective mechanisms—such as virtually institutionalized summit negotiations—for working out their differences.[15] Divided government favors cooperative outcomes in many cases. In policy conflicts with partisan cleavages, it tends to preclude one-sided outcomes. It thus discourages hard-line partisan or ideological positions and promotes moderate, negotiated outcomes.

In addition, the postreform Congress developed several internal features that facilitated cooperative negotiation. The expanded committee and members' staffs played a major role in negotiations. Indeed, because negotiation is a time-consuming activity, much of Congress's negotiating is handled by staff (Malbin 1980). This use of staff substantially increased Congress's ability to work out agreements. One result was longer bills: Instead of resolving contentious issues through the traditional device of ambiguity, Congress negotiated increasingly detailed and specific agreements—evidently reducing uncertainty and increasing satisfaction for all sides.[16]

Congress also developed mechanisms for linking action on multiple issues to permit agreement or pursue collective goals. In the House, the development of multiple referral improved the handling of bills that fall within two or more committee jurisdictions (Collie and Cooper 1989) and made it easier to draft complex legislative packages as a means of achieving agreement. To avoid the awkward situation of different committees drafting separate parts of a negotiated package, the Speaker may refer complex measures jointly or sequentially to multiple committees, with each committee reporting its own version of the entire package. Under recent Rules Committee procedures, the several committees then negotiate a single measure for consideration on the floor (Bach and Smith 1988).[17]

Omnibus legislation, aside from its partisan uses, is also a device for achieving agreement through linkage. For example, an omnibus appropriations bill can tie together spending cuts in a number of unrelated programs to ensure that the pain is widely shared. If the chamber considers the measure under procedures that restrict amendments, support for the general objective of budget cutting can be used to enact the entire package.

In addition, Congress developed flexible practices for assembling appropriate groups of negotiators. By adjusting or bypassing formal structures, these practices bring together legislators whose policy views, institutional roles, and disposition to cooperate facilitate the negotiation and implementation of an agreement. Several devices provide such flexibility.

Multiple referral is one such device. In addition to its usefulness for linking issues, multiple referral avoids making formalistic decisions among committees with rival claims to jurisdiction on a particular bill. It allows direct participation in negotiations by more of the members who are likely to offer amendments, exercise influence, or obstruct action on the floor.

In certain circumstances, Congress found it useful to narrow participation in negotiations by using *ad hoc* groups instead of the standing committees to draft bills. As Gilmour (this volume, Chapter 12) describes, the federal budget increasingly is made in summit negotiations, which bring together House and Senate budget leaders and White House officials to work out a budget that the standing committees are expected to implement. This practice allows the principal opposing forces—the Republican White House and the Democratic majority in Congress—to negotiate the central issues before the committees try to work out the details. *Ad hoc* negotiations have not been limited to budgeting, however. The Senate drafted the 1990 Clean Air amendments not in the Energy and Environment Committee but in informal negotiations organized by the majority leader.

In other circumstances, Congress found it more advantageous to broaden participation beyond the principal standing committees concerned with a bill. As Weingast (this volume, Chapter 8) argues, the drafting of a restrictive rule for floor action in the House is often a negotiation between the committee and other legislators who may have the votes to defeat the committee on the floor. They agree on a rule that produces a bill that amounts to a compromise between the committee and the floor majority. The drafting of time agreements in the Senate presumably involves the same kind of negotiation. An even more dramatic expansion of participation takes place in the contemporary conference committee. Rather than being limited to a few members of a single standing committee in each chamber, recent conference committees often included numerous members from several committees (Oleszek, this volume, Chapter 10). For massive omnibus bills, conference committees had over two hundred members, divided into subcommittees. In effect, postreform conference committees are designed to bring directly into negotiations enough legislators to ensure favorable action on the floor.

At the same time, however, other changes during the reform and postreform periods hindered cooperation on issues with attentive mass constituencies. As with deliberation, the central problem is increased exposure of decision making to public view. Open committee meetings require that negotiations be conducted either in public, where constituency pressures encourage rigidity, or else in separate informal meetings, which add to the costs of the decision process. Recorded votes on floor amendments increase the visibility and political costs of concessions; that is, if committee members responsive to an important constituency back away from one of its demands to reach agreement in committee, some legislator will offer a floor amendment to reverse the decision. To sustain the negotiated solution, they will then have to defend the concession explicitly, and persuade a majority to endorse it, on the floor. Moreover, as argued earlier, it will be difficult to use postreform restrictive procedures to insulate decision making from mass constituencies. Thus there will be a strong tendency for posturing and rigidity to diminish the chances for constructive negotiations on salient issues.

Performance   The strengths and weaknesses of the contemporary Congress in resolving conflict are evident in the policy outcomes. On the one hand, Congress certainly resisted one-sided legislative victories. On intensely conflictual issues like immigration reform and renewal of the Clean Air Act, for example, it persisted for years in seeking negotiated settlements rather than imposing terms on the weaker groups. If anything, Congress has been unduly confined to cooperative solutions. It has also demonstrated virtuosity in designing, analyzing, and negotiating legislative provisions for the sake of accommodating numerous groups. The transition rules incorporated in the 1986 Tax Reform Act are a case in point. Although Congress may take a long time to act, it eventually produces bills that are veritable monuments of mutual adjustment.

On the other hand, Congress has had great difficulty negotiating constructively on highly salient issues. The most important case is the handling of the budget deficit, the major domestic policy failure of recent years. The structural pressures toward cooperative policy-making are evident: considerable bipartisan collaboration occurred, and deficit cutting allocated burdens broadly across groups, regions, and social classes. Nevertheless, the results have been limited. Legislators have refused to recognize the necessity for compromise and instead have made party programs of demaguery: Democrats rejecting cuts in domestic programs, Republicans holding out against tax increases or cuts in defense (Gilmour, this volume, Chapter 12). It is likely that a less exposed decision-making environment would likely have allowed Congress to make greater progress in reducing the deficit.

CONCLUSION

The postreform Congress has distinct virtues and vulnerabilities as a policy-making institution. The structural changes of the reform and postreform periods brought about some significant improvements over the previous post–World War II Congresses. Judged by the criteria suggested in the chapter, the postreform Congress significantly improved its capabilities for representation. It provides less advantage to randomly selected groups or localities; it gives less deference to narrow group or local interests and more weight to diffuse, unorganized interests; and it usually strikes a reasonable balance between liberal and conservative interests, rather than swinging sharply between them or favoring one side permanently. As a result, some of the notorious policy failures of post–World War II Congresses—for example, the placid maintenance of anticompetitive regulatory programs and prolonged inaction on civil rights policy—would be much less likely in the contemporary Congress. Of course, narrow interests still have important advantages in the legislative process; in all likelihood, they always will. But the power of such interests in Congress is not what it used to be (see Peterson 1991).[18]

In some respects, the postreform Congress also improved its capabilities for deliberation and conflict resolution. Through the growth of its staffing, it acquired remarkable ability to analyze complex issues, design intricate bills, and transmit detailed and technical information among the legislators. In the current era, Congress probably makes very few important policy mistakes because of failure to obtain or recognize available information.

Congress also has considerable facility in putting together deals. It can transcend jurisdictional boundaries in negotiations and draft complex packages of provisions; it can either delegate negotiation to a few leaders or involve all interested legislators as circumstances require; and it can establish budget targets and general policies with enforcement mechanisms to ensure implementation. On a measure like the 1990 renewal of the Clean Air Act, the postreform Congress was able to deal with dozens of regulatory issues and hundreds of industrial, environmental, and regional interests not merely through broad generalizations but through painstaking negotiation of specific provisions.

Unfortunately, the limitations of the postreform Congress are as important as its strengths, if not more so. It has great difficulty deliberating responsibly or resolving conflict constructively on issues that elicit strong feelings from mass constituencies. The reforms of the 1970s exposed congressional decision making to exceptionally immediate public observation. The political pressures inherent in such observation were intensified by the recent prominence of issue-oriented campaign advertising. Moreover, the recentralizing and closing up of decision processes in the postreform period provided only limited means of escaping these pressures. Closed processes require acquiesence by large numbers of legislators—indeed, for Senate time agreements, by the entire Senate. Because legislators are tempted to seek visible identification with popular positions, such acquiescence is often hard to obtain.

Accordingly, when Congress is forced to deal with issues like whether to cut Social Security payments, tolerate moderate levels of environmental pollution, ration high-technology health care, or especially, raise taxes, it is under exceedingly heavy pressure to act in conformity to the public's sentiments and prejudices about these subjects. When it is called on to resolve conflicts among such sentiments—for example, to adopt a balanced program of benefit cuts and tax increases—this pressure leads to prolonged or permanent stalemate. Ultimately, the weaknesses of the postreform Congress in deliberating and resolving conflict on salient issues may outweigh its enhanced capacity for representation.

Acknowledgments

The analysis in this chapter benefited from discussion of an earlier related paper at the Conference on the New Politics of Public Policy at the Gordon Public Policy Center, Brandeis University, April 1990. Stella Herriges Quirk provided skillful and, on the whole, tactful editorial advice.

Notes

1. The first two conditions—equal power and informed choice—are derived from a similar discussion by Mansbridge (1983). The additional condition of constructive negotiation requires Congress to avoid destructive conflict, pursue efficient outcomes, and moderate differences in gains between winners and losers. The stipulation of unanimous consent implies that Congress, ideally, should weigh all citizens' preferences rather than merely choosing among them; it assumes that choosing among preferences is not inherently desirable but rather is justified by, and to the extent of, its practical necessity. This does not mean that the three conditions would produce uniquely suitable policy outcomes or that everyone should approve of those outcomes. For one thing, one may disapprove of the public's policy preferences.

2. In general, see Pitkin (1967); on Congress, see Kuklinski (1979).

3. In this context *randomly* means owing to accidental circumstances rather than to any fundamental advantages in political resources.

4. It can be argued that equality exists if the opposing ideological factions have equal opportunity to obtain influence—even though one side will have the bad luck not to be associated with the majority party. This argument is an appeal to the fairness of a lottery; it is unconvincing, however, because the lottery in this case is involuntary.

5. Commentators have often failed to see the ambiguity, recommending instead either open or closed processes depending on which policy questions they happened to study (see, for example, Destler 1986). The terms *autonomy* and *countervailing power* are from McFarland (1987).

6. Party government theorists often exaggerate this difference between party leaders and other members, however (see Quirk 1990).

7. The principal works are Maass (1983); Bessette (1982); Muir (1986); and Mansbridge (1988). For illuminating case studies of legislative deliberation, see Katzmann (1986); and Landy, Roberts, and Thomas (1990).

8. However, floor debate is a good time for negotiation—an activity that, unlike deliberation, is often improved by time pressure. Sometimes the procedural maneuvering during Senate floor debate is designed merely to provide time for negotiation; sometimes it is a means of holding up action as a negotiating tactic. Either way this maneuvering is an appropriate use of the occasion.

9. Compare the discussions of these conditions in Muir (1986) and Mansbridge (1988).

10. In a narrower, primarily administrative context, a number of studies have examined the effectiveness of institutional innovations designed to promote negotiated solutions to policy problems (see, for example, Sullivan's 1984 study of regulatory negotiation).

11. Two clarifications are important here. First, because many policy conflicts cut across party and institutional cleavages, the opposing issue factions may not be associated with different political parties or institutional entities. Second, the dimension of cooperation overlaps that of deliberation, yet the two dimensions are nevertheless distinct: Cooperative bargaining often requires effective mutual deliberation, and effective deliberation often requires the moderation of conflict. Yet deliberation can fail even without conflict, and cooperation can fail despite full recognition of the consequences. For a discussion of the difficulties of distinguishing cooperative from conflictual outcomes in a setting with voting rather than unanimous consent, see Quirk (1989).

12. For a study of the mediating role in Congress, see Perotti (1990).

13. As the collapse of the savings and loan industry has proven, there were some unfortunate deregulatory excesses, but most of the reforms enhanced efficiency and benefited consumers.

14. Contributions cover only a modest fraction of benefits. The program effects a large transfer of income from employees, including the poor, to retirees, including the wealthy (see Derthick 1979).

15. An imposing empirical investigation by Mayhew (1990) shows that Congress passed as much important legislation during periods of divided party control as during periods of unified control.

16. The long bills also cause difficulty for administrators subjected to ever-increasing and often inconsistent legislative constraints (see Derthick 1990; and Wilson 1989).

17. In the Senate, the majority leader formally has the power to make multiple referrals but has not exercised it. Arrangements for considering bills that affect multiple jurisdictions are generally worked out among the committee chairs.

18. For a study that refutes claims of the immobilism of recent American politics, see Harris and Milkis (1989).

References

Aberbach, Joel D. 1990. *Keeping a watchful eye; the politics of congressional oversight.* Washington, D.C.: Brookings Institution.

Achenbaum, W. Andrew. 1986. *Social Security: Visions and revisions.* Cambridge, Engl.: Cambridge Univ. Press.

Adamany, David. 1984. Political parties in the 1980s. In *Money and politics in the United States,* ed. Michael J. Malbin, 70–121. Chatham, N.J.: Chatham House.

Agranoff, Robert, ed. 1972. *The new style in election campaigns.* Boston: Holbrook.

Albright, Robert C. 1956. Minority 47 summoned to weekly discussions. *Washington Post,* Nov. 11, 1–2.

Aldrich, John, and Richard G. Niemi. 1990. The sixth American party system: The 1960s realignment and the candidate-centered parties. Unpublished manuscript.

Alston, Chuck. 1990. Senate GOP has a big problem: How to spend all that cash. *Congressional Quarterly Weekly Report* 48:3087–92.

Arieff, Irwin B. 1980. House, Senate chiefs attempt to lead a changed Congress. *Congressional Quarterly Weekly Report* 38:2695–700.

Arnold, R. Douglas. 1983. The local roots of domestic policy. In *The new Congress,* ed. Thomas E. Mann and Norman J. Ornstein, 250–287. Washington, D.C.: American Enterprise Institute.

———. 1990. *The logic of congressional action.* New Haven, Conn.: Yale Univ. Press.

Axelrod, Donald. 1988. *Budgeting for modern government.* New York: St. Martin's.

Axelrod, Robert. 1984. *The evolution of cooperation.* New York: Basic Books.

Bach, Stanley. 1981. The structure of choice in the House of Representatives: The impact of complex special rules. *Harvard Journal of Legislation* 18(Summer):553–602.

———. 1986. Representatives and committees on the floor: Amendments to appropriations bills in the House of Representatives, 1963–1982. *Congress and the President* 13(Spring):41–53.

———. 1988. The amending process in the House of Representatives. Report 87–178. Washington, D.C.: Congressional Research Service.

Bach, Stanley, and Steven S. Smith. 1988. *Managing uncertainty in the House of Representatives.* Washington, D.C.: Brookings Institution.

Baker, Bobby, with Larry King. 1978. *Wheeling and dealing: Confessions of a Capitol Hill operator.* New York: Norton.

Baker, Ross K. 1989. *House and Senate.* New York: Norton.

Barnes, James A., and Richard E. Cohen. 1988. Unity—Will it last? *National Journal,* 20(Sept. 30).

Baron, David, and John Ferejohn. 1989. Bargaining in Legislatures. *American Political Science Review* 83(Dec.):1181–1206.

Barrett, Laurence. 1984. *Gambling with history: Ronald Reagan in the White House.* New York: Penguin.

Barry, John M. 1989. *The ambition and the power.* New York: Viking.

Baumer, Donald C. 1990. Senate Democratic leadership in the 101st Congress. Paper presented at the annual meeting of the American Political Science Association, San Francisco, Aug. 30–Sept. 2.

Bawn, Kathleen. 1990. Ex Post Vetoes after Multiple Referral: A Case Study of Committee Power in the Post-Reform House. Department of Economics, Stanford University.

Bennett, Robert A. 1987. Wall Street sees market drop in a small budget cut. *New York Times,* Nov. 19.

Bessette, Joseph M. 1982. Is Congress a deliberative body? In *The United States Congress,* ed. Dennis Hale, 3–11. Chestnut Hill, Mass.: Boston College.

Bianco, William T. 1991. Representation and incomplete information. Paper presented at the 1991 Midwest Political Science Association meetings, Chicago, Ill.

Bibby, John F. 1983. *Congressmen off the record.* Washington, D.C.: AEI Press.

———. 1990. Party organization at the state level. In *The parties respond,* ed. L. Sandy Maisel, 21–40. Boulder: Westview Press.

Birnbaum, Jeffrey H. 1987. Backbenchers like Schumer leap to the fore in House where seniority is sovereign no more. *The Wall Street Journal,* June 29, 54.

Biskupic, Joan. 1990. For critics of flag measure advance work pays off. *Congressional Quarterly Weekly Report* 48:1962–64.

Blechman, Barry M. 1990. *The politics of national security.* New York: Oxford Univ. Press.

Bond, Jon R., and Richard Fleisher. 1990. *The president in the legislative arena.* Chicago: Univ. of Chicago Press.

Bone, Hugh A. 1956. An introduction to the senate policy committees. *American Political Science Review* 50(June):339–59.

———. 1958. *Party committees and national politics.* Seattle: Univ. of Washington Press.

Bowles, Nigel. 1987. *The White House and Capitol Hill.* Oxford: Clarendon Press.

Brady, David, Richard Brody, and David Epstein. 1989. Heterogenous parties and political organization: The U.S. Senate, 1880–1920. *Legislative Studies Quarterly* 14(May):205–23.

Brady, David W., Joseph Cooper, and Patricia A. Hurley. 1979. The decline of party in the U.S. House of Representatives, 1887–1968. *Legislative Studies Quarterly* 4:381–407.

Brady, David W., and John Ettling. 1984. The electoral connection and the decline of partisanship in the 20th century House of Representatives. *Congress and the Presidency* 11:19–36.

Brady, David W., and Morris Fiorina. 1990. The ruptured legacy: Presidential-congressional relations in historical perspective. In *Looking back on the Reagan presidency,* ed. Larry Berman, 268–87. Baltimore: Johns Hopkins Univ. Press.

Broder, David S. 1975. The new realities of power. *Washington Post,* Apr. 2, A20.

———. 1987a. Block tax cuts for rich, Wright says; House Speaker charges Reagan budget would burden the poor. *Washington Post,* Jan. 10.

———. 1987b. Democrats find taxes treacherous territory; Wright, Rostenkowski at odds on revenue. *Washington Post,* Mar. 15.

Bullock, Charles S. III, and David W. Brady. 1983. Party, constituency and roll-call voting in the U.S. Senate. *Legislative Studies Quarterly* 8:29–43.

Burns, James MacGregor. 1956. *Roosevelt: The lion and the fox.* New York: Harcourt.

———. 1963. *The deadlock of democracy.* Englewood Cliffs, N.J.: Prentice-Hall.

Bush, George. 1987. Remarks to the Federalist Society on January 30, 1987. *Congressional Record* 133:3467–68.

———. 1990. Memorandum of disapproval for the Intelligence Authorization Act, fiscal year 1991. *Weekly Compilation of Presidential Documents* 26:1958–59.

Byrd, Lee. 1986. After 34 years in Congress, O'Neill to hang up his hat. *Los Angeles Times,* Oct. 19, 2.

Calmes, Jacqueline. 1985. House, with little difficulty, passes '86 budget resolution. *Congressional Quarterly Weekly Report* 43:971, 973–75.

———. 1987. Byrd struggles to lead deeply divided Senate. *Congressional Quarterly Weekly Report* 45(July 4):1419–23.

The campaign sewer overflows. 1990. *New York Times,* Nov. 7.

Canon, David T. 1990. *Actors, athletes, and astronauts: Political amateurs in the United States Congress.* Chicago: Univ. of Chicago Press.

Carmines, Edward G., and Lawrence C. Dodd. 1985. Bicameralism in Congress: The changing partnership. In *Congress reconsidered,* 3d ed., ed. Lawrence C. Dodd and Bruce I. Oppenheimer, 414–36. Washington, D.C.: CQ Press.

Carmines, Edward G., and James A. Stimson. 1989. *Issue evolution: Race and the transformation of American politics.* Princeton, N.J.: Princeton Univ. Press.

Carroll, Holbert N. 1966. *The House of Representatives and foreign affairs.* Rev. ed. Boston: Little, Brown.

Center for Responsive Politics. 1988. *Congress speaks—A survey of the 100th Congress.* Washington, D.C.: Center for Responsive Politics.

Clapp, Charles L. 1963. *The congressman: His work as he sees it.* Washington, D.C.: Brookings Institution.

Clark, Timothy B. 1981. Saving Social Security—Reagan and Congress face some unpleasant choices. *National Journal,* June 13.

Coase, Ronald H. 1937. The nature of the firm. *Economica* 4:386–405.

———. 1960. The problem of social cost. *Journal of Law and Economics* 3(Oct.):1–44.

Cohen, Richard E. 1989. Setting the Senate Democrats' agenda. *National Journal,* Feb. 25, 484.

———. 1990. Rumblings in the ranks on budget deal. *National Journal,* Oct. 6, 2416.

Cohen, Richard E., and William Schneider. 1989. Slim pickings. *National Journal.* Jan. 28, 203–31.

Collie, Melissa P. 1986. New directions in congressional research. *Legislative Studies Section Newsletter* 10(Nov.–Dec.):90–92.

———. 1988. Universalism and the parties in the U.S. House of Representatives, 1921–80. *American Journal of Political Science* 32:865–83.

Collie, Melissa P., and David W. Brady. 1985. The decline of partisan voting coalitions in the House of Representatives. In *Congress reconsidered,* 3d ed., ed. Lawrence C. Dodd and Bruce I. Oppenheimer, 272–87. Washington, D.C.: CQ Press.

———. 1989. Multiple referral and the "new" committee system in the House of Representatives. In *Congress reconsidered,* 4th ed., ed. Lawrence C. Dodd and Bruce I. Oppenheimer, Washington, D.C.: CQ Press.

Collie, Melissa P., and Joseph Cooper. 1989. Multiple referral and the "new" committee system in the House of Representatives. In *Congress reconsidered,* 4th ed., ed. Lawrence C. Dodd and Bruce I. Oppenheimer, 245–72. Washington, D.C.: CQ Press.

Congressional Budget Office. 1990a. *An analysis of the president's budgetary proposals for fiscal year 1991.* Washington, D.C.: CBO, Mar.

Congressional Budget Office. 1990b. *The economic and budget outlook: An update.* Washington, D.C.: CBO, July.

Congressional Quarterly. 1990. Clean air conferees finally named. *Congressional Quarterly Weekly Report.* 30 June:2044.

Congressional Quarterly Almanac. 1989. Washington, D.C.: Congressional Quarterly Press.

Conlan, Timothy J., Margaret T. Wrightson, and David R. Beam. 1990. *Taxing choices: The politics of tax reform.* Washington, D.C.: CQ Press.

Cook, Rhodes. 1988. '88 vote: Stress persuasion over registration. *Congressional Quarterly Weekly Report* 46(Oct. 1):2702–5.

Cooper, Joseph. 1981. Organization and innovation in the House of Representatives. In *The House at work,* ed. Joseph Cooper and G. Calvin Mackenzie, 319–55. Austin: Univ. of Texas Press.

Cooper, Joseph, and David W. Brady. 1981. Institutional context and leadership style: The House from Cannon to Rayburn. *American Political Science Review* 75:411–25.

Cooper, Joseph, David W. Brady, and Patricia A. Hurley, 1977. The electoral basis of party voting: Patterns and trends in the U.S. House of Representatives, 1887–1969. In *The impact of the electoral process,* ed. Louis Maisel and Joseph Cooper, 133–65. Beverly Hills: Sage Publications.

Corwin, Edward S. 1957. *The president: Office and powers, 1787–1957.* New York: New York Univ. Press.

Cotter, Cornelius P., and Bernard C. Hennessy. 1964. *Politics without power: The national party committees.* New York: Atherton Press.

Cowan, Edward. 1981. Constitutional prerogatives are an issue. *New York Times,* July 13, D1.

Cox, Gary, and Mathew McCubbins. 1990. *Parties and Committees in the U.S. House of Representatives.* Berkeley: Univ. of California Press.

Crabb, Cecil V., and Pat M. Holt. 1989. Invitation to struggle: Congress, the president, and foreign policy. Washington, D.C.: CQ Press.

Cranford, John R. 1988. Party unity scores slip in 1988, but overall pattern is upward. *Congressional Quarterly Weekly Report* 46(Nov. 19):3334–37.

Crovitz, L. Gordon. 1990. Micromanaging foreign policy. *Public Interest* 100:102–16.

Davidson, Roger H. 1981. Subcommittee government: New channels for policymaking. In *The new Congress,* ed. Thomas E. Mann and Norman J. Ornstein, 99–133. Washington, D.C.: American Enterprise Institute.

———. 1985. Senate leaders: Janitors for an untidy chamber? In *Congress reconsidered,* 3d. ed., ed. Lawrence C. Dodd and Bruce I. Oppenheimer, 225–52. Washington, D.C.: CQ Press.

———. 1986a. Congressional committees as moving targets. *Legislative Studies Quarterly* 11(Feb.):19–33.

———. 1986b. The legislative work of Congress. Paper presented at the annual meeting of the American Political Science Association, Washington, D.C.

———. 1988a. The impact of agenda on the postreform Congress. Paper presented at the annual meeting of the American Political Science Association, Atlanta, Aug. 31–Sept. 3.

———. 1988b. The new centralization on Capitol Hill. *Review of Politics* 49(Summer):345–64.

———. 1989. Multiple referral legislation in the U.S. Senate. *Legislative Studies Quarterly* 14(Aug.):375–92.

Davidson, Roger H., and Carol Hardy. 1987a. Indicators of House of Representatives activity and workload. Congressional Research Service Rept. 87-136S, Washington, D.C. June 8.

———. 1987b. Indicators of Senate activity and workload. Congressional Research Service Rept. 87-497S, Washington, D.C. June 8.

Davidson, Roger H., and Walter J. Oleszek. 1976. Adaptation and consolidation: Structural innovation in the U.S. House of Representatives. *Legislative Studies Quarterly* 1(Feb.):37–65.

———. 1977. *Congress against itself.* Bloomington: Indiana Univ. Press.

———. 1985. *Congress and its members.* 2d ed. Washington, D.C.: CQ Press.

———. 1987. From monopoly to interaction. Paper presented to the annual meeting of the Midwest Political Science Association, Chicago, Ill.

———. 1990. *Congress and its members.* 3rd ed. Washington, D.C.: CQ Press.

Davidson, Roger H., Walter J. Oleszek, and Thomas Kephart. 1988. One bill, many committees: Multiple referrals in the House of Representatives. *Legislative Studies Quarterly* 13(Feb.):3–28.

Deering, Christopher J. 1989. *Congressional politics.* Chicago: Dorsey Press.

Deering, Christopher J., and Steven S. Smith. 1981. Majority party leadership and the new House subcommittee system. In *Understanding congressional leadership,* ed. Frank H. Mackaman, 261–92. Washington, D.C.: CQ Press.

Denzau, Arthur, William H. Riker, and Kenneth A. Shepsle. 1985. Farquharson and Fenno: Sophisticated voting and home style. *American Political Science Review* 79:1117–34.

Derthick, Martha. 1979. *Policymaking for Social Security.* Washington, D.C.: Brookings Institution.

———. 1990. *Agency under stress.* Washington, D.C.: Brookings Institution.

Derthick, Martha, and Paul J. Quirk. 1985. *The politics of deregulation.* Washington, D.C.: Brookings Institution.

Deschler, Lewis, and William Brown. 1984. *Procedure in the U.S. House of Representatives.* 4th ed. Washington, D.C.: Government Printing Office.

Destler, I. M. 1986. *American trade politics: System under stress.* New York: Twentieth Century Fund.

Destler, I. M., et al. 1984. *Our own worst enemy.* New York: Simon & Schuster.

Dewar, Helen. 1981. Senate unanimously rebuffs president on Social Security. *Washington Post,* May 21.

———. 1989a. At finish of slow-starting session, lawmakers end up eyeball to eyeball. *Washington Post,* Nov. 21, A18.

———. 1989b. Congress off to slowest start in years. *Washington Post,* May 13, A4.

Dewar, Helen, and Edward Walsh. 1986. Reagan, Hill regenerate fiscal debate. *Washington Post,* Jan. 22, A8.

Dewar, Helen, and Ann Devroy. 1990. Senate votes to speed up rights bill. *Washington Post,* July 18, A1.

Dodd, Lawrence C., and Bruce I. Oppenheimer. 1989. Consolidating power in the House: The rise of a new oligarchy. In *Congress reconsidered,* 4th ed., ed. Lawrence C. Dodd and Bruce I. Oppenheimer, 39–64. Washington, D.C.: CQ Press.

Donovan, Beth. 1989. Parties aggressively court absentee-voter bloc. *Congressional Quarterly Weekly Report* 47(Oct. 28):2894–96.

Donovan, Robert J. 1977. *Conflict and crisis: The presidency of Harry S Truman, 1945–1948.* New York: Norton.

Drew, Elizabeth. 1983. *Politics and money: The new road to corruption.* New York: Macmillan.

Dyson, James, and John Soule. 1970. Congressional committee behavior in roll call votes: The U.S. House of Representatives, 1955–64. *Midwest Journal of Political Science* 14:626–47.

Edwards, George C., III. 1989. *At the margins: Presidential leadership of Congress.* New Haven: Yale Univ. Press.

———. 1991. Director or facilitator? Presidential policy control of Congress. In *The managerial presidency,* ed. James P. Pfiffner, 214–24. Pacific Grove, Calif.: Brooks/Cole.

Eisner, Robert. 1986. *How real is the federal deficit?* New York: Free Press.

Ellwood, John W. 1985. The great exception: The congressional budget process in an age of decentralization. In *Congress reconsidered,* 3d ed., ed. Lawrence C. Dodd and Bruce I. Oppenheimer, 315–42. Washington, D.C.: CQ Press.

Epstein, Leon D. 1986. *Political parties in the American mold.* Madison: Univ. of Wisconsin Press.

Evans, C. Lawrence. 1991. *Leadership in committees.* Ann Arbor: Univ. of Michigan Press.

Farnsworth, Clyde H. 1986. The balance of payments has a political fulcrum. *The New York Times,* Mar. 9, E4.

Federal Election Commission. 1989. Press release, Mar. 27.

————. 1990a. Press release, Feb. 2.

————. 1990b. Press release, Feb. 16.

————. 1990c. Press release, Nov. 1.

Fenno, Richard F., Jr. 1962. The House Appropriations Committee as a political system: The problem of integration. *American Political Science Review* 56:310–24.

————. 1966. *Power of the purse.* Boston: Little, Brown.

————. 1973. *Congressmen in committees.* Boston: Little, Brown.

————. 1975. If, as Ralph Nader says, Congress is "the broken branch," how come we love our congressmen so much? In *Congress in Change: Evolution and Reform.* ed. Norman J. Ornstein, 277–87. New York: Praeger Publishers.

————. 1978. *Home style.* Boston: Little, Brown.

————. 1982. *The United States Senate: A bicameral perspective.* Washington, D.C.: American Enterprise Institute.

————. 1989a. *The making of a senator: Dan Quayle.* Washington, D.C.: CQ Press.

————. 1989b. The Senate through the looking glass: The debate over television. *Legislative Studies Quarterly* 14(Aug.):313–48.

Ferejohn, John. 1986. Logrolling in an institutional context: A case study of food stamp legislation. In *Congress and policy change,* ed. Gerald Wright, Leroy Rieselbach, and Lawrence Dodd, 223–53. New York: Agathon Press.

Ferejohn, John, and Keith Krehbiel. 1987. The budget process and the size of the budget. *American Journal of Political Science* 31(May):296–320.

Fessler, Pamela. 1982. House sends tax bill directly to conference. *Congressional Quarterly Weekly Report* 40(July 31):1808.

————. 1990a. Read my lips: No conditions, Bush tells Democrats. *Congressional Quarterly Weekly Report.* 48:1447–63.

————. 1990b. Senate plan faces uphill fight: Exploratory talks are set. *Congressional Quarterly Weekly Report* 48:1329–32.

Feuerbringer, Jonathan. 1987a. Accord held near on deficit figures. *New York Times,* Nov. 11.

————. 1987b. Agreement signed to reduce deficit $30 billion in 1988. *New York Times,* Nov. 21.

Fiorina, Morris P. 1981. *Retrospective voting in American national elections.* New Haven: Yale Univ. Press.

————. 1989a. An era of divided government. Occasional paper 98-6. Cambridge, Mass.: Harvard Univ., Department of Government.

————. 1989b. *Congress: Keystone of the Washington establishment.* 2d ed. New Haven: Yale Univ. Press.

Fisher, Louis. 1984. The Budget Act of 1974: A further loss of spending control. In *Congressional budgeting: Politics, process and power,* ed. Thomas W. Wander, F. Ted Hebert, and Gary W. Copeland, 170–89. Baltimore: Johns Hopkins Univ. Press.

————. 1991. Congress as micromanager of the executive branch. In *The managerial presidency,* ed. James P. Pfiffner, 225–37. Pacific Grove, Calif.: Brooks/Cole.

Ford, Paul L., ed. 1898. *The federalist.* New York: Henry Holt.

Franck, Thomas M., and Edward Weisband. 1979. *Foreign policy by Congress.* New York: Oxford Univ. Press.

Freeman, J. Leiper. 1977. Investigating the executive intelligence: The fate of the Pike Committee. *Capitol Studies* 5:103–18.

Froman, Lewis A. 1967. *The congressional process: Strategies, rules, and procedures.* Boston: Little, Brown.

Galloway, George B. 1946. *Congress at the crossroads.* New York: Crowell.

———. 1953. *The legislative process in Congress.* New York: Crowell.

———. 1962. *History of the U.S. House of Representatives.* Washington, D.C.: Government Printing Office.

Gamarekian, Barbara. 1988. From House to Senate: Into another world. *New York Times,* Apr. 11, B6.

Gates, Robert M. 1987. The CIA and foreign policy. *Foreign Affairs* 66:215–30.

Gawthrop, Louis C. 1966. *Bureaucratic behavior in the executive branch.* New York: Free Press.

Gilmour, John B. 1990a. Bargaining between Congress and the president: The bidding-up phenomenon. Paper presented at the American Political Science Association Convention, San Francisco.

———. 1990b. *Reconcilable differences?* Berkeley: Univ. of California Press.

Gingrich, Newt, and Frank Gregorsky. 1985. How the House deck is stacked. *Washington Times,* Jan. 22, 1D.

Gist, John R. 1982. "Stability' and "competition" in budgetary theory. *American Political Science Review* 76(Dec. 1982):859–72.

Godwin, R. Kenneth. 1988. *One billion dollars of influence: The direct marketing of politics.* Chatham, N.J.: Chatham House.

Granat, Diane. 1983. Leaders introduce "clean bill": House appropriations loads money bill with controversy. *Congressional Quarterly Weekly Report* 41(Sept. 24):1973.

Gregg, Gail. 1980. Balanced budget drive wins broad support on Capitol Hill. *Congressional Quarterly Weekly Report* 38:641.

Griffith, Ernest S. 1967. *Congress: Its contemporary role.* 4th ed. New York: New York Univ. Press.

Haas, Lawrence J. 1991. Byrd's big stick. *National Journal* 23(Feb. 9):316–20.

Hager, George. 1990. Defiant House rebukes leaders; new round of fights begins. *Congressional Quarterly Weekly Report* 48:3183–88.

Hall, Richard L., and C. Lawrence Evans. 1989. The Power of Subcommittees. *Journal of Politics,* 52:335–55.

Hamby, Alonzo L. 1989. The mind and character of Harry S Truman. In *The Truman presidency,* ed. Michael J. Lacey, 19–53. Cambridge, Mass.: Woodrow Wilson International Center for Scholars and Cambridge Univ. Press.

Harris, Richard A., and Sidney M. Milkis. 1989. *The politics of regulatory change: A tale of two agencies.* New York: Oxford Univ. Press.

Hart, John. 1987. *The presidential branch.* New York: Pergamon Press.

Havemann, Judith. 1987. President activates budget-cut mechanism; without deal, $23 billion will be slashed. *Washington Post,* Nov. 21.

Heclo, Hugh. 1984. Executive budget making. In *Federal Budget policy in the 1980s,* ed. Gregory B. Mills and John L. Palmer, 255–91. Washington, D.C.: Urban Institute Press.

Herrnson, Paul S. 1988. *Party campaigning in the 1980s.* Cambridge, Mass.: Harvard Univ. Press.

———. 1989. National party decision-making, strategies, and resource distribution in congressional elections. *Western Political Quarterly* 42:301–23.

———. 1990. Investing in America's future. Democratic Caucus, U.S. House of Representatives, Washington, D.C.

———. 1990a. Campaign professionalism and fundraising in congressional elections. Paper presented at the annual meeting of the American Political Science Association, San Francisco.

o. Reemergent national party organizations. In *The parties respond,* ndy Maisel, 41–66. Boulder: Westview Press.

Paul S., and David Menefee-Libey. Forthcoming. The transformation of ican political parties. *Midsouth Journal of Political Science.*

rand, William F. 1985. Oral history interview, United States Congress, Sen- e Historical Office, Mar. 20–May 6.

H. ckley, Barbara. 1978. *Stability and Change in Congress.* 2nd ed. New York: Harper & Row.

———. 1981. *Congressional elections.* Washington, D.C.: CQ Press.

Hoffer, John L., Jr. 1984. The origination clause and tax legislation. *Boston University Journal of Tax Law* (May):1–22.

Hook, Janet. 1986. House GOP: Plight of a permanent minority. *Congressional Quarterly Weekly Report,* June 21, 1393–96.

———. 1989. How the pay-raise strategy came unraveled. *Congressional Quarterly Weekly Report* 47(Feb. 11):264–67.

———. 1990a. Anatomy of a budget showdown: The limits of leaders' clout. *Congressional Quarterly Weekly Report* 48:3187–91.

———. 1990b. Senate Republican conference takes a step to the Right. *Congressional Quarterly Weekly Report* 48(Nov. 17):3871–72.

Houston, Paul. 1982. House bypasses Constitution on tax boost. *Los Angeles Times,* July 29, 8.

Hunter, Robert E., et al. eds. 1986. *Making government work.* Boulder: Westview Press.

Huntington, Samuel P. 1965. Congressional responses to the twentieth century. In *The Congress and America's future,* ed. David B. Truman, 5-31. Englewood Cliffs, N.J.: Prentice-Hall.

Hurley, Patricia A. 1989. Parties and coalitions in Congress. In *Congressional politics,* ed. Christopher J. Deering, 113–34. Chicago: Dorsey Press.

Hurley, Patricia A., and Rick K. Wilson. 1989. Partisan voting patterns in the U.S. Senate, 1877–1986. *Legislative Studies Quarterly* 14(May):225–50.

Inman, Bobby. 1987. *A conversation with Admiral B. R. Inman on congressional oversight.* Washington, D.C.: Center for Excellence.

Isaacson, Walter, and Evan Thomas. 1986. *The wise men.* New York: Simon & Schuster.

Jackson, Brooks. 1988. *Honest graft.* New York: Knopf.

Jacobson, Gary. 1987. *The politics of congressional elections.* 2d ed. Boston: Little, Brown.

———. 1985–86. Party organization and campaign resources in 1982. *Political Science Quarterly* 100:604–25.

———. 1990. *The electoral origins of divided government.* Boulder: Westview Press.

Jeffreys-Jones, Rhodri. 1989. *The CIA and American democracy.* New Haven, Conn.: Yale Univ. Press.

Jewell, Malcolm E. 1982. *Representation in state legislatures.* Lexington: Univ. of Kentucky Press.

Johnson, Loch K. 1980. The U.S. Congress and the CIA: Monitoring the dark side of government. *Legislative Studies Quarterly* 4:477–99.

———. 1985. *A season of inquiry: The Senate Intelligence investigation.* Lexington: Univ. of Kentucky Press.

———. 1989. *America's secret power: The CIA in a Democratic society.* New York: Oxford Univ. Press.

Jones, Charles O. 1968. Joseph G. Cannon and Howard W. Smith: An essay on the limits of leadership in the House of Representatives. *Journal of Politics* 30:617–46.

———. 1970. *The minority party in Congress.* Boston: Little, Brown.

———. 1976. Senate Party leadership in public policy. In *Policymaking role of leadership in the Senate,* 18–33. Washington, D.C.: Commission on the Operation of the Senate, 94th Cong., 2d Sess., Government Printing Office.

———. 1981. House leadership in an age of reform. In *Understanding congressional leadership,* ed. Frank H. Mackaman, 117–34. Washington, D.C.: CQ Press.

———. 1988. *The trusteeship presidency: Jimmy Carter and the United States Congress.* Baton Rouge: Louisiana State Univ. Press.

Jones, Clayton. 1990. US and Japanese legislators get earful from constituents on trade. *Christian Science Monitor,* Nov. 19, 4.

Kaiser, Frederick M. 1977. Oversight of foreign policy: The House Committee on International Relations. *Legislative Studies Quarterly* 2:255–79.

———. 1988a. Congressional oversight of the presidency. *Annals* 499:75–89.

———. 1988b. Congressional rules and conflict resolution: Access to information in the House Select Committee on Intelligence. *Congress and the Presidency* 15:49–73.

Kassebaum, Nancy Landon. 1988. The Senate is not in order. *Washington Post,* Jan. 27.

Katzmann, Robert A. 1986. *Institutional disability: The saga of transportation policy for the disabled.* Washington, D.C.: Brookings Institution.

———. 1990. War powers: Toward a new accommodation. In *A question of balance,* ed. Thomas Mann, 35–69. Washington, D.C.: Brookings Institution.

Keller, Bill. 1981. Congressional rating game is hard to win. *Congressional Quarterly Weekly Report* 39 (Mar. 21):507–29.

Kenworthy, Tom. 1987a. Democrats ask Reagan to be "realistic" on budget. *Washington Post,* Feb. 18.

———. 1987b. Democrats plan new tactics on fiscal front; gamesmanship between Hill and president may have major implications for 1988. *Washington Post,* July 6.

———. 1987c. $1 trillion Hill budget blueprint nears final passage in the Senate. *Washington Post,* June 25.

———. 1987d. Reagan, Hill agree to cut $76 billion; outline of 2-year deficit-cutting pact set. *Washington Post,* Nov. 21.

———. 1987e. Wright launches push for tax rise support; Democrats given "pep talk" on deficit. *Washington Post,* Mar. 5.

———. 1987f. Wright suggests taxing stock transactions. *Washington Post,* Mar. 4.

———. 1988. Hill Democrats draft nonlethal Contra aid. *The Washington Post,* Feb. 24, 1, 22.

———. 1990. GOP files complaint against representative Annunzio. *Washington Post,* Sept. 27.

Kernell, Samuel. 1986. *Going public: New strategies of presidential leadership.* Washington, D.C.: CQ Press.

Key, V. O. 1965. *The responsible electorate.* New York: Vintage.

Kieweit, Roderick, and Mathew McCubbins. 1991. *The spending power.* Berkeley: Univ. of California Press.

Kingdon, John. 1981. *Congressman's voting decisions.* 2nd. ed. New York: Harper & Row.

Koh, Harold Honju. 1990. *The national security constitution: Sharing power after the Iran-contra affair.* New Haven, Conn.: Yale Univ. Press.

Kolodny, Robin. 1990. Incumbents and challengers in congressional elections: The problem of setting functional priorities for the CCCs. Paper presented at the annual meeting of the American Political Science Association.

ıgman, Paul. 1990. We're no. 3—So what? *Washington Post*, Mar. 24, C1–2.

ıklinski, James H. 1979. Representative-constituency linkages: A review article. *Legislative Studies Quarterly* 4:121–40.

Landy, Mark K., Marc J. Roberts, and Stephen R. Thomas. 1990. *The Environmental Protection Agency: Asking the Wrong Questions*. New York: Oxford Univ. Press.

LeLoup, Lance T. 1980. *The fiscal Congress*. Westport, Conn.: Greenwood Press.

Light, Paul C. 1982. *The president's agenda*. Baltimore: Johns Hopkins Univ. Press.

———. 1985. *Artful work: The politics of Social Security reform*. New York: Random House.

Lofton, John. 1982. Interview: Dole terms his big tax bill a reform, not raise. *Washington Times*, Aug. 27, 2A.

Longley, Lawrence D., and Walter J. Oleszek. 1989. *Bicameral politics: Conference committees in Congress*. New Haven, Conn.: Yale Univ. Press.

Loomis, Burdett. 1988. *The new American politician*. New York: Basic Books.

Lynch, Thomas D. 1985. *Public budgeting in America*. 2d ed. Englewood Cliffs, N.J.: Prentice-Hall.

Maass, Arthur. 1983. *Congress and the common good*. New York: Basic Books.

Mackaman, Frank. 1981. *Understanding congressional leadership*. Washington, D.C.: CQ Press.

Madison, Christopher. 1989. Congressional focus: Speaker at work. *National Journal* 21(Aug. 12):2067.

Malbin, Michael J. 1977. The Senate Republican leaders—Life without a president. *National Journal* 9(May 21):776–80.

———. 1980. *Unelected representatives: Congressional staff and the future of representative government*. New York: Basic Books.

Mann, Thomas E., ed. 1990a. *A question of balance*. Washington, D.C.: Brookings Institution.

———. 1990b. Making foreign policy: President and Congress. In *A question of balance*, ed. Thomas E. Mann, 1–34. Washington, D.C.: Brookings Institution.

Mann, Thomas E., and Norman J. Ornstein, eds. 1981. *The new Congress*. Washington, D.C.: American Enterprise Institute.

Manning, Bayless. 1977. The Congress, the executive and intermestic affairs: Three proposals. *Foreign Affairs* 55 (Jan.):306–24.

Mansbridge, Jane. 1983. *Beyond adversary democracy*. Chicago: Univ. of Chicago Press.

———. 1988. Motivating deliberation in Congress. In *Constitutionalism in America*, vol. 2, ed. Sarah Baumgartner Thurow. New York: Univ. Press of America.

Mathiasen, David G. 1990. The politics of deficit reduction. *Government Executive* 22 (9):42–51.

Matthews, Donald R. 1960. *U.S. Senators and their world*. New York: Vintage.

Matthews, Donald R., and James A. Stimson. 1975. *Yeas and nays*. New York: Wiley.

Mayhew, David. 1974. *Congress: The electoral connection*. New Haven, Conn.: Yale Univ. Press.

———. 1989. Does it make a difference whether party control of the American national government is unified or divided? Paper presented at the American Political Science Association Convention.

———. 1990. Divided party control: Does it make a difference? Unpublished manuscript, Yale University.

McCubbins, Mathew D., and Thomas Schwartz. 1984. Congressional oversight overlooked: Police patrols versus fire alarms. *American Journal of Political Science* 28:165–79.

McFarland, Andrew S. 1987. Interest groups and theories of power in America. *British Journal of Political Science* 17:129–47.

McKenzie, Richard B. 1990. Taxes and America's flight capital. *Christian Science Monitor,* Nov. 26, 18.

Merry, Robert W. 1982. House unit stalls in push for fast action on tax increases, but may succeed today. *The Wall Street Journal,* July 28, 3.

Mezey, Mike. 1989. *Congress, the president, and public policy.* Boulder: Westview Press.

Milgrom, Paul, and John Roberts. 1991. *Economics, Organization, and Management.* New York: Prentice Hall, (forthcoming).

Mills, Michael. 1989. Raising member's pay: A 200-year dilemma. *Congressional Quarterly Weekly Report* 47(Feb. 4):209–12.

Moe, Terry M. 1984. The new economics of organizations. *American Journal of Political Science* 28(Nov.):739–77.

———. 1989. The politics of structural choice. Stanford University. Mimeo.

Muir, William. 1986. *Legislature.* Berkeley: Univ. of California Press.

Myers, Robert J. 1985. *Social Security.* 3d ed. Homewood, Ill.: Irwin.

Nash, John. 1950. The bargaining problem. *Econometrica.*

Nathan, Richard P. 1983. *The administrative presidency.* New York: Wiley.

Neustadt, Richard E., and Ernest R. May. 1986. *Thinking in time.* New York: Free Press.

Nie, Norman H., Sidney Verba, and John R. Petrocik. 1979. *The changing American voter.* Cambridge, Mass.: Harvard Univ. Press.

Nivola, Pietro S. 1990. Trade policy: Refereeing the playing field. In *A question of balance: The president, Congress, and foreign policy,* ed. Thomas E. Mann, 201–53. Washington, D.C.: Brookings Institution.

North, Douglass. 1981. *Structure and change in economic history.* New York: Norton.

Ogul, Morris S. 1976. *Congress oversees the bureaucracy: Studies in legislative supervision.* Pittsburgh: Univ. of Pittsburgh Press.

Office of Management and Budget. Executive Office of the President. 1989. *United States budget in brief: Fiscal year 1990.* Washington, D.C.: Government Printing Office.

———. 1990. *Budget of the United States government: Fiscal year 1991.* Washington, D.C.: Government Printing Office.

Oleszek, Walter J. 1983. Integration and fragmentation: Key themes of congressional change. *Annals of the American Academy of Political and Social Science* 466(Mar.):193–205.

———. 1984. *Congressional procedures and the policy process.* 2d ed. Washington, D.C.: CQ Press.

———. 1985. *Majority and minority whips of the Senate: History and development of the party whip system in the U.S. Senate.* S. Doc. 98-45, 98th Cong. 2d sess. Washington, D.C.: Government Printing Office.

———. 1989. *Congressional procedures and the policy process.* 3d ed. Washington, D.C.: CQ Press.

O'Neill, Thomas P. 1980. How House leader views elections, Carter, Congress. *U.S. News & World Report,* Aug. 11, 23–24.

Oppenheimer, Bruce I. 1980. Policy effects of U.S. House reform: Decentralization and the capacity to resolve energy issues. *Legislative Studies Quarterly* 5 (Feb.): 5.

———. 1981. The changing relationship between House leadership and the committee on rules. In *Understanding congressional leadership,* ed. Frank Mackaman, 207–25. Washington, D.C.: CQ Press.

Ornstein, Norman J. 1981. The House and the Senate in a new Congress. In *The *new Congress,* ed. Thomas E. Mann and Norman J. Ornstein, 363–83. Washington, D.C.: American Enterprise Institute.

Ornstein, Norman J., Thomas E. Mann, and Michael Malbin. 1990. *Vital statistics on Congress, 1989–1990.* Washington, D.C.: CQ Press.

Ornstein, Norman J., Robert L. Peabody, and David W. Rohde. 1985. The Senate through the 1980s: Cycles of change. In *Congress reconsidered,* 3d ed, ed. Lawrence C. Dodd and Bruce I. Oppenheimer, 13–33. Washington, D.C.: CQ Press.

Parker, Glenn R. 1986. *Homeward bound: Explaining changes in congressional behavior.* Pittsburgh: Univ. of Pittsburgh Press.

Parker, Glenn R., and Suzanne L. Parker. 1989. Why do we trust our congressman, and why does it matter? Paper presented at the annual meeting of the American Political Science Association.

Patterson, Samuel C. 1990. Party leadership in the United States Senate. In *Leading the Senate: New styles, new strategies,* ed. John J. Kornacki, 35–55. Washington, D.C.: CQ Press.

Patterson, Samuel C., and Gregory A. Caldeira. 1988. Party voting in the United States Congress. *British Journal of Political Science* 18:111–31.

Peabody, Robert L. 1976. *Leadership in Congress.* Boston: Little, Brown.

———. 1981. Senate party leadership: From the 1950s to the 1980s. In *Understanding Congressional Leadership,* ed. Frank H. Mackaman, 51–115. Washington, D.C.: CQ Press.

Penner, Rudolph G., ed. 1981. *The Congressional budget process after five years.* Washington, D.C.: American Enterprise Institute.

Penner, Rudolph G., and Alan J. Abramson. 1988. *Broken purse strings: Congressional budgeting, 1974–1988.* Washington, D.C.: Urban Institute Press.

Perotti, Rosanna. 1990. Beyond logrolling: Integrative bargaining in immigration reform. Paper delivered at the annual meeting of the Midwest Political Science Association, Chicago, Apr. 1990.

Peterson, Bill. 1985. Study says senators do less with more. *Washington Post,* Dec. 25, A13.

Peterson, Mark A. 1990. *Legislating together: The White House and Capitol Hill from Eisenhower to Reagan.* Cambridge, Mass.: Harvard Univ. Press.

Peterson, Paul E. 1985. The new politics of deficits. In *The new direction in American politics,* ed. John E. Chubb and Paul E. Peterson, 365–97. Washington, D.C.: Brookings Institution.

———. 1990. The rise and fall of special interest politics. Occasional paper 90-3. Cambridge, Mass.: Center for American Political Studies, Harvard University.

Petrocik, John R. 1987. Realignment: New party coalitions and the nationalization of the South. *Journal of Politics* 49:347–75.

Pfiffner, James P. 1979. *The President, the budget, and Congress: Impoundment and the 1979 Budget Act.* Boulder: Westview.

———. 1986a. *The president and economic policy.* Philadelphia: ISHI Press.

———. 1986b. The Reagan budget juggernaut. In *The president and economic policy,* ed. James P. Pfiffner, 108–34. Philadelphia: ISHI Press.

———. 1988a. The president's legislative agenda. *Annals* 499(Sept.):2–36.

———. 1988b. *The strategic presidency.* Pacific Grove, Calif.: Brooks/Cole.

———. 1991a. Divided government and the problem of governance. In *Divided government,* ed. James A. Thurber, 39–60. Washington, D.C.: CQ Press.

———. 1991b. *The managerial presidency.* Pacific Grove, Calif.: Brooks/Cole.

Pitkin, Hannah. 1967. *The concept of representation.* Berkeley: Univ. of California Press.

Polsby, Nelson W. 1988. Modernization of the U.S. Senate. Univ. of California: Aug. 15. Mimeo.

Porter, Roger. 1988. The president, Congress, and trade policy. *Congress and the Presidency* 15(Autumn):165–84.

Powell, Linda W. 1982. Issue representation in Congress. *Journal of Politics* 44:659–77.

Pressman, Jeffrey L. 1966. *House vs. Senate: Conflict in the appropriations process.* New Haven, Conn.: Yale Univ. Press.

Pressman, Steven. 1986. In Capitol marketplace: Trade expansion bills. *Congressional Quarterly Weekly Report* 44(Mar. 8):554–58.

Price, David E. 1984. *Bringing back the parties.* Washington, D.C.: CQ Press.

Putnam, Robert. 1988. Diplomacy and domestic politics: The logic of two-level games. *International organization* 42:427–60.

Putnam, Robert, and Nicholas Bayne. 1987. *Hanging together: Conflict and cooperation at the seven power summits.* Rev. ed. Cambridge, Mass.: Harvard Univ. Press.

Quirk, Paul J. 1988. In defense of the politics of ideas. *Journal of Politics* 50:31–41.

———. 1989. The cooperative resolution of policy conflict. *American Political Science Review* 83:905–21.

———. 1990. Deregulation and the politics of ideas in Congress. In *Beyond self-interest*, ed. Jane J. Mansbridge, 183–99. Chicago: Univ. of Chicago Press.

Raiffa, Howard. 1982. *The art and science of negotiation.* Cambridge, Mass.: Harvard Univ. Press.

Rasky, Susan F. 1990. The operative word in America: Deficit. *New York Times*, Aug. 5, E1, E5.

Rasmussen, Eric. 1989. *Games and information.* New York: Basil Blackwell.

Rich, Spencer. 1981. Plight of Social Security is being exaggerated, Democrats charge. *Washington Post*, July 8.

Richardson, Sula P. 1987. National observances and other commemorative legislation. CRS Rept. 87-878GOV, Oct. 30. Washington, D.C.: Congressional Research Service.

———. 1989. Caucuses and legislative service organizations of the 101st Congress: An informational directory. CRS Rept. 89-277, Apr. 24, pp. 23–32. Washington, D.C.: Congressional Research Service.

Rieselbach, Leroy, ed. 1978. *Legislative reform: The policy impact.* Lexington, Mass.: Lexington Books.

———. 1986. *Congressional reform.* Washington, D.C.: CQ Press.

Ripley, Randall. 1967. *Party leaders in the House of Representatives.* Washington, D.C.: Brookings Institution.

———. 1969a. *Majority party leadership in Congress.* Boston: Little, Brown.

———. 1969b. *Power in the Senate.* New York: St. Martin's.

Roberts, Steven V. 1987. Parley on budget opened. *New York Times*, Oct. 29.

———. 1988. The foreign policy tussle: House Speaker Jim Wright bids for control. *New York Times Magazine*, Jan. 24, 34.

Robinson, Donald Allen. 1976. If the Senate Democrats want leadership: An analysis of the history and prospects of the majority policy committee. In *Policymaking role of leadership in the Senate*, 40–57. Washington, D.C.: Commission on the Operation of the Senate, 94th Cong., 2d sess., Government Printing Office.

Rohde, David W. 1988. Variations in partisanship in the House of Representatives, 1953–1988: Southern Democrats, realignment and agenda change. Paper presented at the annual meeting of the American Political Science Association, Washington, D.C.

———. 1989. "Something's happening here; what it is ain't exactly clear": Southern Democrats in the House of Representatives. In *Home style and Washington work: Studies in congressional politics,* ed. Morris P. Fiorina and David W. Rohde, 137–63. Ann Arbor: Univ. of Michigan Press.

———. 1990. "The reports of my death are greatly exaggerated": Parties and party voting in the House of Representatives. In *Changing perspectives on Congress,* ed. Glenn R. Parker (forthcoming).

———. 1991a. Agenda change and partisan resurgence in the House of Representatives. In *The Atomistic Congress,* ed. Ronald M. Peters and Alan Hertzke, Armonk, N.Y.: M. E. Sharpe, (forthcoming).

———. 1991b. *Parties and leaders in the postreform House.* Chicago: Univ. of Chicago Press.

Rohde, David W., and Kenneth A. Shepsle. 1987. Leaders and followers in the House of Representatives: Reflections on Woodrow Wilson's *Congressional government. Congress and the Presidency* 14:111–33.

Rosenbaum, David E. 1989. Why the deficit is paralyzing Congress. *New York Times,* Oct. 22, E1.

Rothman, David. 1966. *Politics and power: The U.S. Senate, 1869–1901.* Cambridge, Mass.: Harvard Univ. Press.

Rovner, Julie. 1990a. Congress clears sweeping bill to guard rights of disabled. *Congressional Quarterly Weekly Report* 48(July 14):2227–28.

———. 1990b. Disability-rights legislation headed for conference. *Congressional Quarterly Weekly Report* 48(May 26):1657–59.

———. 1990c. House is nearing passage of disability-rights bill. *Congressional Quarterly Weekly Report* 48(May 19):1559–60.

———. 1990d. Last-minute snag means delay for disabled rights measure. *Congressional Quarterly Weekly Report* 48(June 30):2071–72.

———. 1990e. Pepper Commission splinters over health financing. *Congressional Quarterly Weekly Report* 48(Mar. 3):667–68.

Rubin, Irene S. 1990. *The politics of public budgeting: Getting and spending, borrowing and balancing.* Chatham, N.J.: Chatham House.

Sabato, Larry J. 1984. *PAC power.* New York: Norton.

Salisbury, Robert H. 1984. Interest representation: The dominance of institutions. *American Political Science Review* 77:64–76.

Schelling, Thomas. 1960. *The strategy of conflict.* Cambridge, Mass.: Harvard Univ. Press.

Schick, Allen. 1980. *Congress and money: Budgeting, spending and taxing.* Washington, D.C.: Urban Institute Press.

———. 1981. *Reconciliation and the congressional budget process.* Washington, D.C.: American Enterprise Institute.

———. 1983. The distributive Congress. In *Making economic policy in Congress,* ed. Allen Schick, 257–73. Washington, D.C.: American Enterprise Institute.

———. 1990. *The capacity to budget.* Washington, D.C.: Urban Institute Press.

Schlesinger, Joseph. 1985. The new American political party. *American Political Science Review* 79:1151–69.

Schlozman, Kay Lehman, and John T. Tierney. 1986. *Organized interests and American democracy.* New York: Harper & Row.

Schultze, Charles L. 1990. Not to cut the deficit. *Washington Post,* Sept. 6, A27.

Shepsle, Kenneth. 1988. The changing textbook Congress, Department of Government, Harvard University.

———. 1989. The changing textbook Congress. In *Can the government govern?,* ed. John E. Chubb and Paul E. Peterson, 238–66. Washington, D.C.: Brookings Institution.

Shepsle, Kenneth A., and Barry Weingast. 1987. Foundations of committee power. *American Political Science Review* 81:85–104.

————. 1981. Structure and strategy. Paper delivered at the annual meeting of the American Political Science Association, New York.

Shuman, Howard E. 1984. *Politics and the budget: The struggle between the president and the Congress.* Englewood Cliffs, N.J.: Prentice-Hall.

————. 1991. *Politics and the budget.* 3d ed. Englewood Cliffs, N.J.: Prentice-Hall.

Simon, Paul. 1985. Trying on the Senate for size. *Chicago Magazine,* Nov., 150.

Sinclair, Barbara. 1981a. Majority party leadership strategies for coping with the new U.S. House. In *Understanding congressional leadership,* ed. Frank H. Mackaman, 181–205. Washington, D.C.: CQ Press.

————. 1981b. The Speaker's task forces in the postreform House of Representatives. *American Political Science Review* 75:397–410.

————. 1982. *Congressional Realignment, 1925–1978.* Austin: Univ. of Texas Press.

————. 1983. *Majority party leadership in the U.S. House.* Baltimore: Johns Hopkins Univ. Press.

————. 1989a. The changing role of party and party leadership in the U.S. House. Paper delivered at the annual meeting of the American Political Science Association, Atlanta.

————. 1989b. House majority party leadership in the late 1980s. In *Congress reconsidered,* 4th ed., ed. Lawrence C. Dodd and Bruce I. Oppenheimer, 307–30. Washington, D.C.: CQ Press.

————. 1989c. *Transformation of the U.S. Senate.* Baltimore: Johns Hopkins Univ. Press.

————. 1991. Strong party leadership in a weak party era—The evolution of party leadership in the modern House. In *The Atomistic Congress,* ed. Ronald Peters and Allen Herzke Armonk, N.Y.: M. E. Sharpe (in press).

Smist, Frank J. 1990. *Congress oversees the United States intelligence community, 1947–1989.* Knoxville: Univ. of Tennessee Press.

Smith, Hedrick. 1988. *The power game: How Washington works.* New York: Random House.

Smith, Steven S. 1982. Budget battles of 1981: The role of the majority party leadership. In *American politics and public policy,* ed. Allan P. Sindler, 43–78. Washington, D.C.: CQ Press.

————. 1985. New patterns of decisionmaking in Congress. In *The new direction in American politics,* ed. John E. Chubb and Paul E. Peterson, 203–34. Washington, D.C.: Brookings Institution.

————. 1986. Revolution in the House: Why don't we do it on the floor? Discussion paper no. 5, Government Studies. Washington, D.C.: Brookings Institution.

————. 1989. *Call to order: Floor politics in the House and Senate.* Washington, D.C.: Brookings Institution.

————. 1990. Informal leadership in the Senate: Opportunities, resources, and motivations. In *Leading the Senate: New styles, new strategies,* ed. John J. Kornacki, 71–83. Washington, D.C.: CQ Press.

Smith, Steven S., and Christopher J. Deering. 1985. Subcommittees in Congress. In *Congress reconsidered,* 4th ed., ed. Lawrence C. Dodd and Bruce I. Oppenheimer. Washington, D.C.: CQ Press.

————. 1990. *Committees in Congress.* 2nd ed. Washington, D.C.: CQ Press.

Smith, Steven S., and Marcus Flathman. 1989. Managing the Senate floor: Unanimous consent agreements since the 1950s. *Legislative Studies Quarterly* 14 (Aug.):349–74.

Sorauf, Frank J. 1980. Political parties and political action committees: Two life cycles. *Arizona Law Review* 22:445–64.

————. 1988. *Money in American elections.* Glenview, Ill.: Scott, Foresman/Little, Brown.

Sorauf, Frank J., and Scott A. Wilson. 1990. Campaigns and money: A changing role for the political parties? In *The parties respond*, ed. L. Sandy Maisel, 187–203. Boulder: Westview Press.

Stanfield, Rochelle L. 1990. Floating power centers. *National Journal* 22(Dec. 1): 2917–19.

Stanley, Harold W. 1988. Southern partisan changes: Dealignment, realignment or both? *Journal of Politics* 50:3–30.

Stanley, Harold W., William T. Bianco, and Richard Niemi. 1986. Partisanship and group support over time. *American Political Science Review*, 80(Sept.): 969–76.

Steinberg, Alfred. 1968. *Sam Johnson's boy: A close-up of the president from Texas*. New York: Macmillan.

Stewart, John G. 1975. Central policy organs in Congress. In *Congress against the president*, ed. Harvey C. Mansfield, Sr., 20–33. New York: Praeger.

Stockman, David. 1986. *The triumph of politics*. New York: Harper & Row.

Strahan, Randall. 1988. Agenda change and committee politics in the postreform House. *Legislative Studies Quarterly* 13(May):177–97.

———. 1990. *New Ways and Means: Reform and change in a congressional committee*. Chapel Hill, N.C.: Univ. of North Carolina Press.

Sullivan, Terry. 1987. The Impact of Procedural Reforms in Congress. Manuscript, Department of Government, University of Texas.

Sullivan, Timothy J. 1984. *Resolving development disputes through negotiation*. New York: Plenum Press.

Sundquist, James L. 1968. *Politics and policy: The Eisenhower, Kennedy, and Johnson years*. Washington, D.C.: Brookings Institution.

———. 1981. *The decline and resurgence of Congress*. Washington, D.C.: Brookings Institution.

———. 1989. Needed: A political theory for the new era of coalition government in the United States. *Political Science Quarterly* 103:613–35.

Superdiplomat Jim Wright. 1988. Editorial. *Washington Post*, May 8, B6.

Swardson, Anne. 1987. Tax bill drafting session halts after GOP balks. *Washington Post*, Oct. 2.

Tate, Dale, 1982a. Keys to budget compromise emerge from leader's talks. *Congressional Quarterly Weekly Report* 40:787–89.

———. 1982b. Use of omnibus bills burgeons despite members' misgivings; long-term impact is disputed. *Congressional Quarterly Weekly Report* 40(Sept. 25):2379–83.

———. 1983. Pragmatism is the watchword as House Budget Committee heads into 1984 fiscal storm. *Congressional Quarterly Weekly Report* 41:1295, 1297–99.

———. 1984. Hill deficit reductions hinge on conference deliberations. *Congressional Quarterly Weekly Report* 42:1295, 1297–99.

Thurber, James A. 1976. Congressional budget reform and new demands for policy analysis. *Policy Analysis* 2 (Spring):198–214.

———. 1986. Assessing the congressional budget process under Gramm-Rudman-Hollings and the 1974 Budget Act. Paper delivered at the annual meeting of the American Political Science Association, Chicago.

———. 1989. Budget continuity and change; An assessment of the congressional budget process. In *Studies of modern American politics*, ed. D. K. Adams, 78–118. Manchester, Engl.: Manchester Univ. Press.

———. 1991a. *Divided democracy*. Washington, D.C.: CQ Press.

———. 1991b. The impact of budget reform on presidential and congressional governance. In *Divided democracy*, ed. James A. Thurber, 145–70. Washington, D.C.: CQ Press.

Thurber, James A., and Samantha Durst. 1991. Delay, deadlock, and deficits: Evaluating congressional budget reform. In *Federal budget and financial management reform,* ed. Thomas D. Lynch, Westport, Conn.: Greenwood Press.

Thurow, Lester C. 1980. *The zero-sum society.* New York: Basic Books.

Tiefer, Charles, and Hyde Murray. 1989. Congressional elite become take-charge managers in new era. *Legal Times,* Sept. 18, 38–39.

Tolchin, Martin. 1982. Howard Baker: Trying to tame an unruly Senate. *New York Times Magazine,* Mar. 20, 17–19, 66–74.

———. 1983. In the face of controversy, packaging. *New York Times,* Feb. 21, B6.

Torcom, Jean E. 1973. Leadership: The role and style of Senator Everett Dirksen. In *To be a congressman: The promise and the power,* ed. Sven Groennings and Jonathan P. Hawley, 185–224. Washington, D.C.: Acropolis Books.

Treverton, Gregory F. 1990. Intelligence: Welcome to the American government. In *A question of balance,* ed. Thomas E. Mann, 70–108. Washington, D.C.: Brookings Institution.

Tsebelis, George. 1988. Nested games: The cohesion of French electoral coalitions. *British Journal of Political Science* 18:151.

———. 1990. *Nested Games: Rational Choice in Comparative Politics.* Berkeley: Univ. of California Press.

U.S. Commission on CIA Activities in the United States. Rockefeller Commission. 1975. *Report to the president.* Washington, D.C.: Government Printing Office.

U.S. Commission on the Organization of the Government for the Conduct of Foreign Policy. Murphy Commission. 1975. *Report.* Washington, D.C.: Government Printing Office.

U.S. Congress. 1987. *Report of the congressional committees investigating the Iran-contra affair.* Washington, D.C.: Government Printing Office.

———. Church Committee. Senate Select Committee to Study Governmental Operations with Respect to Intelligence Activities. 1976. *Final report.* S. Rept. 94-755, 94th Cong. Washington, D.C.: Government Printing Office.

———. House. 1983. *Constitution, Jefferson's Manual and Rules of the House of Representatives.* 98th Cong., H. Doc. 97-271; 97th Cong. 2d sess.

———. House Committee on the Budget. 1987. *The whole and the parts: Piecemeal and integrated approaches to congressional budgeting.* Washington, D.C.: Government Printing Office.

———. House Judiciary Committee. 1974. *Impeachment of Richard M. Nixon, president of the United States.* H. Rept. 93-1305, 93d Cong. Washington, D.C.: Government Printing Office.

———. House Permanent Select Committee on Intelligence. 1990. *Intelligence Authorization Act for fiscal year 1991.* H. Rept. 101-725. pt. 1, 101st Cong. Washington, D.C.: Government Printing Office.

———. House Select Committee on Committees. 1980. *Final report.* H. Rept. 96-866, 96th Cong. 2d sess., Apr. 1.

———. Iran-Contra Committees. House Select Committee to Investigate Covert Arms Transactions with Iran; Senate Select Committee on Secret Military Arms Assistance to Iran and the Nicaraguan Opposition. 1987. *Report.* H. Rept. 100-433; S. Rept. 100-216. 100th Cong. Washington, D.C.: Government Printing Office.

———. Pike Committee. House Select Committee on Intelligence. 1976. *Recommendations of the final report.* Washington, D.C.: Government Printing Office.

———. Senate Committee on Rules. 1977. *Committee systems reorganization amendments of 1977.* S. Rept. 95-2. Washington, D.C.: Government Printing Office.

———. Senate Select Committee on Intelligence. 1983. *Report.* S. Rept. 98-10, 98th Cong. Washington, D.C.: Government Printing Office.

———. Senate Select Committee on Intelligence. 1987. *Nomination of Robert M. Gates.* Washington, D.C.: Government Printing Office.

———. Stevenson Committee. Senate Temporary Select Committee to Study the Senate Committee System. 1976. *First report with recommendations.* S. Rept. 94-1395, 94th Cong. Washington, D.C.: Government Printing Office.

———. Watergate Committee. Senate Select Committee on Presidential Campaign Activities. 1974. S. Rept. 93–981, 93d Congress. Washington, D.C.: Government Printing Office.

Van Doren, Peter M. 1990. Can we learn the causes of congressional decisions from roll-call data? *Legislative Studies Quarterly* 15:311–40.

Walker, Jack L. 1984. The origin and maintenance of interest groups in America. *American Political Science Review* 77:390–406.

Washington Star. 1964. Legislator is taught how Congress works. Mar. 12, A-2.

Weaver, R. Kent. 1986. The politics of blame avoidance. *Journal of Public Policy* 6:371–98.

———. 1988. *Automatic government: The politics of indexation.* Washington, D.C.: Brookings Institution.

Wehr, Elizabeth. 1987. Budget negotiators report only small shifts. *Congressional Quarterly Weekly Report* 45:2707.

Weingast, Barry R. 1984. The congressional-bureaucratic system: A principal-agent perspective (with applications to the SEC) *Public Choice* 44:147–91.

———. 1989. Floor behavior in Congress: Committee power under the open rule. *American Political Science Review* 83(Sept.):795–815.

———. 1990. Restrictive rules and committee floor success in the postreform House. Unpublished manuscript. Hoover Institution, Stanford University.

Weingast, Barry R., and William Marshall. 1988. The industrial organization of Congress. *Journal of Political Economy* 96:132–63.

Wekkin, Gary D. 1985. Political parties and intergovernmental relations in 1984. *Publius* 15:19–37.

Whalen, Charles, and Barbara Whalen. 1985. *The longest debate: A legislative history of the 1964 Civil Rights Act.* New York: Mentor.

Whelan, Joseph. 1988. *Soviet diplomacy and negotiating behavior—1979–1988: New tests for U.S. diplomacy,* vol. 2. Washington, D.C.: Government Printing Office.

White, William S. 1957. *Citadel: The story of the U.S. Senate.* New York: Harper & Brothers.

Wildavsky, Aaron. 1966. The two presidencies. *Trans-Action* 4(Dec.):7–14.

———. 1984. *The politics of the budgetary process.* 4th ed. Boston: Little, Brown.

———. 1988. *The new politics of the budgetary process.* Glenview, Ill.: Scott, Foresman.

Williamson, Oliver. 1985. *Economic Institutions of Capitalism.* New York: Free Press.

Wilson, James Q. 1989. *Bureaucracy: What government agencies do and why they do it.* New York: Basic Books.

Wilson, Woodrow. [1885] 1956. *Congressional government.* Reprint. New York: Meridian Books.

Witte, John F. 1985. *The Politics and Development of the Federal Income Tax.* Madison: University of Wisconsin Press.

Yang, John E. 1991. Budget battle set to begin on new terrain. *Washington Post,* Feb. 3, A12.

Contributors

William T. Bianco, an assistant professor at Duke University, has written articles that have appeared in *American Political Science Review, Journal of Politics,* and *Legislative Studies Quarterly.*

Roger H. Davidson is professor at the University of Maryland and coeditor of *The Encyclopedia of the United States Congress.* He is the author of *The Role of the Congressman* (1969) and *The Politics of Comprehensive Manpower Legislation* (1972). Professor Davidson is also coauthor of *Congress against Itself* (1977) and *Congress and Its Members* (3d ed., 1990).

John B. Gilmour, an assistant professor at Washington University in St. Louis, is the author of *Reconcilable Differences? Congress, the Budget Process, and the Deficit* (1990).

Paul S. Herrnson, an assistant professor at the University of Maryland, is the author of *Party Campaigning in the 1980s* (1988), which won the Genevieve Gorst Hurford Award, and has written articles that have appeared in *Journal of Politics, Polity,* and *Western Political Quarterly.*

Frederick M. Kaiser is a specialist in American National Government at the Congressional Research Service. His articles have appeared in *Administrative Law Review, Annals, Congress and the Presidency, Journal of Law and Politics,* and *Legislative Studies Quarterly.*

Walter J. Oleszek, a senior specialist in the Legislative Process at the Congressional Research Service, is the author of *Congressional Procedure and the Policy Process* (3d ed., 1989). He is also coauthor of *Congress against Itself* (1977), *Congress and Its Members* (3d ed., 1990), and *Bicameral Politics* (1989).

Daniel J. Palazzolo is an assistant professor at the University of Richmond. His major area of current study is congressional leadership and budget politics.

James P. Pfiffner, a professor at George Mason University, is the author of *The Strategic Presidency* (1988) and *The President, the Budget, and Congress: Impoundment and the 1974 Budget Act* (1979). He is also the editor of *The President and Economic Policy* (1986) and *The Managerial Presidency* (1991), and the coeditor of *The Presidency in Transition* (1989).

Paul J. Quirk is an associate professor in the Department of Political Science and the Institute of Government and Public Affairs, University of Illinois, Urbana-Champaign. He is the author of *Industry Influence in Federal Regulatory Agencies* (1981) and coauthor of *The Politics of Deregulation* (1985), which won the Louis Brownlow Award. His articles have appeared in the *American Political Science Review* and *Journal of Policy Analysis and Management*.

David W. Rohde is a professor at Michigan State University. He is the author of *Parties and Leaders in the Postreform House* (1991) and the coauthor of *Change and Continuity in the 1988 Elections* (1990). He has also been editor of the *American Journal of Political Science*.

Barbara Sinclair is a professor at the University of California, Riverside. She is the author of *The Transformation of the U.S. Senate* (1989), which received the Richard Fenno Prize, *Majority Leadership in the U.S. House* (1983), and *Congressional Realignment, 1925–1978* (1982).

Steven S. Smith is a professor at the University of Minnesota. He is the author of *Call to Order* (1989) and the coauthor of *Managing Uncertainty in the House of Representatives* (1988) and *Committees in Congress* (2d ed., 1990).

James A. Thurber is a professor at the American University, where he also directs the Center for Congressional and Presidential Studies. He is the editor of *Divided Democracy: Cooperation and Conflict between the President and Congress* (1991), coauthor of *Setting Course: Congress in Transition* (1991), and a contributor to *Interest Group Politics* (1991).

Barry R. Weingast is a senior fellow at the Hoover Institution, Stanford University. His articles have appeared in, among others, *American Political Science Review, Journal of Economic History,* and *Journal of Political Economy*.

Index